THE SIX SIGMA WAY

THE SIX SIGMA WAY

How GE, Motorola, and Other Top Companies Are Honing Their Performance

PETER S. PANDE
ROBERT P. NEUMAN
ROLAND R. CAVANAGH

Tata McGraw-Hill Publishing Company Limited
NEW DELHI

McGraw-Hill Offices

New Delhi New York St Louis San Francisco Auckland Bogotá Caracas
Kuala Lumpur Lisbon London Madrid Mexico City Milan Montreal
San Juan Santiago Singapore Sydney Tokyo Toronto

Tata McGraw-Hill

Tata McGraw-Hill Edition 2003

Tenth reprint 2006
RZLQCDRKRCLZZ

Reprinted in India by arrangement with The McGraw-Hill Companies, Inc., New York

Sales territories: India, Pakistan, Nepal, Bangladesh, Sri Lanka and Bhutan

Library of Congress Cataloging-in-Publication Data
Pande, Peter S.
The Six Sigma way : how GE, Motorola, and other top companies are honing their performance / by Peter S. Pande, Robert P. Neuman, Roland R. Cavanagh.
p cm.
Includes bibliographical references.
ISBN 0-07-135806-4
1. Quality control —Statistical methods. 2. Production management—Statistical methods. I. Neuman, Robert P II. Cavanaugh, Roland R. III. Title.
TS156.P263 2000
658.5'62—dc21

00-027237

ISBN 0-07-053321-0

Published by Tata McGraw-Hill Publishing Company Limited,
7 West Patel Nagar, New Delhi 110 008, and printed at
Sai Printo Pack, New Delhi 110 020

*The **McGraw-Hill** Companies*

To Anne and Al Pande, who've been
"Six Sigma" parents and my best friends.

—P.S.P.

To my dear wife, Mabel.

—R.P.N.

To my dad, Hale Cavanagh,
who would have been pleased and proud
to see the results of this undertaking.

—R.R.C.

Contents

PART III
Implementing Six Sigma: The Roadmap and Tools 153

Preface

THIS BOOK is designed to help business leaders—from CEOs to supervisors—tap into the power of the Six Sigma movement that's transforming some of the world's most successful companies. Six Sigma initiatives have tallied billions of dollars in savings, dramatic increases in speed, strong new customer relationships—in short, remarkable results and rave reviews.

Are these results for real? And is it really possible for you and your business to achieve some of the same gains?

The answer is "yes." It can happen in any type of business and, contrary to many people's fears, you don't have to have an in-depth background in statistical analysis. Six Sigma can contribute not only to how your company measures and analyzes its performance, but also to improving your basic approach to managing the business.

Six Sigma: Changing Business Habits

A story from our early experiences implementing Six Sigma illustrates how this new approach to business impacts the very habits that drive an organization. We were working with leaders and Six Sigma project teams at one of largest business units of GE Capital (the first totally service-based company to launch Six Sigma).

It was during a "Gallery Walk"—at which the teams were explaining their progress to company leaders—that the firm's CEO began challenging one of the team leaders. "If you think that's the problem," the

CEO suggested, "why don't you just...?" and he suggested a solution. The team leader tried to explain that their analysis and data were preliminary, and that more work was needed to confirm their suspicions. The executive persisted over several minutes, however, in arguing for his proposed solution. In the face of grilling from his "boss's boss's boss," the team leader grew increasingly flustered and unsure of how to respond.

At that moment, in an act of corporate courage, one of the firm's "Black Belts," a financial services manager we had trained to coach Six Sigma teams, literally stepped between the CEO and the team's charts. He declared, in so many words: "We're not going to jump to a solution because we're using the Six Sigma process!"

Immediately the company leader recognized his mistake. Instead of getting angry, he laughed and apologized. Later, speaking to the entire group, he related the story and gave credit to the Black Belt for defending the Six Sigma Way. "We're not in the 'Just Do It' mode anymore," he noted. "Taking the time to understand a problem and process before we fix it is better—but you may have to *remind* us from time to time until we get used to this new way."

That company went on to achieve millions of dollars in savings through Six Sigma projects, and to totally revamp their approach to strategic and new product planning. While they still haven't lost all their old, "just do it" spirit, they are approaching processes and problems with better questions, and better solutions.

So, What Is Six Sigma?

If you've read this far, you already know that "Six Sigma" is not some kind of new sorority or fraternity. On the other hand, there are different perspectives on what "Six Sigma" is. Business media often describe Six Sigma as a "highly technical method used by engineers and statisticians to fine-tune products and processes." True, in part. Measures and statistics are a key ingredient of Six Sigma improvement—but they are by no means the whole story.

Another definition of Six Sigma is that it's a goal of near-perfection in meeting customer requirements. This also is accurate; in fact, the term "Six Sigma" itself refers to a statistically derived performance target of operating with only 3.4 defects for every *million* activities or "opportunities." It's a goal few companies or processes can claim to have achieved.

Still another way to define Six Sigma is as a sweeping "culture change" effort to position a company for greater customer satisfaction, profitability, and competitiveness. Considering the companywide commitment to Six Sigma at places like General Electric or Motorola, "culture change" is certainly a valid way to describe Six Sigma. But it's also possible to "do" Six Sigma without making a frontal assault on your company culture.

If all these definitions—measure, goal, or culture change—are at least partly but not totally accurate, what's the *best* way to define Six Sigma? Based on our experience—and examples set by the growing number of companies seeking Six Sigma improvement—we've developed a definition that captures the breadth and flexibility of Six Sigma as a way to boost performanc

> SIX SIGMA: A comprehensive and flexible *system* for achieving, sustaining and maximizing business success. Six Sigma is uniquely driven by close understanding of customer needs, disciplined use of facts, data, and statistical analysis, and diligent attention to managing, improving, and reinventing business processes.

This is the definition that will provide the foundation for our efforts to unlock the potential of Six Sigma for your organization. The types of "business success" you may achieve are broad because the proven benefits of the Six Sigma "system" are diverse, including

- Cost reduction
- Productivity improvement
- Market-share growth
- Customer retention
- Cycle-time reduction
- Defect reduction
- Culture change
- Product/service development

And many more.

Is Six Sigma *Really* Different?

Some people, when first exposed to Six Sigma concepts, complain that it's similar to the "Total Quality" efforts of the last 15 to 20 years. Indeed, the origins of many Six Sigma principles and tools are found in the teachings of influential "quality" thinkers like W. Edwards Deming and Joseph Juran. In some companies—GE and Motorola among them—the terms "quality" and "Six Sigma" often go together. So it's true that in some ways Six Sigma's expansion is heralding a rebirth of the quality movement. Cynics who gave up on "TQM" might choose to think of Six Sigma as that generic horror movie plot: the beast that wouldn't die.

But as we'll see, Six Sigma makes for a new and very much *improved* beast. If you've been through TQM, CQI, BPR, ABC, LMNOP (that's a joke), etc. you'll probably find some familiar material in *The Six Sigma Way.* However, we're sure you'll also find a lot that's new, and that you'll see familiar tools applied with greater impact on the business's competitiveness and bottom-line results. A foundation in "TQM" can give you or your business an advantage in ramping-up a successful Six Sigma effort. So, for the time being, it's perfectly okay for you to think of Six Sigma as "TQM on steroids."

To help you unlock the value of Six Sigma, we need to uncover some truths that have been missed in most of the Six Sigma literature so far. Understanding them means Six Sigma can offer some unexpected benefits to you and your organization.

Six Sigma's Hidden Truths—and Potential Payoff

Hidden Truth #1

Six Sigma encompasses a broad array of business best practices and skills (some advanced, some common sense) that are essential ingredients for success and growth. Where it's shown the most impressive impact, "Six Sigma" is much more than a detailed statistics-based analytical method. We'll address the full range of Six Sigma as it's being applied in these diverse and growing organizations.

The Payoff: You'll be able to apply Six Sigma to many different business activities and challenges—from strategic planning to operations to customer service—and maximize the impact of your efforts.

Hidden Truth #2

There are many "Six Sigma Ways." Following a fixed prescription, or modeling your effort after another company, is guaranteed to fail—or come close. This book will offer customizable options and guidelines, not rigid formulas, that take into account your level of influence, your business needs and priorities, and your organization's readiness for change.

The Payoff: The benefits of Six Sigma will be accessible whether you lead an entire organization or a department. Moreover, you'll be able to scale your efforts, from tackling specific problems to renewing the entire business.

Hidden Truth #3

The potential gains from Six Sigma are equally significant (if not greater) in service organizations and non-manufacturing activities as they are in "technical" environments.

The huge opportunities outside the plant floor (in order management, finance, customer service, marketing, logistics, IT, etc.) exist for two main reasons. First, these activities are key to today's sustained competitive advantage, as tangible products turn into commodities in short order. Second, there's a lot to gain, because most non-manufacturing activities are only about 70 percent effective/efficient (if that).

We won't ignore manufacturing, but a high priority in this book will be to explain how to make Six Sigma work in commercial, transactional, or administrative areas that require a special approach and mix of tools.

The Payoff: You'll be prepared to achieve breakthroughs in these untapped gold mines of opportunity—and to broaden Six Sigma beyond the realm of the engineering community.

Hidden Truth #4

Six Sigma is as much about people excellence as it is about technical excellence. Creativity, collaboration, communication, dedication—these are infinitely more powerful than a corps of super-statisticians. Fortunately, the fundamental ideas of "big picture" Six Sigma can inspire and motivate better ideas and performance from people—and create synergy between individual talents and technical prowess.

The Payoff: You'll gain insights into how to strike a balance between push and pull—accommodating people and demanding performance. That balance is where real sustained improvement is found. On either side—being "too nice," or forcing people beyond their understanding and readiness—lie merely short-term gains or no results at all.

Hidden Truth #5

Done right, Six Sigma improvement is thrilling and rewarding. We've seen people rave about the positive changes that have come to their organization, thanks to the new, smarter way they are running their business. We've watched executive teams abandon their decorum, as they race around trying to speed up and perfect a "broken" process in a Six Sigma workshop.

It's a lot of work, too. And it's not without its risks. Any level of Six Sigma effort takes an investment in time, energy, and money. In this book, we'll try to share some of the fun and enthusiasm we've seen and feel about Six Sigma as we describe how to make the investment and ensure big returns. (If at times our attempts at sparkling wit fall flat, we apologize in advance.) We'll also make a big effort to warn you away from the dangers and mistakes that can derail a Six Sigma initiative.

The Payoff: The good news is, Six Sigma is a lot more fun than a root canal. Seriously, the significant financial gains from Six Sigma may be exceeded in value by the intangible benefits. In fact, the changes in attitude and enthusiasm that come from improved processes and better-informed people are often easier to observe, and more emotionally rewarding, than dollar savings. It's very exciting, for example, to talk to front-line people who are energized and enthusiastic because they've gained confidence, learned new skills, and improved their process. Each individual Six Sigma improvement is a success story in itself.

Key Features of the *Six Sigma Way*

This book is designed with maximum customer satisfaction in mind. We hope that by reading it you'll gain a complete picture of what's behind the Six Sigma movement, how it's paying off, and how you can implement the system so as to best fit your circumstances. Our goal is to provide a flexible resource and reference, whether you've been engaged in Six Sigma for several years or are just starting to learn and apply it.

Here are some of the features that will help you get the most out of the book:

1. A guide to finding just what you need. Following this Preface, you'll find an overview of each section and chapter, with tips on which pieces to use (or skip over) depending on your objectives and circumstances.

2. Practical implementation guidelines. Whether it's fixing a process problem or implementing Six Sigma companywide, we'll review important information to help you get started and keep moving.

3. Insights, comments, and examples from real people—business leaders, experts, and managers—who are using Six Sigma in their organizations. These thoughts have helped reinforce and refine our ideas; we're confident you'll learn a lot from them, too.

4. Checklists for a number of the essential steps in Six Sigma improvement. We hope to prepare you to go out and do Six Sigma activities, so we've mapped out key steps to help you make the right choices.

5. An introduction to advanced techniques. This is not a technical manual; plenty of other texts cover the nuances of process statistics and advanced experimental design. We will, however, help anyone understand what the "sophisticated" tools of Six Sigma are, why and how they're used, and when they should be applied.

6. Our own perspectives and advice. In giving you a guide to Six Sigma best practices, we've had to synthesize different viewpoints, guided by our experience and understanding of what works best, when and how. Some of our thoughts challenge the views of Six Sigma "experts"—where they do, we'll give evidence for our perspective. Because we've worked with some of the most visible Six Sigma companies and have applied these concepts in many types of businesses, we believe our views can make Six Sigma even more powerful than it might otherwise be.

A Final Philosophical Word

Lastly, we'd like to offer you a theme that we think represents one of the most important aspects of Six Sigma and hence will be key to your success in applying it to your business.

In their book ***Built to Last,*** James Collins and Jerry Porras provide insights into many of the most successful and admired companies of the 20th century. The dimension that they found most remarkable among these firms is their ability—and willingness—to simultaneously adopt two seemingly contrary objectives *at the same time.* Stability and

Table P.1 "Genius of the And" Examples.

We can...	*AND* we can...
Reduce errors to almost none	Get things done faster
Engage people in understanding and improving their processes and procedures	Maintain control of how work gets done
Measure and analyze what we do	Apply creative solutions to "push the envelope"
Make customers extremely happy	Make a lot of money

renewal, big picture and minute detail, creativity and rational analysis—these forces, working together, make organizations great. This "we can do it all" approach they call the "Genius of the And."

You can see this genius in action in everyday business if you look closely. The best managers, for example, are usually those who set broad goals and direction (big picture), yet who can still offer effective input and ask tough questions (the details). In a larger business context, an example of the "Genius of the And" would be a company's constant attention to *both* long-term growth and quarterly results.

The opposite effect, to which lesser organizations fall victim, Collins and Porras dub the "Tyranny of the Or."[1] That's the paralyzing view that we can have it one way or the other, but not *both.*

Six Sigma, we believe, depends on your business learning to exhibit the Genius of the And—and it offers a way to unlock this genius in your own people and processes. Table P.1 provides some examples of those seemingly opposing ideas we encounter in this book that *in fact* are key to success.

As you learn about the what, why, and how of Six Sigma in this book, try to remember that the success you're seeking will be based on your ability to focus on the "And" and not the "Or." The key to unlocking the "Genius of the And" in you and your organization can be found in these pages....

[1] James Collins and Jerry Porras, *Built to Last* (New York: Harper Business, 1994), p. 44.

A Guide to the *Six Sigma Way*

THIS BOOK is organized for use by a variety of readers, from Six Sigma novices to people right in the thick of improvement efforts. While you may prefer to read it from cover to cover, the content is organized in three parts to help you learn about Six Sigma now at just the level of depth you need—you can read the rest of the book later when you need it.

Here's a guide to the content, first by part, then by chapter.

The Major Sections

Part One: An Executive Summary of Six Sigma

For the executive or the newcomer to Six Sigma, Part One provides a thorough overview of key concepts and background including success stories, themes, measurement, improvement strategies, and the Six Sigma Roadmap—a five-phase model for building the Six Sigma organization. We also look at how Six Sigma efforts can avoid some of the mistakes that hurt "Total Quality" efforts—and how to apply Six Sigma in Service as well as Manufacturing processes or businesses.

Part Two: Gearing Up and Adapting Six Sigma to Your Organization

This section looks at the organizational challenges of launching, leading, and preparing people for the Six Sigma effort. We examine the key question of whether or not to start a Six Sigma effort—and where to begin your effort. This is also where you can find out about responsibilities of business leaders, Black Belts, and other roles. Finally, we explore how to choose the right improvement projects.

Part Three: Implementing Six Sigma—The Roadmap and the Tools

This section focuses on the "How-to" of the major components and tools in the Six Sigma system. For those who want to begin doing the work of making Six Sigma gains—or just want to know more about what's really involved in the effort—this section should answer many of your questions. If your concern is about measurement, for example, you can concentrate on Chapter 14; if you're looking at redesigning a process, Chapter 16 will be your focus. We cover some of the more important advanced tools of Six Sigma in this section as well. As a conclusion, we offer a list of 12 Keys to Success for your Six Sigma journey.

The Appendices: Practical Support

In addition to worksheets and checklists for key Six Sigma activities, the appendix features basic instructions on some of the more common Six Sigma improvement tools and a generic "implementation plan" as a starting point for launching your effort. A glossary of key terms and references by topics are included as well.

The Chapters

Here's a quick summary of each chapter, focused on the questions addressed in each.

Chapter One: A Powerful Strategy for Sustained Success

How does Six Sigma apply to the business challenges of the new century? What are some of the results and successes that have brought Six Sigma to the forefront of business leadership today—including at GE, Motorola, and AlliedSignal? What are some of the key organizational benefits it offers—and the themes that drive Six Sigma improvement?

Chapter Two: Key Concepts of the Six Sigma System

What kind of organizational "system" can Six Sigma create and how does in apply to short- and long-term success? What does the *measure* "Six Sigma" mean? What role do customers and defects play in measuring Six Sigma performance? What are the core improvement and management methodologies of Six Sigma? What is the "DMAIC" model? What really is—or should be—a "Six Sigma Organization"?

Chapter Three: Why Is Six Sigma Succeeding Where Total Quality "Failed"?

What aspects of the Total Quality legacy are still alive in businesses today? How can Six Sigma–focused companies avoid some of the most crucial mistakes that gave TQM a black eye?

Chapter Four: Applying Six Sigma to Service and Manufacturing

Why does Six Sigma hold as much—if not more—promise in Service processes and organizations than in Manufacturing? What are the keys to making Six Sigma work well and provide results in a Service environment? What are the unique challenges that can arise in applying Six Sigma in Manufacturing functions, and how do you address them?

Chapter Five: The Six Sigma Roadmap

What's the best sequence for implementing the "core competencies" of Six Sigma? What are the advantages of the "ideal" Six Sigma Roadmap? What is the value provided by each component to a responsive, competitive organization?

Chapter Six: Is Six Sigma Right for Us Now?

What key questions should we ask to determine if our organization is ready for and can benefit from Six Sigma? When would Six Sigma *not* be a good idea for a business? What are the cost/benefit considerations when deciding whether to embark on a Six Sigma initiative?

Chapter Seven: How and Where Should We Start Our Efforts?

What options can we consider in planning our Six Sigma launch? What are the "on-ramps" to the Six Sigma roadmap? How do we scale our effort to meet our needs? How can we use an assessment of our strengths and weaknesses to focus our resources? Why is a piloting strategy essential, and how should it work?

Chapter Eight: The Politics of Six Sigma: Preparing Leaders to Launch and Guide the Effort

What are the key responsibilities for organizational leaders in guiding the effort? How do communication, demand for results, and "change marketing" impact our potential for success?

Chapter Nine: Preparing Black Belts and Key Roles

What roles are typically needed in a Six Sigma implementation? What is a "Black Belt," and what are the options for defining his/her function? How can the various roles be structured, and conflicts be avoided? What are the key considerations when choosing members for team projects?

Chapter Ten: Training the Organization for Six Sigma

Why doesn't Six Sigma necessarily demand weeks and weeks of training to start? What are the keys to effective Six Sigma training? What are the common elements in a Six Sigma "curriculum"?

Chapter Eleven: The Key to Successful Improvement: Selecting the Right Six Sigma Projects

What are the key steps in choosing and setting up Six Sigma improvement projects? How do we decide which improvement "model"—DMAIC or some other approach—is best for our business?

Chapter Twelve: Identifying Core Processes and Key Customers (Roadmap Step 1)

What are "core processes," and how have they become a key to understanding businesses? What are some common types of core processes and how do you identify those in your organization? How do you identify the key customers and outputs of your core processes? What is a SIPOC model and diagram, and how can they be applied to a better understanding of our business?

Chapter Thirteen: Defining Customer Requirements (Roadmap Step 2)

Why is having a Voice of the Customer (VOC) system so critical in business today? What are the key actions and challenges in strengthening your VOC system? How do we identify and specify Output and Service requirements of our customers? How does better understanding of customer needs link up to our strategy and priorities?

Chapter Fourteen: Measuring Current Performance (Roadmap Step 3)

What are the basic concepts in business process measurement? What are the basic steps in implementing customer- and process-focused measures? How do you effectively carry out data collection and sampling? What types of defect and performance measures are fundamental to the Six Sigma system? How do you calculate "Sigma" for your processes?

Chapter Fifteen: Six Sigma Process Improvement (Roadmap Step 4—A)

How do you Define, Measure, Analyze, and Improve a key business process, while focusing on identifying and eliminating root causes? What are the basic tools of process improvement, and when can each be used effectively? What are some of the key obstacles to executing a Six Sigma improvement project?

Chapter Sixteen: Six Sigma Process Design/Redesign (Roadmap Step 4—B)

How is Six Sigma Process Design/Redesign different—and why is it a critical element in maximizing business performance? What conditions are essential to take on a process design or redesign project? How does redesign differ in execution from improvement? What special tools and challenges come into play when you are designing/redesigning a business process? How do you test and overcome assumptions that limit the value of redesigned processes?

Chapter Seventeen: Expanding and Integrating the Six Sigma System (Roadmap Step 5)

How do you measure and solidify the gains made through Six Sigma improvement projects? What are the methods and tools of Process Control? What are the specific responsibilities of and considerations for a Process Owner? How does the evolutionary discipline of Process Management support the Six Sigma system and long-term improvement?

Chapter Eighteen: Advanced Six Sigma Tools: An Overview

What are some of the most prevalent "power tools" of Six Sigma improvement? What role does each play in helping you to understand and improve processes and products/services? What are the basic steps to these sophisticated techniques?

Conclusion: 12 Keys to Success

What are some of the key actions and considerations any company or leader should keep in mind to make Six Sigma pay off?

Acknowledgments

We now understand why the awards shows on TV always run long. Partly, of course, it's due to slow delivery of canned jokes by the presenters. Usually, though, it's that the winners need to thank so many people. We haven't won an award, but we could go on for a while thanking people. Our friends at McGraw-Hill have threatened to cut to a commercial if we run long, however, so we'll try to keep this brief.

The most important acknowledgment is to the person who put in hours of tireless, good-natured, and indispensable work to make this book a reality: Percy Madamba. She kept everything organized, proofread, offered countless suggestions, laughed at jokes (we're hoping her sense of humor is representative of the general reading public), did graphics and countless other small acts, including shipping out the manuscript. (Our worry now is that Percy will quit and go write her own d__n book.)

Carolyn Talasek, Kelly Fisher, Carla Queen, Chet Harmer, Mona Draper, and Amanda Dutra—along with other members of the great team at Pivotal Resources—contributed graphics, editing help, suggestions, and research, as well as many ideas and insights. That group (the "Pivotal Pack") has been instrumental in bringing together a vast amount of experience and success that we've "channeled" into these pages. Other key contributors to that well of knowledge have included Pamela Schmidt-Cavaliero, Fred Kleiman, Mercie Lopez, Greg Gibbs, Jane Keller, and Rosalie Pryor. Also thanks to our colleague Larry Holpp, for advice and publishing contacts that helped us to bring this book to life.

There are dozens of people in our client organizations, practicing Six Sigma here and in other parts of the world, to whom we owe special thanks. These are the people who are making Six Sigma pay off, and who are learning how to make it work in many different environments. Some of the individuals we thank in particular for their support include all our friends at GE Capital's Center for Learning and Organizational Excellence—Mike Markovits, Mo Cayer, Hilly Dunn, Jenene Nicholson, Kelly Babij, Mike Mosher, and many others. This book would not exist without the terrific work the folks at GE have done, and without their commitment to Six Sigma. Thanks also to: the great people at Employers Reinsurance, including Kaj Ahlmann, Alan Mauch, Tom Felgate, Lee Tenold, Julie Hertel, Mike Nichols, and many others there, too; John Eck and the QNBC people at NBC, where we got to watch the *Tonight Show* live and help introduce Six Sigma to a prime-time organization; at Cendant Mortage, a whole group of great people including our pal Pat Connolly, Tanya DeLia, Suzanne Wetherington, and many others; at Auspex Systems, where process redesign has been part of quality for years, Tamas Farkas and Charlie Golden (who's actually now at Genentech).

People who've offered special insights into this book, whom we'd like to thank for their time, include Dave Boenitz, Chuck Cox, Bob Golitz, Barbara Friesner, Aldie Keene, Alan Larson, Rich Lynch, Celeste Miller, and Jessica Shklar.

At McGraw-Hill, much appreciation to our editor, Richard Narramore, for coaching us through, getting this project off the ground, and put to bed. We're aiming for Six Sigma performance!

Our families deserve loving mention, and sincere thanks, for putting up with the hours of time spent watching daddies and husbands hunched over a computer. (To Olga, Stephanie, and Brian Pande: *Now* the book is finished. Let's go play!)

Finally, we'd like to make a special dedication of this book to the memory of our great friend and colleague, Bill Lindenfelder. Bill was not only our partner in helping teach people about Six Sigma, but taught everyone who knew him about enthusiasm, encouragement, and boundless energy. We're among the many people who miss Bill enormously, and we hope he'd be proud to see some of his ideas and so much of his influence in these pages.

1

An Executive Overview of Six Sigma

CHAPTER

1

A Powerful Strategy for Sustained Success

THE MOST CHALLENGING question confronting business leaders and managers in the new millennium is not "How do we succeed?" It's: "How do we stay successful?"

Business today offers the spectacle of a succession of companies, leaders, products, and even industries getting their "15 minutes of fame" and then fading away. Even corporate powerhouses—the IBMs, Fords, Apples, Kodaks, and many others—go through dramatic cycles of near-death and rebirth. It's like riding the wheel of fortune as consumer tastes, technologies, financial conditions, and competitive playing fields change ever-more-quickly. In this high-risk environment, the clamor for ideas on how to get the edge, stop the wheel (while on top, of course), or anticipate the next change gets louder and louder. Hot new answers are almost as common as hot new companies.

Six Sigma can seem like another "hot new answer." But looking closer, you'll find there is a significant difference: Six Sigma is not a business fad tied to a single method or strategy, but rather a *flexible system* for improved business leadership and performance. It builds on many of the most important management ideas and best practices of the past century, creating a new formula for 21st-century business success. It's not about theory, it's about action. Evidence of the power of the Six Sigma Way is already visible in the huge gains tallied by some very high-profile companies and some not-so-high-profile ones, which we'll examine in a moment. Just as important, though, is the role Six Sigma plays in building new structures and practices to support *sustained* success.

The goal of *The Six Sigma Way* is to enable you to understand *what* Six Sigma is (both a simple and a complex question), *why* it's probably the best answer to improved business performance in years, and *how* to put it to work in the unique environment of your organization. In our mission to demystify Six Sigma for the executive and professional, we hope to show you that it's just as much about a passion for serving customers and a drive for great new ideas as it is about statistics and number-crunching; that the value of Six Sigma applies just as much to marketing, service, human resources, finance, and sales as it does to manufacturing and engineering. In the end we hope to give you a clearer picture of how Six Sigma—the *system*—can dramatically raise your odds for staying successful, even as you watch other companies ride one wave of good times only to wipe out on the next. (Our first and last surfing analogy!)

Some Six Sigma Success Stories

Seeing the impact that Six Sigma is having on some leading companies sets the stage for understanding how it can impact *your* business. As we relate some of these results, we'll also be reviewing the history that has brought Six Sigma to the forefront.

General Electric

Six Sigma has forever changed GE. Everyone—from the Six Sigma zealots emerging from their Black Belt tours, to the engineers, the auditors, and the scientists, to the senior leadership that will take this Company into the new millennium—is a true believer in Six Sigma, the way this Company now works." —*GE Chairman John F. Welch*[1]

When a high-profile corporate leader* starts using words like "unbalanced" or "lunatics" in connection with the future of the com-

* Since launching GE's effort in 1995, Jack Welch has urged his top lieutenants to become "passionate lunatics" about Six Sigma. He has described GE's commitment to Six Sigma as "unbalanced."

pany—you might expect a plunge in the company's share price. At General Electric, however, that passion and drive behind Six Sigma have produced some very positive results.

The hard numbers behind GE's Six Sigma initiative tell just part of the story. From an initial year or so of break-even efforts, the payoff has accelerated: $750 million by the end of 1998, a forecasted $1.5 billion by the end of 1999, and expectations of more billions down the road. Some Wall Street analysts have predicted *$5 billion* in gains from the effort, early in the decade. GE's operating margins—for decades in the 10 percent range—continue to hit new records quarter after quarter. The numbers are now consistently above 15 percent, and even higher in some periods. GE leaders cite this margin expansion as the most visible evidence of the financial contribution made by Six Sigma.

Improvements from Services to Manufacturing

The financial "big picture," though, is just a reflection of the many individual successes GE has achieved through its Six Sigma initiative. For example:

- A Six Sigma team at GE's Lighting unit repaired problems in its billing to one of its top customers—Wal-Mart—cutting invoice defects and disputes by 98 percent, speeding payment, and creating better productivity for both companies.
- A group led by a staff attorney—a Six Sigma team leader—at one of GE Capital's service businesses streamlined the contract review process, leading to faster completion of deals—in other words, more responsive service to customers—and annual savings of $1 million.
- GE's Power Systems group addressed a major irritant with its utility company customers, simply by developing a better understanding of their requirements and improving the *documentation* provided along with new power equipment. The result: Utilities can respond more effectively to their regulatory agencies, and both the utilities and GE have saved hundreds of thousands of dollars a year.
- The Medical Systems business—GEMS—used Six Sigma design techniques to create a breakthrough in medical scanning technology. Patients can now get a full-body scan in half a minute, versus three minutes or more with previous technology. Hospitals can

increase their usage of the equipment and achieve a lower cost per scan, as well.

- GE Capital Mortgage analyzed the processes at one of its top performing branches and—expanding these "best practices" across its other 42 branches—improved the rate of a caller reaching a "live" GE person from 76 to 99 percent. Beyond the much greater convenience and responsiveness to customers, the improved process is translating into millions of dollars in new business.

The Actions behind the Results

GE's successes are the result of a "passionate" commitment and effort. Notes Welch: "In nearly four decades with GE I have never seen a Company initiative move so willingly and so rapidly in pursuit of a big idea."[2] Tens of thousands of GE managers and associates have been trained in Six Sigma methods—a hefty investment in time and money (which is appropriately deducted from the gains cited earlier). The training has gone well beyond "Black Belts" and teams to include every manager and professional at GE—and many front-line people as well. They've instilled a new vocabulary revolving around customers, processes, and measurement.

While dollars and statistical tools seem to get the most publicity, the emphasis on *customers* is probably the most remarkable element of Six Sigma at GE. As Jack Welch explains it:

> **The best Six Sigma projects begin not inside the business but outside it, focused on answering the question—how can we make the customer more competitive? What is critical to the customer's success? . . . One thing we have discovered with certainty is that anything we do that makes the customer more successful inevitably results in a financial return for us.[3]**

Motorola—and Some Six Sigma History

Today, the very existence and success of electronics leader Motorola is tied to Six Sigma. It's the company that *invented* the concepts that have evolved into this comprehensive management system. And while GE has used Six Sigma to strengthen an already thriving company, for Motorola it was an answer to the question: How do we stay in business?

In the 1980s and early 1990s, Motorola was one of many U.S. and European corporations whose lunch (along with all other meals and snacks) was being eaten by Japanese competitors. Motorola's top leaders conceded that the quality of its products was awful. They were, to quote one Motorola Six Sigma veteran, "In a world of hurt." Like many companies at the time, Motorola didn't have one "quality" program, it had several. But in 1987, a new approach came out of Motorola's Communications Sector—at the time headed by George Fisher, later top exec at Kodak. The innovative improvement concept was called "Six Sigma."

What Six Sigma offered Motorola—though it involves much more today—was a simple, consistent way to track and compare performance to customer requirements (the Sigma *measure*) and an ambitious target of practically-perfect quality (the Six Sigma *goal*).

As it spread throughout the company—with the strong support of chairman Bob Galvin—Six Sigma gave Motorola extra "muscle" to drive what at the time seemed like impossible improvement goals: An initial target in the early 1980s of ten times improvement (noted as 10X, and pronounced "ten-ex") over five years, was dwarfed by a goal of 10X improvement every *two* years—or 100X in *four* years. While the objective of "Six Sigma" was important, much more attention was paid to the *rate* of improvement in processes and products.

Motorola's "turnaround" has been just as remarkable over the long term as GE's results in just a few years. Only two years after launching Six Sigma, Motorola was honored with the Malcolm Baldrige National Quality Award. The company's total employment has risen from 71,000 employees in 1980 to over 130,000 today. Meanwhile, in the decade between Six Sigma's beginning in 1987 and 1997, achievements have included the following:

- Five-fold growth in sales, with profits climbing nearly 20 percent per year
- Cumulative savings based on Six Sigma efforts pegged at $14 billion
- Motorola stock price gains compounded to an annual rate of 21.3 percent.

All this, in a business whose future was in jeopardy in the early 1980s. (While the late 1990s presented some tough challenges for

Motorola—based largely on setbacks and competition in the cellular and satellite telephone businesses—the company seems to be turning the corner in late 1999, with most areas back in the black.)

The results Motorola has achieved at the corporate level again have been the product of hundreds of individual improvement efforts affecting product design, manufacturing, and services in all its business units. Alan Larson, one of the early internal Six Sigma consultants at Motorola who later helped spread the concept to GE and AlliedSignal, says projects affected dozens of administrative and transactional processes. In customer support and product delivery, for example, improvements in measurement and a focus on better understanding of customer needs—along with new process management structures—made possible big strides toward improved services and on-time delivery.[4]

More than a set of tools, though, Motorola applied Six Sigma as a way to transform the business, a way driven by communication, training, leadership, teamwork, measurement, and a focus on customers (themes we'll be seeing plenty of throughout this book). As Larson notes: "Six Sigma is really a cultural thing—a way of behavior."

AlliedSignal/Honeywell

AlliedSignal—with the new name of "Honeywell" following its 1999 merger—is a Six Sigma success story that connects Motorola and GE. It was CEO Larry Bossidy—a longtime GE executive who took the helm at Allied in 1991—who convinced Jack Welch that Six Sigma was an approach worth considering. (Welch had been one of the few top managers not to become enamored of the TQM movement in the 1980s and early 1990s).

Allied began its own quality improvement activities in the early 1990s, and by 1999 was saving more than $600 million a year, thanks to the widespread employee training in and application of Six Sigma principles.[5] Not only were Allied's Six Sigma teams reducing the costs of reworking defects, they were applying the same principles to the design of new products like aircraft engines, reducing the time from design to certification from 42 to 33 months. The company credits Six Sigma with a 6 percent productivity increase in 1998 and with its record profit margins of 13 percent. Since the Six Sigma effort began, the firm's market value had—through fiscal year 1998—climbed to a compounded 27 percent per year.

Allied's leaders view Six Sigma as "more than just numbers—it's a statement of our determination to pursue a standard of excellence using every tool at our disposal and never hesitating to reinvent the way we do things."[6]

As one of Allied's Six Sigma directors puts it: "It's changed the way we think and the way we communicate. We never used to talk about the process or the customer; now they're part of our everyday conversation."

AlliedSignal's Six Sigma leadership has helped it earn recognition as the world's best-diversified company (from *Forbes* global edition) and the most admired global aerospace company (from *Fortune*).

The Six Sigma Wave

As we've noted, it might be easy to dismiss Six Sigma as a fad—if it weren't for the caliber of the results it's producing and the companies adopting it. In almost an antifad mentality, in fact, a number of prominent companies in industries from financial services to transportation to high-tech are *quietly* embarking on Six Sigma efforts. They're joining others who have been more vocal about their efforts, including Asea Brown Boveri, Black & Decker, Bombardier, Dupont, Dow Chemical, Federal Express, Johnson & Johnson, Kodak (which had taken in $85 million in savings as of early 2000), Navistar, Polaroid, Seagate Technologies, Siebe Appliance Controls, Sony, Toshiba, and many others.

From these and other Six Sigma companies come a wide variety of other impressive improvements, benefiting both customers and shareholders. A sample from the hundreds of Six Sigma projects underway at organizations around the world includes the following:

Developing New Products

A telecommunication products company used Six Sigma Design techniques to enable greater flexibility and faster turnaround at a key manufacturing facility. At the plant, several specialized products are built on a single production line. Since each customer's order may require different circuit boards, the need to avoid retooling was critical. Working through alignment of customer needs, product design, and process specifications, retooling was dramatically reduced. The plant was also able to institute parallel processing so that if one area of the line wasn't functioning, work-in-process could be easily rerouted without adding to cycle time.

Under the new plant design, customer orders are transmitted electronically, where "virtual design" applied to speed quick response. Altogether, these innovative changes improved overall cycle time from days to hours, as well as improving productivity and resource management.

Sending the Message Faster and Cheaper

Customers of a telecommunications service company were dismayed over the handling of their orders. Every request—for a few minutes of satellite time to a long-term, dedicated up-link—passed through several levels of legal and technical review before being approved. The process not only upset customers, but wasted resources and money.

A Six Sigma team measured and analyzed the problem. While proposed solutions were counter to the "tried and true" way of doing things, the team was able to sway opinions from solid data and knowledge of customer needs. After 6 months of effort the process was streamlined and $1 million in savings was tallied.

Providing a Prompt Answer

A credit financing center used a Six Sigma team approach to analyze and improve call center operations. The focus was on two objectives: (1) reducing average call answer time; and (2) increasing the percentage of customer issues and questions resolved in the initial call. The team "centralized and simplified" the call answering system, cutting average times from 54 seconds to 14 seconds. "First Call Resolution" jumped from 63 percent to 83 percent.

Thinking outside the Box

The spare parts marketing and logistics group for an aerospace manufacturing company was looking for ways to take costs and time out of their service to customers. One major cost element was parts packaging: Bulk parts shipments from manufacturing plants were unpacked, placed on warehouse shelves, then picked and repackaged for shipment to customers.

By focusing the process design on customer needs and value-adding activities, the spare parts packaging operation was moved from the warehouse to the plants. Packaging material cost savings alone were cut by half-a-million dollars per year. The change also contributed to major improvements in on-time-delivery, which have jumped from less than 80% to over 95% in about three years.

The Benefits of Six Sigma

These stories by themselves may be appealing, but if your company is doing okay—as GE was in 1995, when Jack Welch launched their effort—why should you consider a Six Sigma initiative? What's prompting so many businesses, prominent and modest, to invest in this funny-sounding business approach? Drawing from these success stories and those of other companies—and by looking behind the raw dollars—we can define several benefits that are attracting companies to the Six Sigma Way. Six Sigma:

1. *Generates sustained success.* John Chambers, CEO of Cisco Systems, the networking equipment powerhouse that's been one of the fastest-growing companies of the past decade, recently commented on the tenuous hold many companies have on their success: "There is the realization that you can be out of business in three years."[7] The only way to continue double-digit growth and retain a hold on shifting markets is to constantly innovate and remake the organization. Six Sigma creates the skills and culture for constant revival—what we'll describe in the next chapter as a "closed-loop system."
2. *Sets a performance goal for everyone.* In a company of any size—let alone a multibillion-dollar global corporation—getting everyone working in the same direction and focusing on a common goal is pretty tough. Each function, business unit, and individual has different objectives and targets. What everyone has in common, though, is the delivery of products, services, or information to customers (inside or outside the company). Six Sigma uses that common business framework—the process and the customer—to create a consistent goal: Six Sigma performance, or a level of performance that's about as close to perfect as most people can imagine. Anyone who understands their customers' requirements (and who shouldn't?) can assess their per-

formance against the Six Sigma goal of 99.9997 percent "perfect"—a standard so high that it makes most businesses' previous views of "excellent" performance look pretty weak. Figure 1.1 contrasts the number of problems that would be found with a goal of *99 percent quality* versus a goal of Six Sigma performance (99.9997 percent). The difference is pretty startling.

3. *Enhances value to customers.* When GE began its Six Sigma effort, executives admitted that the quality of the company's products was not what it should be. Though its quality was perhaps better than that of its competitors, Jack Welch stated that "We want to make our quality so special, so valuable to our customers, so important to their success that our products become their only real value choice."[8] With tighter competition in every industry, delivering just "good" or "defect-free" products and service won't guarantee success. The focus on customers at the heart of Six Sigma means learning *what* value means to customers (and prospective customers) and planning *how* to deliver it to them profitably.
4. *Accelerates the rate of improvement.* Motorola's goal of "100X improvement in four years" set an example for ambitious, driven organiza-

Performance Goals - What You'd Get ...	
For every 300,000 letters delivered:	
with 99%	*with Six Sigma*
3,000 misdeliveries	1 misdelivery
Out of every 500,000 computer restarts:	
with 99%	*with Six Sigma*
4,100 crashes	< 2 crashes
For 500 years of month-end closings:	
with 99%	*with Six Sigma*
60 months would not balance	.018 months would not balance
For every week of TV broadcasting (per channel):	
with 99%	*with Six Sigma*
1.68 hours of dead air	1.8 seconds of dead air

Figure 1.1 99% quality versus Six Sigma performance

tions to emulate. With information technology setting the pace by doubling its performance to cost ratio every 18 months, the customer expectation for improvement gets ever more demanding. The competitor who improves the fastest is likely to win the race. By borrowing tools and ideas from many disciplines, Six Sigma helps a company not only improve performance, but improve *improvement.*

5. *Promotes learning and "cross-pollination."* The 1990s saw the birth of the "Learning Organization," a concept that appeals to many but seems hard to put into action. AlliedSignal leaders have commented that "everyone talks about learning, but few succeed in weaving it into the fabric of everyday life for so many employees."[9] Six Sigma is an approach that can increase and accelerate the development and sharing of new ideas throughout an organization. Even in a company as diverse as GE, the value of Six Sigma as a learning tool is seen as critical. Skilled people with expertise in *processes* and how to manage and improve them can be shifted from, say, GE Plastics to GE Capital, not only with a shorter learning curve but actually bringing with them *better* ideas and the ability to apply them more quickly. Ideas can be shared and performance compared more readily. GE's vice president for Six Sigma, Piet van Abeelen, has noted that in the past, a manager in one part of the organization could discount input from a counterpart in another area: " 'Your ideas won't work, because I'm different.' " Van Abeelen says Six Sigma eliminates those defenses: "Well, cry me a river. The commonalities are what matter. If you make the metrics the same, we can talk."[10]
6. *Executes strategic change.* Introducing new products, launching new ventures, entering new markets, acquiring new organizations—what were once occasional business activities are now daily events in many companies. Better understanding of your company's processes and procedures will give you a greater ability to carry out *both* the minor adjustments and the major shifts that 21st-century business success will demand.

The Tools and Themes of Six Sigma

Like most great inventions, Six Sigma is not "all new." While some themes of Six Sigma arise out of fairly recent breakthroughs in management thinking, others have their foundation in common sense.

Before you dismiss that origin as no big deal, we'd remind you of a saying we picked up once while working in Europe: "Common sense is the least common of the senses." From a "tools" perspective, Six Sigma is a pretty vast universe. Figure 1.2 summarizes many—but by no means all—of the most important Six Sigma methods.

The more we have learned over the years about the Six Sigma system, the more we have come to see it as a way to link together—and even to implement—many otherwise disconnected ideas, trends, and tools in business today. Some of the "hot topics" that have direct application or can complement a Six Sigma initiative include:

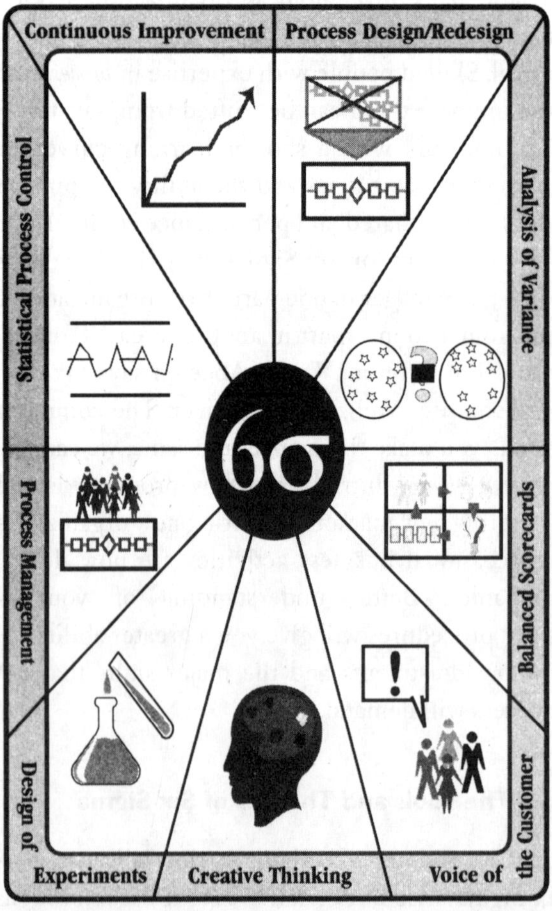

Figure 1.2 Essential Six Sigma methods and tools

- e-Commerce and Services
- Enterprise Resource Planning
- Lean manufacturing
- Customer Relationship Management systems
- Strategic business partnerships
- Knowledge management
- Activity-based management
- The "process-centered organization"
- Globalization
- Just-in-time inventory/production

Six Themes of Six Sigma

We'll close out this introductory look at Six Sigma by distilling the critical elements of this leadership system into six "themes." These principles—supported by the many Six Sigma tools and methods we'll be presenting throughout this book—will give you a preview of *how* we'll help you make Six Sigma work for your business.

Theme One: Genuine Focus on the Customer

During the big Total Quality push of the 1980s and 1990s, dozens of companies wrote policies and mission statements vowing to "meet or exceed customer expectations and requirements." Unfortunately, however, few businesses tried very hard to improve their *understanding* of customers' requirements or expectations. Even when they did, customer data-gathering typically was a one-time or short-lived initiative that ignored the dynamic nature of customer needs. (How many of your customers want the same stuff today as five years ago? Two years ago? Last month?)

In Six Sigma, customer focus becomes the top priority. For example, the measures of Six Sigma performance begin with the customer. Six Sigma improvements are defined by their impact on customer satisfaction and value. We'll look at why and how your business can define customer requirements, measure performance against them, and stay on top of new developments and unmet needs.

Theme Two: Data- and Fact-Driven Management

Six Sigma takes the concept of "management by fact" to a new, more powerful level. Despite the attention paid in recent years to measures, improved information systems, knowledge management, etc., it should come as no shock to you to hear that many business decisions are still being based on opinions and assumptions. Six Sigma discipline begins by clarifying *what* measures are key to gauging business performance; then it applies data and analysis so as to build an understanding of key variables and optimize results.

At a more down-to-earth level, Six Sigma helps managers answer two essential questions to support fact-driven decisions and solutions:

1. What data/information do I *really* need?
2. How do we *use* that data/information to maximum benefit?

Theme Three: Process Focus, Management, and Improvement

In Six Sigma, processes are where the action is. Whether designing products and services, measuring performance, improving efficiency and customer satisfaction—or even running the business—Six Sigma positions the *process* as the key vehicle of success.

One of the most remarkable breakthroughs in Six Sigma efforts to-date has been convincing leaders and managers—particularly in the service-based functions and industries—that mastering processes is not just a necessary evil but actually a way to build competitive advantage in delivering value to customers. There are many more people to convince—with huge dollar opportunities tied up in those activities.

Theme Four: Proactive Management

Most simply, being "proactive" signifies acting in advance of events—the opposite of being "reactive." In the real world, though, proactive management means making *habits* out of what are, too often, neglected business practices: defining ambitious goals and reviewing them frequently; setting clear priorities; focusing on problem prevention versus firefighting; questioning *why* we do things instead of blindly defending them as "how we do things here."

Being truly proactive, far from being boring or overly analytical, is actually a starting point for creativity and effective change. Reactively bouncing from crisis to crisis makes you very busy—giving a false impression that you're on top of things. In reality, it's a sign of a manager or an organization that's lost control.

Six Sigma, as we'll see, encompasses tools and practices that replace reactive habits with a dynamic, responsive, proactive style of management. Considering today's slim-margin-for-error competitive environment, being proactive is (as the airline commercial said) "the only way to fly."

Theme Five: Boundaryless Collaboration

"Boundarylessness" is one of Jack Welch's mantras for business success. Years before launching Six Sigma, GE's chairman was working to break down barriers and improve teamwork, up, down, and across organizational lines. The opportunities available through improved collaboration within companies and with their vendors and customers are huge. Billions of dollars are left on the table (or on the floor) every day, because of disconnects and outright competition between groups that should be working for a common cause: providing value to customers.

As noted above, Six Sigma expands opportunities for collaboration as people learn how their roles fit into the "big picture" and can recognize and measure the interdependence of activities in all parts of a process. Boundaryless collaboration in Six Sigma does not mean selfless sacrifice, but it does require an understanding of both the real needs of end users and of the flow of work through a process or a supply chain. Moreover, it demands an attitude that is committed to using customer and process knowledge to benefit all parties. Thus, the Six Sigma system can create an environment and management structures that support true teamwork.[11]

Theme Six: Drive for Perfection; Tolerance for Failure

This last theme may seem contradictory. How can you be driven to achieve perfection and yet also tolerate failure? In essence, though, the two ideas are complementary. No company will get anywhere close to Six Sigma without launching new ideas and approaches—which always involve some risk. If people who see a possible path to better service, lower costs, new capabilities, etc. (i.e. ways to be closer-to-perfect) are too afraid of the consequences of mistakes, they'll never try. The result: stagnation, putrefaction, death. (Pretty grim, eh?)

Fortunately, the techniques we'll review for improving performance include a significant dose of risk management (if you're gonna fail, make it a safe failure). The bottom line, though, is that any company that makes Six Sigma its goal will have to constantly push to be ever-more-perfect (since the customer's definition of "perfect" will always be changing) while being willing to accept—and manage—occasional setbacks.

Where You Stand

We would be surprised if you weren't saying to yourself right about now: "We're already *doing* some of those things." But remember, we've already noted that much of Six Sigma is not brand-new. What *is* new is its ability to bring together all these themes into a coherent management process.

As you review this introduction and guide to the Six Sigma way, we encourage you to take stock of what you are already doing that supports the themes or tools of Six Sigma—and keep doing them. Meanwhile, be honest about your business's strengths and weaknesses. One thing we've noticed about Six Sigma is that results come much faster when an organization is willing to admit to its shortcomings, learn from them, and start setting priorities to correct them.

Businesses or managers who puff out their chests and claim to have all the answers are invariably the ones in greatest danger; they stop learning, fall behind, and end up having to scramble to catch up—if it isn't too late.

CHAPTER

2

Key Concepts of the Six Sigma System

LIKE ALL SYSTEMS, Six Sigma is made up of essential components that combine to drive improved business performance. Having taken a look in Chapter 1 at some of the results and key themes of Six Sigma, we'll now dig deeper into the questions "What is Six Sigma?" and "Why Six Sigma?" by describing in greater detail some of the key elements of the system.

A Six Sigma Vision of Business Leadership

Creating a Closed-Loop System[1]

Imagine a young child is learning how to ride a bike, and that you as parent, relative, neighbor, are there to help and offer encouragement. You want to see the kid succeed—much as an investor wants to see its business offspring thrive. You give the kid a push, and for a while you watch him or her ride beautifully: balanced, head erect, proud. "Look, I'm doing it!", you hear—just before the kid runs off the path and into a bush. Of course, you're well aware that kids learning to ride bicycles fall off and run into the bushes pretty often at first, so you just pick the child up and put him/her back onto the bike.

Businesses, too, get off course, fall down, run into the bushes. And if they're lucky—or if they catch themselves fast enough—companies too can just brush themselves off and get back on the path. If the mistake is too serious, however, its bike riding days are over; the company is out of business for good.

Biking and the Art of Six Sigma Management

Both successful bike riding and successful business management (over the long term) rely on the same thing: a "closed-loop system" in which both the internal and external sorts of information ("feedback" or "stimuli") tell the rider/manager how to correct course, stay upright, and steer successfully. A good closed-loop system should work even on a winding path, or in a treacherous business environment. But as we can see around any schoolyard, bike riding comes a lot more naturally than managing a business. Long after most kids are riding with no hands—or even getting into "extreme" bike stunts—businesses are still wobbling uncertainly down the path, hoping no one has decided to put in a curve lately.[2]

Six Sigma is based in large measure on creating a closed-loop business system that is sensitive enough to reduce the company's "wobbling" and keep it safely on the often-twisted path to performance and success (see Fig. 2.1). In this case, though, instead of a bike the vehicle is the *process* (or actually, many processes). The internal "stimuli" (like the inner ear) are the measures of activity inside the process. As for the external feedback elements, the ones that tell the company if it has met its goals and is still on the right path, they include profits, customer satisfaction, and a variety of other data sources.

In the vocabulary of Six Sigma, the wobbling or inconsistency of a business system is "variation." The types of bad variation that have a negative impact on customers we'll call "defects." And the approaches used to create, monitor, and *improve* that closed-loop business system we'll call "process management," "process improvement," and "process design/redesign."

System Alignment: Tracking the Xs and Ys

Some concepts from algebra are commonly used to describe this closed-loop concept in Six Sigma companies. (This isn't too technical,

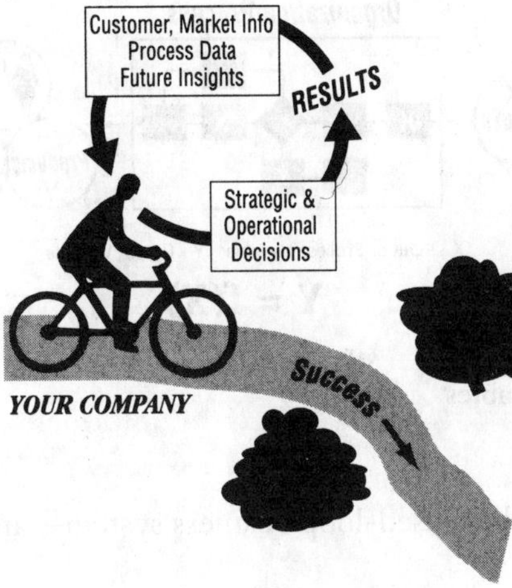

Figure 2.1 A closed-loop system: staying on the path to success

so hang in there.) In Fig. 2.2 you see a model of a company as seen from a process-flow perspective. On the far-left are the inputs to the process (or system); in the middle is the organization or process itself (depicted as a process map or flowchart). Finally, on the far-right, are the all-important customer, end products, and (let's hope) profits. In Fig. 2.3 we've added some letters, which represent measures or "variables" at different points in the system. The "Xs" that show up in the Input and Process flow would be indicators of change or performance in the "upstream" portions of the system. The "Ys" on the right represent measures of the business's performance—like the final score in a game. The formula $Y=f(X)$ ("Y is a function of X") is just a mathematical way of saying that changes or variables in the inputs and process of the system will largely determine how the final score—or Ys—turn out.

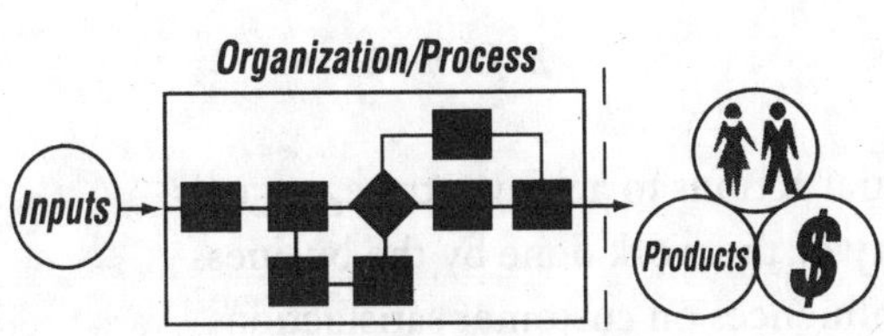

Figure 2.2 The business process model

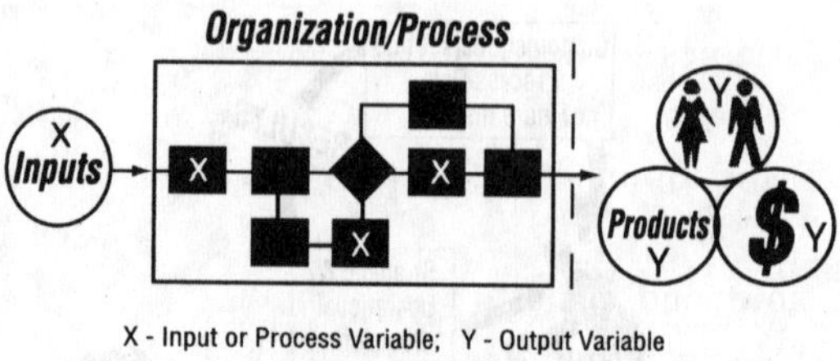

$$Y = f(X)$$

Figure 2.3 Upstream (X) and downstream (Y) variables

The trick of the closed-loop business system—and it ain't easy—is twofold:

1. To figure out *which* of the Xs or variables in the business process and inputs have the biggest influence on the Ys or results.
2. To use the changes in the overall performance of the process (the Ys, as well as other external factors) to adjust the business and keep it moving on a profitable path.

At Six Sigma companies, this language of Xs and Ys becomes routine. Still, these variables tend to take on a variety of meanings; for example:

Y Can Mean:

Strategic goal
Customer requirement
Profits
Customer satisfaction
Overall business efficiency

X Can Mean:

Essential actions to achieve strategic goals
Quality of the work done by the business
Key influences on customer satisfaction

Process variables such as staffing, cycle time, amount of technology, etc.

Quality of the inputs to the process (from customers or suppliers)

Most companies and managers have a pretty weak understanding of the relationship between their own Xs and Ys. They keep their corporate bikes on the path just through luck, or else by making a lot of *major* corrections as they go. But by using Six Sigma methods to understand the system and the variables, a company can learn to monitor and respond to the feedback so that its path forward feels smoother and faster. Like a skilled bicycle rider, it can "automatically" respond to signals from its processes, suppliers, employees, and especially customers and competitors, thereby achieving new levels of strength and performance.

An Introduction to Sigma Measurement (aka "the Big Y")

It's time to explain in more detail both the original meaning of the term "Six Sigma" and the measure it describes. At this point we'll look only at some of the concepts behind Six Sigma measures and what those measures *are.* For more on how to calculate it, you can take a look at Chapter 14.

Sigma, Standard Deviation, and Eliminating Variation

The lower-case letter "sigma" in the Greek alphabet—σ—is a symbol used in statistical notation to represent the "standard deviation" of a population. Standard deviation—as you may recall from statistics courses—is an indicator of the amount of "variation" or inconsistency in any group of items or process. For example when you buy fast food that's nice and hot one day, lukewarm the next—that's variation. Or if you buy three shirts of the same size and one is too small, that's also variation. In fact there are infinite examples of variation because *everything* varies to some degree or another; variation is a part of life.[3]

The Evils of Variation

In discussing variation, Six Sigma people tend to use words like *evil* and phrases like "the enemy"—almost as if the diabolical Professor Variation (Dr. Evil's cousin?) were plotting to take over the world. In fact, however, variation is no joke when it affects customers. If I'm asking for a home loan, for example, and the lending company says it'll take "about two or three weeks" to get an answer (indicating a lot of variation in their process), that may have a big impact on whether I decide to do business with that lender. For if I do, who knows if I'll get the money on time? Another example: When you arrive at an airport, you never know if it'll be 5 minutes or 20 before your luggage gets to baggage claim—so you may wait around for 15 minutes when you could have been making phone calls, reading, buying frozen yogurt, or engaging in some other useful activity.

Variation in products is a critical concern, too. With complex electronics or mechanical parts, variations in current or width or weight from item to item can add up (this is sometimes called "tolerance stacking") until the whole thing falls apart. Or if your company makes a part that another company puts into their product, your inconsistency/variation may require them to exert an extra effort just to get your part to work—not a good value proposition for your customer. Finally, if a consumer buys a toaster that browns one piece of toast but burns the next—and you never touched the settings—that can waste a lot of bread.

The Advantages of Taking a Variation Perspective

Looking at variation helps management to much more fully understand the *real* performance of a business and its processes. In the past—and still often today—organizations measure and describe their efforts in terms of "averages": average cost, average cycle time, average shipment size, etc. But averages can actually *hide* problems by disguising variation.

For example, if you were promising customers that orders for custom parts would be filled within six working days of the date they were ordered, you might find it good news to learn that your *average* order-to-delivery performance is at 4.2 days. *But,* that average number could miss the fact that—due to wide variation in your process—more than 15 percent of orders are arriving in *more* than six days (i.e., *late!*). Without reducing the overall variation, you'd have to reach an average delivery time of *two* days just to get all orders to meet your six-day commitment. By significantly reducing the variation, however, you could have achieved an average delivery time of five days while having *no* late deliveries. Thus, understanding and addressing variation can benefit both you and your customers, because you no longer have to *compensate* for unpredictable efforts just to meet customers' requirements. (In most cases, for example, a five-day average delivery time is less expensive to achieve than a two-day).

The objective in driving for Six Sigma performance is to reduce or narrow variation to such a degree that six Sigmas—or standard deviations of variation—can be squeezed within the limits defined by the customer's specifications. For many products, services, and processes that means a huge, and tremendously valuable, degree of improvement.

Six Sigma Commuting

We can use another example to illustrate the variation idea in a bit more detail.

Let's say that you've decided to evaluate your "process" for getting to work, with the goal of ensuring you get to work on time, every day. "On time" means arriving at work at 8:30 a.m.—give or take a couple of minutes. Let's first assume (just to keep this simple) that you *always* leave the house precisely at 8:12 a.m. You know, therefore, that your "target" commute time is 18 minutes. For you, the 18-minute commute is ideal anyway, because it gives you a chance to get your mind geared up for work and review your plans for the day.

Since it's acceptable to arrive two minutes before or after 8:30, the "specification limits"—or customer requirements—range from a 16- and 20-minute commute. Any time within that range is acceptable to you, the customer of your commuting process. (We note these limits as LSL for "lower specification limit" and USL for "upper specification limit".)

The next question is: How much time does it *really* take to get to work? To find out, you gather some data, timing your trips each workday for several months. A few people wonder what you're doing with that stopwatch, but you've been eccentric all your life and it comes with the territory. When you first compile your data, it looks pretty good: Your average commute time is *exactly* 18 minutes, which is "perfect"!

But taking a closer look, things aren't so rosy. Putting all the data into a "histogram" (aka bell-shaped curve), you see that there's really a *lot* of variation in the time it takes you to get from home to office. As you can see in Figure 2.4, there are plenty of days outside your specification limits when you arrive more than two minutes early or more than two minutes late. "No wonder," you exclaim, "that on some days the coffee isn't ready and on others there are no parking spaces left!"

To confirm the amount of the variation in your commute process, you calculate the standard deviation for the data you gathered (a pretty easy task using spreadsheet or statistics software). It turns out your standard deviation (σ) equals 2.7 minutes (as shown on Fig. 2.4)—meaning less than one "sigma" fits within your specification limits of +/− 2 minutes from the average.

Clearly, this is *not* good! If you *always* wanted to be early, you'd have to start leaving home well before your accustomed 8:12 departure time. But then, of course, many days you'd be all alone, wasting time—and you'd *always* be the one to have to make the coffee. Besides, having listened to Six Sigma inspirational cassettes on your trips to the office, you know that variation like this is the *enemy* and needs to be eliminated.

So you take action to improve your commuting process: no more shortcuts, for example. You have your car's cruise control recalibrated so you can set a precise speed. You discipline yourself not to sit in the parking lot listening to just one more Golden Oldie before going into the building. *Et cetera.* After your improvements are implemented, you anxiously gather more data on the trip time.

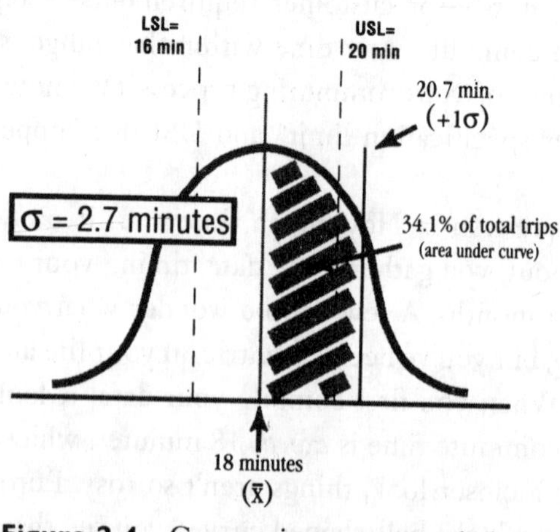

Figure 2.4 Commuting process variation: before improvement

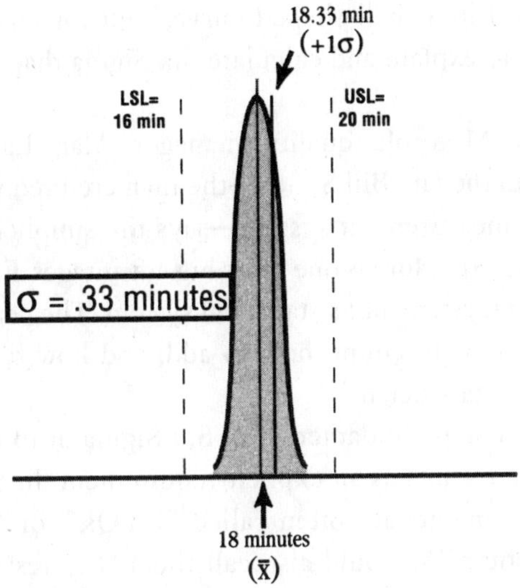

Figure 2.5 Commuting process variation: improved to 6σ

As you can see in Fig. 2.5, your efforts worked! The average commute time is still 18 minutes, but the variation is *much* reduced. If you can maintain this range consistently (i.e., keep good control of your commuting process), the chances of arriving at work in less than 16 or more than 20 minutes is *almost zero.*

Statistically speaking, you've reduced the standard deviation from 2.7 minutes to just .33 minutes—meaning you can fit *six* standard deviations of performance from the average (still 18 *within* your specification limits). Now that's Six Sigma performance!

Any *business* that can reduce its variation to that degree gains a huge edge in efficiency, not to mention customer satisfaction. Put this way, it's really no wonder that Six Sigma is an attractive target for so many company leaders.

Customers, Defects, and Sigma Levels

In the preceding example, we've described Six Sigma performance in terms of reducing the sigma (i.e. standard deviation) of a process—or narrowing the range of variation—so as to fit all the output within customer specifications.[4] Of course, not every problem or set of data can be displayed in a "bell-shaped curve;" but fortunately we can use an easier way to explain and calculate Six Sigma that works for most situations.

Former Motorola quality manager Alan Larson, who worked closely with the late Bill Smith—the man credited with developing the Six Sigma measurement system—says the simplicity of the approach we're about to explore is one of its big advantages. Explains Larson: "It's really a *math* system, not a statistical system. The beauty is, all you need to know is how to count, how to add, and how to divide—you don't have to be a statistician."

The first step, fundamental to Six Sigma, it to clearly define what the customer wants as an explicit requirement. In Six Sigma language these requirements are often called "CTQs," for "critical to quality" characteristics. (We could also call them "key results," or "Ys" of the process, or "specification limits.") The next step is to count the number of *defects* that occur. We've used that term a lot already, but we need to give it a clear definition now:

> *A* defect *is any instance or event in which the product or process fails to meet a customer requirement.*

Once we've counted defects, we can calculate the "yield" of the process (percentage of items *without* defects), and use a handy table to determine the "Sigma level."

Sigma levels of performance are also often expressed in "Defects per Million Opportunities" or "DPMO"—also shown in Fig. 2.6. DPMO simply indicates how many errors would show up if an activity were to be repeated a million times. By factoring in opportunities for defects in the calculation, Motorola made it more realistic to equate performance across different processes. We cover DPMO calculation in Chapter 14, but for now you can think of it simply as another way to describe the quality or capability of a process.

Summary of Sigma Measure Benefits

Companies adopting the Six Sigma system have found that the "Sigma scale" approach to evaluating process performance offers them some significant advantages. To recap, Sigma measures

Simplified Sigma Conversion Table:

If your Yield is ...	Your DPMO is ...	Your Sigma is ...
30.9 %	690,000	1.0
69.2	308,000	2.0
93.3	66,800	3.0
99.4	6,210	4.0
99.98	320	5.0
99.9997	3.4	6.0

Figure 2.6 Simplified Sigma Conversion Table

1. *Start with the customer.* Sigma measures demand a clear definition of what the customer's requirements are. That clarity can benefit both you *and* the customer, in terms of thinking through what's really important.
2. *Provide a consistent metric.* With their focus on defects and defect opportunities, Six Sigma measures can be used to measure and compare very different processes throughout an organization—or between organizations. Once you've defined the requirement clearly, you can define a "defect" and measure almost any type of business activity or process. Here's just a tiny sample:

   - Typos in a document
   - Long hold times in a Call Center
   - Late deliveries
   - Incomplete shipments
   - Medication errors
   - Power outages
   - Systems crashes
   - Parts shortages
   - Post-sale repairs
   - Expense check discrepancies

3. *Link to an ambitious goal.* Having an entire organization focused on a performance objective of 99.9997 percent perfect can create significant momentum for improvement. The Six Sigma measurement approach—provided you invest some thought and effort in setting it

up properly—can create a common "measurement language" usable in all parts of a business.

Sigma Measures: Considering Your Options

It's important to note that there's nothing *mandatory* about using the Sigma scale. It's possible, first of all, to achieve Six Sigma performance and never look at a Sigma conversion table. Also, there are other valid ways to measure and express the performance of a process or product/service. For example, manufacturing quality people have been using various measurement methods for years—control charts and process capability indicators, for example—that can give you a similar perspective on process quality.

You should also be aware of some of the "logistical" issues that surround Six Sigma measures:

- For Six Sigma measures to be applied effectively across an organization, guidelines need to be established. Otherwise they can be calculated inconsistently—making it potentially unfair if two groups are compared based on different assumptions. At Motorola, for example, a committee was used to establish guidelines for calculating Sigma measures.
- Sigma measures are not "static." As customer requirements change, Sigma performance will change—usually looking worse. For example, if your customer calls to inform you that they can no longer get by with next-day delivery but now need everything the *same* day, your performance is likely to take an immediate hit. In some Six Sigma organizations, calculations continue to be made simultaneously on "old rules" and "new rules" for a while, to make the transition smoother.
- As is true with all measures, getting Sigma scores on processes throughout an organization takes time and resources. You'll need to set priorities on what can and should be measured: Don't expect to have a full slate of accurate Sigma performance data for every part of a company in the short term.

Overall, you should think of Sigma-scale measures as an optional element of the Six Sigma system. We know of quite a few businesses—

including some units of GE—that express their overall measures as DPMO and only occasionally translate them to the Sigma scale.

A final point: None of these measures of results—or Ys—will improve your performance by themselves. Without methods for analysis and improvement—and data to determine what makes the organization work more effectively—DPMO or Sigma represent just a final report card. Let's look next at the methods that drive Six Sigma improvement.

Six Sigma Improvement and Management Strategies

Customer knowledge and effective measures are the fuel of the Six Sigma system. The engine they propel is made up of three basic elements (see Fig. 2.7), all of them focused on the *processes* of your organization. The linking up of these approaches is one of the most important (and least recognized) innovations that Six Sigma brings.

Process Improvement: Finding Targeted Solutions

The term "process improvement" refers to a strategy of developing focused solutions so as to eliminate the root causes of business performance problems. Other terms that have been used synonymously include "continuous improvement," "incremental improvement," or "*Kaizen*" (Japanese for "continuous improvement"). In essence, a

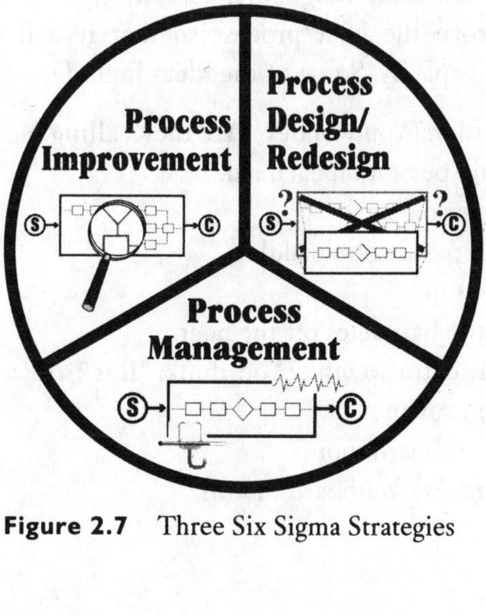

Figure 2.7 Three Six Sigma Strategies

Process Improvement effort seeks to *fix* a problem while leaving the basic structure of the work process intact. In Six Sigma terms, the emphasis is on finding and targeting solutions to address the "vital few" factors (the Xs) that cause the problem or pain (the Y). Thus, the vast majority of Six Sigma projects are Process Improvement efforts.

The Sigma Shores Transportation Company

Imagine that you're in the water transportation business and your market niche is to row people in a small boat across a quarter-mile-wide channel. Your typical customer is on a weekday picnic or a weekend outing, so the leisurely row across the channel meets their requirements perfectly.

On some weekdays, though, you're getting more and more of a new kind of customer: *commuters* trying to avoid traffic to and from the bridge over the channel. Their speed requirements are a little more stringent; these folks want to get to the other side pretty quickly. Plus, since you can only take three people at a time, a line is starting to form on the landings on either side of the channel.

As you gather data, you find it's taking you an average of 7.5 minutes in each direction to cross the channel—and that your slow cycle time is creating the backups at the dock. Your problem is obvious: The boat (your process) is currently too slow.

In a brainstorming meeting with your management team (your spouse, kids, and some neighbors, actually), you develop a list of ways to improve the boat/process so that it will go faster and increase your capacity. Some of the ideas include:

- Row harder! (You wonder: "Are they calling me lazy?")
- Have one person on each oar.
- Get bigger oars.
- Give the passengers paddles.
- Put up a sail.
- Scrape the barnacles off the boat.
- Toss out extra weight. (You think: "But I *like* to bring a beer when I'm rowing!")
- Add an outboard motor.
- Add a *big, huge* outboard motor!

At first, you're not sure which idea is best. So you gather some more data, and find that two solutions are most cost-effective and address the real root causes of your slow trips. You decide to scrape the boat and to increase your stroke rate by 10 per minute; and sure enough, you cut your round-trip time by three minutes.

In a few months, though, you've attracted more business and the "problem" is back: lines at the dock. Your next solution is to buy a moderate-sized outboard motor—which you can afford now, thanks to your increased revenues. The motor works great, and now the boat/process is really humming along. You've managed to take a 15-minute round trip and cut it to 5. The *Sigma Shores Transportation Company* (your new company name) is thriving. Customers are thrilled! And you've just successfully implemented two rounds of Process Improvement.

Process Design/Redesign: Building a Better Business

One of the reasons business leaders lost patience with "quality" initiatives back in the 1980s, was the slow pace of improvement they seemed to generate. That frustration opened the door to a new fad: the "reengineering" boom of the early to mid 1990s. While reengineering ended up producing its own disappointments, it did offer an important perspective on driving better business performance: Incremental improvements alone don't allow you to keep up with the rapid pace of change in the areas of technology, customer demands, and competition.

That's why Six Sigma brings together *both* Process Improvement and Design/Redesign, incorporating them as essential, complementary strategies for sustained success. In the design/redesign mode, the objective is not to *fix* but rather to *replace* a process (or a piece of a process) with a new one. It also ties into product and service design—often called "Six Sigma Design"—in which Six Sigma principles are used to create new goods and services tightly linked to customer needs and validated by data and testing.

In today's business world, no company is likely to stay on top for long that doesn't rethink at least some key processes on a regular basis. Chuck Cox, a speaker, consultant, and co-author of a book on process and product design, says there should probably be a rule of thumb to "redesign major processes every five years. Things change that fast." Even reengineering champion Michael Hammer has noted that continuous improvement "and reengineering fit together over time in the life story of a process. First the process is enhanced [improved] until its useful lifetime is over, at which point it is reengineered. Then, enhancement is resumed and the entire cycle starts again."[5]

Major Redesign at Sigma Shores Transportation

The success of Process Improvement at your water transportation business is exceeding your wildest dreams. Lines at the landings are even longer than before. Also, you're getting requests from customers to transport them down the channel and out into the bay—not only a long trip, but dangerous for your little boat. It's becoming clear that your boat/process isn't up to the job anymore. It has reached what process design experts would call its "entitlement"—the limit of its capability as currently designed. When a work process hits that barrier—i.e., when the structure or basic premises of a process aren't keeping up with changing needs or opportunities—the only real recourse is to design a new process. In other words: Time to get a *new* boat!

Just making that fairly simple decision can open up a whole new panorama of innovations that weren't there for you when you were limited to "fixes." The implications of process design or redesign—as here, in getting a new boat—can be enormous. First of all a new boat, or a new process, can be a big investment. But there are plenty of other considerations as well:

- *Skills.* Do you know how to operate a bigger boat? You, or anybody who's working with you, will need to be trained and perhaps even certified to handle the new equipment and procedures. People may find themselves in completely new jobs they hadn't expected to be filling—or may not even want.
- *Customers.* How will they respond to a new boat? Will the intimate service and easy access of the rowboat be missed too much? Can you continue to attract enough customers to your crossing? Why do your customers really come to you—for the transportation, or the "rowboat experience"?

- *Competitors.* Will major ferry companies or other boating entrepreneurs invade your market? Will you sustain enough business to fully engage the new, bigger boat?
- *Other Processes and Facilities.* You and a few helpers have been able to handle ticket-taking, reservations, embarkation and debarkation, and the maintenance of your outboard-powered rowboat. With a big new boat, however, processes on either side of the channel will need to be improved or redesigned, too.

Still, in spite of all these worries and considerations, you realize you have no choice. Without the significant (exponential) leap in performance that your new boat surely will bring, your business will stagnate, and likely lose its edge in the local transportation market. So you go ahead and make the major investment in time, money and creativity to upgrade your processes, and you buy a shiny new, 30-passenger mini-ferry. Through careful design, planning, and testing, the new Sigma Shores Ferry is successfully launched—and you've reached a whole new level of performance.

Process Management: The Infrastructure for Six Sigma Leadership

The third key strategy of Six Sigma is the most evolutionary. It involves a change in focus from oversight and direction of *functions* to the understanding and facilitation of *processes,* the flow of work that provides value to customers and shareholders. In a mature Process Management approach, the themes and methods of Six Sigma become an integral part of running the business:

- Processes are documented and managed "end-to-end"—and responsibility has been assigned in such a way as to ensure cross-functional management of critical processes.
- Customer requirements are clearly defined and regularly updated.
- Measures of outputs, process activities, and inputs are thorough and meaningful.
- Managers and associates (including "process owners") use the measures and process knowledge to assess performance in "real time" and take action to address problems and opportunities.

- Process Improvement and Process Design/Redesign—built around the improvement tools of Six Sigma—are used to constantly raise the company's levels of performance, competitiveness, and profitability.

We've described Process Management as "evolutionary," because it is an approach that organizations tend to learn and develop slowly. The growth of Process Management as a practice actually parallels the expansion of Six Sigma into a complete management system.

Sigma Shores Institutes Process Management

Having totally revamped your business and processes in upgrading to a new ferry, you now make a vow: "Never again will I let an opportunity as big as what we've had sneak up on me." So you take steps to establish a more proactive, customer- and process-focused approach to managing the business. You assign your top staff members to take charge of key activities: promotions and sales, customer reservations and embarkation, on-board operations, landing and debarkation. Rather than "departments" you describe these as "processes," each defined by a process map and tracked by key measures.

At Sigma Shores Ferry, each manager keeps track of his or her critical process, communicating with counterparts so as to ensure smooth handoffs (of customers, in particular) and to share useful data. Your "Customer Acquisition" (i.e., sales) process owner expands your customer and competitive research efforts, thereby giving you better, more up-to-date information on how your service is performing and on any opportunities or threats. Having key measures on arrival times, service factors, customer boarding, boat efficiency (e.g., fuel usage) helps you make a healthy profit while maximizing customer satisfaction. Your organization is no longer lurching from crisis to crisis; it's a finely-tuned *machine.*

As you begin to solidify your Six Sigma–based management system, new employees are trained in a common model that guides any Process Improvement or Design/Redesign project. This model—which you call "DMAIC"—gives your people a consistent way to manage change and improvement in your growing organization.

The DMAIC Six Sigma Improvement Model

There have been many "improvement models" applied to processes over the years since the quality movement began. Most of these are based on the steps introduced by W. Edwards Deming—Plan-Do-Check-Act, or P-D-C-A—which describes the basic logic of data-based process improvement:[6]

- *Plan.* Review current performance for issues and gaps. Gather data on key problems. Identify and target root causes of problems. Devise possible solutions, and plan a test implementation of the highest potential solution.
- *Do.* Pilot the planned solution.
- *Check* (or *study*). Measure the results of the test to see if the intended results are being achieved. If problems arise, look into the barriers that are obstructing your improvement efforts.
- *Act.* Based on the test solution and evaluation, refine and expand the solution to make it permanent, and incorporate the new approach wherever applicable. *Start over. . . .*

Define-Measure-Analyze-Improve-Control, or DMAIC

In *The Six Sigma Way,* we will use and refer to a five-phase improvement cycle that has become increasingly common in Six Sigma organizations: Define, Measure, Analyze, Improve, and Control—or DMAIC (pronounced "deh-MAY-ihk") (see Fig. 2.8).[7] Like other improvement models, DMAIC is grounded in the original PDCA cycle; however, we will be using DMAIC to apply to *both* Process Improvement and Process Design/Redesign efforts. Therefore, whenever we refer to "DMAIC projects" throughout the remainder of this book, we are talking about efforts using either Six Sigma improvement strategy. Figure 2.9 provides a diagram of the major DMAIC activities, comparing the "Process Improvement" to the "Process Design/Redesign" paths.

Defining the "Six Sigma Organization"

To close out this discussion of the key concepts of Six Sigma, let's take a brief look at the notion of a "Six Sigma Organization." In the follow-

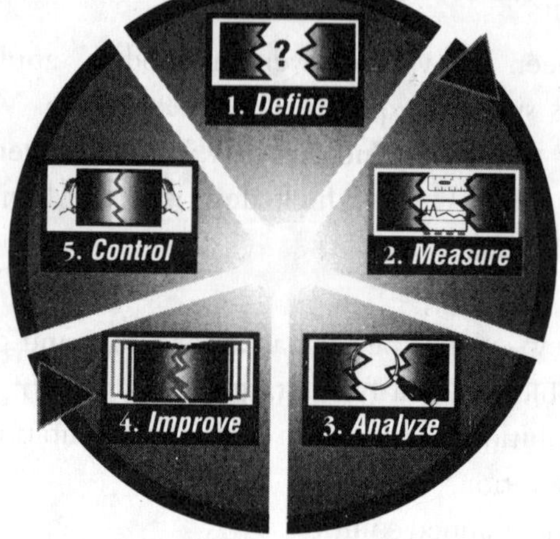

Figure 2.8 The DMAIC Six Sigma improvement model

ing chapter, as we compare TQM efforts to Six Sigma, you'll be able to see more clearly what a Six Sigma organization looks like.

Our proposed definition of a *Six Sigma Organization*—and the one we'll be sticking with in this book—is this:

> *An organization that is actively working to build the themes and practices of Six Sigma into its daily management activities, and is showing significant improvements in process performance and customer satisfaction.*

Now for a few notes to accompany that definition.

1. To qualify, *you do not need to have achieved actual Six Sigma levels of performance* (99.9997 percent perfect) *on any process.* Some people draw the false conclusion that a "Six Sigma organization" like GE or Motorola has actually reached this quality nirvana all across the board—which is far from the truth. They may have accomplished it in some processes (at GE's Americom satellite communications company, we heard of some Six Sigma performance levels), but no company has more than a few processes at that level (yet). But don't get discouraged: Just taking all your processes to *Four* Sigma—99.37 percent yield—would be an enormous achievement for any company we can think of.

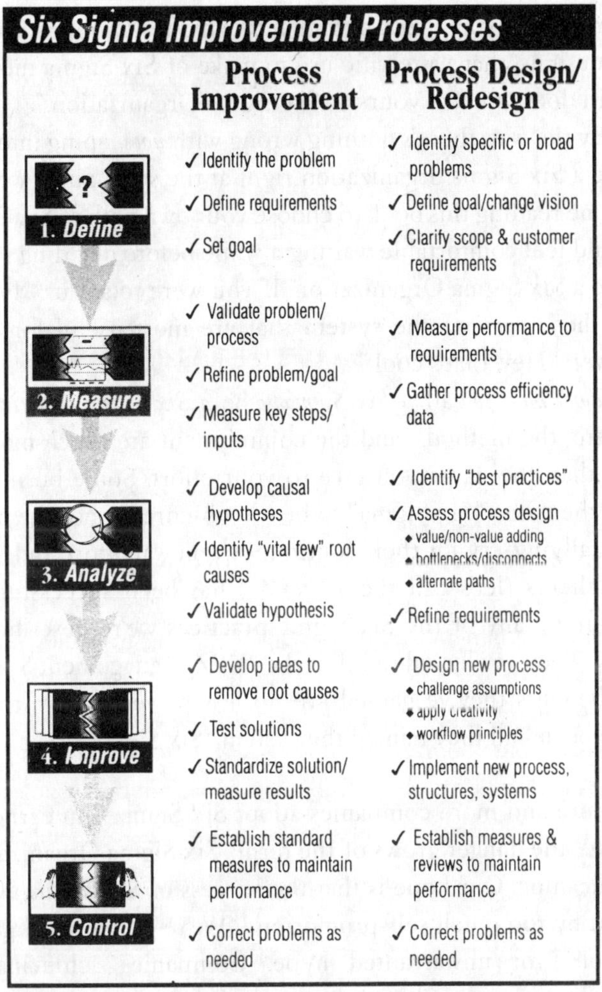

Figure 2.9 Overview of Process Improvement and Process Design/Redesign "paths" in DMAIC model

2. *Simply using Sigma measures or a few tools does not qualify a company to be a "Six Sigma Organization," either.* Our definition makes the criteria tougher by demanding a *broad scope* of activity and commitment. A real "Six Sigma Organization" should be one that has taken up the challenge of measuring and improving *all* processes, with the objective of building that responsive, closed-loop system for business leadership we've described. Or to borrow a theme from AlliedSignal, to "create a culture of continuous renewal." If, for example,

your company applies Six Sigma techniques to improve new product designs, that's a terrific use to make of Six Sigma methods. But it still doesn't make yours a "Six Sigma Organization."

By the way, there's nothing wrong with *not* leaping into the effort to be a Six Sigma organization right at the start. Since we're urging anyone reading this book to choose your own path to Six Sigma, you should feel comfortable waiting a while before deciding if you *want* to be a Six Sigma Organization. If you were to ask us: "Is it okay to use those *parts* of the system that are most useful for us?", we'd answer: "Hey, that's cool."

3. *You don't have to* call *it Six Sigma to* be *a Six Sigma organization.* The system, the methods, and the commitment are much more important than the name you give to your effort. Some businesses may find the name "Six Sigma" to be too obscure, or not the best to use as a rallying-cry for their continuous renewal effort. Indeed, one of our clients (let's call them "XYZ") has been successfully implementing many of the Six Sigma practices we're describing in this book. They've elected to call it the "XYZ Management System," but the benefits they've gained are no less powerful than they would have been had they named the system "Six Sigma."

As more and more companies adopt Six Sigma—in earnest or just for show—the danger grows of the term "Six Sigma Organization" losing its meaning. Our hope is that the success of Six Sigma efforts isn't undercut by too much self-promotion ("We're doing Six Sigma—isn't that cool?") or unwarranted hype. Companies achieving success through Six Sigma should see the results in their bottom lines and with their customers—and shouldn't need to oversell their efforts.

CHAPTER

3

Why Is Six Sigma Succeeding Where Total Quality Failed?

We complain about hype one minute, then indulge in a little bit of our own the next. For the title of this chapter, we must admit, does contain a bit of exaggeration.

First of all, while Six Sigma definitely is succeeding in creating some impressive results and culture changes in some influential organizations, it certainly is not yet a *widespread* success—not at a time when many companies are still just starting their Six Sigma initiatives. Then too, although Total Quality Management or Continuous Process Improvement is less visible in many businesses than it was in the early 1990s, we can't out-and-out say: "TQM is dead." Many companies are still engaged in improvement efforts based on the principles and tools of TQM. And Six Sigma—as the history we reviewed in Chapter 1 shows—is in many ways a vigorous rebirth of quality ideals and methods, as these are applied with even greater passion and commitment than often was the case in the past.

Still, the basic premise of our chapter title is accurate: Six Sigma is revealing a potential for success that goes beyond the levels of improvement achieved through the many TQM efforts. Past quality programs often fell victim to mistakes that hurt both their results and the reputation of TQM—errors that could easily be repeated by the firms now taking a crack at Six Sigma.

Thus, if nothing else, we hope the examples and broad-based approach we're providing you with here in *The Six Sigma Way* will help those companies already engaged in "quality" or "process improvement" to improve their existing efforts by gaining a better understanding of the entire Six Sigma system.

Six Sigma and the Pitfalls of TQM

If TQM has left behind it a positive legacy, is still alive in many organizations, and has provided the impetus for the creation of the Six Sigma system, why does it still have a black eye? In part the negative view is just perception, the price TQM has had to pay for being so highly touted in its early years. Just as importantly, though, the way many of the efforts were introduced and managed left a bad taste in the mouths of many TQM veterans. Thus, people who've seen and done "Quality" may be the toughest to convince that Six Sigma really does have something new and superior to offer.

Some of the mistakes of yesterday's TQM efforts certainly might be repeated in a Six Sigma initiative if you aren't careful. Table 3.1 provides you with a review of some of the major TQM gaffes, as well as hints on how the Six Sigma system can keep them from derailing your effort.

Table 3.1 Six Sigma versus TQM.

TQM Pitfall: Lack of Integration	Six Sigma Solution: Links to the Business and Personal "Bottom Line"
Quality often was a "sidebar" activity, separated from the key issues of business strategy and performance. Warning signs included a "quality council" made up of delegates rather than of the core management team, or a staff quality "department" with no links to P&L or other bottom-line considerations. Another "integration gap" arose when a company's middle	Six Sigma organizations are putting Process Management, Improvement, and Measurement into action as part of the daily responsibilities *especially* of their operating managers. Incentives—like GE's well-publicized 40 percent of bonus money being tied to Six Sigma—help reinforce the message that Six Sigma is "part of the job." One area that still demands

Table 3.1 *(Continued)*

TQM Pitfall: Lack of Integration	Six Sigma Solution: Links to the Business and Personal "Bottom Line"
managers were left out of the decision process, and problem-solving authority was handed to teams over which they had no official control. True integration was undermined as well when, despite the term "total" quality, the effort actually was limited to product and manufacturing functions.	attention is the application of Six Sigma to administrative or service processes; however, some terrific successes have been achieved at GE's Capital Services financing unit.
TQM Pitfall: Leadership Apathy	**Six Sigma Solution: Leadership at the Vanguard**
In every TQM effort that has thrived, leadership was actively engaged in leading the process. Much more often, however, top management's skepticism has been apparent, or their willingness to drive quality ideas has been weak. In those organizations quality felt "temporary"—and when the leaders who had initiated it left the company, quality was *proven* to be temporary.	Passion for and belief in Six Sigma at the very top of the business is unquestioned in companies like Bombardier, AlliedSignal, and GE. Along with that passion—and a readiness to beat the drum for the Six Sigma system almost constantly—is a leader's recognition that Six Sigma is synonymous with constant reinvention of the business. We always say the signs are ripe for a company or department to take on Six Sigma only when its top people have made a decision that *change* is essential to continued success, let alone survival.
TQM Pitfall: A Fuzzy Concept	**Six Sigma Solution: A Consistently Repeated, Simple Message**
The fuzziness of TQM started with the word *quality* itself. It's a familiar term with many shades of meaning. In many companies, Quality was an existing department with specific responsibilities for "quality control" or "quality assurance," where the discipline tended to focus more on	On this score, Six Sigma may have some of the same difficulties as TQM. After all, the words "Six Sigma" aren't perfectly descriptive of this system we're presenting. The quick definition we've suggested we think can do a pretty good job: "Six Sigma is a business system for achieving and

(Continued)

Table 3.1 *(Continued)*

TQM Pitfall: A Fuzzy Concept	Six Sigma Solution: A Consistently Repeated, Simple Message
stabilizing rather than improving processes. The whole idea of quality "philosophies" also made the whole concept seem mysterious to many people. The vagueness of TQM was aggravated when, as new approaches emerged—e.g. ISO9000 certification or reengineering—they were not integrated into the existing quality effort.	sustaining success though customer focus, Process Management and Improvement, and the wise use of facts and data." Clear, accurate and fairly specific. By continuing to communicate that definition, and avoiding debate about which tools are mandatory or which Six Sigma philosophy you're following, you can keep the focus from getting diffused or confusing.

TQM Pitfall: An Unclear Goal	Six Sigma Solution: Setting a No-Nonsense, Ambitious Goal
Many companies made quality even fuzzier by having positive-sounding goals like "meeting or exceeding customer requirements," with no way to track progress toward that goal. Quality methods taught in the 1980s and 1990s also did a pretty poor job of dealing with the reality of diverse and changing customer requirements. Without tools to really understand customer needs, TQM in action was liable to become an "open-loop" system in which a company might meet today's customer requirements but not be ready for tomorrow's. (In fact, that seems to be what happened to a number of quality "success stories" that later turned into corporate "horror stories.")	A clear goal is the centerpiece of Six Sigma. It's an extremely challenging goal, but still believable, unlike past campaigns for "zero defects." Whether the goal is expressed in yield (99.9997 percent perfect), Defects per Million Opportunities (3.4 DPMO), or Sigma (6σ), people involved in Six Sigma initiatives can see their results grow; and they can equate them to dollar impact as well. Just as importantly, by focusing on ways to track changes in customer needs and requirements, Six Sigma companies are building a dynamic system for measuring performance based on the latest and most stringent demands of the customer. While the goal may change over time, the closed-loop Six Sigma system will help the organization to adjust.

TQM Pitfall: Purist Attitudes and Technical Zealotry	Six Sigma Solution: Adapting Tools and Degree of Rigor to the Circumstances
One of the most frustrating effects of TQM "expertise" was the creation of	As long as you and your business leaders recognize that Six Sigma is a

Table 3.1 *(Continued)*

TQM Pitfall: Purist Attitudes and Technical Zealotry	Six Sigma Solution: Adapting Tools and Degree of Rigor to the Circumstances
what one might call "Quality Police": individuals who would insist on doing things a certain way (*only*). Deviate from that way, or that belief, and you were betraying the ideal of quality or the teachings of such-and-such a guru. The effects of quality purism were twofold: 1) resources were used to analyze problems using tools that were not appropriate or necessary; and even worse, 2) the "regular" people trying to apply quality (the non-experts) were alienated from the effort. At the risk of stereotyping, those attitudes seemed to arise the most from people favoring the more complex techniques or tools, who would insist that those techniques be applied even when they weren't really needed. Simplify a tool to your needs, and beware their wrath! For too many people who became quality "enforcers," the means *were* the end.	way to create and run a more successful organization—demanding a great diversity of skills, not just technical expertise—you can avoid this problem. There are many "Six Sigma Ways." The healthiest attitude to adopt is: "We'll use the tools and approaches that get results with the greatest ease and simplicity." Not: "We'll require everybody to do an in-depth analysis whether it's needed or not." There's nothing wrong with having consistent methods, or applying advanced techniques to measure and improve processes—it's the *foolish* consistencies that make up the hobgoblin. Six Sigma, because it encompasses so many ideas and methods, can overcome the "purity problem." Still, we would warn any organization that the zealotry that hurt TQM still lurks as a danger in the Six Sigma system. Beware the Six Sigma Police!

TQM Pitfall: Failure to Break Down Internal Barriers	Six Sigma Solution: Priority on Cross Functional Process Management
When TQM was in its heyday, it still was a "departmentalized" activity in most companies. That's not all bad, since there are departmental customers and departments that have processes that can be measured and improved. But most of the talk about "Total" quality—encompassing an entire organization-spanning process—	The most enlightened Six Sigma practitioners place silo-busting near the top of their priority list. It's important both as an objective—to help create a smoother, more effective, and efficient company—and as a tool to eliminate rework created by disconnects and miscommunication. Even so, Six Sigma's success at

(Continued)

Table 3.1 *(Continued)*

TQM Pitfall: Failure to Break Down Internal Barriers	**Six Sigma Solution: Priority on Cross Functional Process Management**
was just talk. Improvement projects were done in isolated chunks: Engineering had its projects, so did Finance, Manufacturing, or HR. TQM became more cross-functional as it evolved, but in many cases it targeted small conflicts, not major, customer-critical issues.	breaking down organizational barriers will be determined over the long term; a few successes don't mean victory. That's why the discipline of process *management* is as central to the Six Sigma system as are ways to measure or improve processes.[3]
TQM Pitfall: Incremental vs. Exponential Change	**Six Sigma Solution: Incremental Exponential Change**
TQM teachings often emphasized that change would be driven by an abundance of small improvements. There was no explicit exclusion of more radical change in the TQM -toolkit, but it can't be denied that an impatience had built up among many corporate leaders when the "reengineering" concept broke loose. This turned into a classic case of the "Tyranny of the Or," as described in the Preface of this book. The TQM advocates trashed reengineering for being a sledge-hammer that left companies devastated, while the reengineering folks ridiculed TQM as "wimpy." No middle ground existed. It was a battle that in plenty of companies left both parties badly wounded or dead.	One of the great opportunities of Six Sigma is to begin afresh, with the recognition that *both* small improvements *and* major change are an essential part of the survival and success of 21st-century businesses.
TQM Pitfall: Ineffective Training	**Six Sigma Solution: Blackbelts, Greenbelts, Master Blackbelts**
We use the term "ineffective" as a catch-all for the variety of problems that can arise during roll-out of TQM	Six Sigma companies are setting very demanding standards for learning, and are backing them up with the

Table 3.1 *(Continued)*

TQM Pitfall: Ineffective Training	Six Sigma Solution: Blackbelts, Greenbelts, Master Blackbelts
training. In truth, there's no perfect way to train an organization for TQM—or Six Sigma. There are always challenges around timing (When is it appropriate to give people new skills?), depth (How detailed does this need to be?), and resources (How much time and money can we afford to devote to training?). By no means was TQM training always ineffective, but it did tend to be "light" and focused much more on teaching tools than on providing a clear *context* about how to make improvement work. As a result, people knew the tools, but not when and how to best apply them. The emphasis of TQM training was on projects—time-bounded, off-line improvement efforts—and therefore didn't appear relevant to people's daily responsibilities (another factor in the lack of integration noted earlier). Perhaps worst of all, quality training often fell victim to a numbers game, with success being determined by "number of people trained" or "teams formed."	necessary investments in time and money to help people meet those standards. Whereas most organizations scream in agony when training takes more than two hours, GE's Blackbelts—the primary drivers of Six Sigma improvements—take three weeks of training, with follow-up exams and continued learning through conferences and other forums. Even more impressive is the "Greenbelt" commitment: every management employee being given a minimum of two weeks training in Six Sigma methods. It's easy (and we've heard many do it) to dismiss GE's effort as being possible only because of its tremendous resources. But it isn't fair to assume that the GE people getting these skills are any less busy than your people may be. The truth is, the training commitment is a sacrifice—an investment—that's being made consciously. You don't need to match GE or any other Six Six Sigma company course-for-course to be successful, but the principle of continuous renewal and improvement does demand a heavier investment and higher learning expectations than most companies traditionally have assumed. The other challenges—linking training to people's jobs, and creating results measures that go beyond "butts in seats" (the standard training metric)—are

(Continued)

Table 3.1 *(Continued)*

TQM Pitfall: Ineffective Training	Six Sigma Solution: Blackbelts, Greenbelts, Master Blackbelts
	being addressed both in the design of the training and in the expectations placed on the trainees before and after their learning experiences.
TQM Pitfall: Focus on Product Quality	**Six Sigma Solution: Attention to All Business Processes**
Despite the "total" descriptor, many quality efforts were concentrated on production or manufacturing processes, not on service, logistics, marketing, or other equally critical areas. We know, for example, of a printing company that was focusing its teams on eliminating millimeters of deviation in trimming paper (an important quality factor, granted), while their order-tracking processes were a mess. Even if the product quality was excellent, customers wouldn't *get* them on time.	As we'll see in Chapter 4, Six Sigma not only works in Service and in transactional processes, but probably offers *more* opportunities there than in Manufacturing. Thus, Six Sigma has the potential to be more "total" than Total Quality!

The final "pitfall" that can entrap any improvement-minded organization—TQM, Six Sigma, you name it—is complacency. Sure, it would be ill advised for a company that has successfully integrated quality improvement into its business practices to abandon it and "replace it" with Six Sigma. It's just as shortsighted, though, to ignore the advances in tools and in business management principles that have been made by the Six Sigma system, just because "we're already doing quality."

GE, for example, has confessed it needs to redouble its efforts to ensure that its major savings have real value to customers, who are asking: " 'When do I get the benefits of Six Sigma?' " GE leaders have noted: "Improvement to our internal processes is of no interest to the customer."[4] Allied/Honeywell's leaders, similarly, have admitted that "the initial euphoria over our early Six Sigma successes had left us somewhat self-satisfied, dulling our awareness of how much more we were leaving on the table."[5] Thus if your only reason to ignore Six Sigma is because you think your existing improvement efforts are "good enough," that should be a warning in itself.

So we'd urge you to keep an open mind and look for ways—big or small—to improve your Improvement effort. In the remaining sections of the book we'll be showing you, first in an overview, and then in greater depth, how to find your own route on the Six Sigma Way.

CHAPTER

4

Applying Six Sigma to Service and Manufacturing

A COMMON CONCERN of managers and business leaders is this: "How can Six Sigma apply to *my* organization?" The question seems to come most often from people in service- or transaction-based areas, who wonder how this supposedly manufacturing-oriented discipline will help them. But manufacturing managers have their doubts as well, especially because many manufacturing processes have already been through intense *quality* scrutiny. Thus in this chapter we'll be looking at some compelling reasons why *both* service and manufacturing operations can benefit from a Six Sigma discipline, and showing you how to adapt your approach to meet unique challenges in either arena.

Clarifying "Service" and "Manufacturing"

First let's clarify the terms we'll be using:

- "Service" processes and businesses. When throughout this chapter we talk about "Services" or "service and support" processes, what we mean is any part of a company not directly involved in designing or producing tangible products. That can mean sales, finance, marketing, procurement, customer support, logistics, or human resources—and more—in *any* organization, from a steel company to a bank to a retail store. A few of the other words used to describe these activities include: *transactional, commercial, nontechnical, support* and *administrative.*

- "Manufacturing" processes. By "Manufacturing" we mean only those activities relating to the development and production of tangible products. Other terms used to describe these are "plant floor," "production," "a fab," and sometimes "engineering" and "product development."

These categories are quite broad, of course. For instance, there's actually a lot of large variation among Service processes, as between a call center and a consulting firm. Likewise there are many differences between a company that manufactures coffee cups and another that makes microchips. Nevertheless, all of the issues pertaining to making Six Sigma effective tend to be most similar *within* these two categories of Service and Manufacturing. Although as we will see, it's likely that it is your Service activities that will benefit most from the Six Sigma approach.

The Changing Role of Manufacturing

These days, there are almost no purely "Manufacturing" companies.

Designing, producing, and/or selling manufactured products is still, of course, the core business of many companies. And the need to provide defect-free products (those that work as expected and meet customer requirements) is more important than ever. But the success of a manufacturing firm is hardly guaranteed solely by producing defect-free goods. A successful manufacturing business needs to master many competencies, including:

- Keeping track of new technologies, and being able to develop them rapidly into viable products.
- Understanding existing and emerging customer needs that can be met by improved processes and/or new/improved products.
- Establishing and managing supplier networks so as to ensure a timely supply of parts and raw materials.

- Taking, processing, and filling customer orders accurately—including building to unique specifications as needed—and profitably.
- Adapting to shifting market conditions.

An increasing number of businesses have handed over responsibility for manufacturing to a vendor/partner so that they can focus on product design, development, and marketing. One of the most dramatic examples of this shift is the change in strategy at Qualcomm. In 1999, this cellular telephone powerhouse announced its decision to sell-off *all* its manufacturing and product businesses so that it could focus on research and technology development and licensing—which already was accounting for much of its profits. The reaction from Wall Street: a more-than-1000-percent stock-price surge.[1]

This example signals a change to a world where manufacturing capability is a specialized service (even a commodity), and where the abilities to design products to meet new or emerging needs, and to establish flexible supply chains—and then fill them with the right products—become the real keys to competitiveness. (After all, if your competitors can buy the services of the same or similar manufacturing outsource vendor, what other edge is left?)[2]

Even the specialist firms who supply manufacturing "muscle" to design-and-marketing-only clients must have processes capable of planning and setting up for production, managing order flow and capacity, and building effective interfaces with customers—all of them "service" activities.

Finally, the trend in the U.S. from a manufacturing- to a predominantly service-based economy has been apparent for quite a while. Already by the early 1970s, services accounted for more than 65 percent of employment in the United States. In the late 1990s the Bureau of Labor Statistics pegged service-based jobs at about 80 percent, with that number projected to grow. Though there may be debate as to the political and social implications of this decline or movement of manufacturing jobs, the fact remains that if you want to create a more competitive company in North America or Europe today, you're going to have to upgrade the capability of your Service operations.

Service Process Opportunities—and Realities

As the role played by Services in boosting business competitiveness grows, so too does the evidence of there being plenty of untapped potential in these activities. Consider the following factors:

- Research has shown that the costs of poor quality (rework, mistakes, abandoned projects, etc.) in service-based businesses and processes typically run as high as 50 percent of total budget. (In manufacturing operations, it's estimated at about 10 to 20 percent.)
- This cost data matches with our experience and that of many others who've found that administrative and service processes, prior to improvement, perform in a range of 1.5 to 3 sigma (yields of 50 to 90 percent).
- Analyses of Service processes often reveal that less than 10 percent of total process "cycle time" is devoted to real work on tasks that are important to paying customers. The remainder of the effort and time is used up in waiting, rework, moving things around, inspecting to catch defects, and non-essential activities.

What Makes "Six Sigma Services" More Challenging?

Are people outside manufacturing just out of touch, or less competent than the folks in the plant? We don't believe they are (and there's no way we're going to debate that point, anyway). Actually there are some important, understandable reasons why service-based processes often have more pent-up opportunities for improvement than manufacturing operations. Such as:

1. *Invisible work processes.* In most fabs and factories, you can see, touch, and even follow work product through a process. Take a simple "production process" like making a hamburger. When you order a meal at a fast-food place, you expect to receive it in just a little more time than it takes to cook and assemble the burger—and usually that's what happens. Buns, patties, and ingredients, once they've been picked up to make your burger, are cooking or moving most every second on the way to your tray or paper bag. It's hard to hide a patty and a bun in your "out basket" or credenza on the burger production line.

Likewise on a typical plant floor, bottlenecks, slowdowns, scrap, rework show up pretty quickly to the naked eye. Here's a vivid example. We worked at a bottling plant that would divert any unfilled bottles into a large glass recycling bin: Every defective bottle would loudly *crash* and shatter as it fell into the scrap pile! So too, if you've ever seen a flame (or "flare") burning over an oil refinery, it's not there as a decoration: it's a sign something isn't working right in the plant.

By contrast, the "work product" of most Service processes is much harder to spot with the naked eye: information, requests, orders, proposals, presentations, meetings, signatures, invoices, designs, ideas. And now, as more and more Service processes revolve around information handled in computers and networks, the work product becomes "virtual," flowing from screen to screen or server to server as mere electrons. In fact, with e-mail, the Web, and other networks, a service-based process can jump from location to location all around the world instantly. That can be a big advantage, of course, in the globalized economy, but it sure does make an understanding of how the work gets done even harder to come by.

Just as big a challenge can be Service-people's beliefs about their work. Because their processes aren't tangible and can be driven by personal style and circumstance, people working at key functions like sales, marketing, and even software development are notorious for commenting: "We don't have a process." Actually, they do—usually several of them. But these people are so close to the processes that it can be a challenge to get them to recognize them.

Evolving workflows and procedures. When you make a change in a production process, it usually takes some work: things get moved, raw materials are sent to different locations, toolings and procedures are changed. For that reason, changes to manufacturing processes usually are given a pretty high level of deliberation.

Outside of manufacturing, though, a process can be changed quickly—especially if it's a simple change and hasn't gotten itself too ingrained in people's habits. Responsibilities can be shifted, forms revised, new steps added, guidelines altered, and so on, without any capital investment or serious deliberation. Many changes arise out of individual, even spur-of-the-moment decisions, with ramifications that may be small. Add up all the individual choices and changes, though, and the overall impact can be huge. As a result, service processes in many businesses evolve, adapt, and *grow* almost continuously (not exactly like viruses—but it's a tempting analogy).

3. *Lack of facts and data.* In light of the above, it isn't astonishing that the hard facts on the performance of service processes often are pretty skimpy-looking. The data that do exist are narrowly focused, anecdotal, and/or subjective. It's just that the nature of these processes makes them inherently more difficult to measure—though it can be done, and done well, once the process itself begins to be better understood.

   Noting and tracing problems in a service process, for example, is usually more challenging than in a plant or production facility. Big stacks of untouched documents (and who doesn't have those?) may be easy to see, but backlogs, rework, delays, and the costs of working on them are hard to spot. It's possible to track expenses on a department or work group, but tying those costs to specific process activities is still tricky.[3]

   Pick up almost any manufacturing or quality engineering trade publication and you'll see a slew of ads for production-monitoring and -testing equipment. Measurement for manufacturing is a multibillion-dollar industry. In action, manufacturing measurement can be impressive. For example, a medical products plant in Texas has a display showing various aspects of its production line including a continuous readout on cost-per-unit, in fractions of a cent, updated every few seconds.

   Except for volume measurement in computer networks and customer call centers, though, Service process managers can't just plug in a machine to do their measurements for them. For instance, one of our clients has been working on streamlining a loan document closure process. They've learned—surprise!—that dozens of people independently have been checking up on and trying to solve problems with loan packets, resulting in a significant amount of redundant time and effort. However, accurately *measuring* the time and cost of the rework and redundancy is difficult, since those tasks make up a relatively small slice of many different peoples' work days.

4. *Lack of a "head start."* Inspectors, quality-control staff, quality engineers, and process improvement "gurus" have been prowling man-

ufacturing floors for decades. After all, it was the discipline of maximizing efficiency that helped to make the United States the productivity leader of the world in the two decades after World War II. It was as other economies caught up with and passed key industries in the effectiveness or quality of their products that American corporate leadership received a startling wake-up call. When the "Quality Circles" first arrived in the 1970's, they were mainly a production-floor phenomenon. Even as TQM bloomed in the 1980s and 1990s, as noted in Chapter 3, the real action was still in the product quality arena. Even today, the membership of the American Society for Quality (ASQ) is over 60 percent in the manufacturing area, though we've already noted that 80 percent of U.S. jobs are in Services.

Of course, Service Process Improvement is not unknown. Motorola, for example, has had dozens of success stories in its Six Sigma efforts, with some notable cutting of costs, defects, and time out of "white-collar" processes. Nevertheless, the vast majority of Service activities have not been touched by the powerful methods of Process Measurement and Improvement. Which means there's a lot of catching up to do. And if you want to do so, you're going to have to be ready to adapt the Six Sigma approaches to the special conditions of a Service environment.

Making Six Sigma Work in Services

The following "tips" for making Six Sigma more effective in Services are really just broad suggestions. It's up to you to make them fit your specific organization, products, customers, and so on. Overall, however, these ideas should help you to get results in a Service arena faster, with greater positive impact, and with better buy-in from the "this doesn't apply to us" skeptics you're likely to run into.

Services Tip #1: Start with the Process

Ever go to a dance or a party where at the end, someone turns up the lights? It's usually a bit of a shock, maybe a little sad, but also gives you a chance to see things more clearly. Some of the discoveries might include:

- What the people at the party (including you) really look like.
- Who's there whom you may not have seen before.
- How the room has been arranged.
- Where the games or activities were held that you missed.
- What a mess the place is!

What we're saying is that in most Service organizations, starting to investigate processes is like turning up the lights. Though often something of a rude awakening, it also can be an enlightening event that gets the Six Sigma effort off to a fast start. As people discover what's really going on, they can recognize that one party seems to be over but that another one—cleaning the place up—is just getting under way.

Services Tip #2: Fine-tune the Problem

When the bright lights come on, it takes a few seconds for your eyes to adjust. So too, when you shine a light on service processes, it takes a while for a group to see and understand the issues around them as clearly as they should. That's to be expected, and the only way to get a really clear perspective is to get to work detailing your processes and customer requirements, and the issues affecting them. In the meantime, though, fuzzy vision and an over-eagerness to "straighten this place up" can lead to projects or improvement initiatives that aren't well defined. The temptation may be to tackle large, unwieldy issues or to launch dozens of minor projects simultaneously—which can raise frustration levels and thereby damage your credibility.

The discipline of effective project selection and problem definition is essential in manufacturing, too. It just tends to be more difficult to choose and scale projects in Service environments at the outset of the Six Sigma effort. (For more on the "how-to" of project selection, see Chapter 11.)

Services Tip #3: Make Good Use of Facts and Data to Reduce Ambiguity

One of the biggest obstacles between you and clarifying issues, measuring performance, and generating improvement in the Service arena is the fact that things often are not well described or defined. For example, product specifications in manufacturing often are noted very precisely—literally in milliseconds and microns—while in Services they're usually sketchy if they exist at all. That means that as you start to shed light on processes and customers in a Service environment, a high priority should be to translate ambiguity into clear performance factors and measures throughout your operations. The ability to define and measure intangibles, the more subjective factors, is one of those unique skills that is a must in Service processes but often is a non-issue in manufacturing. In fact, we've worked with quite a few Six Sigma and quality experts with terrific skill and experience in Manufacturing, who have trouble adjusting to the greater ambiguity of Services. One of the concepts covered in Chapter 14—"operational definitions"—becomes critically important to create meaningful Service process requirements and measures.

Lower volumes in some Service processes pose an extra challenge—as they can in Manufacturing, too. (See the Applied Materials example later in this chapter, on page 64.) If you're completing only a few dozen "deals" in a month, or you have a tightly focused, intimate customer base, getting large amounts of hard data will be difficult if not impossible. But that shouldn't excuse you from managing your business on a basis of facts and data—you will just need to gather and analyze the data differently. You will still be able to *improve* your processes, too. (For more on that, see "Measuring Low Volume or Rare Activities" in Chapter 14 on page 205.)

Services Tip #4: Don't Overemphasize Statistics

This will be the most controversial of our suggestions, so we'll review this one in a bit more depth, beginning with a case history.

The Six Sigma–based improvement initiative at a financial services company—a client of ours—began in late 1998. This firm has enjoyed tremendous growth; when we began working with them, they were turning *away* business and hiring over 200 new people per month (a rate usually seen only at Internet start-ups). It was, however, a good news/bad news scenario: Senior management of the company recognized that too many of the new people were being put to work just to deal with the problems created by a chaotic environment.

Less than a year after the launching of several high-priority improvement projects and the introducing of Six Sigma and teamwork skills, this company has been able to significantly shift its management approach, making it more proactive, fact-based, and cooperative. They've achieved major savings and streamlining of inefficient processes, and are now in a much better position to handle the company's aggressive growth targets. Fortunately they've retained their fast-paced, entrepreneurial spirit—it's just that they're channeling those energies more effectively. We've heard many of their people comment on how greatly the Six Sigma skills have improved their approach to problems and processes—and the whole atmosphere of the company.

As we talked over their keys to success with the company's quality VP, he quickly focused on one of them: "I'd say one of the best choices we made was not to push people into heavy statistics right away." His reason was simple, if twofold: that the people who aren't used to technical processes and measurement aren't ready for more sophisticated tools, and that the data they have available isn't ready for advanced analysis.

To some purists, deemphasizing statistics is tantamount to "dumbing down" Six Sigma. But as they say about comedy, so we say about Six Sigma: Timing is everything. Like our client, many Service groups aren't ready for detailed statistics at the outset.

Fortunately, many of the problems in a Service environment—especially in the early stages of the Six Sigma effort—can be solved, with terrific results, with only occasional need for advanced statistics.

This perspective is supported by the experience of GE Capital, where we've worked for several years. There, Black Belts have received a version of Six Sigma training which is less technical than that given to their counterparts in GE's industrial businesses. Still, GE Capital has, overall, been able to generate about $800 million in net gains from Six Sigma through the end of 1999. And over time the rigor of the concepts is being increased, with more people being given a path to advanced or "Master Black Belt" training.

Encouragingly, we've worked in a number of Service organizations where once people began to use *basic* measurement and data-analysis methods—and saw the value of the tools—they started to actually *ask* for more *advanced* data-gathering and -analysis tools. It's like having people show up eagerly at a party instead of having to be dragged there; guess who's going to have more fun?

Some Valid Issues—and Responses

We've heard arguments, especially from people in manufacturing companies, that it's "not fair" for some people to be able to avoid having to learn the "tough" skills. Or that there are risks if people miss out on an opportunity to apply advanced statistical methods. These are reasonable concerns, which we think we can address by making the following three points:

1. Our suggestion is not "statistics never"—it's to provide statistical skills and tools when the people and processes need them. In fact one of the Motorola alums who's become one of the better-known Six Sigma statistical experts, Dr. Mikel Harry, admits he used to think "the sun rose and set on statistics," but now recognizes that *how* those tools are used is more important.[4]
2. There are actually *other* skills needed by people in Service areas—such as an ability to deal with the ambiguity of intangible processes—that aren't as critical in Manufacturing or technical environments. Once they have been mastered, more opportunities arise to apply advanced tools in Services.
3. If people fail to use advanced analysis methods when they could have, there are three possible outcomes. They may 1) Draw false conclusions based on incomplete analysis; 2) draw correct conclusions, but not back them up with statistical validation; or 3) make process, product, or service design decisions that are not "optimum." In our experience the risks of making a mistake can be minimized—as long as one's conclusions are based on good logic and the risks are managed properly during implementation.

Overall, it's most important to Six Sigma improvement that people in Services *or* Manufacturing learn to ask critical questions about their processes and customers: "How do we really know that?" "Is there some way we can test our assumptions?" "What are the data telling us?" "Is there a *better* way to do this?"

Manufacturing Challenges

Your attempt to apply Six Sigma to Manufacturing will bring with it some unique challenges, too. The following are some of the most prevalent difficulties you should be mindful of, along with some suggestions to help you overcome them.

Manufacturing Challenge #1: Adopting a Broader Perspective

People on the plant or shop floor have always tended to be somewhat isolated from the rest of the business. And as manufacturing activity becomes an ever-smaller proportion of the overall activity of a business, the risks of isolation—from other groups in the company and from external customers—increase. The Six Sigma system, though, demands communication and coordination all along your company's critical processes, as well as the demolition of the barriers between manufacturing and the rest of the world. Two key messages arise when manufacturing groups can begin to see their role as integrated into the entire business:

1. *Most problems are not manufacturing problems.* Folks in production will benefit when they and others in the business begin to see data proving what they already had suspected: that unclear orders, last-minute changes, parts and staffing shortages, engineering/design errors, and so on have a greater impact on delivering the right stuff to the customer on-time than do defects on the plant floor. (See the GE Power Systems example in Chapter 1 on page 5.)
2. Manufacturing needs to become an active participant in the entire process. Just because barriers to Six Sigma often are not the production group's "fault," doesn't mean that Improvement isn't their responsibility. The Manufacturing folks in many organizations need to be educated on their role in helping to solve "upstream" issues as well as dealing with challenges faced by such "downstream" activities as warehouses and customer service.

One way to change the internal focus of Manufacturing is to target Six Sigma improvement projects that demand cross-functional cooperation, including Manufacturing. Involving people from the plant floor to, for example, improve order fill rates, will help change the view that *making* the product is a distinct and unrelated activity from selling or delivering it.

The other terrific opportunity for a broader perspective comes through using Six Sigma methods to better integrate Product Design and Manufacturing. Some of the most impressive success stories in Six Sigma annals involve using key customer feedback to create refined or totally new products, and then using advanced Six Sigma methods to ensure that the new products can be produced at a 6σ level of quality.

Manufacturing Challenge #2: Moving Past "Certification" to Improvement

A few years back we heard a manager at a computer systems manufacturer complain about his problem in getting new production and testing equipment properly calibrated. As we probed into the problem, he described their equipment acquisition process, which surprisingly involved receiving new equipment *twice:* once when it was delivered by the manufacturer, and the second time from a vendor who had calibrated the equipment.

We were asking some obvious questions (such as, "Why don't you have the equipment vendor send the items *directly* to the calibrator?" Or better yet, "Why not make the *vendor* responsible for calibrating it?"). Then a manager from the company's quality group spoke up: "ISO9000 requires us to do it this way," he explained.[5]

The growing emphasis in recent years on various manufacturing certifications and audits—ISO-9000 being the most prevalent—have, in our experience, hampered many company's *improvement* efforts. And clearly, in the present instance, the excuse that certification *requires* a circuitous (and problem-filled) process is just not true. It is true, however, that once a process has been "certified," it tends to be perceived as "law." The too-common case in a certified environment is that once a process has been documented and approved, it's heck-on-earth to improve it.

Certification activities have drawn resources away from Process Improvement efforts, too. Quite a few organizations have a team of full-time staff dedicated to maintaining certification documents and conducting internal compliance audits—but fewer or no people focused on actually *improving* the processes. Of course, more enlightened companies do use their certification efforts to examine and improve their processes; unfortunately in our experience, however, such instances are relatively rare. Tying Six Sigma to certification efforts offers some impressive potential improvement synergies.

Manufacturing Challenge #3: Adapting Tools to Your Manufacturing Environment

So far we've talked about "Manufacturing" as if every production operation were the same—which of course is not at all the case. Making auto engine parts is a very different process from assembling an SUV; bottling bleach is very different from building computer monitors. We can't of course even begin to tell you just how you will need to adapt Six Sigma methods so as to optimally fit every type of manufacturing environment. It's important to recognize, though, that you *will* need to flex Six Sigma techniques to make them do their best for you.

We can use one company's experience as a great example here. Applied Materials, the world's leading manufacturer of equipment for semiconductor plants (or "fabs" as they're usually called) first got involved in Six Sigma back in the late 1980s.

The challenge for Applied Materials Manufacturing in adopting Six Sigma, however, was in using concepts like Defects per Million Opportunities. "We manufacture pieces of equipment that are room-sized," explains Dave Boenitz, head of the Applied Materials Quality Institute, "We deal in hundreds of units, not millions. Each unit is comprised of eight, ten, twelve, fifteen *thousand* parts. So if you were to look at a Sigma level per unit, it would be very difficult comparing apples to apples. You could definitely look at a million opportunities in one of our systems, but it's a matter if finding out *which* million opportunities you're going to measure."

The approach Applied has concentrated on to reduce defects, has been "Mistake Proofing"—a diligent effort to find and prevent all kinds of mistakes and errors in a process. (See Chapter 18, page 372.) "We just have not put energy into the Sigma or DPMO measures, because we don't see what the value-add is going to be." But the improvements Applied makes are just as valid.

Making Six Sigma Work Best for You

If there's one theme we're likely to overstate in this book, it's the need to select, apply, and adapt Six Sigma methods and ideas to fit your organization's needs and readiness. As soon as any consultant, guru, or author tells you "Here's how you have to do it," we recommend that you politely excuse yourself and leave the room. The *real* answer to how you can best implement Six Sigma in your business is, as we've noted: "It depends."

Fortunately, Six Sigma is a very robust system; even with the challenges likely to arise in your organization—whether in Service or Manufacturing—you can be successful if you remember, and remind others, that this is not really a program or a technique. It's a flexible but essential way to make your business more responsive, efficient, competitive, and profitable.

CHAPTER

5

The Six Sigma Roadmap

In this chapter we conclude our Executive Overview with a look at the ideal Roadmap for establishing the Six Sigma system and launching improvements. These five steps, depicted in Fig. 5.1, feature what we would suggest are "core competencies" for a successful 21st-century organization:

1. Identify core processes and key customers.
2. Define customer requirements.
3. Measure current performance.
4. Prioritize, analyze, and implement improvements.
5. Expand and integrate the Six Sigma system.

Advantages of the Six Sigma Roadmap

The Roadmap is not the only path to Six Sigma improvement; you will very likely need to adjust the order of these steps, or even start more than one of them simultaneously. In Part Two we'll look at ways to adapt the Roadmap, based on your organization's specific needs and goals. What makes this path "ideal," however, is that, taken in this order, these activities build up the essential foundation that will then support and sustain Six Sigma *improvement*. Specifically, the Roadmap's advantages include:

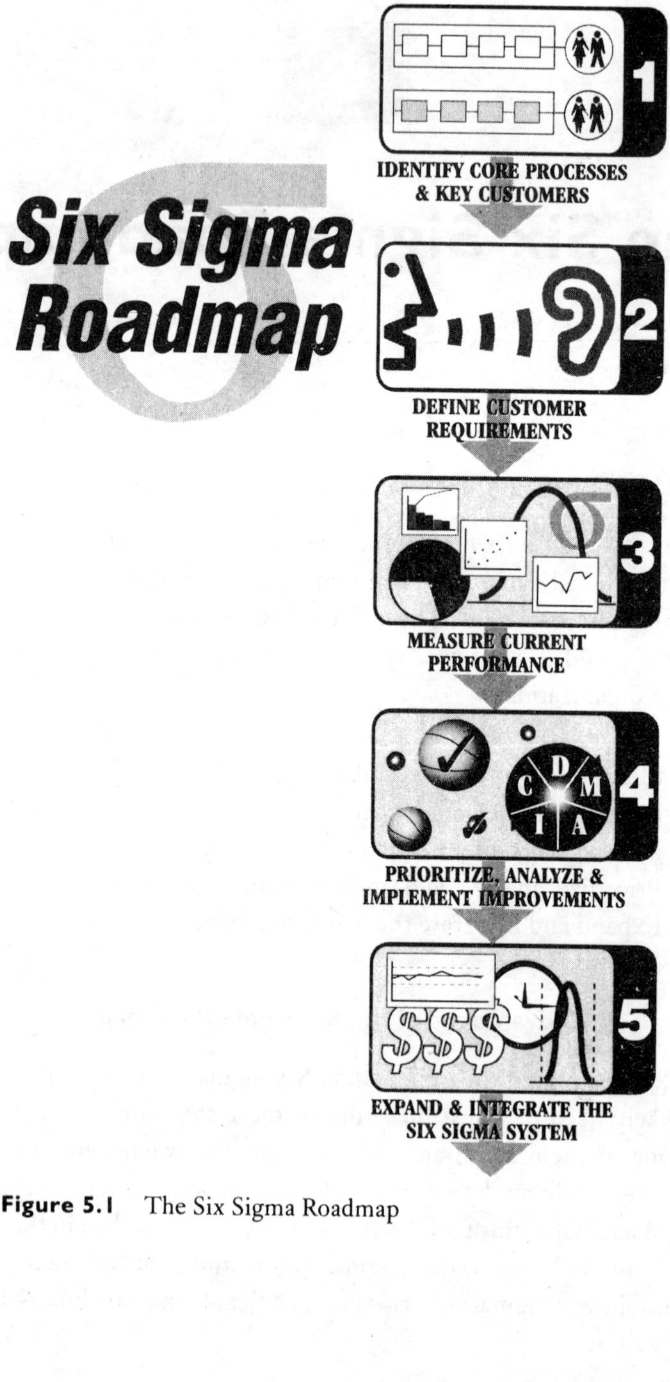

Figure 5.1 The Six Sigma Roadmap

- A clearer understanding of the business as an interconnected system of processes and customers.
- Better decisions and uses of resources, to get the greatest possible amount of benefit out of your Six Sigma improvements.
- Shorter improvement cycle times, thanks to better upfront data and selection of projects.
- More accurate validation of Six Sigma gains—whether in dollars, defects, customer satisfaction, or other measures.
- A stronger infrastructure, to support change and sustain results.

This Roadmap is guaranteed to win a poll as the "ideal" implementation approach among Six Sigma veterans, as well. Everyone we've worked or spoken with who has been involved in a Six Sigma launch—executives, implementers, and team members—agrees that this is the path they *should* have followed in the past and *would* follow if given the chance to in the future.

As an example here, one of our clients (a unit of GE) spent nearly two years launching dozens of Six Sigma improvement projects—in essence, starting at Roadmap "Step 4." But despite their best intentions and efforts to make those projects pay off, the rate of success did not meet expectations. Projects took longer than expected, and results tended to dissipate after the teams had disbanded. Over time, the firm's top leaders began to realize that one source of their trouble was that, in the words of their number-two executive: "We didn't really know what we should be working on. Like other companies, most of our projects were *internally* focused." Having gained that insight the hard way, this company had to backtrack in order to fulfill some of the earlier tasks on the Roadmap. For example, they've now installed systems and processes to gather real-time "Voice of the Customer" data (Step 2), as well as measures to evaluate performance against customer "Critical to Quality" criteria or "CTQs" (Step 3). That means their improvements now are focused on *real* customer needs, firmly backed up by data.

The Roadmap, Step by Step

Step One: Identify Core Processes and Key Customers

As businesses become ever more dispersed and global, customer segments more narrow, and products and services more diverse, it gets tougher and tougher to see the "big picture" of how the work actually gets done. By taking Step One, you begin to bring that big picture into clearer focus by defining your critical activities and getting a grasp of the broad structure of your business system.

Step One Overview

The objectives described in Table 5.1 are applicable to an entire organization or any segment of it. Even a department or function that serves internal customers—Human Resources, Information Technology, or Facilities, for example—has its own "core processes" that deliver products, services, and value to customers.

Step One Rationale

The knowledge to be gained from Step One is important as a prerequisite for the customer knowledge-building activities of Step Two. A more significant benefit of this high-level inventory, however, is the new, clearer understanding gained about the organization as a whole. If it's already clear to you how and why this is such a great idea, you can jump down to Step Two.

If you're still not sure why the "big picture" of your customers and core processes is needed, come with us on a trip to Company Island.

The Story of Company Island

Company Island is a land much like many corporations or even departments. On the island are several rivers (processes) that flow to

Table 5.1 Step One Overview.

Objectives	Deliverables
To create a clear, "big-picture" understanding of the most critical cross-functional activities in your organization, and of how they interface with external customers.	A "map" or inventory of value-delivering activities in your organization, driven by three questions: 1. What are our core or value-adding processes? 2. What products and/or services do we provide to our customers? 3. How do processes "flow" across the organization?

the sea and deliver nutrients (products and services) to various and sundry fishes (customers). Life is pleasant, though very busy, on Company Island. Most of the time, people spend their days tending to their small stretch of a river, or helping make sure the fishes come get their nutrients. (Other nearby islands—Competitor Island, Upstart Island, Cash Cow Island, etc.—also are trying to lure the fish).

The trouble is, life on Company Island is a lot more complicated than even the island's leaders are aware of. Along the shore, for example, it turns out that the rivers don't come to the sea in a single broad channel. Instead it's more like a delta, with lots of small rivulets. Some of these may deliver lots of good food to the fish, others may be dumping toxic waste. Big fish get a lot of attention, while the smaller ones are ignored (or sometimes vice versa).

On shore, it's equally complicated. There are some streams that end nowhere; others meander so much that they take forever to get to the sea. Some tributaries are uncharted and untended by the professional managers (Company Island has a great business school), so they get overgrown and silted up. In fact, in some places well-intentioned islanders have actually built dams that block a river's flow, leaving downstream islanders mighty thirsty and unhappy with their upstream colleagues.

Sometimes, a few folks on Company Island see the problems that need attending to and fix them; unfortunately, a good proportion of those fixes actually hurt things going on downstream or in other rivers. (Islanders who work the shore and tend the fishes tend to yell loudest when that happens).

If those folks could just get more people together to talk about what's happening in the various regions of Company Island, they could piece together a true, complete map of the place. With that "bird's-eye view" it would be much easier to identify where the fish are well fed and where they're "fed up" and ready to head for another island. Also, Company Islanders could then figure out which rivers are the most treacherous or slow-moving, and shift their attention to those major trouble-spots.

"Mere myth!" you may shout. "Our 'island' is a paradise by comparison!" another may claim. Cold reality would indicate, however, that very few organizations really have a true understanding of the "lay of the land." The existing maps often are woefully inaccurate, particularly since organizational islands, unlike physical ones, can and do change pretty quickly.

Anyway, we hope you get the point of Company Island: It's pretty hard to manage, let alone improve, an organization, when working with only a ground-level, incomplete picture of how it works and what it does. Step One of the ideal Six Sigma Roadmap is the place where you begin to chart your island.

Step Two: Define Customer Requirements

One of the discoveries often admitted to by business leaders and managers, after embarking on Six Sigma, is that, to quote one executive, "We really didn't understand our customers very well." Getting good customer input on your company's needs and requirements may be the most challenging aspect of the Six Sigma approach. And as we'll see in Chapter 13, it takes much more than the occasional survey to figure out what your customers really want, as of this moment.

Step Two Overview

See Table 5.2.

Table 5.2 Step Two Overview.

Objectives:	Deliverables:
1. To establish standards for performance that are based on actual customer input, so that process effectiveness/capability can be accurately measured—and customer satisfaction predicted. 2. To develop or enhance systems and strategies devoted to ongoing "Voice of the Customer" data gathering.	A clear, complete description of the factors that drive customer satisfaction for each output and process—aka "requirements" or "specifications" in two key categories: • "Output Requirements" tied to the end product or service that make it work for the customer (what quality gurus have called "fitness for use"). • "Service Requirements" describing how the organization should interact with the customer.

Step Two Rationale

If you don't know what customers want, it's pretty darned hard to give it to them. Moreover, in the context of achieving Six Sigma performance, you can't develop meaningful measures until you have clear, specific requirements. You may gather data while turning up relatively few defects—but entirely ignore other areas where you are falling short.

The further rationale for Step Two is one of attitude. What's gotten many companies—even entire industries—into serious trouble in the past is a "we know what's best for the customer" mentality.[1] Almost as bad is the misguided belief that "we're really tuned in to the needs of our market," when in fact the company is out of touch with changing demands. Arrogance or ignorance may have been tolerable 20 years ago, but in today's competitive environment either one is a sure predictor of trouble.

In the 21st century, it will be the companies that really listen to their customers that are most likely to see long-term survival and success.

Step Three: Measure Current Performance

While Step Two defines what customers want, Step Three looks into how well you're delivering on those requirements today—and how likely you are to do so in the future. On a broader level, performance measures focused on the customer serve as the starting point for establishing a more effective measurement system.

Step Three Overview

First, see Table 5.3. Then note that measurement systems should also capture data on the efficiency of your processes: costs per output, energy or material consumption, rework, etc. You can have very happy customers and highly inefficient operations—an unprofitable formula.

Step Three Rationale

The need for an accurate "grade" of performance against customer requirements should be pretty obvious. There are several other benefits of Step Three, however, that make this much more valuable than a report card:

Table 5.3 Step Three Overview.

Objectives:	Deliverables:
To accurately evaluate each process's performance against definable customer requirements, and to establish a system for measuring key outputs and service features.	• Baseline Measures—quantified evaluations of current/recent process performance. • Capability Measures—assessment of the ability of the current process/output to deliver on requirements. These include "Sigma" scores for each process that allow comparison of very different processes. • Measurement Systems—new or enhanced methods and resources for ongoing measurement against customer-focused performance standards.

1. *Creating a measurement infrastructure.* This gives you the power to follow changes in performance—good or bad—and to respond promptly to warning signs and opportunities. Over time, these data become key inputs to the responsive, always-improving Six Sigma Organization.
2. *Setting priorities and focusing resources.* Even in the short term, knowledge derived from these measures drives decisions as to where to make the most urgent and/or high-potential improvements. The impact is a higher return on investment for Process Design, Redesign, or Improvement projects (Step 4).
3. *Selecting the best improvement strategies.* Having accurate process capability measures allows you to gauge the real nature of performance issues: Are they occasional problems or minor issues, or situations implicitly demanding that an entire product line or process be revamped?
4. *Matching commitments and capabilities.* Ever hear salespeople wonder in frustration, "How come we can't do this for the customer?" Or people in operations complaining about "impossible commitments" made by the sales force? Better communication alone won't resolve these disconnects, which in many businesses are some of the most

challenging and costly. You need to have the added advantage of the knowledge gained through Six Sigma methods—both about what customers really want and what the organization can actually *deliver*.

Step Four: Prioritize, Analyze, and Implement Improvements

Now that you're equipped with facts and measures, not just anecdotes and opinions, you're ready at Step 4 to start cashing in on the real payoff of Six Sigma.

Step Four Overview

See Table 5.4.

Step Four Rationale

The rationale for improving business processes probably needs no explanation. A key to success in the Six Sigma system is to choose your improvement priorities carefully and not to "overload" the organization with more activities than it can handle. The value of the improvement methods applied in Step Four is that they encompass the best techniques for driving out defects and improving process efficiency and

Table 5.4 Step Four Overview.

Objectives:	Deliverables:
To identify high-potential improvement opportunities and develop process-oriented solutions supported by factual analysis and creative thinking. Also, to effectively implement new solutions and processes and provide measurable, sustainable gains.	• Improvement Priorities. Potential Six Sigma projects assessed based on their impact and feasibility. • Process Improvements. Solutions targeted to specific root causes (aka "continuous" or "incremental" improvements). • New or Redesigned Processes. New activities or workflows created to meet new demands, incorporate new technologies, or achieve dramatic increases in speed, accuracy, cost performance, etc. (aka Six Sigma Design or Business Process Redesign).

capacity. Six Sigma techniques and tools can be applied to large, complex business problems or to fairly simple Process Improvement opportunities.

Step Five: Expand and Integrate the Six Sigma System

Real "Six Sigma performance" will not come to you through a wave of Improvement projects—it can be achieved only through a long-term commitment to the core themes and methods of Six Sigma.

Step Five Overview

See Table 5.5.

Step Five Rationale

Perhaps the strongest rationale for Step 5—the place where you take on the chore of building a long-term vision of a Six Sigma organization—is to consider the possibility of *not* doing it.

Table 5.5 Step Five Overview.

Objectives:	Deliverables:
To initiate ongoing business practices that drive improved performance and ensure constant measurement, reexamination, and renewal of products, services, processes, and procedures. core and Step Five is the place where your organization works hard to achieve the vision of a Six Sigma . Organization	• Process Controls. Measures and monitoring, to sustain perfor mance improvement. • Process Ownership and Management. Cross-functional oversight of support processes, with input from Voice of Customer, Voice of Market, Voice of Employee, and process measurement systems. • Response Plans. Mechanisms to act based on key information so as to adapt strategies, products/services, and processes. • Six Sigma "Culture." An organization positioned for continuous renewal, with Six Sigma themes and tools an essential part of the everyday business environment.

It's a few years from now. You've been watching more than a few customers defecting to an upstart competitor, a company that claims to have put a "Six Sigma system" in place. As you investigate, you learn that this growing business does in fact have some advantages over your older, less responsive company; such as:

- An accurate, well-channeled customer feedback system
- Well-integrated, "seamless" processes, with smooth handoffs and cooperation up and down the line
- Timely measurement systems that track not just dollars but also defects, changes in key activities, variations in key inputs like raw materials, etc.
- Expertise in correcting problems and making improvements—either by fine-tuning processes or by creating entirely new processes, products, or services to meet changing customer needs

How comfortable would you be with that type of competition? Can you be confident that tomorrow a similar firm won't start making inroads into your profits or market share? How would you defend yourself against that type of competitor? If such questions make you squirm even a bit, it's an indication that Step 5 should be made a key element in your Six Sigma efforts.

Recapping the Executive Summary

As we close out Part One of *The Six Sigma Way*, we offer you five summarizing subsections just as a reminder of *what* Six Sigma is and *why* it offers so many potential benefits to any organization.

Definition of Six Sigma

Six Sigma can be defined in several ways. It's a way of measuring processes; a goal of near-perfection, represented by 3.4 Defects per Million Opportunities (DPMO); an approach to changing the culture of an organization. Most accurately, though, Six Sigma is defined as a broad and comprehensive *system* for building and sustaining business performance, success, and leadership.

In other words, Six Sigma is a context within which you will be able to integrate many valuable but often disconnected management "best practices" and concepts, including systems thinking, continuous improvement, knowledge management, mass customization, and activity-based management.

Six Essential Themes

The "vision" of a Six Sigma organization embraces all of these six themes:

1. *A genuine focus on the customer,* backed by an attitude that puts the customers' needs first, as well as by systems and strategies that serve to tie in the business to the "Voice of the Customer."
2. *Data- and fact-driven management,* with effective measurement systems that track both results and outcomes (Ys) and Process, Input, and other predictive factors (Xs).
3. *Process focus, management, and improvement,* as an engine for growth and success. Processes in Six Sigma are documented, communicated, measured and refined on an ongoing basis. They are also *designed* or *redesigned* at intervals, to stay current with customer and business needs.
4. *Proactive management,* involving habits and practices that anticipate problems and changes, apply facts and data, and question assumptions about goals and "how we do things."
5. *Boundaryless collaboration,* featuring cooperation between internal groups and with customers, suppliers, and supply chain partners.
6. *A drive for perfection, and yet a tolerance for failure,* that gives people in a Six Sigma organization the freedom to test new approaches even while managing risks and learning from mistakes, thereby "raising the bar" of performance and customer satisfaction.

History and Evolution

Six Sigma was developed at Motorola in the late 1980s, as a way of providing a clear focus on Improvement and of helping to accelerate the *rate* of change in a hard-pressed competitive environment. The concept, tools, and system of Six Sigma have evolved and expanded through the years—most recently through the examples set by GE and AlliedSignal/Honeywell—and this has helped to continually rekindle interest and redouble efforts at process and quality improvement.

Thus, even though Six Sigma is based on many of the ideas and tools of the "quality" movement of the 1980s and 1990s, a savvy company implementing Six Sigma can avoid the pitfalls that have given TQM a bad name in many organizations.

Results and Opportunities

In the case of Motorola, Six Sigma helped to bring back the company from the brink of extinction in the late 1980s and early 1990s. As for GE and AlliedSignal, Six Sigma has brought them billions in gains in less than four years, and is expected to bring sustained and expanding bottom-line benefits well into the new century. As other firms' efforts gain momentum, additional success stories begin to emerge.

The opportunities open to your business will depend on your current performance and "defect levels," your competitive position, and so on. If yours is a *Service*-based process or organization, you may actually have a much greater potential for improvement than does a Product or Manufacturing organization.

At the same time, however, Six Sigma is not an automatic cure for an ailing business. GE Appliances, for example, has been struggling with poor performance for several years. It has found that Six Sigma has taken longer to deliver on the needed turnaround than had been hoped.[2]

Implementation

It is essential that your organization develop its own strategy and plan for launching and integrating Six Sigma. Still, the five basic steps are these:

1. Identify core processes and key customers.
2. Define customer requirements.
3. Measure current performance.
4. Prioritize, analyze, and implement improvements.
5. Manage processes for Six Sigma performance.

Still, as we'll see in the chapters of Part Two, there are many options open to you, as you seek to define goals and to execute Six Sigma.

2

Gearing Up and Adapting Six Sigma to Your Organization

CHAPTER

6

Is Six Sigma Right for Us Now?

Assessing Your Six Sigma Readiness

Embarking on a Six Sigma initiative begins with a decision to *change*—specifically, to learn and adopt methods that can boost the performance of your organization. In its most ambitious applications, Six Sigma can be a more fundamental change than, say, a major acquisition or a new systems implementation, because Six Sigma affects *how* you run the business. The depth of impact on your management processes and skills will vary, of course, with how extensively you want to apply Six Sigma tools and the results you're seeking.

The starting point in gearing up for Six Sigma is to verify that you're ready to—or need to—embrace a change that says "There's a better way to run our organization." This shouldn't be a rote, number-crunching-based decision, but there are a number of essential questions and facts you'll have to consider in making your readiness assessment.

I. Assess the Outlook and Future Path of the Business

A first step is a general review of the condition of your organization today and its outlook for the future, both in the short and the long term. Key questions include:

- *Is the strategic course clear for the company?* Do we have a strong sense of what value we offer to the market and to our customers? Is there a plan to adapt the strategy to potential or pending changes in our markets, technologies, etc.?
- *Are our chances good for meeting our financial and growth goals?* Is the business in a healthy enough state that is has the needed cash and capital to provide customer and shareholder value? Can we meet the expectations of analysts and investors? Is there a strong theme or vision for the future of the organization that is well understood and consistently communicated?
- *Is the organization good at responding effectively and efficiently to new circumstances?* Will we be able to plan and manage change (new products, acquisitions, growth, etc.), or are we more likely to be reacting to internal and external events? Are we creating truly innovative new products and services that will keep us in the lead? How stable are our customers' needs? Our technologies? How able are we to maintain and improve our "intellectual capital"?

What the Answers Mean

Generally good prospects make it less likely that you need Six Sigma to sustain your success—as long as you're being realistic about your future. Complacency and/or overconfidence, however, always are dangerous in the 21st-century business environment. Thus it's a good idea to "discount" any rosy predictions as a hedge against unforeseen events. When the head of a company as successful as Intel writes a book called *Only the Paranoid Survive,* that should probably be taken as a warning.[1]

In fact, a positive outlook can also be seen as a compelling reason in *favor* of Six Sigma. Along with those companies that have embarked on Six Sigma to stave off future disaster (see Motorola's story in Chapter 1 on page 6), there are plenty who have taken on Six Sigma in the midst of strong growth and positive projections. For example, one of our clients—an integrated logistics company—has grown tenfold over the past decade and has good reason to project similar gains as large firms continue to outsource their logistics and warehousing efforts. Nonetheless, they are taking on Six Sigma to help leverage and guarantee their growth and competitive position.

2. Evaluating Your Current Performance

Even if the "future's so bright you gotta wear shades," existing problems increase the potential value of a Six Sigma effort. Six Sigma makes it easier to be more concrete in an assessment of where you are today; and the more you can use hard data to answer the following questions, the better:

- *What are our current overall business results?* Are we meeting sales and profit goals? Are there areas (products, business units) that are underperforming? What's our yield, Sigma level, or DPMO—estimated, or based on real data? Is there a lot of variation in our output performance?
- *How effectively do we focus on and meet customer requirements?* Do we even *understand* what our customers need? How would we describe our relationships with key customers/segments? What would *they* say? Do we compete mainly on price—and might there be ways to better convey value to our customers? Does our service match the quality of our products, and vice versa? How successful are our new products or services when released to the market? Are we able to satisfy one player in our supply chain but not others?
- *How efficiently are we operating?* What level of rework and waste exists in our processes? Are we so "busy" solving problems and fighting fires that we never take time to improve things? What's our cost per "unit"—is the trend improving or getting worse? Are our support processes—finance, human resources, facilities, information technology—enhancing our ability to deliver value to customers, or simply enforcing rules and policies? How smoothly do our new products or services reach the market?

What the Answers Mean

There are actually several conclusions you can draw from this current performance assessment. (Some of these will come in handy in the next chapter, when we discuss coming up with your own Six Sigma implementation strategy.)

A. *Is there enough room for improvement to make Six Sigma worthwhile?* If everything is humming along just fine and the money is rolling in, you may decide the potential payoff from Six Sigma isn't worth the effort. On the other hand if you see some major Improvement opportunities—financial and/or competitive—that's a sign that Six Sigma may be a worthwhile option. For some organizations, too, the potential value of Six Sigma lies in improving the culture or habits of the business; for example, converting from a reactive, "seat-of-the-pants" style to a more responsive or proactive management approach. However, since the negative impact of a reactive culture will show up in increased costs, you should be able to back up the need to "improve our culture" by pointing to concrete financial benefits to be gained.

B. *Where are the best opportunities for improvement?* This part of the assessment can give you initial insights into those high-priority needs on which your first Six Sigma projects may focus.

C. *How effective are our customer knowledge and measurement systems?*

The harder you have found it to answer these three questions, the more seriously you should consider adopting Six Sigma methods to help you strengthen your "Voice of the Customer" and measurement capabilities.

3. Reviewing Systems and Capacity for Change and Improvement

A third major factor in deciding whether to launch Six Sigma is the organization's existing improvement processes and its ability to undertake a new initiative. Questions here include the following:

- *How effective are our current improvement and "change management" systems?* Do we already have efforts under way to improve our performance, measures, systems, etc.? Are the improvement efforts well coordinated, or are they disconnected (aka "shotgun") solutions? Are there sufficient data to support the choice of improvement priorities and to measure results? How well do we implement solutions and changes—both from a technical and a people perspective? Have we integrated continuous improvement into our business culture? Are we good at making changes and flexing to meet new business challenges? Is our "quality" effort/group focused on improvement, or just on control?

- *How well are our cross-functional processes managed?* Do our people understand the entire process or just their own narrow slice? Do we provide enough opportunities for our people to learn more about the business as well as about the key skills that drive people's performance? Would we be able to adapt quickly to new customer demands or tighter requirements? Do functional groups interact well, or are there barriers between departments? Are there a lot of reviews or checks on decisions, or do we trust our people to "make the call"?
- *What other change efforts or activities might conflict with or support a Six Sigma initiative?* Are recent acquisitions, new product introductions, strategy changes, systems implementations, or other "big" initiatives likely to consume people's attention and resources? Would other changes make potential Six Sigma solutions obsolete? Can Six Sigma be used to help leverage a new initiative—for example, to help integrate processes in a merger or redesign activities for a new information system?

What the Answers Mean

The purpose of this third assessment element is to test the *timing* and readiness of the business for a possible Six Sigma effort. Even if assessment factors 1 (future prognosis) and 2 (current performance) make a strong case to initiate Six Sigma, your business may already be capable of dealing with the challenges. Or your people, systems, and resources may already be all wrapped up in making other efforts or changes—in which case you'd have trouble making the commitment of leadership, time, and energy, not to mention money, that a Six Sigma effort demands.

When Six Sigma Is *Not* Right for an Organization

First, let's remind ourselves that Six Sigma can be applied as a *targeted* approach, so a limited implementation may always be feasible. Nevertheless, we can look at the flipside of the preceding assessment to identify conditions in which it probably would be best to say "No thanks" (for now) to Six Sigma efforts. Conditions that might indicate a "no-go" decision on Six Sigma include the following:

- *You already have in place a strong, effective performance and process improvement effort.* If there are systems and tools in place to support ongoing problem solving and process design/redesign, Six Sigma may not add much value—and might even *confuse* people.

- *Current changes already are overwhelming your people and/or resources.* An organization can handle only so much turmoil at once. Lumping Six Sigma on top of one or more other major business upheavals could prove to be the proverbial straw on the camel's (your company's) back. *However,* beware of making the "we're too busy" argument—a copout for never doing the tough work it takes to become a truly world-class organization. Just as with getting married or having children, there's never a "perfect" time. That means your success will have a lot more to do with how well you integrate and use Six Sigma to support other, existing changes.
- *The potential gains aren't there.* Six Sigma demands an investment. If you can't make a solid case for future or current return, it may be best to stay away—at least until you have figured out exactly how and when it might pay off.

Summarizing the Assessment: Three Key Questions

At the end of a review of your business, including its future and current state, and its organizational factors, the objective is to decide "Should we take on—or at least seriously consider—a Six Sigma initiative for our organization?" We can boil all the specifics down to three key questions, as follows:

1. Is change (whether broad or targeted) a critical business need now, based on bottom-line, cultural, or competitive needs?
2. Can we come up with a strong strategic rationale for applying Six Sigma to our business? (Which is another way of saying, "Will it get and hold the commitment of business leadership?")
3. Will our existing improvement systems and methods be capable of achieving the degree of change needed to keep us a successful, competitive organization?

If your answers are *Yes, Yes,* and *No,* you may well be ready to explore further how to adopt Six Sigma in your organization. By the way, these three questions also may be found in the Six Sigma Start-Up Worksheet in the Appendix on page 380. (The lower half of the worksheet focuses on finding the type of effort that makes the best sense for you, based on our discussions in the following chapter.)

Six Sigma from a Cost/Benefit Perspective

Though we've touched so far on several factors relating to the potential value and feasibility of Six Sigma, the blunt question we often hear posed by executives and managers is this: "Exactly what is Six Sigma going to cost, and what kind of return can we expect it to bring us?" Unfortunately, there's no way to answer that question without examining the improvement opportunities present in your business, and then planning your implementation to see what the relative payoff will be. We can, however, offer you a bit of guidance on how to estimate—and manage—your likely return.

Estimating Potential Benefits

You can most accurately define possible dollar-gains from Six Sigma by evaluating the costs of rework, inefficiency, unhappy or lost customers, and so on, and then estimating the amount by which you think you can *reduce* them. For example, if you've developed measures of Defects per Million Opportunities (DPMO), you would determine the average cost of each defect (taking into consideration people, material, and other factors) and the total savings for an X percent defect reduction. The more specifically you can define these numbers, called "Costs of Poor Quality" or "COPQ," the more accurate will your estimates be.

The type of assessment will never be perfect, however, for the following reasons among others:

1. Since it would be a huge amount of work to quantify costs for *all* the problems in any organization, instead you'll likely have to rely on guesstimates—or the broader, overview assessment described above.
2. "Knowing" what extent of savings is possible (what "X percent" really means) will really be just a guess, until someone actually starts analyzing the problem and the possible solutions to it—in other words, only *after* you've started doing the real work of Six Sigma improvement.

3. External impacts are hard to quantify. For example, it's very challenging to project just how many *new* customers you'll gain, or existing ones you'll prevent from defecting, simply by improving a key process. A certain level of Six Sigma effort is based on *faith* that better management and data will translate into better market image and customer loyalty.
4. You won't be able to work on everything, and the choice of improvement projects will significantly impact the early success—and financial benefit—of the Six Sigma initiative. We cover Improvement Project Selection in detail in Chapter 11, as we seek to ensure that you will target the optimal opportunities.

Probably the best way to get good dollar estimates of potential Six Sigma benefits is to take a combined approach. First, conduct a detailed financial benefit assessment of several representative improvement opportunities. Then, project how many similar opportunities exist across the organization. The answer will give you a more solid answer to the "How much can we gain?" question—but it will still be an estimate.

Determining Lead Time for Results

We once had a colleague who displayed the following saying on her desk: "Everything takes longer than you expect, even when you expect it to take longer than you expect." That wonderful truism could be applied to many things, but it sure can hold true for Six Sigma results. Improvement projects can exceed their predicted completion times by months—especially when those projects haven't been well defined to begin with. Predicting when you'll see real dollars, or major customer impact, will depend a lot on *what* you choose to work on.

Still, it's relevant and important to wonder what the lead time for a payoff will be. Generally you should figure *six to nine months* for the first wave of DMAIC projects to be completed and results to be concrete. Of course, you *can* push teams for faster results. Giving them extra help or coaching as they work through their "learning curve" can be a good way to accelerate their efforts (though it also may boost your costs). But based on our experience and the companies we've observed, it would be a mistake to forecast big tangible gains much sooner than that.

We know of one company that launched its Six Sigma projects early in its second quarter and hoped to have significant results by the end of the fiscal year—but the gains came too late. Thus if a pay-as-you-go implementation is critical, you may want to consider how to schedule your Six Sigma launch so as to achieve your results time-window. You can also consider how to manage your *costs* so that the urgency of a payoff won't be as great.

The Costs of Six Sigma Implementation

Tapping in to the potential gains you've identified will demand an up-front investment. Which means that if you can't clear *some* budget for a Six Sigma start-up effort, your Go/No-go debate probably is over for now. However, the attraction of gains to be made through Six Sigma will usually prompt business leaders to at least consider making the investment. The challenge at that point is to determine what the costs are likely to be.

Some of the most important Six Sigma budget items can include the following:

- *Direct payroll.* Individuals dedicated to the effort full-time. (See Chapter 9, Preparing Black Belts and Other Key Roles).
- *Indirect payroll.* The time devoted by executives, team members, process owners, and others to such activities as measurement, Voice of the Customer data gathering, and improvement projects.
- *Training and consulting.* Teaching people Six Sigma skills and getting advice (from folks like us) on how to make the effort successful can be a significant investment, too.
- *Improvement implementation costs.* Expenses to install new solutions or process designs can range from a few thousand dollars to millions—especially for IT-driven solutions.

Other expenses that can add up include travel and lodging, facilities for training, and office and meeting space for teams.

Estimating and Managing Your Costs—and Returns

Estimates of *your* Six Sigma costs will depend on your implementation speed, the scale of your effort, and your general "risk profile" when it comes to investing in the potential gains of the initiative. Many of the factors impacting your investment decisions—including your overall objective, staffing, training and project selection—are covered in the subsequent chapters of Part 2.

The example of our client, GE Capital Services (GECS), may be encouraging. GECS launched Six Sigma in 1996 and spent about $53 million the first year—a number driven more by speed and scale than by a concern for controlling costs. However, the initiative paid for itself that same year, with a reported $53 million in gains and savings. In year two, 1997, Six Sigma expenditures at GECS rose to $88 million, but gains were pegged at $261 million—a $173 million *profit.* For 1998, the last full year of the effort as of this writing, the profit reported was $310 million over expenses of $98 million.[2]

You can maximize your Six Sigma ROI by making careful decisions as to where the investment is most likely to pay off. We've observed and worked with companies who have probably spent more than was necessary to get results from their Six Sigma efforts. On the other hand, trying to do Six Sigma "on the cheap" can be a bad move. It can adversely affect the quality of the training and advice you receive, of course, but more importantly it sends the wrong message to the organization about the seriousness of your commitment. When you ask people to invest their energy and enthusiasm in improving the business—which often involves sacrifices to their personal time, potentially risky career decisions, and stepping outside their "comfort zone" to try new skills and tools—the company has to show its willingness to sacrifice, too.

Cost/Benefit and Your Six Sigma Launch

The question raised at the start of this section was: "Exactly what is Six Sigma going to cost, and what kind of return will it bring?" By now we hope you understand why we believe that a strictly Cost/Benefit–based decision on a Six Sigma start-up is usually not the best approach. (The exception would be for a limited, one-or-two-project effort.) For most companies, the issues that affect potential return are much too broad—and the cost/benefit estimates too sketchy—to base your decision on that ratio alone. We'd suggest that the culture and climate factors cited earlier in this chapter—the organization's readiness for change, the ability to track and understand customer needs, the tendency to go with "firefighting" versus fire *prevention,* etc.—should have as much influence on your Go/No-go decision as any hard dollar estimates.

If Six Sigma continues to look attractive to your organization at this point, the next meaningful question you should be asking is "How do we ensure that our Six Sigma effort works well and yields a significant return—both short-term and long-term?" That will be our focus through the remainder of Part Two.

CHAPTER

7

How and Where Should We Start Our Efforts?

THE FIRST IMPORTANT choice you have to make in your Six Sigma launch—one affecting your costs and the potential size and speed of your return on investment—boils down to asking "Where do we begin?" We'll use the Six Sigma Roadmap—introduced in Chapter 5—to frame and guide these start-up decisions. We'll actually look at two ways in which you can approach your initial implementation decisions. The first is based on criteria impacting the scale and urgency of your effort; the second, on an assessment of your strengths and weaknesses in what we call the "core competencies" of the Six Sigma system.

Where to Start: Objective, Scope, and Timeframe

So, how *should* your organization begin its push toward Six Sigma performance? When tough questions like this are posed about Six Sigma, we tend to fall back on one of these two answers: "It depends," and "God only knows."

Since the second answer leaves us unable to consult further, we'll have to try to narrow down "It depends." Fortunately for us, it has become clear that decisions on how to tailor your approach rest on three primary factors: your Objective, your Scope, and your Timeframe. These elements are interrelated, but by looking at them one at a time you can get some guidelines on how to make your start-up decisions. As we review these criteria, you should recognize that information drawn from the Six Sigma readiness assessment, covered in Chapter 6, can be a big help in your implementation choices.

Clarifying Your Objective

What do you want your Six Sigma efforts to accomplish?

Every business wants "results" from Six Sigma, but the type of result or change that is needed (or feasible) can vary a lot. For example, Six Sigma may be attractive as a way to address nagging problems in terms of product failures or gaps in customer service. Then again, you may be part of a profitable, growing business, but recognize that your success is creating a reactive management culture that threatens future growth. Each of those scenarios could lead to different types of Six Sigma efforts.

We've defined three broad levels of Objective—Business Transformation, Strategic Improvement, and Problem Solving (see Fig. 7.1)—based on the scale of impact you want to make on the organization. It's tempting, of course, to say "I want it *all!*" But identifying which is your

Objective	Description
Business Transformation	A major shift in how the organization works; aka "culture change." Examples: • creating a customer-focused attitude • building greater flexibility • abandoning old structures or ways of doing business
Strategic Improvement	Targets key strategic or operational weaknesses or opportunities. Examples: • speeding up product development • enhancing supply chain efficiencies • building e-commerce capabilties
Problem Solving	Fixes specific areas of high cost, rework or delays. Examples: • shortening application processing time • reducing parts shortages in West • decreasing volume of past-due receivables

Figure 7.1 Three levels of Six Sigma objective

primary driver for Six Sigma (for now, at least) will help you to arrive at the best start-up strategy.

Assessing Your Scope

What segments of the organization can or should be involved in your initial Six Sigma efforts?

Scope can be influenced a lot by your position in the organization. If for example you head an Information Technology group, you may have the authority and resources to launch a Six Sigma change effort in IT but certainly not across the entire corporation. Even so, it's possible you will want to try to influence your organization's leaders to begin a companywide effort. In fact, one of our clients did begin to implement their Six Sigma effort based just on some early suggestions coming from their vice president of IT.

Another element of Scope revolves around the basic question "What's feasible?" It may not be realistic to take on every business activity simultaneously. Even at GE, some businesses and processes were not included in the initial Six Sigma wave. Sales processes, for instance, didn't receive any focused attention until over a year into the effort. Businesses like NBC started a little later, too. Scrutiny of your core processes or business operations can provide valuable input as you seek to focus your initial scope.

Determining feasibility always involves tradeoffs (as we said, "it depends"). The three main factors that come into play in most cases are the following:

- *Resources.* Who are the best candidates to participate in the effort? How much time can people spend on Six Sigma efforts? What budget can be devoted to the start-up? What other activities will compete for resources? Etc.
- *Attention.* Can the business focus on many start-up efforts at the same time? Will you or other leaders be overwhelmed as you try to guide too many activities simultaneously?
- *Acceptance.* If people in a certain area (function, business unit, department, etc.) are likely to resist, for whatever reason, it may be best to involve them later. It's the organizational change version of the adage "Choose your battles."

Defining Your Timeframe

How long are you—or the "powers-that-be"—able/willing to wait to get results?

In other words, "Urgency" or "Patience" or "Degree of Panic" might be more accurate here than "Timeframe." A long lead-time for a payoff can be frustrating; companies can be like kids on a car trip ("Are we there yet?"). The time factor, in fact, has the strongest influence on most Six Sigma start-up efforts—and for good reason.

Chuck Cox, who heads quality efforts for the Server Division of the French computer firm Groupe Bull, teaches advanced Six Sigma tools. Cox has witnessed many quality and Six Sigma launches through the years, and he notes: "You can't persuade the senior guys to break loose the resources and lead the charge unless they see a pretty immediate return on the investment." To Cox, getting gains in a "quick-start" mode is the best way to prove both the concept and value of Six Sigma.

Cox also agrees with us, however, that short-term gains aren't the main point. The real goal is to create an organization that can effectively hang on to "a loyal customer base"—something that can happen only with a long-term, integrated effort. The danger of a purely project-based, problem-solving approach is that you never raise the scope of your work so as to really capitalize on the Six Sigma system.

On-Ramps to the Six Sigma Roadmap

Possible starting points—corresponding to the "Objective" for your Six Sigma effort—are presented in Fig. 7.2 as "on-ramps" to the Roadmap. It's even possible to take more than one on-ramp at a time—a neat trick, as long as you're careful not to spread your resources and energies too thinly. After we've explained the on-ramps we'll present a Start-Up Scenario to illustrate each category.

Business Transformation On-Ramp

The top on-ramp is for those who have the need, vision and patience to launch Six Sigma as a full-scale change initiative. At the outset it may be more feasible—and a worthwhile learning exercise—to concentrate on developing a map of a few core processes, rather than trying to identify and define all processes at once. In addition, taking the Busi-

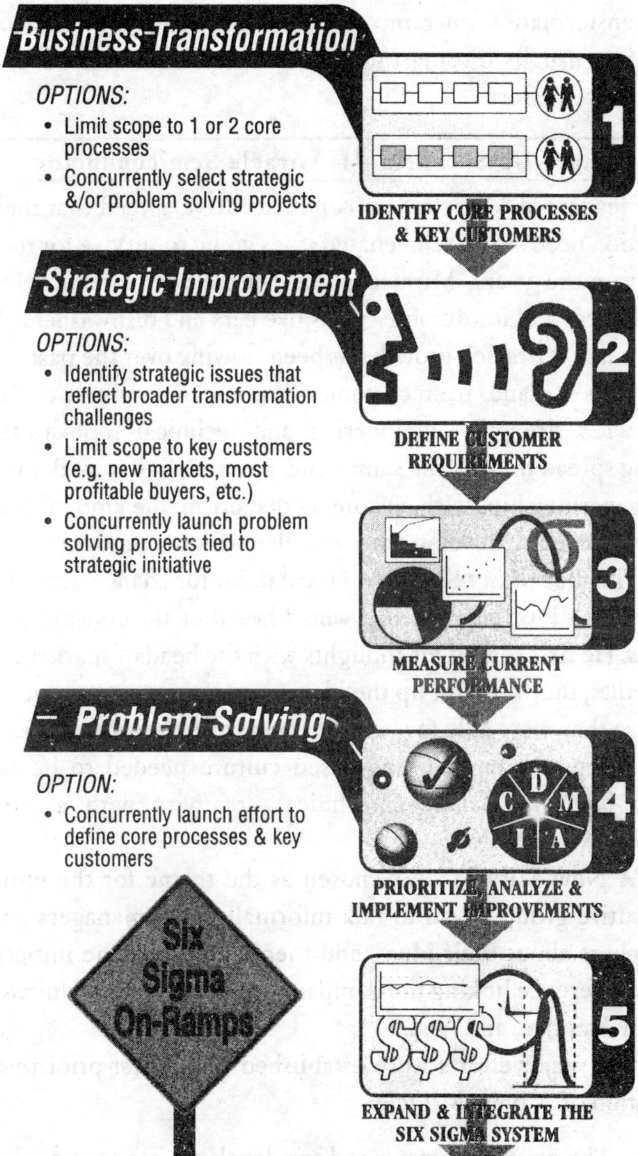

Figure 7.2 On-ramps to the Six Sigma Roadmap

ness Transformation on-ramp doesn't close down the other ones for you. In fact, usually it's smart to approach any organizational change as a multifaceted effort.

Start-Up Scenario #1: Miracle Semiconductor

The leaders of Miracle Semiconductor have agreed that their organization needs to be rejuvenated if it's going to survive for more than a few more years. Miracle makes specialty microchips for small appliances and for durable goods like cars and dishwashers. Though profitable, Miracle's growth has been slowing over the past couple of years. As demands from customers become increasingly challenging, Miracle's strength—engineering and technical sophistication—is being spread thin. At the same time, the company is weak in creating those partnerships with customers that create the kind of "give-and-take" needed to develop truly excellent custom products.

The idea of Six Sigma as a focal point for change actually began with the VP of engineering, who'd heard of the concept at a trade show. He first shared his thoughts with the head of marketing. Then together, they brought up the idea in a senior management meeting, where they were able to get agreement from the other top execs that the company's engineering-based culture needed to be replaced with one that balances technical creativity with a customer-responsive attitude.

"A New Miracle" was chosen as the theme for the effort. The executive group began to talk informally with managers and team members about their ideas, and then announced the initiative at a teleconference linking the company's locations in the United States, Latin America, and Asia.

Two major efforts were established as the first priorities in the creation of A New Miracle:

- The executive group and two levels of management began to hold a series of meetings designed to create a high-level "map" of the businesses, showing links between departments and critical interfaces with customers and prospective customers.
- A cross-functional team was formed to assess issues relating to development of proposals for prospective customers, with

the goal of identifying three to four specific improvement projects by the end of the quarter.

"I know we need to beef up our technical resources," said Miracle's company president, "but we'll just be wasting our time if we don't get these things done first."

The Strategic Improvement On-Ramp

The "middle" on-ramp is the one that offers the most options. A Strategic Improvement effort can be limited to one or two key pilot improvement projects, or it can engage a whole wave of teams and training aimed at addressing a strategic weakness. It can set the stage for a more ambitious Business Transformation initiative, or simply involve a focused improvement campaign that exists in no longer-term context.

Strategic Improvement also can be aimed at building one of the key "infrastructure" elements or core competencies of the Six Sigma system: measurement, for example, or Voice of the Customer systems.

Start-Up Scenario #2: Safety Zone Insurance

Safety Zone Insurance is a life and casualty insurer that sells policies through independent agents in the upper Midwest. Despite several waves of belt-tightening, Safety Zone has one of the highest cost-profiles in its market. Its claims service is considered to be outstanding—insured customers actually are quite happy—but it takes Safety Zone a lot of time, with high labor costs, to perform underwriting activities and to issue policies. The delays are an aggravation for agents, who complain about them regularly.

The company's Chief Operating Officer, Eleanor Zone, has concluded that just telling people to "cut costs" again won't cut it. "We've got to get smarter about how we handle applications," she exclaimed in frustration, while preparing for the company's shareholder meeting. (Safety Zone stock had just dropped 10 percent over the prior month.)

After the meeting, Zone met with the director of underwriting and suggested that they try a Six Sigma approach to cut costs and application processing time.

"Isn't that a whole 'culture change' thing?" the director asked. "From what I'm hearing," Zone responded, "we can use Six Sigma methods just to help with critical issues—like fixing our costs. If that works, we can look for other ways to expand it." Since several agents in Michigan had recently written a letter threatening to stop representing Safety Zone, a team was formed right away to address the problem. Meanwhile, a review committee was formed to gather data about the high costs and the slow processing, with a deadline for a report in two weeks....

The Problem Solving On-Ramp

With an urgency of results driving nearly every Six Sigma start-up, most organizations choose to jump on the Problem Solving on-ramp first. And yet, while that's usually the quickest way to a payoff, doing *only* Problem Solving can also be the riskiest shortcut on the Six Sigma way. The dangers come in two categories:

1. *Poor project selection.* Without process or customer data, business leaders choose their projects based on mere guesses and assumptions. That means you may well end up targeting issues that are annoying, but not really critical to the business or its customers. There's a common temptation, as well, to launch too many projects simultaneously.
2. *Limited gains.* The "problem-solving" methods of Step 4—Process Improvement and Process Design/Redesign—are most powerful when driven by a wider focus and a long-term perspective. A real vision of broader change often was missing from TQM problem-solving efforts, which is a big reason why so many companies lost momentum.

If you're among the majority of organizations who'll want to start Six Sigma improvement projects (Step 4) right away, your best bet is to try to balance the push for immediate results with attention to longer-term goals (Steps 1, 2, 3, and 5). But if *all* you want to do is solve some critical problems, that's okay too.

Start-Up Scenario #3: Acme Products Company

The head of finance for Acme Products Company was surprised to see Joe Check, eager head of Acme's accounts receivable group, hovering outside her office door. "Come in, Check," she called, "What's up?"

"I've got some interesting stuff I wanted to show you," Joe said. "I've had a couple of people on my staff working on trying to cut the number of accounts sent to collections. We all figured the problems would be with the shakier customers—but we found it's really the *top* accounts that have outstanding invoices most often."

"You mean we're sending Collection Agents after our better customers?"

"Almost twice as often as the ones we call the 'deadbeats,' " Joe confirmed.

"Oops," said the finance VP. "But hey, if they aren't paying on time, we have to go after them anyway."

"Well, if the invoices had been correct, I'd agree with you. We also found that there were some discrepancies between the sales reps' price book and the invoicing system. Almost 80 percent of the delayed payments included items that had mismatched pricing."

"How'd you figure all this out?"

"Well," Joe explained, "I'd been reading about this Six Sigma improvement stuff, and it seemed interesting. I mean, we spend a lot of time just fixing problems around here that I suppose we shouldn't have. So I decided to try it out. We didn't do anything really sophisticated, but the guys in the department were pretty impressed."

"I'm pretty impressed, too," the VP admitted. "I can think of quite a few other areas we could work on."

By the end of the following month, the VP had announced a pilot Six Sigma effort in Finance, involving Accounts Receivable and Investor Relations.

The Roadmap and Your Strengths and Weaknesses

An alternative way of defining your Six Sigma priorities—still based on the Six Sigma Roadmap—is to assess your capabilities at each Step, which as we've noted represent the "core competencies" for a successful organization in the 21st century. As you ponder your responses to the following questions, you will begin to see where your greatest weaknesses lie—and where your initial activities might be concentrated:

- *Step One.* Do we have a clear understanding of how our organization "fits together"? For example, what are the core processes? Which key customers do they serve? Are the interfaces or handoffs between groups clear and well managed?
- *Step Two.* How well do we *really* understand our customers? Our competitors' customers? Do we have an effective, broad-based Voice of the Customer strategy? Are mechanisms in place to capture customer and market input so that we can review and analyze it? Is our focus on *both* Service and Output requirements, or are we ignoring one or the other? Have we translated customer feedback into clear requirements or specifications?
- *Step Three.* Are we accurately *measuring* our performance against customer requirements? (Do we really know how well we're doing?) Do measures encompass both Service and Output specifications? Are there too few measures, or too many? Is the data accessible? How well do we use measurement data to evaluate and fine-tune our processes/performance? Do the people working in the process understand the measures and what to do with the information? Are input or process measures in place, to help us see potential problems or opportunities *before* they happen?
- *Step Four.* Do we have any critical problems or opportunities that are calling out for attention? Conversely, is every problem "urgent," or are we setting effective improvement priorities? What's the likely payoff from these problems? Are necessary resources being deployed to tackle the problems, or are we solving them with "band-aids"? Is there a clear, proactive process in place to develop root-cause-focused solutions? Are we able and willing to design or redesign processes when their current design is no longer viable? Are key leaders engaged in and supporting the improvement efforts? Are we measuring results and ensuring that solutions pay off?
- *Step Five.* Have we established responsibility for ongoing assessment and management of our key processes? Have steps been taken to ensure that improvements are maintained and that results are being

met? Are measures captured and reported so we can tell "at a glance" how the business is performing? Are we prepared to manage the business as a "closed-loop" system?

In some ways, these questions offer a more reasoned way of identifying your Six Sigma priorities. Rather than being driven by current issues or concerns—which is the emphasis in the choice of "On-Ramps"—this assessment focuses on the *systemic* strengths and weaknesses of your organization. For example, by improving your knowledge of customer needs, or by strengthening your measurement systems, you create a stronger business while giving Six Sigma teams a better environment—not to mention better data—for improvement.

Realistically, though, current issues usually take precedence over systemic challenges. The trick is to focus on the immediate needs of your business even while ensuring that your initial projects lay the groundwork upon which you can build your Six Sigma "core competencies."

Piloting Your Six Sigma Effort

Regardless of the scale or scope of your Six Sigma start-up, a "piloting strategy" should be an essential component of your effort. The reality is, some problems and surprises will crop up in *every* Six Sigma implementation. Piloting, however, allows you to minimize the challenges that arise and to *learn* from them. Of course, if you're still not really sure whether Six Sigma will be effective in your business, a pilot also is the best way to test the overall approach.

The common arguments *against* piloting include a need to move fast, lack of resources, and/or a loss of momentum and enthusiasm around the Six Sigma effort. But a well-thought-out piloting plan shouldn't delay your progress much, and by working out the "bugs" in your training, projects, teamwork, etc., you pave the way for greater results faster. Piloting typically *saves* money in the long run, by helping you understand sooner where your resources are being used most effectively. When you *don't* pilot—or at least include time to incorporate improvements in your Six Sigma processes—you simply prolong and expand the impact of unforeseen problems.

Among the problems we've seen that *could* have been minimized through a piloting strategy are Improvement Project selection, training design, and the failure of improvement results to "stick." In many of these cases the problems dragged on for months, because not enough attention or time was paid to fine-tuning the effort early on.

What Should You Pilot?

Piloting can be applied to any aspect of Six Sigma, including solutions derived from Process Improvement or Design/Redesign projects. Some of the comment elements of a Six Sigma start that can be considered for piloting include:

- Orientation of business leaders
- Project selection
- Project team makeup
- Team leader selection
- Measurement methods
- Training design and content (for audiences including executives, team leaders, team members, etc.)
- Training logistics and scheduling

Clearly, the most important pilot subject will be the *results* achieved from the Six Sigma effort. Those may take a while to measure, however. So by keeping an eye on some of the factors noted here, you can boost the probability of a strong final payoff.

Key Questions for a Piloting Strategy

A piloting strategy starts with the *attitude* that you will manage problems and adopt a "continuous improvement" approach to your Six Sigma effort. Specifics of a piloting strategy depend on your objective; however, asking some basic questions can help to drive any pilot planning:

- ✦ *How can we test our plan or approach, to ensure that it will work?* Look for opportunities for a limited, lower-risk trial of key aspects of the Six Sigma effort. Make sure, though, that any test replicates "normal conditions" as much as possible, otherwise your pilot data may not represent what will happen later.

- *What will we need to measure/observe to see how well our effort is working?* The more specific you can be, the better. Piloting needs to be accompanied by a careful, focused review of "what worked" and "what didn't." Without it, your "improvements" will be based as much on guesses as on real learning from the pilot.
- *How much time will be needed to respond to what we learn from the "pilot"?* This is always a challenge. Most companies, once they've decided to launch Six Sigma, want to get it done *yesterday.* But some time for review and refinement is key, if a pilot strategy is to pay off. Therefore we strongly recommend that a period be set aside in your rollout to assess, identify, and implement improvements. Usually (depending on what you're piloting), the review/refinement time can be a couple of weeks or less—after which you can move forward aggressively and with much more confidence that your efforts will pay off.

As noted, piloting is an important part of Six Sigma improvement efforts. For more detail on piloting approaches, see Chapter 16, page 327.

Six Sigma Start-Up Summary

Let us begin here by reminding you that some of the basic questions relating to preparing your effort are found on the Six Sigma Start-Up worksheet in the Appendix. Now let's summarize some of the most important things you should remember:

- *Plan your own route.* There are many paths to Six Sigma, and the best is the one that works for your organization. Steer clear of those who say they have *the* way to implement Six Sigma.
- *Define your objective.* Priorities are important. It's okay to apply Six Sigma to solve key problems; it also can be a driver of "culture change." Start at the level (or levels) that best make the sense given your needs and readiness.
- *Stick to what's feasible.* Set up your plans so that they match your influence, resources, and scope. If that means trying Six Sigma methods on a small scale in an area you can manage—hey, that's often a great way to start.

- *Use a piloting strategy.* You'll save time and effort in the long run if you test and improve key aspects of your effort before you roll them out full-scale.
- ***Balance short- and long-term considerations.*** The big drawback of aiming for quick results is the risk of getting stuck working only on short-term projects. Building the core competencies of Six Sigma into your organization—customer knowledge, measurement, proactive improvement, etc.—needs to be a focus as well.

CHAPTER

8

The Politics of Six Sigma: Preparing Leaders to Launch and Guide the Effort

As WE DISCUSSED in Chapter 3, one of the difficulties that undermined the TQM movement in many organizations was the weak commitment of business leaders. Top management would—to use the common phrase—"talk the talk" but not "walk the walk." Some quality efforts never really got off the ground. Others were very successful for a while, then faded away as the company and its leaders lost focus in the face of other fads or challenges.

The same goes for Six Sigma. Six Sigma initiatives launched today could easily fizzle out quickly—or, they could enjoy a successful engagement and then close like a tired theater production. The key for you and your company's leadership is to keep *both* questions in mind:

1. How do we successfully launch a Six Sigma effort and achieve momentum for improvement?
2. What do we do to ensure that Six Sigma concepts and methods continue to sustain our success over the long term?

Key Practices vs. Role Models

It would be a copout for us to say "Do what Jack Welch did." Exactly what worked for GE under Welch's leadership would not make sense in most (if any) other companies. For example, while GE was very bold about promising major gains from Six Sigma early on, we know of several other large corporations that feel more comfortable with a strong commitment but a low-key external profile to their Six Sigma processes. Still, by borrowing from a variety of leaders and initiatives—including GE's—we can put together a list of key leadership actions that are essential to any Six Sigma effort—with an eye *both* to a successful start-up *and* building a lasting, integrated management system.

Leading the Six Sigma Launch

We would suggest that the following are the eight most important responsibilities for top managers to take on in the early stages of the Six Sigma process:

1. *Develop a strong rationale.* As an output of the soul-searching questions we've just reviewed, leaders should be able to describe—first for themselves, then for others—*why* the Six Sigma system is needed by the business. "It's the latest big thing," or "Wall Street is really hot on Six Sigma companies" won't cut it. The rationale has to be specific to *your* organization and tie in directly to benefits almost anyone in the company can understand.
2. *Plan and actively participate in implementation.* As soon as top leaders implicitly hand over responsibility for decisions on a broad plan and goals to some "Six Sigma manager" or to a consultant, the game is over. We'd be the first to agree that a consultant or internal expert can be a valuable advisor, but the executive group needs to *own* the effort, for three critical reasons:

    a. They're the ones who'll have to sell it, and defend it.
    b. They need to be able to *change* the plan, as needs and knowledge evolve.
    c. They're best positioned to balance all the priorities and challenges of the business with the Six Sigma process.

Note that the plan and strategy can encompass not only the rather broad questions we've already cited—What are our first steps? How much of the business should be involved?—but also more nitty-gritty questions such as "What's our budget?"; "How many people will be trained, to what level, and when?"; and so on.

3. *Create a vision and a "marketing plan."* We've observed through the years that one of the weakest elements in "change management" is what we call change *marketing*. Change will always be scary, traumatic, etc., but the way it's often handled tends to magnify people's cynicism and worry. It's possible, though, to convert at least some of that "fear energy" into excitement and a positive force, if the change is positioned and, well, *marketed* properly.[1]

   With the rationale and implementation strategy as inputs, elements of the marketing plan include the following two:

   a. *The Theme, or Vision.* A name for the effort, a concise vision statement, even a slogan—these can fill the role of "theme" (you may want both a name *and* a theme). One of our favorites from a high-tech client was "Building an Enduring Great Company." We've already mentioned AlliedSignal/Honeywell's "Creating a Culture of Continuous Renewal." GE's quality definition is "Completely Satisfying Customer Needs Profitably." Your own organization's key message should fit your business and people. For example, a more technical message, such as "Driving Down Defects and Vaporizing Variation," might play well in an engineering organization. In a service company, a phrase such as "Measuring What the Customer Cares About" could be more appropriate. We're not saying these are great, but hopefully you get the point: Be sure you send out a clear, positive—inspiring, even—message as to the nature of your Six Sigma effort.

   b. *The Marketing Plan.* Your promotion of Six Sigma should fit your implementation. If you intend to "test" Six Sigma improvement on a few projects, obviously a big companywide splash is not a good idea. Key questions to drive your Six Sigma marketing include: Who are our key audiences—internal and external? How do we best introduce our plans to ensure a positive reaction? How does the message need to be tailored to different groups? What media, events, etc. are appropriate? How do we deal with negative reactions? The plan should include key terms and phrases, too: "launch," "expansion," and "ongoing support," for example.

The challenge is to develop a "marketing plan" for Six Sigma that is appealing and challenging, but realistic. Avoid over-optimistic "hype."

4. *Become powerful advocates.* It may seem paradoxical for executives to *lead* something they're still learning about—but there you have it. If there's one strategy to be borrowed from the likes of Bob Galvin at Motorola, Larry Bossidy of AlliedSignal, and Jack Welch at GE, it's their continued pounding of the Six Sigma drum. All of these leaders—and they aren't alone—constantly pushed Six Sigma as *both* a vehicle for profits and a new but integral approach to running the business. We quoted some of Welch's comments, for example, in Chapter 1. He's been a tireless proponent of Six Sigma, and his example has extended to other top leaders at GE. That passion and evangelism has been witnessed by GE suppliers and customers as well—quite a few of whom are now exploring and/or launching their own Six Sigma initiatives. Veterans of Motorola and AlliedSignal tell similar stories about Galvin and Bossidy. "Strong," "constant," and "energetic" are some of the words we've heard that describe these leaders' efforts. Your own leadership's willingness or even eagerness to follow these models is likely to lend a big boost to your Six Sigma effort.
5. *Set clear objectives.* Your goals can be just as important a feature of the "marketing" effort as your communication plans or theme. Broad business targets—e.g., 10X improvement, Five Sigma in Five Years—are excellent *if* they can be interpreted meaningfully in the trenches. The specific objectives appropriate for your organization will be tailored to the nature and scope of your effort. In any case, they should be understandable, challenging, meaningful, and *not* impossible.
6. *Hold yourselves and others accountable.* In the 1980s we were called in to meet with the president of a client company who was frustrated with their quality effort. "I've been pushing people for two

years," he complained, "and we still aren't seeing any results." When we asked him what were the *consequences* of that lack of results, however, the leader had no answer for us. The same people who *weren't* doing quality were being paid and getting bonuses just like always.

There's no question where accountability starts with Six Sigma: with the *leaders* themselves. If an improvement project fails, for example, questions should focus not just on teams or training, but more importantly on what leaders could have done: Were enough resources provided? Was the project well defined? Did I/we listen when problems were raised? Did we provide the needed sense of urgency? For instance, if *just* the direct reports of the company president quoted above had been held accountable for improvements, a lot more would have been achieved.

One of the boldest, most effective, and most remarked-on aspects of GE's Six Sigma effort was the linking of 40 percent of every executive's "variable compensation" (i.e., bonus money) to successful Six Sigma efforts. That "feet-to-the-fire" incentive sent a strong message to everyone at GE about the importance of Six Sigma—and certainly helped keep Six Sigma projects from getting swamped by other priorities.

Included in executive accountability, and extending throughout the organization, is the whole question of aligning compensation and rewards in a way that will foster Six Sigma results. We've seen a surprising number of instances, in large organizations, where compensation criteria send mixed if not *contrary* signals about what's important. For example:

- A consumer products company paid sales commissions on *shipments* to retailers, prompting salespeople to secure big orders. If goods were returned—and refunds paid to the retailers—salespeople already had their money.
- The information technology group at a unit of a *Fortune* 500 firm is given incentives to cut its budget—with no regard to impact on service levels.
- A product development/marketing department for a large telecommunications company is evaluated on the speed with which new offerings are introduced—meaning that pro-

grams are launched before sales and service people have any information about them.

Addressing these types of misalignment may be one of the most unrecognized, and valuable, benefits of a Six Sigma effort. But while gaining good alignment of goals throughout a company may take a bit of time to achieve, some short-term Improvement Project solutions hinge on a resolving of compensation/goal conflicts.

7. *Demand solid measures of results.* Six Sigma ultimately is all about building a better organization—one that's successful both in the short and in the long term. Too often, TQM companies relied on "soft" measures to gauge the impact of their efforts. With Six Sigma, by contrast, the question of how to judge results should be much less ambiguous. Involving financial experts in your organization, to help quantify potential gains upfront and validate their achievement, can accomplish two objectives:

   a. Help ensure that the results you achieve are *real.*
   b. Boost confidence that you really are serious about seeking—and sticking with—Six Sigma improvements.

   The direct bottom-line impacts of Six Sigma can be directly tied to such metrics as defect reductions (reflected in DPMO, Sigma, etc.), cycle-time improvement, and lower costs (rework, scrap, etc.). Less "hard," but in the long run more meaningful financially, are profit margins, customer loyalty, retention rates, new product sales, etc.

8. *Communicate results—and setbacks.* Constant, honest communication about the gains your company is achieving through Six Sigma, as well as the shortcomings or challenges you've encountered, keep the effort moving forward. Making successes well known, and recognizing key contributors, obviously builds confidence and enthusiasm. On the other hand, publicizing *only* the successes will hurt your credibility by giving the impression you're "sugar-coating" the results. (People will learn about the mistakes, anyway.). Issuing balanced updates that look at both the "pluses" and the "deltas" (things that need to be improved) is the best, most effective form of communication.

There can be no doubt that leaders set the tone and direction for the effort—meaning that their actions have the greatest overall impact on the course of the Six Sigma process. Without the input of other key players, however, no leader can effect change or achieve the results we've suggested a well-executed Six Sigma initiative can offer. In the following chapter, we look at such other essential roles in your implementation.

CHAPTER

9

Preparing Black Belts and Other Key Roles

ONE OF THE best-publicized aspects of the Six Sigma movement is the creation of a corps of process measurement and improvement experts known variously as "Black Belts," "Master Black Belts," and "Green Belts." (We heard of one organization that considered the creation of yet another level—"Yellow Belts"—and felt some relief when they scrubbed the idea!) While the "Belts" are important, they are just the most well-known component in a larger organizational structure and set of roles that support the Six Sigma process.

One of your key tasks, as you start on the Six Sigma Way, will be to define the appropriate roles for your organization, and to clarify their responsibilities. Those decisions should be driven by a variety of factors, including your Six Sigma objectives, implementation plan, budget, and existing staff and resources. In this chapter we'll be probing three key questions:

1. What are the major roles in a Six Sigma organization?
2. What is a "Black Belt," and what are the options in terms of making use of the Black Belt, Master Black Belt, and Green Belt roles?
3. What level and content of training is needed, to get your Six Sigma process "off the ground" and keep it climbing?

Roles in a Six Sigma Organization

We'll set aside terms like "Black Belt," and "Master Black Belt" for a moment, and look first at a variety of important Six Sigma "job descriptions."[1]

The Leadership Group or Council

If they are to fulfill their various leadership responsibilities for Six Sigma (as described in the previous chapter), executives must have a forum in which they can discuss, plan, guide, and learn from the initiative. In most of the organizations we've worked with, such a "Six Sigma Leadership Team" or "Quality Council" is pretty much the same group as the existing top management team—which is the ideal. In the TQM days that role too often was delegated, sending a negative signal about the *real* importance of the initiative to business leaders.

In addition to the planning and marketing tasks we have defined earlier, specific functions of the top management group include:

- Establishing the roles and infrastructure of the Six Sigma initiative
- Selecting specific projects and allocating resources
- Periodically reviewing the progress of various projects, and offering ideas and help (for example, avoiding project overlap)
- Serving (individually) as "sponsors" of Six Sigma projects (see below)
- Helping to quantify the impact of Six Sigma efforts on the company bottom line
- Assessing progress, and identifying strengths and weaknesses in the effort (i.e., avoiding complacency)
- Sharing best practices throughout the organization—and with key suppliers and customers, where appropriate
- Acting as "roadblock removers," when teams identify seeming barriers
- Applying the lessons learned to their own individual management styles

How often a leadership group meets, in its role as Six Sigma Council, can have a big influence on the pace of the overall initiative. Convening monthly, for example, is a common schedule, and may be frequent enough. However, if improvement teams are expected to present their progress reports to the full committee, that may mean several months between "updates"—which can slow efforts and reduce the sense of urgency. Shorter, more frequent sessions may work better, in maintaining the pace and energy behind the improvements.

The "Sponsor" or "Champion"

A Sponsor—a role mentioned in several of our earlier Six Sigma stories—is the senior manager who "oversees" an improvement project. This is a critical responsibility that can require a delicate balance. Teams need the freedom to make their own decisions, but they also need guidance from business leaders on the direction of their efforts. Sponsor responsibilities include:

- Setting and maintaining broad goals for improvement projects under his or her charge—including creating the Project Rationale—and ensuring that they're aligned with business priorities
- Coaching on, and approving changes in, direction or scope of a project, if needed
- Finding (and negotiating) resources for projects
- Representing the team to the Leadership Group and serving as its advocate
- Helping to smooth out issues and overlaps that arise between teams, or with people outside the team
- Working with Process Owners to ensure a smooth handoff at the conclusion of an improvement project
- Applying their gained knowledge of Process Improvement to their own management tasks

Of all these responsibilities, perhaps the most important to the success of an Improvement Project is to help teams refine the scope of their projects. In our experience, many projects slow down or stall simply because the Team Leader and group are hesitant to narrow or shift their focus, for fear of "disappointing" the top leaders. In practice, though, most projects need some refinement—and the Sponsor's help in adjusting the direction is critical.

The Implementation Leader

Unless one of your current top executives plans to add administration of the Six Sigma effort to his or her responsibilities (which can take up a lot of time and energy), resources will need to be dedicated to managing the day-to-day progress and logistics. Depending on the scale of your efforts, one Implementation Leader or "Six Sigma Director" may be enough, or you may need a staff to handle this broad set of tasks:

- Supporting the Leadership Group in its activities, including communication, project selection, and project reviews.
- Identifying and/or recommending individuals/groups to fulfill key roles—including external consulting and training support
- Preparing and executing training plans, including curriculum selection and scheduling and logistics
- Helping Sponsors fulfill their role as supports, advocates, and "nudges" of the teams
- Documenting overall progress and surfacing issues that need attention
- Executing the internal "marketing plan" for the initiative

The talent and energies required for this "administrative" role can be enormous. While often (in our experience) this person is more of a generalist than a Six Sigma "expert," the implementation leader can have a bigger impact on overall success than any other individual.

The Six Sigma Coach

The Coach provides expert advice and assistance to Process Owners and Six Sigma improvement teams, in areas that may range from statistics to change management to process design strategies. The Coach is the technical expert, though the level of expertise will vary from business to business based on how the roles are structured and the level of complexity of the problems.

Since the Coach is really a *consultant,* one of the keys to his or her success is to define clear agreements on people's roles and the extent of their direct involvement with the projects and processes. There can be a fine line between "helping" and "meddling," and often it can be subjectively determined only according to the needs of the "client." In addition to technical help, a Coach may provide guidance on:

- Communicating with the project Sponsor and leadership group
- Establishing and sticking to a firm schedule for the project
- Dealing with resistance or lack of cooperation from people in the organization
- Estimating potential, and validating actual results (defects eliminated, dollars saved, etc.)
- Resolving team member disagreements, conflicts, etc.
- Gathering and analyzing data about team activities
- Helping teams promote and celebrate their successes

The "Team Leader" or "Project Leader"

The Team Leader is the individual who takes primary responsibility for the work and the results of a Six Sigma project. Most Team Leaders focus on Process Improvement or Design/Redesign, but they also can take on efforts tied to Voice of the Customer systems, measurement, or process management. As we'll be seeing in some of our Six Sigma stories in Part III, the Team Leader is critical to keeping a project on track and ensuring that progress continues. Some of his or her specific responsibilities—particularly in an Improvement project—include:

- Reviewing/clarifying the project rationale with the Sponsor
- Developing and updating the Project Charter and implementation plan
- Selecting or helping to select the project team members
- Identifying and seeking resources and information
- Defining and helping others in the use of appropriate Six Sigma tools—as well as team and meeting management techniques
- Maintaining the project schedule and keeping progress moving toward final solutions and results
- Supporting the transfer of new solutions or processes to ongoing operations, while working with functional managers and/or the Process Owner
- Documenting final results and creating a "storyboard" of the project

The "Team Member"

Most organizations use *teams* as the vehicle for the bulk of their improvement efforts. The Team Members provide the extra brains and muscle behind the measurement, analysis, and improvement of a process. They also help spread the word about Six Sigma tools and processes and become part of the "bench strength" for future projects.

The "Process Owner"

This is the person who takes on a new, cross-functional responsibility to manage an "end-to-end" set of steps that provide value to an internal or external customer. He or she receives the "handoff" from improvement teams, or becomes the owner of new and newly designed processes. Note that the Sponsor and the Process Owner may be the same person. (For details, see Chapter 17.)

Options in Defining Roles and Structure

These "generic" roles aren't all mandatory. In fact we would suggest that these be about the *most* you have, as there can be some overlap among these responsibilities as it is. Table 9.1 gives you some of the variations we've seen, including the increasingly common "Belt" titles.

Table 9.1 Examples of variations in generic roles and "Belt" or other titles.

Generic Role	"Belt" or Other Title
Leadership Council	Quality Council, Six Sigma Steering Committee
Sponsor	Champion, Process Owner
Implementation Leader	Six Sigma Director, Quality Leader, Master Black Belt
Coach	Master Black Belt or Black Belt
Team Leader	Black Belt or Green Belt
Team Member	Team Member or Green Belt
Process Owner	Sponsor or Champion

In Fig. 9.1 you will see a diagram showing the two options open to you for deploying these different roles, and how their "reporting structures" might work.

Black Belts, Master Black Belts, and Role Structures

Now that we've reviewed the most common roles in a Six Sigma implementation, and some options as to their use, we can give you a better understanding of what "Black Belt" and "Master Black Belt" mean while also laying out the choices you have for preparing and deploying these individuals.

Black Belts and Master Black Belts

We've run into varying stories as to how the term "Black Belt" emerged. Clearly, though, it originated at Motorola in the early 1990s, and signified individuals possessing special expertise in statistics and technical product/process improvement. The "Black Belt" label, of course drawn from the martial arts suggests a finely-honed skill and discipline, while the different levels—Green, Black, and Master—recognize depth of training and experience. In Six Sigma's early days, certifica-

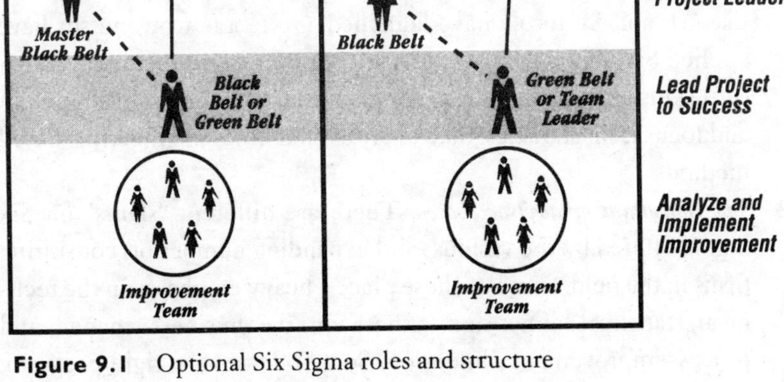

Figure 9.1 Optional Six Sigma roles and structure

tion and training for Six Sigma Black Belts was developed in a joint effort among companies including Motorola, Texas Instruments, IBM, and Kodak. It was almost exclusively a technical role, focused on manufacturing and product-related improvements. Today however there is no "official" job description or certification for Black Belts; the role and the skills that define it have both become much more diverse.

The differences from business to business in Black Belt definitions and preparations seem to arise out of four main factors:

1. *Type of processes/projects to be worked on.* To pick up on one of our themes from Chapter 4: When the processes and products are fairly technical, Black Belts need more technical skills. In many Service environments, where the data is more sketchy and the issues less technical (at least at the outset), other foundational skills—process definition, developing operational definitions, collecting and analyzing data, team skills—take precedence.
2. *Structure of the Black Belt role in the organization.* If Black Belts are to be used primarily as Coaches (providing specialized support to Green Belts and teams, for example), the emphasis will tend to be more technical. If they are drawn from the management/professional ranks and will be leading improvement teams, skills such as problem definition, leadership, and project management tend to become more important than statistical analysis. (Master Black Belts, or others, can provide the technical help when needed).
3. *Objectives of the "Six Sigma" initiative.* Certainly not every company is applying Six Sigma as the organizationwide business leadership system that we're presenting in this book, or that Six Sigma leaders like GE and Motorola have launched. Quite a few businesses have applied Six Sigma as basically just a set of measurement and statistical skills and tools. In these companies a Black Belt's development and focus is on statistics, data analysis, and other engineering-based methods.
4. *The consultant or advisor chosen.* There are different "slants" on Six Sigma offered by the various (and expanding number of) consulting firms in the field. Some of these place a heavy emphasis on the technical/statistical dimension, others on the business change and process improvement dimension. Some offer a very rigid program; others recommend adapting the content and rigor to the organiza-

tion and its needs/implementation plan. This book takes the latter approach.

One other factor has contributed to the variation in Black Belt capabilities. In principle, a Black Belt *candidate* often is supposed to have completed a certain number of successful improvement projects before earning his or her official designation. More often, however, individuals are called "Black Belts" in their organizations as soon as they've finished (or even begun) a training program. Master Black Belts are more consistently experts in statistical tools, though they may take on the role of an internal "change management" consultant as well.

Considerations in Defining the Black Belt Role

How you go about selecting and deploying "Black Belts" will be influenced by some of the issues we've noted.[2] You should also consider how you intend to staff the positions, and their longer-term value to the organization. The following are some options/considerations:

- *Management skill development.* In some businesses, one of the purposes of Black Belt development is to upgrade the skills of current/future managers and leaders. In these cases Black Belt candidates are drawn mainly from the existing ranks, and usually are assigned to lead an improvement project. People placed in Black Belt positions are given opportunities for advancement after they've finished their "tour of duty."

  The pros:
  - Puts people with direct experience of the organization and its processes to work on improvement opportunities.
  - Engages middle managers directly in the Six Sigma effort by assigning them projects.
  - Black Belts drawn from inside the organization usually already are familiar with the politics and people in the organization, which means they can select team members, work with Sponsors more effectively, and so on.
  - If the Black Belts are well known and respected, they can help convince others in the business of the value of the Six Sigma system.

- Instills in management talent the basic Six Sigma knowledge and skills

The cons:

- May draw existing or promising management talent away from day-to-day operations.
- Can lengthen the ramp-up time it takes for inexperienced Black Belts to be trained and to become familiar with Six Sigma methods.

✦ *Building technical expertise.* Another approach is to establish the Black Belt as a permanent position and career path. Companies with this as a priority will tend to either hire in, or select and train, people with Six Sigma–focused skills and aptitudes. Though they may lead a project, the role usually fits better under the heading "Coach," and their advancement would be within the ranks of the Six Sigma "expert" group.

The pros:

- Allows Six Sigma expertise to be applied to projects right away (from people hired in).
- Permits a raising of the level of rigor of the training.
- Keeps trained Six Sigma resources focused on sanctioned projects and initiatives, rather than dispersing them back to the organization.
- May allow more projects, if each Black Belt can take on multiple projects.

The cons:

- Technically oriented Black Belts may have less organizational knowledge or experience.
- Misses out on the opportunity to "seed" management and professional ranks with experienced, trained Six Sigma project leaders.

✦ *A hybrid approach.* A mix of these two approaches can often work best: Having some Black Belts come from existing management and professional groups, and selecting others or bringing them into the organization specifically to be the Six Sigma technical "muscle." In the hybrid model you would have a choice of calling the temporary group "Green Belts" or "Black Belts," and the technical experts "Black Belts" or "Master Black Belts."

Of course, it isn't essential that you adopt the "Belt" naming system at all—you could stick with more common terms like "Coach" and "Team Leader," or create your own names for the roles.

Role-Clarity Issues

Even within a seemingly clear structure, overlapping responsibilities and role confusion can create significant challenges. Sometimes this is due to personal styles or actions. An eager Sponsor, for example, might feel that he or she is showing real commitment by attending every team meeting, when in fact that is making the Team Leader feel uncomfortable and unimportant. Then again, if a Coach takes a hands-off, "you-do-it" approach with a struggling team, the group can get frustrated and disillusioned. Thus it's important both to establish clear guidelines for each role and to encourage communication about how individuals can adapt their roles to their personal styles.

Other role-conflicts can arise when existing functions seem to overlap with those in the Six Sigma structure. For example, some companies have used auditors or organization development staff to help business units and departments with their "improvement" efforts. Factoring these people's current responsibilities into the mix of Six Sigma activities is important; ignoring them will only increase the likelihood of confusion, or even resentment. There are no pat answers as to how you can best resolve role issues, but the most important objective is to make sure all potentially *duplicate* roles are eliminated.

Selecting Project Team Members

Because so much of the work in Six Sigma is done by teams, our review of roles wouldn't be complete without some tips on *choosing* people for those teams.

Being a Smart "Team Traveler"

Probably the most common mistake in establishing teams of all types is to overload them with too many members. You can get an idea of how this works by analyzing the travelers getting on and off an airport rental car bus.

On one end of the spectrum is the man or woman carrying a fairly thin garment bag; perhaps a sample kit, briefcase, or laptop; and that's about it. On the other end of the spectrum is the traveler with two large suitcases and a smaller carry-on bag that's full-to-bursting. Of course, by the time the first customer has leaped onto the rental car bus and taken a seat, the second is just starting to *drag* that first big bag up the . . . *pant*. . . steps of the . . . *unhh!*. . . bus—*Whew! Only two more to go!*

Which would you say is the more experienced traveler?

People who've been on the road quite a bit have learned the hard way that when you go to places other than your home, they have these fancy conveniences called "stores," where if you need something that you didn't happen to bring along, you can "buy it." In marked and often comical contrast, occasional travelers tend to toss any conceivable thing they'll need into the suitcase, including that extra-large bottle of shampoo in case their hair needs washing two or three times a day, and the extra thermal underwear in the event of a freak May snowstorm in Ft. Lauderdale. (Hey, with all this crazy El Niño and LaNiña stuff, who knows?)

You might well say, "Well, the traveler with all the extra stuff is on vacation," and you might just be right. But could you imagine the savvy traveler going on vacation with as much stuff as our friend the over-packer? *We* can't.

Our point is that when it comes to teams, many organizations act like novice travelers: they over-pack a team with every conceivable type of person whose skill or contribution might be needed during the project. Not surprisingly, big teams move more slowly, and their members also tend to be less engaged and enthusiastic. There are plenty of different "rules of thumb" on team size, but a good optimum number for almost any project team is between five and eight. Beyond that, communication tends to get overly complicated, decisions harder to make, and cohesiveness weak.

Here are some key questions for you to ponder, as an aid to selecting team members:

- Who has the best knowledge of the process being improved, and/or contact with the customer?

- Who has the most knowledge about the problem, and/or the best access to data?
- What key skills or perspectives will be needed throughout the course of the project?
- What groups or functions will be most directly affected by the project?
- What degree of management/supervisory/frontline representation is likely to be needed?
- What skills, functions, or organizational levels can be obtained as needed during the project?

It's okay to *adjust* the membership of the Six Sigma team over the course of a project—especially in the transition from developing solutions to implementing them. Indeed, different skills and talents often are needed to make process improvements work successfully. Also, having a flexible approach to team makeup—as long as it doesn't disrupt the cohesiveness of the group—will help you avoid the "over-packing" problem.

Once people are on board the Six Sigma effort, the next challenge is to give them the skills, knowledge, and tools they will require if everyone pulling together is going to achieve meaningful change and improvement.

CHAPTER

10

Training the Organization for Six Sigma

A SIX SIGMA organization *is* a "Learning Organization." That means an organization that is constantly gaining new information and insights from its customers, external environment, and processes, using that knowledge to respond with new ideas, products, services, and improvements, and then measuring the results and learning still more.

Training—both at the outset and on a sustained basis—is a key ingredient to achieving success by following the Six Sigma Way. Returning to one of our earliest messages in this book, there are almost no key management skills that *don't* play a role at some point in building a Six Sigma organization. Training we've delivered to Six Sigma "Black Belts," for example, has included a wide array of topics ranging from project management, change management, and consensus and team building, to the tools and techniques of measurement and process analysis.

Where you should place the emphasis, in your company's Six Sigma training, is on the skills and methods your people most need to fulfill their role(s) in the early phases of the effort—and to plan *continued* learning that will both reinforce early knowledge and add more advanced (or basic) knowledge later on.

Essentials of Effective Six Sigma Training

The keys to good Six Sigma training are not dramatically different from those for any kind of training. As we often saw in the days of TQM training, however, these lessons tend to be ignored in the rush to get people's quality "ticket punched." TQM training tended to be dry, uninspiring, and irrelevant to people's everyday jobs. It also left people with an *awareness*-level understanding of concepts and tools, but without the depth of knowledge to actually *use* them. The following are some of the essentials you should keep in mind when planning your Six Sigma training:

- *Emphasize "hands-on" learning.* From leaders to experts to practitioners, people in a business learn best when they can put concepts and skills into immediate practice. Ideally, such "hands-on" work will include efforts exerted on real processes, projects, and improvement needs.
- *Provide relevant examples and links to the "real world".* If your people are going to internalize how Six Sigma will work in your organization, the examples and exercises you provide will have to reflect your business and its specific challenges. Generally, a Service business or process needs to use service-related examples; a Manufacturing group learns most from plant floor–related scenarios. Even if you haven't done Six Sigma yet, a good training provider who knows the methodologies should be able to come up with some good examples that will work in your environment.
- *Build knowledge.* With so much material to cover, it's easy to fall into the "data dump" trap. The concepts of Six Sigma can be interesting and exciting, but starting with advanced ideas and jargon will turn people off. Establishing a foundation of key principles and ideas—stated in common terms—sets the stage for more sophisticated skills and methods. It's also important to put tools into a context (e.g., an improvement model like DMAIC, the Six Sigma Roadmap) so that their application and relevance is clear.
- *Cater to a variety of learning styles.* Visuals, games, exercises, and so on should be varied and, for most audiences, include some *fun.*
- *Make training something more than learning.* Training is a key element in your Six Sigma "marketing plan." It represents a golden opportunity to gain buy-in, to deputize change agents, and to clarify the

themes of the effort and its value to the business. Look for ways to reinforce those messages during the training.

- *Make training an ongoing effort.* One of the comments we most often hear from participants in Six Sigma training is the suggestion that they get "refreshers" on a regular basis. Businesses, however, tend to offer only "hit-and-run" training. We give kids (ages 5 through 21) about 16 *years* to absorb an education, but people in the working world are expected to learn and master major new concepts and tools in (if they're lucky) three days! Six Sigma (i.e., "learning") organizations will almost certainly have to adopt a practice of continuous education and training, just as their processes themselves are in need of continuous renewal and improvement. Considering the speed of change today, occasional once-off learning or cookie-cutter training won't make it in the 21st century.

Planning a Six Sigma Curriculum

Six Sigma successes in organizations of many types have proven that there's a lot of talent and opportunity waiting to be unleashed on the problem of how to make companies more responsive and efficient. One of the first concerns that arises, though, is "Will it take many weeks of training for us to tap into that potential?" Our answer would be: "It doesn't have to." Some of the more advanced skills of Six Sigma clearly take time to master—especially for those having no background or experience in statistics. On the other hand, people can be prepared in less than two weeks to begin tackling improvement projects—provided that the training is well designed, and tailored to the participant's current skills, processes, etc.

A Model Six Sigma Training Curriculum

We favor a "one-size-fits-*one*" approach to Six Sigma, including Six Sigma training. Still, we can provide you here with a broad plan for developing skills and commitment—based on the approach now in place in a number of companies—that should serve as a guideline for your own training plan. Table 10.1 presents an overview of the generic plan; the ranges of days reflect possible differences in the existing knowledge of participants, the amount of hands-on practice, and the depth of content that may be provided.

Table 10.1 A Model Six Sigma Training Curriculum.

Training Component	Key Content	Audiences	Length
Orientation to the Six Sigma Concepts	Basic Six Sigma principles; review of business need for Six Sigma; brief practice and/or simulation; overview of roles and expectations	All	1–2 Days
Leading and Sponsoring Six Sigma Efforts	Role requirements and skills for Leadership Council and Sponsors; Project Selection; Reviewing team projects	Business Leaders; Implementation Leaders	1–2 Days
Six Sigma Processes and Tools for Leaders	Condensed and adapted instruction in Six Sigma measurement and analysis processes/tools	Business Leaders; Implementation Leaders	3–5 days
Leading Change	Concepts and practices for setting direction, promoting and guiding organizational change	Business Leaders; Implementation Leaders; Coach/Master Black Belts; Team Leaders/ Black Belts	2–5 days
Six Sigma Improvement Basic Skills Training	Process Improvement, Design/Redesign, and core measurement and improvement tools	Team Leaders Black Belts; Managers/Green Belts; Team Members; Project Sponsors	6–10 days

Table 10.1 *(Continued)*

Training Component	Key Content	Audiences	Length
Collaboration and Team Leadership Skills	Skills and methods for developing consensus, leading discussions, conducting meetings, managing disagreement	Business Leaders; Coaches/Master Black Belts; Team Leaders/Black Belts; Managers/Green Belts; Team Members	2–5 days
Intermediate Six Sigma measurement and analytical tools	Technical skills for more complex project challenges: sampling and data collection; Statistical Process Control; Tests of Statistical Significance; Correlation and Regression; basic design of experiments; etc.	Coaches/Master Black Belts; Team Leaders/Black Belts	2–6 days
Advanced Six Sigma tools	Modules in specialized skills and tools: Quality Function Deployment; Advanced Statistical Analysis; Advanced DOE; Taguchi Methods; etc.	Coaches/Master Black Belts; Internal Consultants	Varies by topic
Process Management Principles and Skills	Defining a core or support process; identifying critical Outputs, Requirements, and Measures; Monitoring and Response plans	Process Owners; Business Leaders; Functional Managers	2–5 days

Please note that we are *not* suggesting that every group mentioned requires all of the training elements noted. They should be selected according to current skills and priorities. But at the same time, the message should be clear: Business Leaders launching Six Sigma can't expect to delegate all responsibility for learning new skills and concepts to *other* people in the organization.

Incorporating the Six Sigma system requires new management habits and skills, too. Over time, Six Sigma training ideally will become accepted as basic "business leadership skills," as these practices and tools become a fundamental part of building an outstanding organization.

CHAPTER

11

The Key to Successful Improvement: Selecting the Right Six Sigma Projects

WE ONCE CONDUCTED an informal poll of colleagues who have been involved in Six Sigma and other process improvement initiatives, and found an unanticipated consensus: Each person identified *project selection* as the most critical, and most commonly mishandled, activity in launching Six Sigma. It's a pretty simple equation, really: Well-selected and -defined improvement projects equal better, faster results. The converse equation is also simple: Poorly selected and defined projects equal delayed results and frustration.

In fact, one of the strongest arguments in favor of following the ideal Six Sigma Roadmap (see Figure 5.1) is that doing so allows you to much more effectively select your initial improvements. Even with better process and customer measures, however, choosing projects can be tricky.

Project Selection Essentials

Let's begin by looking at some of the keys to effective project selection. That will set the stage for us to offer you steps to ensure you do it well.

Executive/Leadership Training

There's a lot for leaders to learn when it comes to guiding a Six Sigma initiative. All-too-frequently, however, one of the topics that gets "edited out" of executive development plans is how to choose projects. That's understandable, since identifying problems is usually not a task executives or managers have trouble with. Picking the *right* projects, however, and defining them well, is by no means easy. And other leadership responsibilities—creating a vision; dealing with staffing and resources; and overseeing the projects—all are critical as well. But if Six Sigma projects are ill defined, the impact is immediate. Thus we suggest you make a note in large letters near the top of your Six Sigma implementation plan: TEACH THE SENIOR TEAM HOW TO PICK PROJECTS.

Launching a Reasonable Number of Projects

"But what's wrong with working on lots of things at once?" you may ask. Well, imagine you're standing in front of a group of 15 people and gently tossing three or four basketballs at them. Chances are, someone will reach out and catch the balls. Now let's say you're throwing out more but smaller balls—say 10 or 15 tennis balls. There's a bigger chance one or two will hit the floor, but if you use a gentle toss, most will still be caught.

But, what if you were to ever so gently toss a few handfuls of dried beans at the group? No matter what, of course, most of them would land on the ground or a tabletop (or go down people's clothing, causing even greater embarrassment).[1]

The moral: People and organizations can focus on only so many things at one time.

In the urgency to get results, it's easy to bombard an organization with many basketballs and beans. Too large a wave of projects can drown leaders' ability to track and guide them. Too many projects scatter people's attention and sap their ability to implement them well. We've heard folks at GE admit, for example, that it was a mistake to require every manager learning Six Sigma methods to complete a personal (or "desktop") improvement project. Many of the individual projects were "makeshift," even trivial—in essence reducing the overall benefit of the Six Sigma effort.

"Scope" Projects Properly

Our catch-phrase for a common mistake is "Trying to solve world hunger." Too often, projects are assigned to teams that are major, complex issues. You can't untangle these problems, any more than you can eliminate world hunger, few without a huge, long-term effort. A team can easily spend months trying to follow and measure all the various tendrils of an issue—thereby frustrating the team and trying the leaders' patience. The ideal is to strike a balance between two broad criteria. We suggest your mantra for project selection become: *Meaningful* and *Manageable.* Usually, this means keeping the assignments small and very focused.

We've heard some encouraging news recently, coming out of major companies who are devoting extra attention to defining meaningful and manageable projects—in one case, scrapping an initial list of projects after realizing they came too close to the "world hunger" thing.

Focus on Both *Efficiency and Customer Benefits*

We've worked with executive groups, early in a Six Sigma effort, who have demanded to know when and where their efforts would yield "home runs": quick-strike, big dollar gains. For most businesses, however, early-inning home runs occur only through cost cutting and efficiency improvements. This desire for big dollar savings from Six Sigma is a good thing, as long as it is balanced by an understanding that short-term financial gains are only a part of the potential benefit. There's often much more upside potential through improvements in competitive position and market strength—even though the payoff may take longer.

Let's look now at an example—or dramatization—of how projects tend to be chosen and expectations set.

The Perfecto Pasta Company

Senior managers of the Perfecto Pasta Company were concerned about flat growth in sales and profits. While their market, packaged noodles sold in stores, was growing at double-digit-plus rates, Perfecto's numbers had held steady, meaning that their share of the market had declined from 25 to just 13 percent. Compared to other packaged-pasta companies, Perfecto's profit margins were low as well.

Perfecto's top management was introduced to Six Sigma concepts by a consultant who promised he could deliver them big bottom-line savings within six months. Excited by the concepts they heard and by the prospect of turning around the business, the group decided to launch these three "pilot" Six Sigma efficiency-boosting projects:

- Reduce waste on the number-three vermicelli production line [estimated saving: $100,000/quarter].
- Streamline the order entry and fulfillment process, including implementation of a new, industry-tailored ordering software system, *PastaPower*™, and the likely layoff of 25 people [estimated saving: $250,000/quarter].
- Speed up the invoicing and cash application process to improve cashflow and reduce outstanding receivables [estimated saving: $80,000/quarter].

The announcement of the new initiative was well received by stock analysts, and Perfecto's share price responded with a 15 percent gain in two weeks. "They're going to hit some real home runs with this one," said one of Perfecto's stock watchers as he upgraded the company from "sell" to "maintain."

When the projects paid off, there was initial rejoicing. Total savings were projected to be about $2 million a year. The joy was dampened, however, when Perfecto's *market share* continued to fall, down to below 10 percent.

As it turned out, competitors had gained an edge over Perfecto by tailoring their shipments to retailers so as to fit the noodle preferences of each store's consumers. (In some areas shoppers prefer rigatoni, while in others, manicotti and bow-tie noodles are the leaders.) Perfecto had continued to offer a standard order mix of eight pasta products.

Perfecto finally had to sell out to one of its upstart competitors, the formerly tiny NoodleCorp. Perfecto's president was asked why the Six Sigma effort hadn't addressed the tailored-delivery issue: "Do you know how long it would have taken for us to make any money on that?" he responded angrily.

Now, of course, your company won't necessarily "go under," like Perfecto, if early Six Sigma projects focus only on internally-driven savings. And sure, the gains that can be realized through enhanced efficiencies and reduced rework are tremendous in many organizations. But the push for quick gains alone means delaying those longer-term benefits of Six Sigma which target *customers:* satisfaction, service, value, and product performance. Such a commitment to making *customers* the sole focus of your project selection is rare, and it requires some real executive discipline. We're aware of only one major industrial company, a more recent Six Sigma "convert," which has explicitly stated that efficiency improvement is *not* a priority of their initiative, whereas customer loyalty *is.*

Our best advice is to balance projects so that they include *both* externally- and internally-directed improvement opportunities.

Steps toward Effective Project Selection

Good project selection is itself a process; if you follow it well, you can improve your "hit rate" substantially. Presented below are some key questions and steps that will help drive the project selection process. Our assumption here is that projects are being chosen by a group, usually of senior managers. But even if you're choosing projects on your own for your organization, the same considerations apply.

Choosing Sources for Project Ideas

As is true of any process, inputs are key to an effective result: "garbage in, garbage out." If you take into consideration only a few anecdotal pieces of data as you decide where to focus your Six Sigma efforts, you are that much more likely to have irrelevant or unmanageable projects. Steps One through Three in the Six Sigma Roadmap are designed not only to provide you with a better understanding of your customers, business, and processes, but also solid information on improvement priorities. Absent those steps, sources of project ideas can include the following:

- *External Sources.* These fall into three categories: Voice of the Customer; Voice of the Market; and Comparison with Competitors. In essence, these sources identify opportunities to better meet customer requirements, respond to trends in the market, or counter competitor strategies and capabilities. Sources for this kind of information can vary widely: from trade and business articles, to competitor/market research, to feedback from salespeople. Here's a sample of questions arising out of these sources:

- Where are we falling short in meeting customer needs?
- Where are we behind our competitors?
- How will the market be evolving? Are we ready to adapt?
- What new needs are on the horizon for customers?

✦ *Internal/External Sources.* These inputs help you to identify challenges that your business faces in defining and/or achieving its market and customer strategies. Questions they should help you answer include these:

- What are the barriers between us and our strategic goals?
- What new acquisitions need to be integrated so that they are profitable and aligned with our desired market image?
- What new products, services, locations, or other capabilities do we hope to launch, to better provide value to customers and shareholders?

Some of the best improvement opportunities arise from these questions, because they have clear value both to the company and to its positioning vis-à-vis the outside world.

✦ *Internal Sources.* The frustrations, issues, problems, and opportunities visible inside your operations are the third key source of possible Six Sigma projects. You can label these internal sources "Voice of the Process" and "Voice of the Employee." Questions for you to consider in listening to these voices include:

- What major delays slow down our process?
- Where is there a high volume of defects and/or rework?
- Where are the costs of poor quality (COPQ) increasing?
- What concerns or ideas have employees or managers raised?

The goal here is to pay closer attention to various people's perspectives on ways in which processes can be improved to the benefit of the business, customers, shareholders and employees.

Understanding What Will Qualify as a "Six Sigma" Improvement Project

You can't use DMAIC on just anything. There are three basic qualifications for a Six Sigma improvement project:

1. *There is a gap between current and desired/needed performance.* "Where's the pain?" is how we often pose this question. If you're going to apply DMAIC, you first need a problem to solve or an opportunity to take advantage of. In the case of process design, there's a new activity being launched for which there *is* no existing process.
2. *The cause of the problem isn't clearly understood.* You may have theories, but so far no one has been able to factually pinpoint the root cause; that, or else solutions you *thought* would relieve the pain just aren't working.
3. *The solution isn't predetermined, nor is the optimal solution apparent.* If you've already planned a short-term remedy, there still may be potential for a Six Sigma project; "quick fixes" can help buy time for more rigorous analysis. If a significant effort has already been launched to bridge the "gap," however, a separate, concurrent Six Sigma project would be redundant or worse. You can "skip" DMAIC when quick fixes are adequate, or the solution is legitimately obvious. There's nothing in the Six Sigma philosophy that requires you to ban forever the Nike advertising approach to business improvement ("Just do it") when it's warranted.

Project Selection Scenarios

Some sample situations should help you to see what qualified Six Sigma improvement projects should, and should not, look like. As you'll see, it isn't always black-and-white. In such situations, however, if three questions can be answered Yes, Yes, and No, that pretty much proves that the project is appropriate for Six Sigma.

Project Scenario #1: The Bank of Townville

At the Bank of Townville, the facilities department is working overtime to find and lease 10 new locations as part of the Bank's expansion program. Because of a shortage of storefront space in downtown Townville, they're looking at putting a couple of branches in nearby Burgtown.

Is there a problem or an opportunity here? Sort of. We have fewer locations than called for in our plans, and we need new space for new locations.

Is the cause of the problem unknown? No. We know that the cause is a shortage of appropriate space in Townville.

Is the solution predetermined or obvious? Yes. We already have a plan to put some new branches in Burgtown.

So this would *not* be a good Six Sigma improvement project.

Project Scenario #2: Bullwinkle Medical Equipment

Fifteen new products have been introduced by Bullwinkle Medical Equipment company in the past year. All but two of these have exceeded sales projections, and Bullwinkle is looking at record profits and a double-digit jump in market share. At the same time, as volume has increased, more and more customers are complaining about missed delivery dates. A new Web-based ordering system is in development, to allow Bullwinkle clients to order equipment online and to speed up the delivery process.

Is there a problem or opportunity? Both. The opportunity is to get even more orders. The problem is that promised delivery dates are being missed.

Is the cause of the problem unknown? Actually, yes. While we know customers are complaining about missed delivery dates, the website solution is based on the assumption that the bottleneck is at the order-entry point in the process—which may not be true.

Is the solution predetermined or obvious? It seems predetermined; as we noted, however, it may not really be a solution to this problem. On the other hand, having a Web-based ordering system seems like a worthy improvement.

There are *two* possible Six Sigma projects in this scenario; 1) as a process design effort, to develop new processes to support the order-entry website, and 2) by applying process improvement *or* design (we don't yet know which) to determine the cause(s) of late deliveries and apply solutions so that we can meet our delivery commitments. Of course, another perspective might be to say "we're handling it with the website."

Project Scenario #3: Excellent Insurance Company

The job market in the area near the Excellent Insurance Company's national call center is tight. Competition for new hires is intense, and Excellent's call center director is looking for new ways to attract applicants. To promote referrals, Excellent is scheduling a "Day on the Green" picnic and concert at the Center City amphitheater. Each employee who brings a potential new hire for Excellent will get a free "Day on the Green" T-shirt.

Is there a problem or opportunity? Absolutely. The call center needs people, and there aren't enough to hire.

Is the cause of the problem unknown? No. It's been a strong economy, and several other large employers near the call center have had trouble filling positions.

Is the solution predetermined or obvious? Yes, or at least one possible solution is on the way to implementation.

This scenario is an example of a project that might be assigned to a Six Sigma team when, in fact, it would be very likely to cause frustration to a team. Certainly Six Sigma techniques are not needed to plan the Day on the Green event!

To summarize: You and your leaders should be careful not to shove just any old issue that seems important onto the Six Sigma project list.

Defining Criteria for Project Selection

One of the challenges of project selection—as in many business decisions—is to agree not just on what to do, but also on what *not* to do. As we've noted, you can't do everything all at once—and some potential Six Sigma projects will likely have to be left off your initial list. The key word is *priority;* which problems/opportunities will you tackle *first?*

The best project selection is based on identifying the projects that best match your current needs, capabilities, and objectives. The following subsections provide you with a "generic" list of possible criteria to include in your project selection process, grouped into three categories: Results or Business Benefits; Feasibility; and Organizational Impact.

1. Results or Business Benefits Criteria

- *Impact on external customers and requirements.* How beneficial or important is this problem/opportunity to our "paying customers" or key external audiences (e.g., shareholders, regulators, supply-chain partners)?
- *Impact on business strategy, competitive position.* What value will this potential project have in helping us to realize our business vision, implement our market strategy, or improve our competitive position?
- *Impact on "core competencies."* How will this possible Six Sigma project affect our mix and capabilities in "core competencies"? (Could involve strengthening a core competency, or "off-loading" an activity no longer deemed a key internal skill.)
- *Financial impact (e.g., cost reduction, improved efficiency, increased sales, market-share gain).* What is the short-term dollar gain likely to be? Long-term? How accurately can we project these numbers? (Beware of inflating possible gains beyond what's realistic.)
- *Urgency.* What kind of lead time do we have to address this issue or capitalize on this opportunity? (Note: *Urgency* is distinct from *impact;* a small problem can be urgent, and a huge issue can have a long lead time.)
- *Trend.* Is the problem, issue, or opportunity getting bigger or smaller over time? What will happen if we do nothing?
- *Sequence or Dependency.* Are other possible projects or opportunities dependent on dealing with this issue first? Does this issue depend on other problems being addressed first?

2. Feasibility Criteria

- *Resources needed.* How many people, how much time, how much money is this project likely to need?
- *Expertise available.* What knowledge or technical skills will be needed for this project? Do we have them available and accessible?
- *Complexity.* How complicated or difficult do we anticipate it will be to develop the Improvement solution? To implement it?
- *Likelihood of success.* Based on what we know, what is the likelihood that this project will be successful (in a reasonable timeframe)?

- *Support or Buy-In.* How much support for this project can we anticipate from key groups within the organization? Will we be able to make a good case for doing this project?

3. Organizational Impact Criteria

- *Learning benefits.* What new knowledge—about our business, customers, processes, and/or the Six Sigma system—might we gain from this project?
- *Cross-functional benefits.* To what extent will this project help to break down barriers between groups in the organization and create better "whole process" management?

As extensive as the preceding list of criteria is, you may have other criteria that are relevant to your business. You should *not* use all these factors in your project selection; instead, choose the five to eight that are most relevant criteria for your organization today. Where possible, it's easier to stick to the criteria for which you have more factual answers. Remember: The objective is to target the best projects to fit your specific business and organizational needs, and the goals of your Six Sigma effort.

When you have a very long list of potential projects, it may be a good idea first to narrow the list down by using some qualifying criteria (e.g., minimum potential dollar benefits; benefits to external customers) or some type of group-voting process. To gain a more careful assessment, note that scoring each possible project on each of your chosen criteria will give you a comparison and show which best supports all the factors for a worthwhile project. A "criteria matrix" can help structure your comparison of the projects.

However you use or define the criteria for project selection, remember that there are lots of reasons to consider a project to be worthy of the DMAIC process, as well as many things to watch out for before formally launching a project. Fundamentally, these reasons all go back to our two "macro" criteria: Is the project *Meaningful* and is it *Manageable*?

Creating the Project Rationale

The end-product of the selection effort is a description of the issue, value, and broad goal or expectations of the team assigned to a project. The Project Rationale establishes direction for an improvement team leader in choosing team members (if it's up to him/her to assemble the team) and in developing an initial plan for execution of the project. Done well, the Rationale also becomes a communication tool and even something of an internal "marketing" document, helping to explain the purpose of the project to others in the organization.

Most importantly, the Rationale (sometimes called a "Business Case," "Project Mission," or "Purpose Statement") provides a starting point for an improvement team to create its "Charter" or similar overview document. Common elements of a Project Rationale statement include the following:

- *A description of the issue or concern.* It's important not to assign cause or blame for the problem/opportunity.
- *The focus of this specific project (optional).* Sometimes more than one project can be launched to work on various aspects of a large (world hunger–like) problem/opportunity.
- *A broad goal or type of results to be achieved.* Normally, this should *not* include a target; it's more appropriate for the team to set its own specific goal or target—with the support of the project sponsor or champion.
- *An overview of the value of the effort.* What is the financial, customer, strategic, or other benefit of addressing the project—and why is it being done now?
- *Project parameters and expectations.* This can give the team some understanding of the resources they'll have available to them, what solutions they may *not* consider, and so on.

Your Project Rationale statements may include other elements, or leave some of these out. If you have an existing project definition format or document, it could be used as a Rationale statement. In other words, we recommend you use what works in your own business.

Overall, it's important to strike a balance between giving clear guidelines to a team on project direction and expectations, while not overly narrowing options or dictating solutions. As we'll see in Chapter 15, one of a Six Sigma improvement team's first tasks will be to interpret and prepare its own starting document based on the Project Rationale created by business leaders.

Selecting Project "Dos and Don'ts"

Do—Base your Improvement Project selection on solid criteria.

Balance results, feasibility, and organizational impact issues. Good project selection can be a key to early success.

Do—Balance efficiency/cost-cutting with externally-focused, customer value projects.

The "customer-focus" theme is a source of Six Sigma's strength. Putting your energies into short-term savings only sends the wrong signal and reduces your chance of boosting customer satisfaction and loyalty.

Do—Prepare for an effective "handoff" to the improvement team.

A technique like the Project Rationale can give a good start to a project by defining clear issues and objectives.

Don't—Choose too many projects.

Improvement takes care and feeding on the part of leaders and "experts," especially at the beginning. It's tempting to overextend your resources and capabilities.

Don't—Create "world hunger" projects.

Even more common than "too many" is "too big." Better to get a too-small project done more quickly—as long as the results are meaningful—than to have a too-big project drag on for months.

Don't—Fail to explain the reasoning for the projects chosen.

Everyone has problems they *think should be top-priority. Ensuring support for the ones you choose means providing a good rationale for your priorities.*

Choosing Your Six Sigma Improvement Model(s)

A final consideration in defining your Six Sigma approach is what improvement model to adopt. Although it directly impacts primarily Step 4 in the Six Sigma Roadmap, the choice of models will also affect how you conduct your training and how you "market" the Six Sigma initiative.

Why—and Why Not—to Adopt "DMAIC"

As we explained in Chapter 2, many companies have adopted the DMAIC model—Define, Measure, Analyze, Improve, Control—or some variation of it for their Six Sigma improvement projects. We're using those five steps as our preferred model throughout *The Six Sigma Way.* However, if your organization already uses or has taught people a process improvement or redesign method, it's by no means mandatory in the Six Sigma system that you abandon it in favor of DMAIC.

Many of the various models we've seen in different organizations can serve well as a guide to Six Sigma improvement efforts. All of them, in some way or another, are based on the "Plan-Do-Check-Act" cycle, and each has its relative strengths and weaknesses. If your existing model is familiar and well understood by many people already, changing improvement methods could be confusing. Plus, you'd need to teach people a whole new model to replace the old. If you are likely to *keep* your current improvement process, it should not be difficult to adapt the actions we'll cover in Chapters 15 and 16 to your existing improvement process.

Potential Advantages of DMAIC

On the other hand, there are both organizational and content reasons why you might consider adopting a new improvement model as part of the Six Sigma effort—or if you don't have a current problem-solving process, why DMAIC offers advantages over others.

1. *Making a fresh start.* If your existing continuous improvement model is perceived to be part of a failed or discredited quality initiative—or if it's used only rarely—DMAIC (or some other valid model)

may help you to position Six Sigma as a truly different, better approach to business improvement. This "clean break" may help you avoid opening old wounds or reviving animosities created in a previous push for improvement. Explained properly, it can signal that the business has learned from its past efforts and is embarking on a "new and improved" path: Six Sigma.

2. *Giving a new context to familiar tools.* Introducing a new (and better) improvement model is a positive rationale for giving people a fresh opportunity to learn and practice familiar tools—and to add new ones.
3. *Creating a consistent approach.* A lasting effect of the waves of quality training that assaulted many companies from the 1970s through the 1990s is the existence of *different* improvement models within the same company. But if cross-functional efforts are to work on a process "end-to-end," a common method and vocabulary is essential. Thus a decision to "pick one model and stick with it" may be an important way for your business to tap into the power of Six Sigma.
4. *Putting a priority on "Customer" and "Measurement."* Another potential advantage of the DMAIC model is the emphasis it places on these two critical components of the Six Sigma system. For example, validating customer requirements is a key substep of the "Define" phase, but was not to be found in most of the "older" quality models. Measurement is specifically addressed in other improvement roadmaps, but in the DMAIC process, measurement is presented more as a foundational, ongoing effort than as simply a "task."
5. *Offering both "Process Improvement" and "Process Design/Redesign" paths to improvement.* As we've noted, one of the breakthroughs of the Six Sigma system lies in its ability to get beyond the pointless TQM-versus-reengineering debate. We've found plenty of instances where improvement teams in Six Sigma had a legitimate choice to either "fix" or "redesign" a troubled process. DMAIC, as we'll present it in this book, can help them to make that choice—and to adapt the model to either approach.

In the final analysis, there is no right or wrong improvement model for Six Sigma. If the five steps of DMAIC work for your business, great.

If an existing model or some other one is a better choice for your people or project, that's okay, too. Either way, Six Sigma still can work for your business.

Having laid out many of the key decisions—and some of the challenges, too—associated with defining and designing Six Sigma for your organization, we turn next in Part Three to *making it happen.*

3

Implementing Six Sigma: The Roadmap and the Tools

CHAPTER

12

Identifying Core Processes and Key Customers

(Roadmap Step 1)

Introduction

In Chapter 5 we introduced the example of "Company Island," a place where a lot of stuff is flowing around, but no one really has a grasp of the "big picture." Whether you start your Six Sigma effort with Step One, or loop back to this effort later, the objective here is to develop the high-level view of the organization—in essence, a "map" of your island showing how essential work gets done.

The "map-making" approach we'll describe here is somewhat like putting a puzzle together. We'll begin by forming a basic idea of how the puzzle should look—just as you'd get from the top of the puzzle box. Then we'll assemble the edges of the puzzle first—or, since we're delicately balancing two metaphors, we'll define the "coastline" of the island where it links up with its customers. Then, we'll assemble the internal pieces of the puzzle, adding clarity to the basic image we first described. As with a puzzle this will involve some trial-and-error and, like map-making, some research, too. Usually, as the picture emerges it looks a little different from what you had expected, much as seeing a map of a place you've visited often can reveal facts you never knew.

Step 1 Overview

The following are the three main activities associated with Identifying Core Processes and Key Customers (see Fig. 12.1):

1. Identify the major core processes of your business.
2. Define the key Outputs of these core processes, and the key customers they serve.
3. Create a high-level map of your core or strategic processes.

As we discuss these steps, we'll assume for the most part that the organization we're mapping is an entire business or operating unit. It's possible, though, to use the same approach to map a *segment* of the organization including those areas—for example, finance, human resources, or information technology—that provide services or products primarily to *internal* customers. Even small islands can use the Six Sigma system to improve their performance.

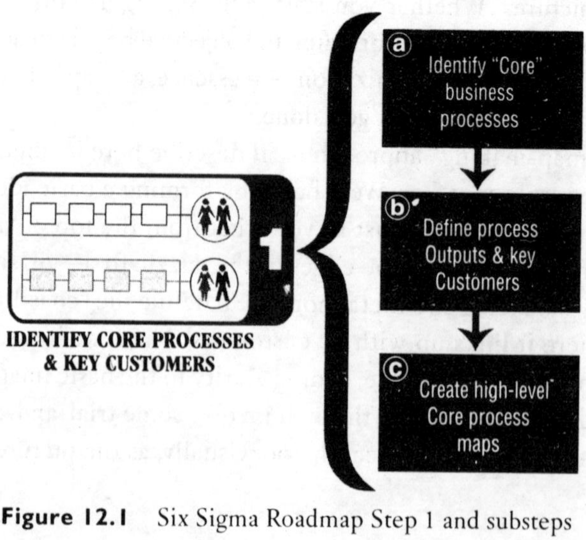

Figure 12.1 Six Sigma Roadmap Step 1 and substeps

Introduction to a Core Process Story

To bring to life many of the key steps, challenges, and tools of the Six Sigma Way, in Part Three we will feature a series of stories or scenarios of real-but-fictionalized companies that are putting their best effort forward to accomplish the tasks we're describing. The first of the organizations we'll meet is a consumer products company. Others will include a transportation company, an electronics marketer/manufacturer, and an insurance company. *Note:* The scenarios we're presenting are based on real events, but the names and organizations have been fictionalized.

FieldFresh Looks at the Big Picture

The FieldFresh company has been packing and selling canned and frozen fruits and vegetables through retail stores in the Midwest for over 60 years. The FieldFresh brand has benefited greatly from its strong reputation for quality and from the loyalty of consumers in its eight-state market area. While FieldFresh is still and always has been profitable, the company is aware that while times have changed a lot in six decades, things at FieldFresh have not.

FieldFresh today is run by a handful of top managers—all with 20 or more years with the company—most of whom are getting close to retirement. It's always been a close-knit, family-oriented company (it's not uncommon for parents and their offspring to both work at FieldFresh), with a strong sense of tradition and a high level of commitment to employees and customers. The heads of FieldFresh's four main functional groups—advertising and promotion, manufacturing, accounting, and personnel—have done an excellent job running their individual departments. Each has a firm grasp of his or her area, but because they've worked together so long and know the business so well, the four have kept operations among the different functions flowing smoothly and effectively.

The biggest concern among the FieldFresh leaders—prompted by pressure from the company's board of directors—is how the company will weather the changes in their industry as well as the pending turnover in top management. "You've been really lucky," commented FieldFresh board member Marla Jones, president of a local bank. "So many companies like FieldFresh have had the rug pulled out from under them because they failed to adapt and prepare for change. You're still doing fine, but the question is: 'How will FieldFresh make it in the new century?' "

Step 1A: Identify "Core" Processes

By "core process" we mean a chain of tasks—usually involving various departments or functions—that deliver value (products, services, support, information) to external customers. Alongside the core processes, each organization has a number of "support" or "enabling" processes that provide vital resources or inputs to the value-producing activities. While the idea of a core process may seem pretty straightforward—and it is—it's interesting that this key organizational "building block" is a relatively recent idea, one of the breakthrough concepts of the Six Sigma system.

Concepts behind the Core Process

1. Work as a Process

Starting with Frederick Taylor and proceeding through the quality gurus of the 1980s and 1990s, the *process* has been an important theme for management theorists and practitioners. In the early days of modern manufacturing, the scale of production and degree of specialization were limited, and the processing of goods for customers was still clearly at the core of the business. As industrial organizations and competition grew, however, the work processes were overlaid—and obscured—by functional management structures and specialization of skills. The work processes were still going on, but the primary management focus was on "our function" and the individual's attention on "my task."

When the quality movement brought "the process" back into focus, it was—and often still is—difficult for people to see their work or organization in this seemingly new way.

Slowly, however, more and more organizations are starting to grasp the distinction between a "function" and a "process." And the idea that business success is driven by understanding and improving work processes has become a basic principle in many organizations.

2. Cross-Functional Management

Frustration with functional and hierarchical business structures is nothing new. Some of the most persistent jokes, satires, and complaints about corporations through the years have been aimed at the "empires" and bureaucracies that hamper good decision making and responsiveness. As early as the 1920s, organizations like General Motors were using "interdivisional relations committees" to deal with the friction generated between line and staff divisions, and between the various functional areas created within GM's decentralized organization.[1]

Efforts to break through the organizational barriers have been made countless times in the history of modern business, through "reorganizations," "restructurings," "management shake-ups," and so on—and they happen often today. Cross-functional project and management teams have been tried, as a force to break down the walls between groups. But while teamwork can help, just forming a team does little to remove the attitudes and structures that create the walls.

As businesses have begun to understand the difference between a process and a department, and to map processes *across* functional boundaries, the real key to the cross-functional cooperation has appeared.

3. The "Value Chain"

Showing how work passes through various departments is terrific; but for there to be a truly powerful model for management, it has to show a clear strategic benefit. Thus, other than eliminating some squabbles and bureaucratic snags, how can cross-functional processes be used to improve business competitiveness and profitability? The third concept, the "value chain," provides the answer.

The "value chain," as defined by Harvard's Michael Porter in his 1985 book *Competitive Advantage*, is a way of representing an organization as "a collection of activities that are performed to design, market, deliver, and support its product."[2] Three dimensions of the value chain concept finally bring the "Core Process" idea into focus:

1. *The value chain reinforces the key interconnectedness of business activities and corporate success.* Each function plays a part (or should) in the basic goal of the organization: to provide some unique value to its market and customers. Any break or weak link in the chain (e.g., inter-functional rivalries) diminishes the value provided.

2. *While each function contributes to value, some play a "primary" role, others a "secondary" one.* Primary functions are "involved in the physical creation of the product [or service] and its sale and transfer to the buyer as well as the after-sale assistance."[3] Functions categorized as "support activities" by Porter include human resources, finance, procurement—even (gasp!) senior management. (Of course, anyone who's worked around large companies for a while knows that "support" functions often have greater clout or get more attention than do the "primary" ones—a corporate case of the tail wagging the dog.)
3. *Value chains are defined at the operating-unit level of an organization.* A "corporate-wide" value chain, encompassing various business units, would be meaningless.

The value chain concept, as presented by Porter, has little to do with work processes. The value chain "activities" he describes are usually much more akin to departments or functions—tied to the traditional "organization chart" view of a business, *not* the process view. But the relevant message for companies trying to define and prioritize their business processes is clear: Those processes that provide products and services to customers are "primary" and others are "secondary."

"Generic" Core and Support Process Descriptions

Core Processes

For any enterprise, certain activities are essential. While in your organization they may be called something different or broken into smaller chunks, the following list is a good starting point to help you ensure you've included all the primary processes:

- *Customer Acquisition.* The process of attracting and securing customers for the organization.
- *Order Administration.* Activities meant to interpret and track requests for products or services from customers.
- *Order Fulfillment.* Creation, preparation, and delivery of the order to the customer.
- *Customer Service or Support.* Activities designed to sustain customer satisfaction after delivery of an order.

- *New Product/Service Development.* Conception, design, and launch of new value-adding services to customers.
- *Invoicing and collections (optional).* Whether "getting paid" is really a core, versus support, process is open to interpretation. While technically it's not part of value-delivery, it also is a key part of a "win-win" relationship with customers, and hence of your financial success. Therefore it certainly is reasonable to consider this a core process.

Support Processes

In the "support" functions of an organization, there are also standard processes that provide key resources or capabilities that enable the core processes to perform. These are a little more specific, as we've taken *departments* and divided them into their key processes:

- *Capital Acquisition.* Provision of financial resources for the organization to do its work and execute its strategy.
- *Asset Maximization.* Deployment of existing capital (especially money) to create the greatest possible return in alignment with the firm's value strategy.
- *Budgeting.* The process of deciding how funds will be allocated over a period of time.
- *Recruitment and Hiring.* Acquisition of *people* to do the work of the organization.
- *Evaluation and Compensation.* Assessment and payment of people for the work/value they provide to the company.
- *Human Resource Support and Development.* Preparation of people for their current jobs and future skill/knowledge needs.
- *Regulatory Compliance.* Processes ensuring that the company is meeting all laws and legal obligations.
- *Facilities.* Provision and maintenance of physical plant and equipment so that the business can perform its functions.
- *Information Systems.* Movement and processing of data and information to expedite business operations and decisions.
- *Functional and/or Process Management.* Systems and activities to ensure effective execution of the work of the business.

It's likely that after reading these Support Process descriptions you're thinking, "This is *weird!*" Well, we've already warned you that the "functional" view of the organization is so deeply ingrained in our minds that, when we change the context to flow of work and value provided, it's strange and disorienting. But it's also true that we've presented just *one* way out of many, to define and "slice" these processes. How *you* do it will almost certainly be different, and make more sense for your organization.

FieldFresh Leaders Consider Their Challenge

While at first they resisted as "meddling" the challenging comments made by some members of their Board of Directors, over time most of the top five executives at FieldFresh—President Elliott Peardale and his four department VPs—began to acknowledge the validity of the issue. "We've got some great people here," said Peardale, "but we've not helped them learn the business to the degree we might have. After all, we've handled every top decision pretty much by ourselves."

At the urging of another board member, who happens to be Chairman Emeritus of the Business department at the state's top university, FieldFresh's top leaders attended a one-day seminar on the concepts behind the Six Sigma approach to business management. After the workshop, the group met at their weekly lunch to share their thoughts on the ideas they'd heard.

"Sounds too much like all that quality b______!" pronounced manufacturing VP Jimmy Haricot.

"Don't judge too fast, Jimmy," responded Brenda Lechosa, head of advertising and promotion. "It got me thinking that we've set this company up for trouble. The only people who really understand this entire company are us. We know the customers, we know the departments, we know the background. And even then, I think we're in the dark on more stuff than we'd like to admit."

"Brenda's right, I'd say." That was accounting VP Hal Krautmeyer. "I can't hand things off to anyone else in the department for more than a couple of weeks. When I come back from vacation I have a stack of backlogged issues to work on. When Millie and I head for Arizona permanently in a couple of years, are you guys going to hang around and pay the bills?"

"We did try some of that TQM stuff, you know, a few years back," commented Peardale, "and it didn't get us much. I can see why Jimmy's skeptical."

"But this seems different to me," persisted Lechosa. "They said Sigma Six, or whatever you call it, is about fixing problems, but I really liked the part about looking at the business in a new way."

"What would be 'new'?" asked Haricot. As the manufacturing head, he typically played the role of nuts-and-bolts skeptic on the FieldFresh team.

Personnel leader Al Funghi finally weighed in: "To me, what's new is a way to show others in the company how we work together. We keep saying we can't hand over responsibility to people, but we haven't really tried. Maybe if we helped them understand the company as well as we do, they *could* do more."

"I don't need any teams to start fixing a bunch of imaginary problems in the plants!" protested Haricot.

"Jimmy," said Peardale, "I don't think that's the suggestion."

"No way," agreed accounting's Krautmeyer. "I don't think fixing problems is the answer for us—at least not right away. But if we could start showing people how the company works—and maybe see ways for it to work better—we might all be able to retire when we want to, instead of working here till we're all eighty-something."

"That's what I'm saying," agreed Lechosa. "But I'd add one thing: I think there's more at stake than our retirement. I just think we can't expect our brand loyalty and tradition to carry us forever. The way we've run the company probably won't work for the next generation."

"You know," said Peardale, almost interrupting the advertising manager. "I guess that's what has been bothering me for quite a while now, but I hadn't been able to explain it. It's hard to admit, but it's time we updated things at FieldFresh if we're going to leave a good situation behind when we leave." The consensus was strong enough that the managers decided to take a first step on the Six Sigma roadmap: to try to create a process-focused "map" of the FieldFresh organization.

Defining and Tailoring Your Core Processes

One of the first things to recognize in trying to list the primary or core processes in your organization, is that there is no "right" or "wrong." In some instances; how you define core processes may be guided, for example, by the need to send a message to the organization. We recently spoke with a senior executive who had reorganized his company under what were called four "pillars"—Create, Deliver, Care, and Support—encompassing three core and various enabling processes. There's a lot of detail under each pillar, but as a unifying theme for the company, it's pretty effective. As another example, one of our clients developed a fairly simple model of what they call their "strategic processes," shown in Fig. 12.2. Each person in the organization is able to identify his or her own contribution to one or more of these core processes.

Key Questions for Core Processes

Putting together your model of core processes may take some time and thought. Then too, how many you identify will vary with your business and with such factors as strategy and history. As a rule of thumb, however, most operating units should have between four and eight really high-level "primary" processes. Asking the following questions can help you to determine them.

1. *What are the major activities through which we provide value—products and services—to customers?* This question gives you a starting point to

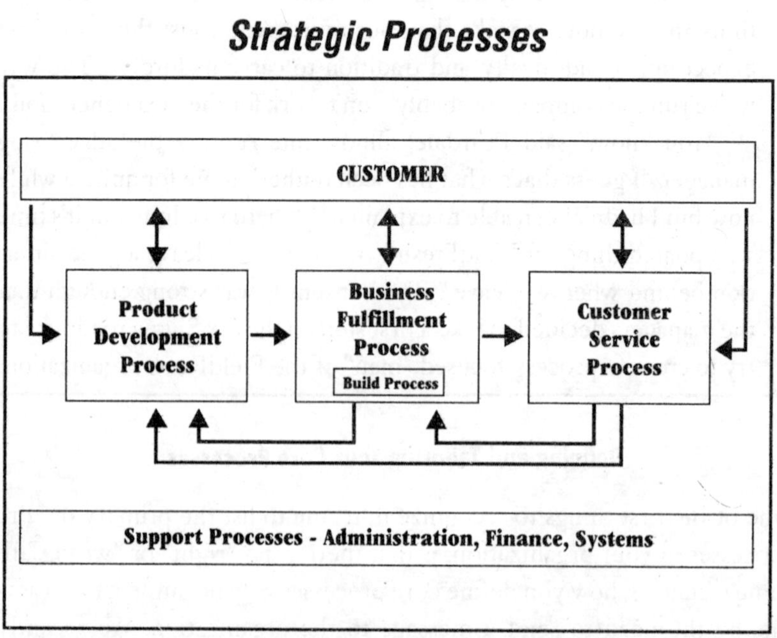

Figure 12.2 Example: simplified "strategic processes" model

identify your core processes—*value* being the primary definer of a "core" activity. Be careful not to include activities that are very important to you—for example, legal or regulatory compliance—but that don't add value to customers. (We'll encounter this notion again when we look at value analysis in Chapter 16.)

2. *How could we best describe or name these processes?* You can refine the names later, but give them a label to start with. Try to avoid using a department or function name—no true core process happens within a single department.
3. *What are the primary (one to three) critical Outputs of each process that we can use to evaluate its performance/capability?* The quality of the end product delivered to the customer is the most important success criterion for a process. If you identify *many* Outputs from a core process, you may not have defined the process specifically enough—or perhaps you've lumped together several "business units."

FieldFresh Gets to the Core of the Matter

It was a month later that the five top managers at FieldFresh arrived at work for an early 7 A.M. meeting. Their agenda: to identify the major or "core" processes of their business. Jimmy Haricot agreed to give it a try; the other VPs were convinced it would be a good idea. They had brought in a facilitator to help them, recommended by one of the Board members.

Their first list was a mix of lots of activities or groups, including: payroll, grower relations, invoicing, media buying, label design, etc. "This is a mess," complained Personnel head Al Funghi. "We're doing something wrong."

"You know," said Jimmy, who was trying to be cooperative, "weren't we supposed to look at the stuff that focuses on the customer *only?*"

Everyone agreed they had gotten off track. With the help of the facilitator, they began to move the non-core activities to a separate list of "support" functions and processes and to reorganize the core processes by major categories. It was a struggle, and by the end of the session at 10:30 A.M. they were exhausted. "We'd better noodle this over a little," said Peardale.

In between meetings, Brenda Lechosa called the people who'd given the initial workshop and got some advice. When they met for another 7 A.M. session a week and a half later, she passed along the input: "They suggested we try to avoid naming any process after a department. We have to think cross-functionally, and focus on the major value-adding activities."

At the end of another couple of hours work—and a fair amount of verbal arm-wrestling—they had reduced the list to the following four core processes:

- Product supply
- Product development
- Production and distribution
- Consumer and retailer marketing

They then created a list of what they decided to call "support" processes, following a simple naming convention:

- People support
- Financial support
- Infrastructure support
- Strategic support

They sketched a diagram of these lists, which the facilitator put into a more presentable graphic (see Fig. 12.3).

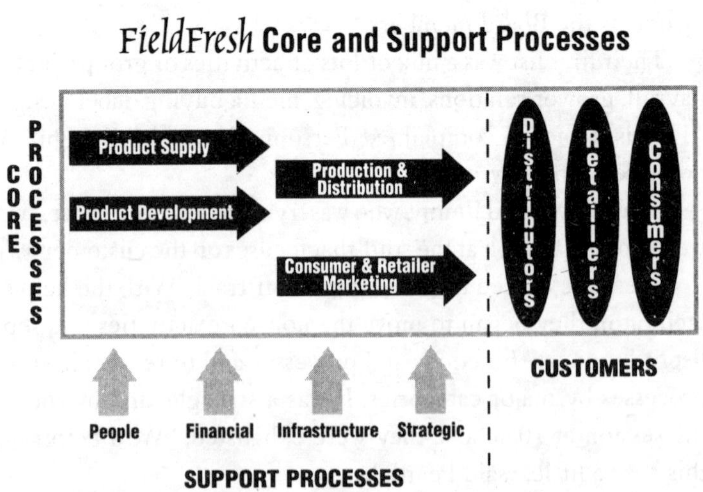

Figure 12.3 FieldFresh core and support processes

Step 1B: Define Your Key Process Outputs, and Key Customers

This is the easiest part of Step One, though it has its traps, too. The challenge is to avoid pushing too many items or work products into the category of "Outputs." If yours is like most organizations, a lot of "stuff" is getting produced every day, and some of that may end up in the hands of your customer. But from a strategic or core process standpoint, only the final product or the primary Output is relevant, for now.

It's not at all mandatory that core process Outputs be delivered to external, paying customers. For example, the Output of a "Customer Acquisition" process is some type of agreement to do business with a customer: an order, distribution agreement, contract, statement of work, policy, etc. The external customer usually receives some verification of the deal, but the primary "customer" of that core process will be the *next* core process—e.g., order administration or production.

The Outputs of the FieldFresh Processes

Each of the vice presidents at FieldFresh was given an assignment: to draft a definition of the major Outputs, and customers, of the core processes they'd identified. Since a customer could be a person or a group of people, they decided that it would be okay to name a department as the "customer" of a core process, even though it might be the first step in another process.

For example, Accounting's Hal Krautmeyer took "Product Development." He listed three Outputs, each with different customers:

Output 1: Product formula; *Customers:* Plant Technical Support, Grower Relations

Output 2: Process specifications; *Customer:* Plant engineering

Output 3: Consumer test data; *Customers:* Promotions Planning, Brokers/Distributors.

Al Funghi of HR was asked to work on "Product Supply." There was one major Output:

Output 1: Produce (raw material); *Customers:* Plant Technical Support (which handles recipe-based products), or Production (which receives any fresh-canned or fresh-frozen items directly).

Step 1C: Create High-Level Core Process Maps

The last step you should take in assembling the process map "puzzle" is to identify the major activities that make up each core process. (As an option, you can create high-level diagrams of support processes as well.)

The "SIPOC" Process Model

A SIPOC diagram is one of the most useful and often-used techniques of process management and improvement. It's used to present an "at-a-glance" view of work flows. The name comes from the five elements in the diagram:

- *Supplier*—the person or group providing key information, materials, or other resource to the process
- *Input*—the "thing" provided
- *Process*—the set of steps that transforms—and ideally, adds value to—the Input
- *Output*—the final product of the process
- *Customer*—the person, group, or process that receives the Output.

Often, key requirements of the Input and Output are added, making it more like "SIRPORC." No one seems to use that term, though—maybe because it sounds like a royally honored pig.

Benefits of SIPOC, or "Sir Pork"

SIPOC can be a big help in getting people to see the business from a process perspective. Among its advantages, it:

1. Displays a cross-functional set of activities in a single, simple diagram
2. Uses a framework applicable to processes of all sizes—even an entire organization
3. Helps maintain a "big picture" perspective, to which additional detail can be added

By linking SIPOCs end-to-end across an organization—where the Output of one process becomes the Input of another—you can develop a high-level process diagram of the entire company.

SIPOC and Completing the Core Processes

The first two tasks covered in this chapter have given us a good start on our SIPOC diagram: We've identified the Process broadly by name, and we've defined the Output and Customer. Now we're interested in the Suppliers and Inputs, and a more detailed description of the Process.

Suppliers and Inputs

To identify the Suppliers and Inputs to a process, you first need to know at what point—where, when, and with what action—the process *starts.* That's usually not too difficult when defining the major processes for an organization; you can simply identify at what point the previous (or "upstream") process leaves off, and what Inputs are passed along to the next process.

Generally it's best to limit Inputs to items consumed during the process and *not* to include equipment, facilities, or other relatively permanent infrastructure. First of all, it's much simpler: If you included every piece of software, desk, telephone, machine, etc. used in most processes, it would be a *long* list. More importantly, an ultimate goal of diagramming the process is to understand the flow and variation in the work over time. Stuff that's more or less permanent actually becomes part of the Process, and we can measure its effect on the work there—but not as an Input.

The following are some easy questions for you to ask, as an aid in identifying Suppliers and Inputs:

- *What key materials, information, or products are provided to the process?* The most critical input to any core process is the "thing" being worked on. In an assembly plant, it's parts; in a lending company, it's a loan request; at an airline company, it's a passenger. Other key inputs will be essential to the success of the process also, such as a "work order" at the assembly plant, customer data at the lending company, and passenger reservations at the airline.
- *Which of these are absolutely essential to the process work as being performed?* Focus only on such *critical* inputs. If the work can get done well without it, it isn't critical.
- *Are they consumed or used during the process, or passed through to the customer as an Output?* If neither is true, it may be a tool, but it probably isn't an Input.

- *Who provides those Inputs?* Once you've defined the Input, it's usually easier to identify the process Suppliers.

Diagramming the Process

The "P" segment of a SIPOC is best done as a "block diagram," with each box representing major activities or "subprocesses." Unlike a more detailed process map or flowchart, a block diagram usually is a simple, straight-line flow, with no decision points, rework loops, or alternate paths shown. To avoid getting into too much detail, you should limit the Process to from 4 to 10 blocks. It can be tricky, though, because the detail tends to come out anyway. For that reason we usually recommend using an "Affinity" method to build the high-level block diagram. In the Affinity technique a group lists ideas and then organizes (or, in the ize-ization of our vocabulary, "affinitizes") them into meaningful categories. What emerges are usually the high-level steps. Once you've named the steps or tasks, you can order them (roughly) into a sequential block diagram—the "P" of SIPOC. For the business's high-level processes, even these process blocks will in most cases be broad and cross-functional.

Taking a SIP at FieldFresh

The FieldFresh management group was happy with the list of Outputs and Customers they each had drawn up individually.

Brenda Lechosa of Advertising offered an idea: "If our next step is to sort of map out these processes, I think some of the directors and managers would be really helpful. And it would save us some time having to do this all ourselves."

The group was willing to give it a try. So they drew up a roster of four "process committees" to identify Inputs and Suppliers and create a series of high-level process maps.

All four committees made presentations of their core process SIPOC maps in an all-managers meeting held at a local conference center. An example, from the Product Supply process, is shown in Fig. 12.4. After the presentation, Peardale announced to the assembled management group that FieldFresh was initiating an effort, which he called "FieldFresh 3000," to position the company for competitiveness and growth "all the way to the *next* millennium."

The process committees that had worked on the core process maps would continue to work on defining and measuring the requirements

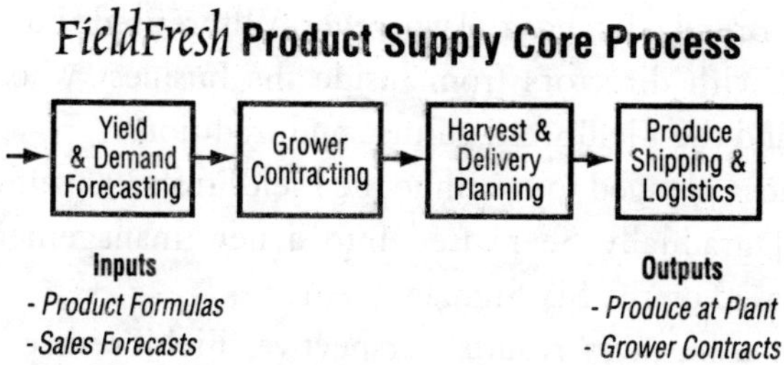

Figure 12.4 FieldFresh Product Supply Core Process

of each key activity. "We're going to take this a step at a time," he cautioned the group. "We still don't know if this Six Sigma approach is really right for FieldFresh. But the signs so far look pretty good."

Using the Core Process Maps

The Core Process definition becomes the starting point for Step Two in the Six Sigma Roadmap, in which we'll begin to identify requirements for the processes. At the same time, the value of the whole-organization view of the business as a network of key processes can help create a new understanding of the business and its interdependencies. Just as at FieldFresh, the act of defining a process model of the organization can be an eye-opener and a way of focusing attention on such questions as "Why do we do it this way?"; "Are these activities really important?"; "How effectively are these two processes connecting?"

These are questions that will arise all the time in a Six Sigma–savvy organization; that's why we've suggested a defining of the core processes as the ideal starting point for the effort.

Epilogue: The Follow-Through at FieldFresh

In the ensuing months, the FieldFresh management group became a much more open place to work. It turned out that a lot of ideas and information has been "bottled up" in the director and manager ranks. Those now began to come forth, as these key people offered ideas on how to measure their performance and how to better communicate with customers.

At the end of the following year, President Elliot Peardale announced his retirement and handed over the reins of the company to Brenda Lechosa. Two other VPs retired, but they were replaced with directors from inside the business who know and understand the FieldFresh culture and tradition.

Lechosa pledged to continue the FieldFresh 3000 effort, but said it would gradually be phased into a new management practice model based on the Six Sigma system.

From a business results perspective, FieldFresh continued to revamp outdated processes, over time establishing better collaborative relationships with its distributors and with retailers. Publicity gained through stories appearing in several regional newspaper business sections ("FieldFresh Refreshes" and "A New President and New Practices") mirrored a sales rebound, as FieldFresh managed to update its brand identity without losing its strong reputation.

Jimmy Haricot, back for a visit to the office after a month of fishing in Wyoming, told his long-time colleague Lechosa that "The place looks just the same, but I can tell the atmosphere is a lot different. I may just come out of retirement to run the plants for you again."

Lechosa looked at him over her glasses.

"Not!" he added.

The former VP and the new president both laughed heartily.

Fade to commercial. . . .

Identifying Core Process and Key Customer "Dos and Don'ts"

Do—Focus on activities that directly add value to customers.

You can include Support processes in your work as well, but the priority should be to understand and improve things that drive the business's success.

Do—Stay at a high level.

As soon as you get into too much detail, you lose the "big picture" perspective that's one of the biggest benefits gained by defining core processes.

Do—Involve a mix of people.

It takes cross-functional input to describe cross-functional processes. Use this opportunity to take a new look at how the business unit operates.

Don't—Overload the process with Inputs and Outputs.

There are rarely more than a few key Inputs, and one to three key Outputs.

Don't—Look upon your core processes as unchangeable.

The point of the Six Sigma system is to make your business more successful by creating skills and structures that support any change needed to meet changing customer and competitive needs.

CHAPTER

13

Defining Customer Requirements

(Roadmap Step 2)

Introduction

This chapter is all about what may be the most important new "core competency" your organization will need to develop in the 21st century. Understanding what customers really want—and how their needs, requirements, and attitudes change over time—will require a combination of discipline, persistence, creativity, sensitivity, science, and, sometimes, luck.

Step 2 Overview

The "final" products of this Six Sigma activity include:

- A strategy and system for continually tracking and updating customer requirements, competitor activities, market changes, etc.—aka, a "Voice of the Customer" (VOC)[1] system.
- A description of specific, measurable performance standards for each key Output, as defined by the Customer(s)

- Observable and (if possible) measurable service standards for key interfaces with Customers
- An analysis of performance and service standards based on their relative importance to customers and customer segments and their impact on business strategy.

The tasks you must undertake to develop these deliverables are shown in Fig. 13.1. Achieving the first task, an ongoing customer feedback system, is really a long-term goal. In the initial stages of a Six Sigma effort you are likely to focus on high-priority input from customers rather than revamp your entire customer-monitoring effort. Because the ability to really listen to the customer is becoming so critical to business success, however, we'll begin with that major initiative.

Step 2A: Gather Customer Data, and Develop a "Voice of the Customer" Strategy

It's easy to assume that most companies have a pretty good handle on their customers' needs, or have people and mechanisms in place to keep tabs on them. Certainly a lot of money is spent on market research and customer surveys by companies of all types—perhaps including yours. We would suggest, however, that many of the practices in use today, to

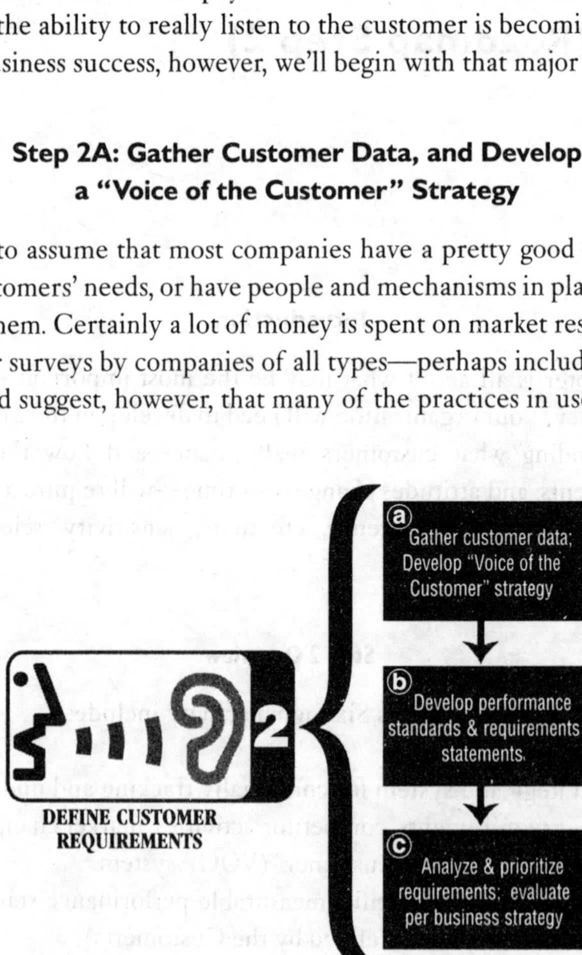

Figure 13.1 Six Sigma Roadmap Step 2 and substeps

keep tabs on customers' needs, create a false sense of security. When they are examined more closely, many companies are likely to come to the same conclusion as that reached by an executive at a large insurance company: "We began to realize we didn't understand our customers as well as we thought we did."

Consider some indirect evidence as to how well companies really use the inputs they receive from their customers:

- While point-of-sale data-gathering technologies (scanners, smart cash registers, credit card systems, etc.) have been around for almost two decades, they've been integrated only rather slowly into daily operations. For example, it's been only in the past few years that data from retail store barcode scanners have been used to create automatic replenishment programs that send computerized "reorder" notices to product manufacturers.
- Despite a lot of press coverage of, and investment in, data warehouses—vast stores of raw facts collected about transactions and customer behaviors—many companies still aren't using these resources consistently. According to a survey that sampled 50 leading U.S. companies, some 72 percent said that as of 1999 they were *not* making use of the customer data provided by their transactional information system (see Fig. 13.2).[2] It's hard to tell if this is because people have yet to figure out how to actually *use* the data, or if companies just haven't yet elected to make the investment—we suspect it's a mix of both. Just as interesting, though, is the fact that the survey results show that *all* the companies queried plan to be using that data in a few years.

More anecdotally, we see the weak grasp that many businesses have on their customer requirements in the way their new product or service development efforts are managed. We've yet to find a company whose product development initiatives aren't always being plagued by shifting demands for features and functions based on "new data" about the customer and new marketing priorities. Some fluidity and guesswork around requirements is to be expected. Still, overall, what we have called "virtual development"—product design and development with constantly changing goals and parameters—is a sign of poor discipline and a failure to gather solid, valid customer input on which to base design decisions.

Uses of Customer Data

How companies plan to use the information they have assembled on their customers . . .

	1999	2001
Marketing	18%	52%
Customer Service	16%	48%
Sales	16%	34%
Process Improvement	2%	22%
Fraud Detection	10%	14%
Product Development	4%	10%
Don't Use Data	72%	0%
Don't Know	0%	18%

How companies expect they will benefit from their wealth of customer information . . .

	1999	2001
Increase Revenue	20%	74%
Cut Expenses	16%	34%
No Impact	72%	0%
Don't Know	0%	20%

Data: Forrester Research Survey of 50 of the 1000 Largest US Companies

Figure 13.2 Current and planned use of data warehouse information

To measure, let alone *achieve* Six Sigma, however, a clear understanding of and attention to the needs of customers is mandatory, since a performance sigma is based on the customer's definition. Even if you work in an internal support organization like IT or Human Resources, your success depends (or should) on how well you help your internal customers reach their key goals.[3]

Key Factors in Voice of the Customer Systems

Whether you develop this core competency internally or rely on outside resources to serve as your "ears to the market," you will need to recognize some of the essentials of an effective Voice of the Customer system.

Making It a Continuous Effort

The first principle of an effective VOC system is that it must become a constant priority and focus. The now-and-then approach that served in the past is no longer sufficient, in light of today's speed of change. Organizations that fail to keep their eyes and ears open are those most likely to be asking "What the heck happened?" as they watch their fortunes fall.

Clearly Define Your "Customers"

In the previous chapter we outlined how to build a more comprehensive view of your core processes and key customers. Looking more carefully at the question "Who are our customers?" can bring a real awakening to a business and its leaders as well.

Quite a few organizations have already been through this awakening. A common discovery, for example, is that a small proportion of customers contributes the lion's share of revenues. Often, too, it's found that the costs of supporting some customers turn out to make them *unprofitable.* Some intelligent strategic improvements have been made in recent years to better "segment" customer groups. Companies are getting more adroit at aligning their product offerings, services, and features—as well as their costs—with the "profile" of each group: a "win-win" strategy. In other instances, the tough decision is made to abandon a customer segment, or to focus efforts on serving those customers whose needs best match the company's strategy.

Our objective in this chapter is to help you design or improve your systems for understanding and defining customer requirements and market trends—not to question your business's strategy. Nevertheless, how you define your strategy and differentiate your customers will have a big impact on the accuracy of your data and the resources needed to establish a "Voice of the Customer" system.

Avoid the Squeaky Wheel Syndrome

It's human nature to pay attention to the unusual—or the annoying. It's not necessarily a bad business practice, either. Upset customers, or those with special needs and demands, can test your organization's ability to rise to challenges and develop new capabilities. And you certainly don't want those squeaky, ticked-off clients and customers running around telling their colleagues/friends about their horrible experience doing business with you.

When the squeaky wheel drowns out everything else, though, it's a serious issue. Your "sample" of customer data is incomplete and the conclusions you're likely to draw about your market or customers are liable to be wrong. Six Sigma Voice of the Customer systems will have to be tuned to hear more than just high-pitched whines. A corollary to the squeaky wheel syndrome is the tendency to interpret "Voice of the Customer" as meaning just your existing customers. An opposite, equally serious mistake is to seek input only from prospective customers while ignoring the people currently helping you to pay the bills (an issue one especially tends to find in sales-driven organizations that are always looking for the "next deal.")

Aldie Keene, a partner with the Indianapolis-based Customer Loyalty Research Center, is a veteran of hundreds of customer-focused research projects done for many of the top companies in the United States. Keene says one of the biggest stumbling blocks that organizations trip over is "getting information from the wrong customers." He often sees companies that design products and services to a specific target customer segment. "Then, of course, they sell to anybody that comes in the door." Later, in testing customer satisfaction, "guess who turns out to be the most dissatisfied? A large percentage are ones that weren't targeted by their product/service strategy."

Beyond talking to and listening to the wrong audience, Keene notes, companies then *react* to the negative data: "They say, 'Whoa, we're really doing a bad job.' And they point fingers: 'You, over there—get better!' All without understanding who's really included in the negative responses and why they're unhappy."

The key, not surprisingly, is to balance and diversify your efforts to learn from a variety of groups, including:

- Current, happy customers
- Current, unhappy customers (that includes both those who complain and those who don't)
- Lost customers
- Competitors' customers

5. *Be detailed, but concise.* One of the big shortcomings of Requirement Statements comes from being too brief. It can be hard to assess a process or service based on "shorthand" requirements. At the same time if they're too wordy, no one reads them. The trick, of course, is to strike a balance.
6. *Match—or be validated by—the Voice of the Customer.* Most importantly, the requirement or specification needs to fit the need/expectation of the customer. Each requirement inside the process should likewise be able to be *linked* to an external customer requirement (or why is it a requirement?).

Some Requirement Statement Examples

Table 13.1 provides some contrasting examples of poor and effective customer performance standards.

Table 13.1 Requirement Statement Examples

Poorly Written:	Well-Written:
Rapid delivery.	Orders delivered within three working days of Purchase Order receipt. (POs must be received by 3 P.M.)
Treat all patients like family. [This is fine as a guiding principle, but not as a requirement statement.]	• Greet patients within 20 seconds of entry into waiting area. • Address all patients by "Mr." or "Ms." and last name. • Address patients by first name if permission is given by patient. Etc.
Make products easy to assemble and not requiring too much technical expertise.	All model 1200 bicycles able to be assembled by any adult in 15 minutes or less, using only a wrench and screwdriver.
Liberal returns policy.	Any returned item retailing for less than $200 accepted with no questions and with full cash refund.
Simple application.	Application form length maximum of two pages.

Some questions you should ask to test your Requirement Statements are these:

- Does this requirement really reflect what's important to our customers?
- Can we check to see whether and/or how well the requirement has been met?
- Has this been stated so that it's easily understood?

Steps toward Defining Requirements

We can break down the process of clarifying customer requirements into six main steps. (See also the worksheet in the Appendix.)

1. *Identify the Output or Service situation.* This is the key starting point: requirement for *what?*
2. *Identify the customer or customer segment.* Who is going to receive the product or service? The more narrowly you can focus, the easier it usually will be. When thinking of external customers, be sure to differentiate between distributors or supply chain partners and "end users" or consumers.
3. *Review available data on customer needs, expectations, comments, complaints, etc.* Use objective, quantified data, where possible, to define the requirements. Try at all costs not to "guess" what's important to customers, or to base requirements on anecdotal input only.
4. *Draft a Requirement Statement.* This is where you confront the big challenge of translating what customers want into something observable, and defining a clear performance standard. After drafting the statement, test it with other people to make sure it's clear, specific, observable/measurable, easy to understand, and so on.
5. *Validate the requirement.* Validation includes any step you can take to "recheck" the requirement to ensure that it accurately reflects customer needs and expectations. One approach might be to give customers an "example" based on the requirement and then gauge their reaction to it—or, just ask them! Requirement validation may also involve checking with the people in the process who will need to interpret and meet the requirement.
6. *Refine and finalize the requirement statement.* When there's a gap between what customers want and what you can actually *do,* the

challenge is to *negotiate* a requirement that is feasible—or even better, improve the process. After the requirement has been finalized, distribute and/or communicate it, to ensure that everyone is aware of the performance expectations and measurement.

If you end up feeling that your initial Requirement Statements are closer to conjecture than to hard reality, you won't be alone. Vague requirements—due to weak knowledge of the customer or of one's process capabilities—are the rule in many processes. It will take time to build up your understanding and solidify your performance standards. A couple of situational examples will help us to illustrate the issues and effort that go into creating a good Requirement Statement.

Requirements Example #1: Attention to the Customer

In the hotel business, one of the more important factors in customer satisfaction is how attentive and responsive staff are to the needs of their guests. Creating a performance standard along the lines of "Be attentive to customers" is not very helpful. Over the years in evaluating keys to satisfying guests, the hotel industry has developed a way to make "attentiveness" measurable, by defining a service requirement for all chance encounters between a guest and staff member.

Called "10, 5, First and Last," the requirement stipulates that hotel personnel: a) make eye contact with a guest by the time they are ten feet away; b) greet the guest no less than five feet away; and c) be the first person to speak and the last person to speak in the conversation. It may not be perfect for every guest, but this standard is a good reflection of the kind of attention that most customers at a high-quality hotel would want and expect.[5]

Requirements Example #2: Designing Packages

Let's say that you manufacture and market disinfecting solutions for contact lenses. It's especially important that your packages be clear and easy for consumers to read—for their convenience, of course, but also with respect to the safety and marketability of your product. Customer data tells you that contact wearers want to be able to find a product easily and to understand quickly what it does for them. Your first draft of a package design Requirement Statement might be "Easy to Read"—but you know that's not nearly concrete enough to be observed and measured.

In cases like this, you will almost certainly want to test how far away customers stand when they are searching for contact solutions on the shelf. Following that research, your requirement might state: "Labels must be legible by persons with normal 20/20 vision no less than six feet from the package."

Note that this requirement statement does not describe the actual design of the label; we've simply established a performance standard or specification that *any* design should meet. One of the advanced Six Sigma methods covered in Chapter 18, Quality Function Deployment, is commonly used to help balance the tradeoffs and relationships between multiple requirements, particularly in the *design* of products and services.

A variety of other tools and data-organizing techniques can help get you through the sometimes arduous process of distilling various customer inputs into tangible performance standards. An Affinity Diagram, for example, can be used to organize a variety of customer issues or comments into logical groupings, and the latter can help you to pick the meaningful requirements out of a sea of customer feedback data. A Tree Diagram helps to link broad features and satisfaction components to specific characteristics and requirements.

Step 2C: Analyzing and Prioritizing Customer Requirements; Linking Requirements to Strategy

We began this chapter looking at the broad objective of creating an effective system for gathering Voice of the Customer input. We also have examined the more concrete activity of attaching specific performance standards to Outputs and customer encounters. In this final section we review some of the issues—and decisions—that arise as you begin to create a more detailed description of what customers want.

All customer requirements clearly are not created equal, nor will customer reactions to a "defect"—a case where a requirement is not met—be the same for every requirement. We may be upset over having to wait in a long line to check in at the airport gate, but we will certainly be even *more* upset if the plane lands at the wrong airport (hey, it's happened!). Another dimension of defining customer requirements, then, is to categorize and prioritize performance standards and their impact on customer satisfaction. This review can also help your business anticipate how customer expectations will *evolve*—giving you a chance to stay ahead of their needs, and your competitors.

A model being used at a growing number of companies to analyze requirements is based on the work of Noriaki Kano, a Japanese engineer and consultant. In the most common application of "Kano analysis," customer requirements are grouped into three categories:

1. *Dissatisfiers,* or *Basic Requirements.* These are factors, features, or performance standards that customers absolutely expect to be met. If you achieve these, you don't get any "extra credit"; if you miss them, you're guaranteed to have an unhappy customer. When you tune in a TV station and see a picture, you don't say "Wow! Great station!" Getting a picture of some kind is your minimum expectation; you will really judge the station on something more.
2. *Satisfiers,* or *Variable Requirements.* The better or worse you perform on these requirements, the higher or lower will be your "rating" from customers. Price certainly is the most prevalent Satisfier; in most cases, the less expensive the price, the happier the customer. Most day-to-day competition takes place over these factors. Assuming that your organization is meeting the basic needs, many of your process improvement priorities are likely to concentrate on boosting your capacity or performance vis-a-vis these requirements.
3. *Delighters,* or *Latent Requirements.* These are features or factors that go beyond what customers expect, or that target needs no one else has addressed. We could provide you with some examples of delighters, of course, but we don't want to give away any of our big-money ideas. Actually, you can easily come up with your own. If you imagine something that you *wish* a vendor would offer you (delighters don't have to be free, but often they are), most likely you're thinking of a delighter.

There are quite a few nuances to the Kano model, the most important of them being that features or requirements will change categories, sometimes quickly. Meals on coach airline flights, for example, used to be Satisfiers: you expected a meal and rated the airline on the quality and quantity of the food. Now, many people would be delighted just to *get* a meal on a flight.

Most of the time, of course, it works the other way; as customers get used to what they initially view as being "special" or "superior," that requirement moves toward the "Dissatisfier" category. Ford's highly successful Taurus was a hit in part because of many "surprise" features it included. Sales slumped in later years, however, when these once-delighters were dropped to cut costs.

This push to offer more—and the tendency of customers to *expect* more—is one of the major drivers of competition and improvement. As your business develops a more objective and complete picture of customer requirements, you can also apply a concept like Kano analysis to get a better idea of what the various features and capabilities mean in terms of your customers' satisfaction and your competitive edge.

Throughout this chapter, we've been treading *awfully* close to those concepts and analyses that directly impact strategic issues—e.g., target markets and customer value propositions. That shouldn't be a surprise; Six Sigma methods can and should drive strategic decisions—or at least provide information that allows you or other company leaders to make better decisions. It would be premature, however, to begin basing key strategy choices simply on an initial inventory of customer requirements.

First, you should have solid data to gauge how well your processes are delivering those requirements to customers. Using those measures will help you be a better chooser of top-priority improvements for your business, and allow you to begin testing the accuracy of your current company strategies. Applying effective measures is our focus in Chapter 14.

Defining Requirements Dos & Don'ts

Do—Have a broad-based system to collect and use customer and market input.

External data is key to meeting today's customer's needs and to getting new ones—as well as to your ability to see change coming. Tune your ear to the Voice of the Customer!

Do—Pay equal attention to Service and Output requirements.

A company with Six Sigma products but lousy service and customer relations may survive—but only until customers have found an alternative.

Do—Make the effort to create clear, observable, and relevant Requirement Statements.

Even if your requirements are fuzzy at first, the learning—and discipline—that comes through building clear, measurable requirements is essential to really understanding your customers and evaluating your own performance.

Don't—Close your mind to new information on what customers *really* want.

Customer data can bring you messages that contradict what you've always believed. At that point, individuals and companies often go into denial—refusing to accept that their assumptions are wrong or no longer valid. It's okay to question the data, but it isn't okay to ignore *it simply because it conflicts with your assumptions.*

Don't—Hold people suddenly responsible for the newly defined Requirements.

If new insights into customer needs reveal a "gap" between what they want and what you're offering, don't just push people to "do better!" without looking at ways to change the process, too.

Don't—Turn new requirements into new "paradigms."

Be prepared to see customer requirements change—and soon. Plan in reviews and mechanisms to redefine performance standards as new Voice of the Customer data warrants.

Don't—Fail to measure and track performance to requirements.

Gaining a better understanding and definition of customer requirements is an essential prelude to asking the next big question—the topic of Chapter 14—"How well are we meeting *these requirements?"*

CHAPTER

14

Measuring Current Performance

(Roadmap Step 3)

Introduction

The focus of this chapter is *measurement.* We'll spend most of the time reviewing the "nuts and bolts" of understanding and carrying out good measures, but the underlying objective is for you to acquire good data that you can use to plan and track your Six Sigma improvement effort. Unfortunately, you can't do that unless you have some solid measures to start with.

Depending on your purpose, measures can be easy, or a major effort. For example, gathering data on specific problems can be fairly quick: If the data already is available, the gathering may take as little as a few hours. On the other hand, getting enough data to use to comparatively measure core business processes can take weeks or even months of effort. Other than training, measurement is probably the biggest "investment" any organization makes in its Six Sigma initiative. The long-term development of a measurement "infrastructure" however, is a key building block for a full organizational Six Sigma system. The huge benefit is an ability to monitor and respond to change in a way that few organizations can lay claim to today.

Step 3 Overview

Figure 14.1 outlines for you the major tasks in this measurement step, and shows the order in which we'll be reviewing them in this chapter. To recap, key deliverables include:

- Data to assess current performance of your process(es) against customers' Output and/or Service requirements.
- Valid measures derived from the data that identify relative strengths and weaknesses in and between your processes—a key input to good project selection in Step 4.

The techniques covered in the chapter—building as they do on some of the foundational concepts introduced in Chapter 2—may be some of the most vital to the Six Sigma Way. We'll start with a look at some of the foundational concepts of business measures.

Understanding Business Process Measurement

Measurement Concept #1: Observe, then Measure

A lot of people, when facing the mere *thought* of measurement, claim "You can't measure what we do!" Our response is that while it may take

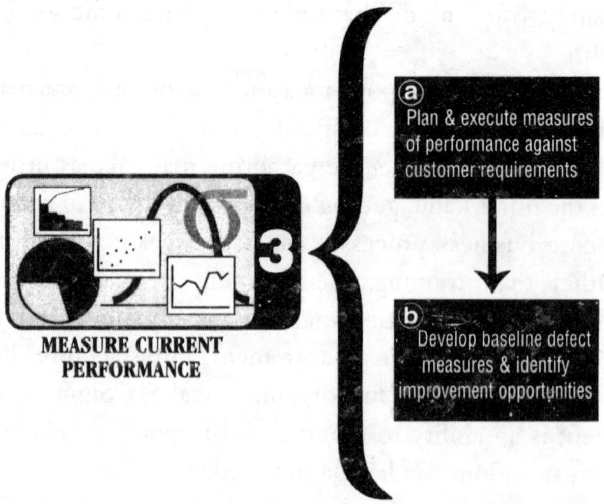

Figure 14.1 Six Sigma Roadmap Step 3 and substeps

a little work, most things that go on in a business *can* be measured. The number-one requirement for measurement is an ability to "observe." In fact "observation" is a technical term in measurement and statistics, referring to an event or a count.

In the previous chapter we introduced a performance standard used in the hotel industry: "10, 5, first and last." (Make eye contact with a guest at 10 feet; greet them at 5 feet; and be the first and last person to speak.) With that clear standard defined, it's fairly easy to observe hotel staff and measure how well this standard is being met. At Loews Hotels, where we learned of this standard, the requirement has become a key to their customer and self-evaluations. Spotters and designated "shoppers" actually roam Loews' hallways and record how they are acknowledged. Gathering specific data on eye contact, greeting distance, and who spoke first and last, the hotel can even break down measures to note which of the four factors is being missed or met most often. Bear in mind, this is a measurement of *attentiveness to customers* in a hotel—one of the seemingly "fuzzier" things you might want to measure.

One of the easiest things to measure—and also one of the most important in today's business world—is time. If you can read a calendar or start and stop a timer, you can gather time-related data. Obviously, dollars are an essential measurable element. Our understanding of how to accurately track costs has been enhanced through better information systems and by paying more attention to Costs of Poor Quality and Activity-Based Costing. The most important step is to get the "thing" being measured boiled down to an objectively observable event or behavior. In the last chapter we introduced the need to make customer requirements observable and measurable, and we'll return to it later when we discuss "operational definitions."

Measurement Concept #2: Continuous versus Discrete Measures

Understanding the difference between "continuous" and "discrete" (or "attribute") measures is important, because it can impact not only how you define your measures but also how you collect data and what you can learn from it. We'll encounter these concepts in sampling and also later, when we look at data analysis and advanced tools.

At times the difference can seem confusing, so we're going to lay down the rule as explicitly as possible:

Continuous measures are only *those factors that can be measured on an infinitely-divisible scale or continuum; e.g., weight, height, time, decibels, temperature, ohms, money.*

A discrete measure is anything else that doesn't fit the criteria for "continuous." Discrete items might include:

- Characteristics or attributes, such as level of education (high school, Bachelor's degree, etc.); or type (for example, an airliner might be a Boeing 737, Boeing 747, or Airbus 300).
- Counts of individual items (e.g., numbers of credit cards, numbers of orders processed).
- Artificial scales, like rating a record from 1 to 5 (good beat, easy to dance to) or describing your level of satisfaction with service.

Discrete measures can appear deceptively continuous, especially counts or attributes that are converted to percentages. For example, gender is a discrete characteristic in most species; an individual will be either female or male (you can add an "undetermined" category if you like). If however you take some gender data and say that a group is 72.3334 percent female, that doesn't make that measure continuous; the source is still discrete. Scaled surveys can also *look* continuous; but again, really they are discrete.

For convenience, continuous measures often are converted into discrete measures, too. For example: Delivery times are recorded as "on-time" or "late" rather than in days and minutes. On car dashboards, oil pressure gauges (continuous) often have given way to warning lights (discrete). But if you don't see a *number* on some kind of measurement *scale* like temperature or time, you know you're dealing with a discrete measure—period. Figure 14.2 provides some examples of common discrete, continuous, and continuous measures, converted to discrete.

Let's now take a look at the *good* side of discrete data:

The Pros of Discrete Measures

- ✦ The most obvious, of course, is that many factors can be defined only as discrete or attribute data. Examples include location (state, city, street); customer type (new or repeat, business versus home user); product number; damaged versus undamaged; etc.

Discrete & Continuous Measure Examples

DISCRETE	CONTINUOUS →	DISCRETE
◆ Number of typographical errors	◆ Hold time per incoming call →	◆ Number of calls on hold past 30 secs
◆ Rating of Service	◆ Average temperature per hour →	◆ Hours with temp over 85 degrees
◆ Units delivered/day	◆ Minutes to board plane →	◆ Delayed boarding incidents
◆ Percent of calls on new service program	◆ Quantity of gas in tank →	◆ Tank Empty/Full
◆ Number of claims in dispute	◆ Width of chip (microns)	◆ Out-of-spec chips
◆ Fill rate (% of on-time, complete deliveries)	◆ Cost per unit →	◆ Units exceeding target cost

Figure 14.2 Measure examples: discrete, continuous and continuous converted to discrete.

- ✦ Intangible factors can often be converted into measurable discrete characteristics. For example, to measure customer perceptions or satisfaction, researchers often use a "rating scale" that is really a discrete measure. If you wanted to gauge the effectiveness of an advertisement, you could ask customers if they recall having seen it. The possible answers—yes, no, not sure—are discrete categories.
- ✦ Generally, it's faster and easier to capture discrete data observations. Noting whether something "is" or "isn't" can be done more quickly (and less intrusively) than measuring it on a scale.
- ✦ One of the most important observations that we all make in the course of Six Sigma and business process improvement—a defect—is a discrete factor. Thus if you're going to reduce defects, you're going to impact a discrete measure.

The Cons of Discrete Measures

Discrete measures do, unfortunately, have their drawbacks too. When you have a choice and can afford the time, resources, and possible disruption, you'll want to capture continuous data whenever possible:

- ✦ You have to make more observations—i.e. do more measuring—with discrete data to get valid information. And the closer your performance is to "perfect," the more items you need to count to get accurate data since defects become so rare. Some statisticians note that continuous data can be accurate with a "sample" of just 200 items, no matter how high the volume of the process or how few the number of defects.[1] So discrete data can be more expensive to collect. (More later in the chapter, on determining sample size.)

- Discrete measures can "bury" important information. If you're coaching a team and you note whether players' weight is "acceptable" or "too heavy," it'll be hard to analyze later. How *much* overweight are they? What kinds of changes might get the results you need? It's a longer road to a more svelte team without specific, continuous measures. (And we haven't even considered if a player might be too *light*. . . .)
- Statistically speaking, you can do many more potentially useful forms of analysis with continuous data versus discrete. Many of the more advanced Six Sigma techniques, for example, are usable only with continuous measures.

All this is not to say that you shouldn't use discrete data. As noted, in many cases you won't have a choice; in others, you may not have the resources or capability to "go continuous." Fortunately, as we'll see a bit later, there are plenty of tools on hand to help you use discrete data when that's all you have.

Measurement Concept #3: Measure for a Reason

Measurement consumes resources, attention, and energy, and that means you don't want to perform any measures you don't *have* to. Unless there's a clear purpose to the measure—a key question you need to answer, or factor you want to track—it may not be valuable or relevant.

You can ensure a better choice and balance of measures when you keep in mind the different categories that are available to you. Next we look at two ways to define measures.

Predictor and Results Measures

We have noted the tenet of Six Sigma measurement that is all about understanding relationships between changes in upstream factors (Xs) (suppliers, raw materials, processes, procedures) and their impact on customer satisfaction, loyalty, and profitability (Ys). Another way to describe the X-Y concept (using more common language) is to consider the following two measure categories.

- *Predictors.* Similar to Xs, predictors are factors we can measure to forecast or anticipate events downstream in the process. For example, if we see an increase in cycle time in ordering raw materials, we might *predict* an increase in late deliveries.
- *Results.* These are similar to "Ys" in focusing on the outcomes of the process. Results can be immediate (e.g., on-time delivery) or longer-term (e.g., customer retention).

Efficiency and Effectiveness Measures

This approach to categorizing measures looks closely at who gets the immediate benefit from the performance: you, the customer, or both.

- *Efficiency.* These measures track the volume of resources consumed in producing products and services. More efficient processes use less money, time, materials, etc. Efficiency has a significant bearing on the budget performance of your organization, and eventually on profitability. But though you might pass along efficiency improvements to customers through lower prices, it's primarily an internally-focused measurement.
- *Effectiveness.* On the other hand, effectiveness looks at your work through the eyes of customers: How closely did you meet their needs and requirements? What defects did they receive? How happy and loyal have they become, based on your performance?

In a full-blown organizational measurement system, you should have a mix of all types: Predictors and Results, Efficiency and Effectiveness. A traditional business "blind spot" has been to look only at Results measures. In improvement efforts, the temptation is to boost Efficiency (with its quick potential bottom-line impact), without sufficient regard for how that will impact Effectiveness in delivering value to customers.

Measurement Concept #4: A Process for Measurement

Measures can and should be continuously improved, just as you would "regular" work processes. The basic steps for implementing any measure are pretty straightforward, as you can see in Fig. 14.3. What follows is an overview of some of the key questions/actions you should ask/take at each of these measurement steps.

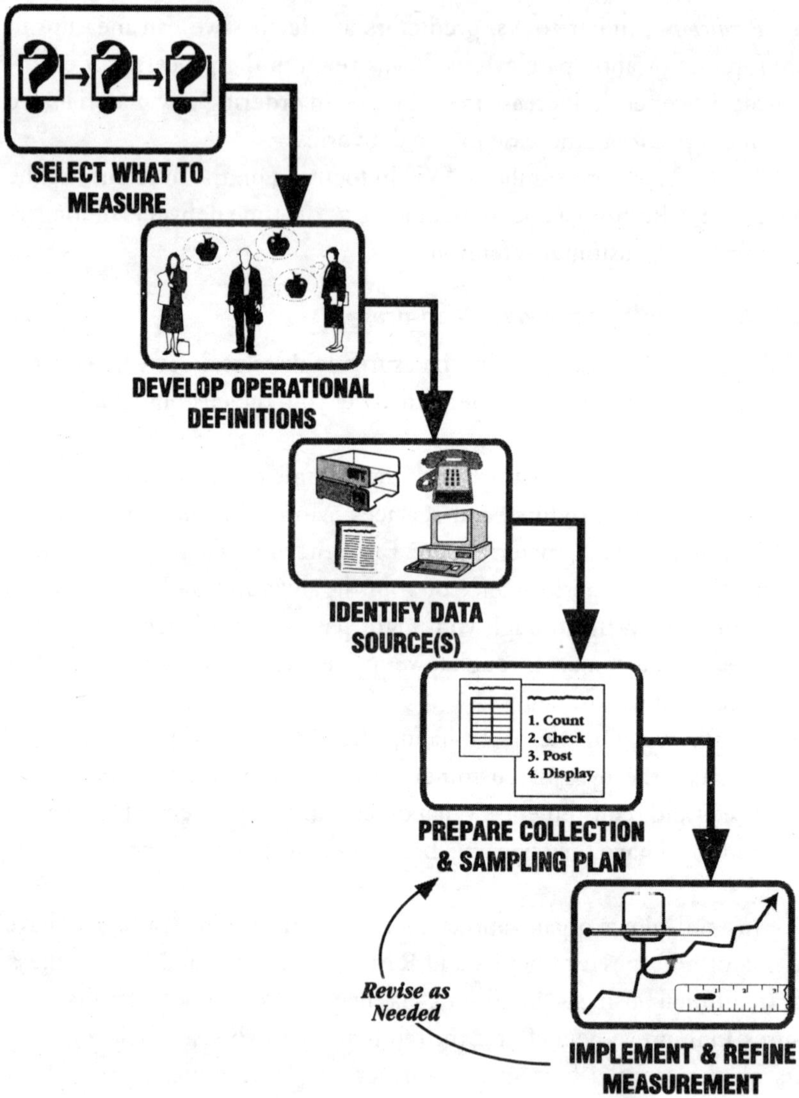

Figure 14.3 A five-step measurement implementation model

- *Select what to measure.* What key questions are we trying to answer? What data will give us the answer? What Output or Service requirement(s) will best help us gauge performance to customer needs? What "upstream" factors might help alert us to problems later on? How will we display, analyze, and/or use the measure?

- *Develop operational definitions.* How can we clearly describe the factor/thing we're trying to track or count? If different people gather the data, will they interpret things in the same way? How can we test our definitions to make sure they're air-tight?
- *Identify data source.* Where can we find or observe data to provide the measure? Is past experience (or "historical" data) valid? Is the data in our information systems accessible and in a useable format? Can we afford (the time, money, disruption) to gather new data?
- *Prepare a collection and sampling plan.* Who will gather and/or compile the data? What forms or tools will they need to capture and organize the data? What other information will we need to be able to analyze the data effectively? How many observations or items will we need to count to get an accurate measure? How often will we need to do measures? How can we best ensure that the data we get are representative?
- *Implement and refine measurement.* Can we test out our measures before going into full-fledged implementation? How will we train the data collectors? How will we monitor the data gathering? What issues may arise (or have arisen), and what can we do about them? What will we change next time?

In the remainder of this chapter we'll cover some of the most important steps and concepts associated with this Measurement Process, to help you select and execute your measures more smoothly. As we do so we'll concentrate on the first priority of an initial Six Sigma effort: evaluating the company's success in meeting customer requirements.

Measuring Rare or Low-Volume Activities

Airliner crashes, fortunately, are quite rare. Then too, the "measures" that have been gathered on them have taken many years to collect. But imagine if a plane were to crash tomorrow and no past data existed. You certainly wouldn't expect officials to say: "We're going to have to let a few more planes crash, so we can get enough data-points to start our investigation."

That comment, however, isn't all that different from the excuse we're always hearing: "This happens too rarely for us to measure it." For if you never *try* to gather data from your process, of course you won't learn much.

Part of the problem here is the exclusive emphasis on *quantitative* data. It's true that rare events or low-volume operations offer less opportunity for numbers-based measures. But it's a mistake to believe that acquiring quantitative data is the only worthy objective. Asking questions and getting factual information, even on a rare or one-time event, is still critical. And although statisticians will rightly assert that there's a danger to drawing conclusions from one-time events—hey, you have to play the cards you're dealt.

Remember, too, that gathering facts is the starting point for measurement. Over time, isolated facts can become meaningful measures.

Step 3A. Plan and Measure Performance against Customer Requirements

Select What to Measure

In an ideal world you would be beginning this measurement fully equipped with a complete description of how customers evaluate your service and/or products. If your Voice of the Customer data and Requirements are not yet very sophisticated, you can still start measurement, but with a somewhat greater risk of using measures that don't pan out.

Selecting just your optimal performance measures (because you can't measure everything) means balancing two major elements: 1) what's *feasible,* and 2) what's most useful or *valuable.* If you've been able to prioritize customer requirements, you have a good starting point for determining value. Areas in which you suspect there are performance gaps can also be good places to begin measures. Figure 14.4 provides you with a partial list of criteria to consider—in the Feasibility and Value categories—as you choose what to measure.

Develop Operational Definitions

If we asked you and a friend to run outside right now (first being sure to bookmark this page) and count all the red cars you see—but not to talk to one another—how similar would your answers be? We think it's likely they would be fairly different, for some of the following reasons:

Criteria for Selecting Measures	
Value/Usefulness	Feasibility
• Link to high-priority customer requirements • Accuracy of data • Area of concern or potential opportunity • Can be benchmarked to other organizations • Can be helpful on-going measure	• Availability of data • Lead time required • Cost of getting data • Complexity • Likely resistance or "fear factor"

Figure 14.4 Measurement selection criteria

- What do you do about pick-ups and SUVs? Are they "cars"? (They seem to outnumber "cars" these days.)
- What is "red?" Some cars that you consider to be red your friend might call "rust" (not *really* red).
- Are you to count only moving vehicles, or parked ones as well? Any variation in that choice is sure to affect the numbers a lot.
- If you jumped in your car (or pickup or SUV) and drove around *looking* for red whatevers, you obviously would get a very different count. (And we didn't say you had to stick together!)

As that example illustrates, one of the biggest pitfalls associated with the quest for effective business process measurement is the failure to create good "Operational Definitions"—and the data collection procedures to go with them. By Operational Definition we mean a clear, understandable, and unambiguous description of what's to be measured or observed, so that everyone can operate, or measure, consistently on the basis of definition.

Here's a real-world example for you of the challenge posed by trying to measure without good "Op Defs." We were working with the publicity group of a large company, which was holding a major press event. The goal was to improve the processes of setting up and managing the event, so as to increase the probability of favorable press coverage. The client decided (at the last minute) to track questions posed to speakers on a variety of factors—for example, "tone" (positive, neutral, or negative) and "topic"—and then to track the answers to the questions. Two or three people were assigned to record the data, using a "checksheet" form with 30 or so options to choose from.

The results, as you might imagine, were more than a bit of a mess. Even the number of questions counted by the data collectors differed, since the reporters often linked several questions together. Defining the "tone" of a question was pretty subjective, and recording the content of answers was a hit-or-miss proposition. Fortunately, the data gathering was not a total loss; enough broad trends were observable that some benefits were indeed gleaned through this tracking of questions and answers. The client learned a valuable lesson about the process (we found that executives ended up answering many more questions in informal hallway conversations than in the press conference per se) and about realistic objectives for measurement. But the "hard data" wasn't really useable, and future measurement activities clearly would demand much tighter Operational Definitions if they were to get some solid quantitative input.

Misunderstood measurement definitions can even have drastic consequences. It was a shock to the U.S. space exploration program when the Mars Polar Orbiter was incinerated in the Martian atmosphere in September 1999. It turned out that the spacecraft flew too low because one group of engineers had calculated course instructions in pounds-per-second, while a computer interpreted the data in *grams*-per-second. As Six Sigma experts might say: "Oops!"

When you're creating Operational Definitions for your measures, there's simply no substitute for focused work and a close scrutiny of your chosen terms.

Identify Data Sources

There are many possible sources of data in an organization. Your most important considerations are to ensure that the source you choose—or can get a hold of—has accurate data and represents the process, product, or service you want to measure. Ideally, you target measures for which there are good sources.

We will venture to offer just a few tips on a very common source of data: the people working in the process. While many managers or teams starting out on measurement these days expect to get data from information systems, it frequently turns out that what you really need to know isn't captured by the system. Or if it is, it can require a lot of work to extract it from other data. A better option in these cases is to gather data manually, from the people and the process. But when you rely on people as your data source, especially individuals measuring their own work, there are obvious risks. Inattention and human error are most common; suspicion and paranoia are forces to be respected and reckoned with, too. If you keep the following pieces of advice in mind, you will ensure that your data are complete and accurate:

- Explain clearly why you're gathering the data.
- Describe what you plan to do with the data—including your plans to share findings with the collectors, keep individuals' identities confidential, and so on.
- Be careful whom you choose to participate; avoid making data collection either a reward or a punishment.
- Make the process as easy as it can be.
- Give data collectors the opportunity to provide input on the data collection process.

Prepare a Collection and Sampling Plan

The ins and outs of executing measures could fill an entire book (can you say "sequel"?), so we'll limit our overview of this step to three major elements: forms, stratification, and sampling.

Data Collection Forms

Well-designed spreadsheets and "checksheets" are the workhorses of data gathering. And while there are some standard types of forms, you really should tailor each form to fit the actual data collection you're going to do. The following guidelines will help you to create a data collection form:

- *Keep it simple.* This will affect how much data you effectively capture. If it's hard to read or crowded, there's a risk of mistakes or noncompliance.
- *Label it well.* Make sure there are no questions as to what piece of data "belongs" where.
- *Include space for date (and time) and collector's name.* These obvious things tend to get left off, causing headaches later.

- *Organize the data collection form and the compiling sheet (the form or spreadsheet you'll use to pull together the data) consistently.* If these two work together, it can make entering raw data much easier and much less prone to mistakes.
- *Include key factors to stratify the data.* More on this in a moment.

Some common types of checksheets include the following:

Defect or Cause Checksheet. Used to record types of defects or causes of defects. *Examples:* reasons for field repair calls; types of operating-log discrepancies; causes of late shipments.

Data Sheet. Captures readings, measures, or counts quantities. *Examples:* transmitter power level; number of people in line; temperature.

Frequency Plot Checksheet. Records a characteristic of an item along a counted scale or continuum. *Examples:* gross income of applicants for a loan; cycle time from order to shipment for each order; weight of a package.

Concentration Diagram Checksheet. Features a picture of the item or document being observed; data collectors then mark where problems, defects, or damage are seen on the item. Examples: damage diagram used by car rental agencies; noting errors on invoices.

Traveler Checksheet. A "traveler" is any kind of checksheet that "moves" with the product or service through the process. Data about that item then are recorded in appropriate places on the form (see Fig. 14.5). *Examples:* capturing cycle-time data for each step of an Engineering Change Order; noting number of people handling a part as it moves through an assembly facility; tracking rework on an insurance claim.

That mention of the "Traveler" checksheet gives us a good opportunity to point out an important factor in collecting data: In process measures, you usually will want to gather various pieces of information about *one thing at a time* as it moves through the process. The temptation can be to grab a bunch of items (parts, forms, orders) at Point A in the process and record data about them, then move to Point B in the process, grab another bunch and record data about *them.* The problem

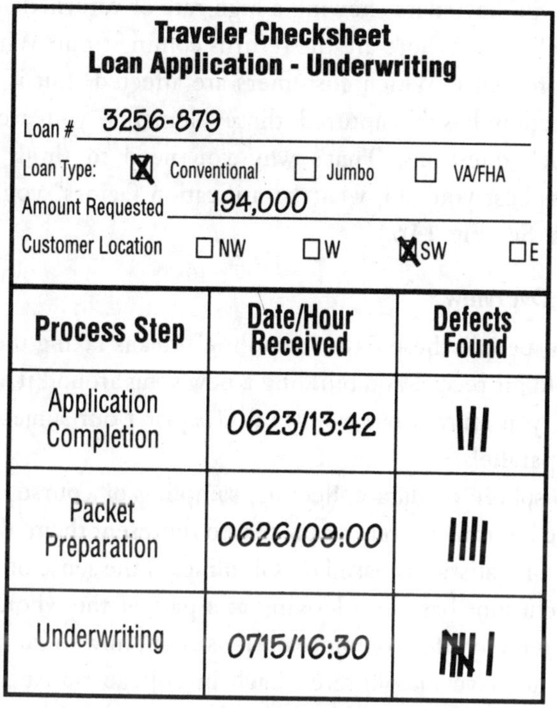

Traveler Checksheet
Loan Application - Underwriting

Loan # 3256-879

Loan Type: ☒ Conventional ☐ Jumbo ☐ VA/FHA

Amount Requested 194,000

Customer Location ☐ NW ☐ W ☒ SW ☐ E

Process Step	Date/Hour Received	Defects Found
Application Completion	0623/13:42	III
Packet Preparation	0626/09:00	IIII
Underwriting	0715/16:30	~~IIII~~ I

Figure 14.5 Example: "traveler" checksheet

is, the items you count at Point B may not be related to those counted at Point A. This issue becomes especially critical when you're trying to identify root causes or determine the impact of upstream variables (predictors or Xs) on downstream results (Ys).

A traveler is one good way of ensuring that you have data that can be correlated at each step in the process.

Stratification

Getting a baseline measure of performance against customer requirements is a key objective in Step 3 of the Six Sigma Roadmap. At some point, however, you are likely to want to know more about that data, and that's where stratification comes in. The word itself denotes layers (or "strata") of data; we prefer to equate it to "slicing and dicing" your measures. Stratification helps you to exercise your curiosity and to clarify what's really happening. If for example, you make computer systems, and you have data showing a high rate of returned systems, you will naturally ask: Where are the returns coming from? Which systems have the problems? Which customers are affected? But if your initial data collection hasn't captured those elements, you aren't able to answer such questions. That's why you need to think through in advance, as best you can, what "stratification factors" you're likely to need later. (See Fig. 14.6.)

Sampling Overview

To a lot of people these days, "sampling" means taking the guitar lick from an old hit record and building a new song around it. (If you have teenagers, you know what we mean). *That* isn't our subject here—but there are parallels.

In the sphere of data collecting, sampling of course means using *some* of the items in a group or process to represent them *all*. The entire discipline of statistics is based on sampling, in the sense of an ability to draw conclusions based on looking at a part of the whole. Six Sigma measures tend to offer you more options about how to sample than you are likely to have encountered back in college statistics courses. If

Data Stratification

Factors	Examples (Slice the data by . . .)
Who	◆ Department ◆ Individual ◆ Customer type
What	◆ Type of complaint ◆ Defect category ◆ Reason for incoming call
When	◆ Month, quarter ◆ Day of week ◆ Time of day
Where	◆ Region ◆ City ◆ Specific location on product *(top right corner, on/off switch, etc.)*

Figure 14.6 Measurement and data stratification factors

you're going to understand why, we need to briefly explain the distinction between population statistics and process statistics:

- *Population statistics.* Most "textbook" statistics courses focus on various methods of sampling and testing relationships between two or more groups—consumers, companies, products, voters, baseball teams, etc. Population sampling is like dipping into a standing pool of water: As long as we know that the water in the dipper is like the rest of the water, we can rest easy that we have a good sample.
- *Process statistics.* Business measures often pose a different challenge, for here, taking a sample from a process is like testing a running stream of water. Besides having fewer frogs, a stream is different from a pool or pond because it's changing from moment to moment. The sample I'm taking at one moment could be different from the one I may take a few moments later. And it could be different again a few moments later. Things in the stream that may change include water temperature, oxygen content, number of fish, rate of flow, etc. Then too, if two of us took samples at the same time but at different places in the stream, they would likely be different as well.

It's possible to do either kind of sampling—population or process—in a business environment. When you draw data from a group of people or items that are just "sitting there"—including a pool of items in a process—you can consider it a population sample. If however you are trying to track changes over time in order to understand the degree and type of variation in the process, you require a process sample. Table 14.1 provides some comparative examples of both types.

Getting a *valid* sample—one that represents the whole—can be a significant challenge in either case. The science (sometimes art) of sampling is a big topic. Thus our goal in the next few pages is just to give you some background and a few rough steps, so you will understand the kinds of decisions that go into devising a sampling plan. Even after in-depth instruction it can still be challenging, so we recommend you consult an expert before you start collecting a lot of data, if your situation looks complicated.

Table 14.1 Some Examples of Population Sampling and Process Sampling

Population Sampling:	Process Sampling:
• Tallying the average loan amount from a group of applications.	• Capturing the average loan amounts requested, by day, week, month
• Recording the age of all parts of inventory currently in stock.	• Tracking the average age of parts inventory by week.
• Conducting a survey of customer perceptions.	• Polling every tenth customer on his/her service experience each day.
• Compiling the reasons for inbound calls among all calls over the past six months.	• Recording inbound call volume every quarter-hour.

Let's turn now to a hypothetical scenario, as a way of introducing some of the key concepts of sampling. Watch for the terms in italics; we'll review them below.

A Sampling Story: Pivotal Logistics

At Pivotal Logistics—a company that provides warehousing and distribution services to a variety of parts and raw-materials firms—a Process Management team was working on an apparent issue with errors in incoming Bills of Lading. Somehow, the paper documents accompanying shipments seemed to have different data from that shown in the logistics tracking system. If true, the problem would create inventory inaccuracies, mis-billings, and a variety of other defects directly impacting Pivotal's customers.

So they could understand the extent and impact of the possible paperwork discrepancies, the group wanted to capture data about the Bills of Lading from the receiving process. With more than 1500 deliveries per day, however, it would be impossible to check every shipment. On the other hand the process team was concerned about avoiding *bias* in the data. For example, if they gathered data from only a few key customers, that might not reflect what was really happening with the paperwork. Or if they took information at the wrong time, that might affect the accuracy of the results. "What we need," said Process Owner Les Lomas, "is a good sampling plan."

As the group sought to come up with a plan to collect a good, representative sample, it considered the following options:

1. *Having Dock Clerks take a look at delivered shipments when they are less busy.* This seemed like a good way to avoid having the measurement disrupt the work and frustrate people in the warehouse. But as Monty Vista, the IT member of the process team, noted, "That's no good—it's a *convenience* sample!"
2. *Picking the shipments that seemed to most resemble the traffic for a particular day.* That would mean that Dock Clerks would take a look at the day's schedule and select a few deliveries that represented the mix for the day. It was Mark De la Salle of the Scheduling group who objected: "How can they make that kind of *judgment* and still get us an accurate sample?"
3. *Having the Dock Clerks check every-so-many deliveries for Bill of Lading defects.* "Now *this* makes more sense," said Les Lomas. "It's a lot more *systematic,* and it seems to me like we can have more *confidence* in the results."

"Isn't it better," asked De la Salle, "to do a *random* sample?"

"I think we'd have a tough time doing this randomly," Lomas answered. "There's no way to pick the shipments without some guesswork, and this way we can keep the data in sequence so we can see if there are patterns during the day."

The Pivotal group felt like they were getting closer to a decent plan for sampling—but there was still some work to be done. . . .

Key Sampling Concepts

As the Pivotal Logistics group has noted so far, there are better and worse ways to sample. Some of the issues they've encountered have included the following:

- *Bias.* This is the iceberg in the shipping lanes of sampling. Having a biased sample means that your data isn't completely valid and that any conclusions you draw from it are likely to be wrong. There will always be some bias; the trick is to keep it to a minimum.
- *Convenience sampling.* Collecting the items that are easiest to get isn't just lazy, it's also a good way to *create* bias in your data. (As the

Church Lady used to say on *Saturday Night Live,* "How conVEEE-nient!").

- *Judgment sampling.* Almost as bad—though it may seem better—is to try to make "educated guesses" about which items or people are representative. Your guess is itself a bias.
- *Systematic sampling.* This is the method recommended for many business measurement activities. In a process, this might mean taking samples at certain intervals (every half-hour; every twentieth item). A systematic population example would be to check every tenth record in a database. The caveat with systematic sampling is to make sure the frequency of sampling doesn't correspond to some pattern that will bias the data.
- *Random sampling.* We've all heard that this is best, but in the real world it's harder than you might think to be *truly* random. Most business applications of random sampling involve computer-based random selections.

Some other relevant sampling concepts include the following:

- *Stratified sampling.* Stratifying your sample helps to ensure that all key groups are represented in the data. If Pivotal Logistics has two major types of shipment, they may want to sample each separately, to ensure adequate data for each.
- *Confidence level.* This term refers to the issue of how certain you want to be that the data you gather and the conclusions you draw reflect the population or process, aka "reality". Confidence usually is expressed in percentages, and a 95 percent confidence level is pretty standard in business process measures.
- *Precision.* The accuracy of the measure you plan to do. This actually links to the type of scale or amount of detail of your operational definition, but it can have an impact on your sample size, too. For example, if you want to measure cycle times down to the second, you will need to ensure that your timer is especially accurate.

Sampling Prerequisites

There's a "Catch-22" to developing a solid sampling plan: You have to *know something* about the data you're gathering. As a result, early measures often are less reliable because they're based on a "best-guess" sampling plan.

The more you measure, and the better you get to know the characteristics of what you're measuring, the better your sample decisions can be.

Here are some of the things you're likely to need to know:

- Is this a continuous or discrete measure?
- If it's continuous, what's the degree of variation (standard deviation) of the process?
- If it's discrete, how often does the thing we're looking for (usually the "proportion defective" in the population or process) occur?
- How many items move through the process each day? Each week? *Or:* How large is the total population?
- What confidence level do we hope to reach through our measure?
- For continuous data, what's the desired precision of our measure?

Other important terms/concepts in sampling are shown in Table 14.2.

Remember that getting your sample will often involve guesswork at the start (until you get some early readings of the data), and unfortunately will be impacted by the feasibility of getting at the things you want to observe. Overall, keep in mind the rule of thumb that (as long as you don't bias your data) the larger your sample, the better your accuracy.

Implement and Refine Measurement

You're always better off if you can run a test of your data collection so as to ensure that forms, sampling plans, and definitions work as

Table 14.2 Other Important Terms in Sampling

TERM	DEFINITION
Sampling Event	The act of extracting items from the process or population to be measured.
Subgroup	The number of consecutive units extracted for measurement at each sampling event. A subgroup can be just one item, or several.
Sampling Frequency	The number of times per day or week a sample is taken; sampling events per period of time. Sampling frequency tends to increase as the number of cycles or changes in a process increase.

planned. If you can't do a trial of the data collection, at least pay careful attention to how it works as you begin to gather the data. If you plan to use many different people to gather or compile data, some kind of training, whether formal or informal, is going to be essential.

Testing Measurement Accuracy and Value

There are various ways to check how accurate your measures are—and to ensure that they're staying accurate. In the manufacturing arena, the most common test of the effectiveness of a measure is known as "Gage R&R." It involves repeating a measure in various environments to test against four important criteria:

1. *Accuracy.* How precise is the measurement or observation?
2. *Repeatability.* If one person or piece of measuring equipment measures or observes the same item more than once, will s/he or it get the same results each time?
3. *Reproducibility.* If two or more people or machines measure the same thing, will they get the same results?
4. *Stability.* Over time, will accuracy or repeatability deteriorate or shift?

While Gage R&R is most commonly done with continuous data measures—and often with measurement instruments (e.g. scales, meters,—similar methods can be used to test discrete data measures. Some form of measurement accuracy check can be used as a test before you implement a measure and as a check if you gather the data over a long period of time.

Step 3B: Develop Baseline Defect Measures and Identify Improvement Opportunities

The tools and methods of data collection are important in any type of business process measurement. At this point on the Six Sigma Roadmap, though, our objective is simply to establish performance "baselines"—to determine how well processes are working *today*—so that we can focus and measure improvement. We'll look first at Output measures, then at measures that take into account internal performance.

Output Performance Measures

As we discussed in Chapter 2, Six Sigma measurement focuses on tracking—and reducing—*defects* in a process. In this review of comparative measurement, we'll again pick up the theme of defect measures and explain the various options and concepts you should be aware of as you go about choosing and implementing your own. The use of defect-related measures has several advantages:

1. *Simplicity.* Everyone can understand "good" and "bad." The calculations of the various types of defect-based measures can be made with just basic math skills.
2. *Consistency.* Defect measures can be applied to any process for which there is a performance standard or requirement, whether for continuous or discrete data, or a Manufacturing or Service process.
3. *Comparability.* Motorola used Six Sigma measures to track rates of improvement on processes of all types, and to compare the performance of efforts in very different areas of the business.

There are some drawbacks to defect measures, too. For one thing, by looking *only* at good and bad, they may hide key information or subtleties in the data—especially with continuous data measures. Our purpose here, however, is to help you build a foundation for measurement that can then be used as a base for evaluating the overall effectiveness of a process. When we get into data analysis in Chapter 15, we'll look at other measurement methods that can provide a more detailed picture of process performance and help you to determine root causes.

Key Concepts of Defect-Based Measurement

A few simple terms need to be reviewed or clarified if we are going to understand defect measures:

- *Unit.* An item being processed, or the final product or service being delivered to the customer—a car, a mortgage loan, a hotel stay, a bank statement, etc.
- *Defect.* A failure to meet a customer requirement/performance standard—a leaky crankcase, a delay in closing the mortgage loan, a lost reservation, a statement error, etc.

- *Defective.* Any unit that contains a defect. Hence, a car with any defect is, technically, just as "defective" as a car with 15 defects.
- *Defect opportunity.* Since most products or services have multiple customer requirements, there can be several chances or opportunities to have a defect. The number of defect opportunities on a car, for example, might be well more than 100.

One final essential: Remember that your data has to include information on performance against customer requirements. Thus if a key requirement is "on-time delivery," and your data captures only "cost per order," you will need to get more data.

Defective and Yield Measures

We'll start with measures that focus on "defectives"—units that contain one defect or ten. Defective measures are especially important in businesses or with products for which *any* defect is serious. For example, any

Proportion Defective

Formula: $\dfrac{\text{Number of Defectives}}{\text{Number of Units}}$

Service Examples:

- 43 of 250 loan applications contain defects

$$\frac{\textbf{43 defectives}}{\textbf{250 units}} = .172 \text{ (or 17.2\% defective)}$$

- 66 of 186 advertising contracts contain defects

$$\frac{\textbf{66 defectives}}{\textbf{186 units}} = .354 \text{ (or 35.4\% defective)}$$

Manufacturing Examples:

- 97 of 750 microchips contain defects

$$\frac{\textbf{97 defectives}}{\textbf{750 units}} = .129 \text{ (or 12.9\% defective)}$$

- 99 of 1150 steel joists contain defects

$$\frac{\textbf{99 defectives}}{\textbf{1150 units}} = .086 \text{ (or 8.6\% defective)}$$

Figure 14.7 Formula and examples: Proportion Defective

typographical error in a magazine ad is going to hurt its credibility. Or any flaw in the stitching of a dress will make it unsellable at full price.

The following are two measurement expressions for Defectives:

- *Proportion Defective.* This refers to the fraction or percentage of item samples that had one or more defects. The formula for, and some examples of, Proportion Defective are shown in Fig. 14.7. We'll use these same examples for each type of defect measure.
- *Final Yield* (noted as Y_{final}). This is calculated as 1 *minus* the Proportion Defective. It tells you what fraction of the total units produced and/or delivered was defect-free. (Multiplying Final Yield by 100 gives you the percentage "good".) (See Fig. 14.8.)

Defect Measures

Defects per Unit, or *DPU.* This measure reflects the average number of defects, of all types, over the *total* number of units sampled. (See the

Final Yield

Formula: 1 - Proportion Defective

Service Examples:

- 43 of 250 loan applications contain defects

  1 - .172 = .828 or 82.8% Yield

- 66 of 186 advertising contracts contain defects

  1 - .354 = .646 or 64.6% Yield

Manufacturing Examples:

- 97 of 750 microchips contain defects

  1 - .129 = .871 or 87.1% Yield

- 99 of 1150 steel joists contain defects

  1 - .086 = .914 or 91.4% Yield

Figure 14.8 Formula and examples: Final Yield

formula and examples in Fig. 14.9.) If you calculated a DPU of 1.0, for example, it would indicate a likelihood that every unit will have one defect—though some items may have more than one, and others, no defects. A DPU of .25 shows a probability that one in four units will have a defect.

These first three measures help you to see both how well or poorly your process is performing, and how defects are distributed in your work efforts.

Determining Defect Opportunities

One of the innovations of Six Sigma measurement noted in Chapter 2 is to adjust measures according to the complexity or number of "opportunities" for defects. The purpose is to level the playing field, so that a complex service or product can be compared in performance to a simpler one. First we'll look at the steps to get to opportunity-based measures, then at how these measures can be expressed. .

Defects/Unit or DPU

Formula: $\frac{\text{Number of Defects}}{\text{Number of Units}}$

Service Examples:

- 52 defects on 250 loan applications (43 defective)

  $\frac{\text{52 defects}}{\text{250 applications}}$ = .208 (or 20.8%) DPU

- 321 defects on 186 advertising contracts (66 defective)

  $\frac{\text{321 defects}}{\text{186 contracts}}$ = 1.73 (or 172%) DPU

Manufacturing Examples:

- 99 defects on 750 microchips (97 defective)

  $\frac{\text{99 defects}}{\text{750 microchips}}$ = .132 (or 13.2%) DPU

- 233 defects on 1150 steel joists (99 defective)

  $\frac{\text{233 defects}}{\text{1150 joists}}$ = .202 (or 20.2%) DPU

Figure 14.9 Formula and examples: Defects per Unit or DPU

To judge by looking at a coffee mug, it isn't a terribly complicated product. But open up a couple's mortgage application for the new home they hope to buy and—though it's apples-and-oranges-different from the mug—it's easy to tell it's a lot more complicated. And even if the calculator in your briefcase is harder to peer inside, chances are it's more complex than the mortgage application. Thus in Six Sigma measures, the word *complex* translates into more opportunities for defects. The challenge is to identify a realistic number of defect opportunities for each product or service. In many cases it's a judgment call, but we can identify three main steps in defining the number of opportunities:

1. *Develop a preliminary list of defect types.* Let's take the coffee mug as our example here (we'll look at a service example in a moment). How many types of defects might there be? Here's an initial list of possibilities:

   - Leaks
   - Glazing/finish blemishes
   - Misshapen container
   - Misshapen handle
   - Broken

2. *Determine which are the actual, customer-critical, specific defects.* We could just make do with our first list, and say that there are five defect opportunities, period. But there may be defects that actually never happen, or that are simply two types of the same defect. So it's a good idea to scrutinize your first draft list. Also, as we'll see when we calculate Sigma measures, including more opportunities will make our *Sigma performance look better.* Being of high integrity, we don't want to "pad" our opportunities just to boost our score; plus, painting an overpositive picture initially would make it harder to show improvement later. With that attitude, and a little common sense, we propose defining just three opportunities for error on a mug, as follows:

   - Glazing/finish blemishes
   - Misshapen (container or handle)
   - Broken

   We've taken out Leaks, because they are so rare that it's not a realistic consideration in terms of day-to-day measuring of our performance. And it's simple, and also realistic, to consider all malformed mugs as falling under one opportunity.

Of course, it wouldn't have been *wrong* to say that there are five opportunities. In defining the number of opportunities, there's a range of "right" answers. We suggest you adopt such criteria as reasonable, realistic, practical, and most importantly *consistent,* when you're determining numbers of opportunities.

3. *Check the proposed number of opportunities against other standards.* If your company makes coffee mugs, over time there most likely would emerge guidelines or conventions for number of coffee-mug opportunities. Motorola, as noted earlier, had a committee set standards for opportunity calculation, so that they could be sure of a consistent comparison of processes.

Having walked through opportunity-counting for coffee mugs, let's take another example: that all-important document, the Invoice. Each keystroke in a document like an invoice could technically be considered a defect opportunity, but to count each one would be neither practical nor consistent. Also, some parts of an invoice will be standard or done from a template, since those will be fixed. We want our search for defects to focus on elements of the invoice that change each time one is issued.

On a generic invoice, you *could* have as many as 17 opportunities, if not more, including:

- Customer name
- Contact name
- Customer address: street and number, city, state, zip code, mail stop
- Account or customer number
- Purchase order number
- Items ordered
- Quantity ordered
- Unit price
- Discounts
- Total price
- Tax
- Shipping costs

- Payment due date
- Remittance address
- Printing errors
- Folding/stuffing errors
- Timeliness

This, arguably, is too long a list. It would be a challenge to track each defect type individually. Also, as we've noted, having many opportunities would make for a too-good-looking Sigma score. So another option might be *four* opportunities, as follows:

1. Customer data (including name, address and P.O. number)
2. Order information (items, quantity, ship-to address)
3. Pricing (unit price, discounts, taxes, etc.)
4. Production (print quality)

So, trimming down from a starting total of 17 defect types, we could arrive at just *four* opportunities. But in fact, as long as we're consistent and our reasoning is sound, either of these numbers—or something in between—could work.

Really complex products can have many more opportunities. An example done at Texas Instruments in the early 1990s for an electronic component shows over 4000 opportunities—understandable, when you think of the numbers of individual items (each of which can have defects) and requirements for such a complex piece of equipment.

We can summarize by giving you some guidelines for figuring opportunities for your products or services:

- *Focus on "standard" problem areas.* Defects that are rare shouldn't be considered opportunities.
- *Group closely related defects into one opportunity.* This both simplifies your work and ensures against any inflating of opportunities.
- *Make sure the defect is important to the customer.* If you've focused on validated requirements/performance standards, this will be easier.
- *Be consistent.* If your business plans to use opportunity-based measures, you should consider setting standards for defining opportunities.
- *Change only when needed.* Each time you change the number of opportunities, you shift the denominator for your Sigma measure—

meaning that your comparison with earlier results is less valid. You should change the rules only when really necessary.

Some organizations we've worked with—for example, an aerospace parts logistics group and an equipment-leasing company—have simplified the issue by defining just *one* opportunity, in essence focusing on *defectives.* The argument in these cases is that customers want *no* defects and that opportunity calculations can make things appear better than they are. On the other hand, the "one-opportunity" choice makes cross-process comparisons less effective.

Calculating Opportunity-Based Measures

There are several ways to calculate and express measures based on defect opportunities:

- *Defects per Opportunity, or DPO.* This expresses the proportion of defects over the total number of opportunities in a group. For

Defects/Opportunity (DPO)

Formula: $$\frac{\text{Number of Defects}}{\text{\# of Units x \# of Opportunities}}$$

Service Examples:

- 52 defects, 250 loan apps, 4 defect opportunities/app

$$\frac{\text{52 defects on applications}}{\text{250 apps. x 4 opportunities/app}} = .052 \text{ DPO}$$

- 321 defects, 186 ad contracts, 8 defect opps/contract

$$\frac{\text{321 defects on contracts}}{\text{186 apps. x 8 opportunities each}} = .216 \text{ DPO}$$

Manufacturing Examples:

- 99 defects, 750 microchips, 150 defect opportunities

$$\frac{\text{52 defects on microchips}}{\text{750 chips x 150 opportunities/chip}} = .00046 \text{ DPO}$$

- 319 defects, 1150 steel joists, 15 defect opportunities

$$\frac{\text{319 defects on joists}}{\text{1150 joists x 15 opps/joist}} = .018 \text{ DPO}$$

Figure 14.10 Formula and examples: Defects per Opportunity or DPO

example, if DPO were .05. it would signify a five-percent chance of having a defect in one category. (See Fig. 14.10.)

- *Defects per Million Opportunities,* or *DPMO.* Most defect opportunity measures are translated into the DPMO format, which indicates how many defects would arise if there were one million opportunities. In manufacturing environments especially, DPMO often is called "PPM," from "parts per million."[2] (See Fig. 14.11.)
- *Sigma Measure.* Getting to Sigma performance equivalents now is a piece of cake. As we showed you in Chapter 2, the easy way to get your number is to translate your defect measure—usually DPMO—by using a conversion table. The numbers for our examples shown in Fig. 14.12 were derived from the Sigma Conversion Table (see Appendix, page 391). If in each example the data is accurate and the opportunity guidelines are consistent, we would conclude the microchip manufacturing process as the one functioning

Defects/Million Opportunities (DPMO)

Formula: DPO x 1,000,000 (10^6)

Service Examples:

- Loan Applications

  $.052 \times 10^6 = 52{,}000$ DPMO

- Advertising Contracts

  $.216 \times 10^6 = 216{,}000$ DPMO

Manufacturing Examples:

- Microchips

  $.00046 \times 10^6 = 460$ DPMO

- Steel Joists

  $.018 \times 10^6 = 18{,}000$ DPMO

Figure 14.11 Formula and examples: Defects per Million Opportunities or DPMO

most effectively, and the advertising contract process as the worst. In the real world, that would be a pretty typical result.

The Difference between Sigma and Standard Deviation

There's an anomaly to the Sigma Conversion table that may be of interest, especially to the statistically savvy or just plain curious. We'll try to explain it briefly in layperson's language, though if you just plan to use a table to get a Sigma performance score, you may find this more than you *need* to know.

The convention in Six Sigma, based on Motorola's original work back in the 1980s, is to use a scoring system that accounts for more variation in a process than will typically be found in a few weeks or even a couple of months of data gathering. As an example, let's say we work in a customer service call center and find that for one quarter we hit a "first-call resolution" rate of 95.44 percent. Out of one million calls we'd have about 45,600 "defects," or calls not resolved in the first conversation.

However, what we see in a single month is usually not representative of what would happen over, say, a year or two. Over the longer term

Sigma

Calculate DPMO, Consult Table

Service Examples:

- Loan Applications

  52,000 DPMO = 3.1 Sigma

- Advertising Contracts

  216,000 DPMO = 2.3 Sigma

Manufacturing Examples:

- Microchips

  460 DPMO = 4.8 Sigma

- Steel Joists

  18,000 DPMO = 3.6 Sigma

Figure 14.12 Sigma measure examples

we'll probably find that our performance is more variable, and perhaps not quite as good. A more realistic "yield"—based on assumptions drawn from electronics manufacturing but now applied to the rest of us—would be about 69.2 percent or 308,000 defects per every million calls. Ouch!

Fortunately, the way this convention is applied is less depressing. Instead of lowering the Sigma score, the scoring itself has been "shifted" so that for our one-month's data of 95.44 percent we'd consider our *short-term* Sigma level to be about 3.2σ (technically noted σ_{ST}). This score reflects a more realistic expectation of your likely defect levels; if we were to perform at 3.2σ over the long term (i.e., without this "shift" in the scoring), normal statistical tables would tell you to expect fewer than 3000 defects—while this table says that if you think you're at 3.2σ now, you should figure on getting over *45,000* defects.

If you think this is enough to make your head swim, we're right in the water with you. This so-called "1.5 Sigma shift" is one of the key bones of contention amongst the statistical experts about how Six Sigma measures are defined. The lucky thing is that when a convention is adopted and applied consistently, it's still valid. Since this is the way every company we know of prepares their Sigma scores, we can assure you that it works just fine. The only challenge comes if you try to equate the accepted Six Sigma scoring system to strict standard deviations under a normal curve.

Total Process Performance Measures

The defect and Sigma calculations we've reviewed here are based on results or measures at the *end* of the process. When your primary concern is to evaluate your processes' effectiveness at meeting customers' needs, these measures may be all you need. On the other hand defective, DPU, or DPMO/Sigma measures give no real indication of how well the "innards" of the process are working.

Internal Yield Measures

Internal or process measures are based on data collected from *inside* your operation. As with Output measures, we'll concentrate here on internal *defect* measures, which quantify the yield or rework going on during the process. These measures can be revealing, if not shocking.

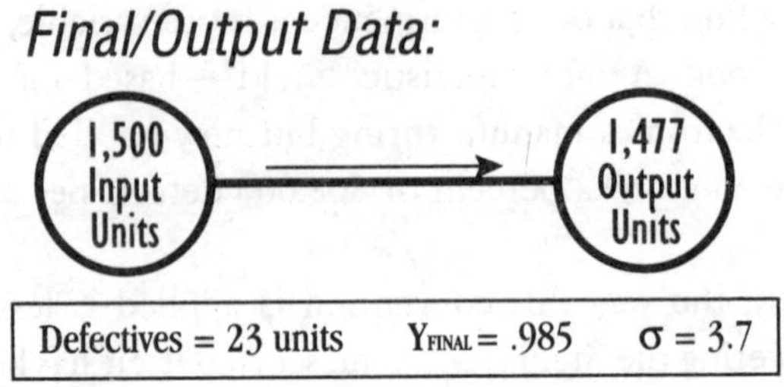

Figure 14.13 Yield example 1: Final Yield

We'll start with an imaginary process (it could be in a Service or Manufacturing business). As shown in Fig. 14.13, data collected at the Output of the process showed a final Yield of .985 (98.5 percent) and a Sigma of 3.7.[3] Of 1500 units (orders, parts, etc.) 1477 were delivered at the end of the process "defect-free."

Now let's look inside the process. We can see in Fig. 14.14 that there are three major "subprocesses," each of which operates with a Yield in the upper 90 percent range. The company has caught the defects and can rework them, but over the course of the process, 89 items have to be reworked. So at the end of the internal data gathering, only 1411 items have *really* gotten through "defect-free," with 89 undergoing some rework.

In Fig. 14.14, we've included the calculation of what's called "First-Pass Yield"—based on the total number of "reworked" items and the total input. Noted Y_{NORM}, this shows a yield in this example quite a bit

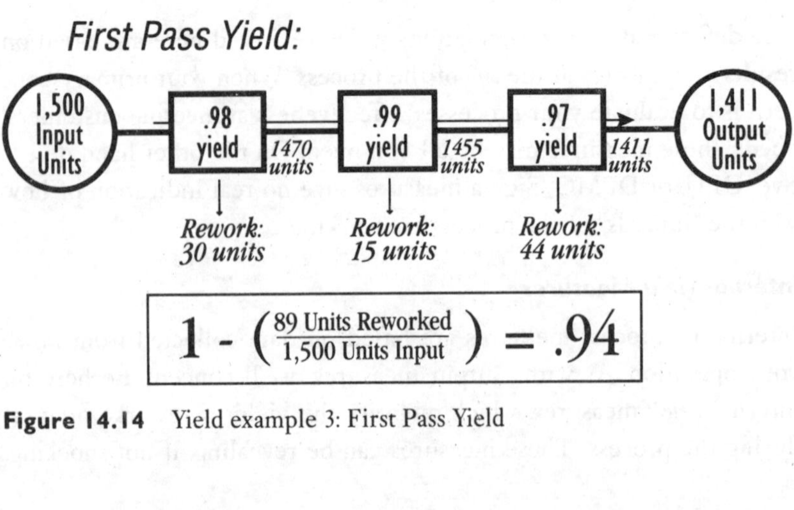

Figure 14.14 Yield example 3: First Pass Yield

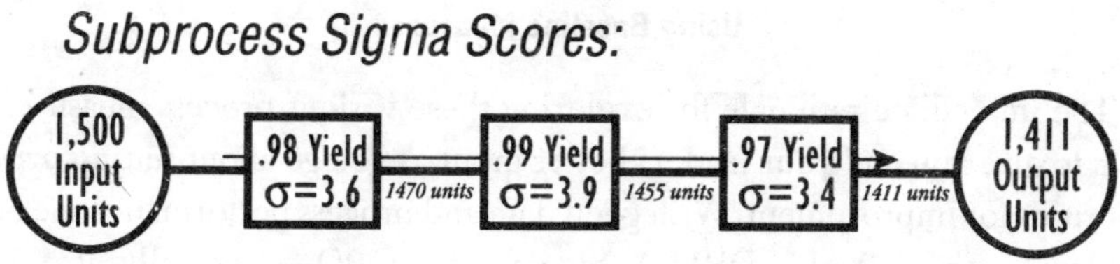

Figure 14.15 Yield example 4: Subprocess yield and Sigma scores

worse than the Y_{FINAL}: .94 compared to .985. In other words, the final yield numbers are hiding defects being fixed in the process.[4]

Lastly, we can develop Sigma performance figures for each substep in the process, based on the defect data we've been examining. As we can see, based both on the yield and on the Sigma numbers shown in Fig. 14.15, the third step in the process shows the most need of attention.

Including "Cost of Poor Quality"

An important performance dimension not captured by defect or Sigma measures is the *dollar impact* of defects, often called "Cost of Poor Quality" or "COPQ."[5] For example, if you have two processes both performing at 3.5 Sigma, their defect-based performance seemingly is equal. However, adding up the *dollars* lost to defects in both processes, you may find the bottom-line impact of one process far higher than the other.

For this reason, we urge teams and Six Sigma implementers to make COPQ a key part of their measurement efforts early on. This entails some work in translating problems or defects into dollar costs per incident—including labor and materials for rework or customer handholding—as well as opportunity or lost business costs. But COPQ numbers are often *more* meaningful to the business leaders or others having no Six Sigma background because—unlike Sigma or DPMO—they speak a language almost anyone understands: *money.* COPQ measures can represent a very useful way of strengthening consensus for improvement and of helping you to select problems with clear bottom-line benefits. If you can include reasonable dollar estimates on the *external* impact of problems—for example, quantify the volume of business lost for every point decrease in a customer satisfaction rating—COPQ can make an even stronger case for customer-directed improvement.

Using Baseline Measures

The immediate rationale for exploring these various process measures is to give you and your leaders better input as you go about setting priorities for improvement. With good data and process performance measures such as Yield, DPMO, Sigma, or COPQ—especially if the measures cover most of your key customer-focused processes—the organization can look for areas of greatest "gap" or concern. Also, you have a head start on getting projects started more quickly, since current performance data already is available. Finally, these measures are a great starting point to track improvement down the road, allowing you to document gains and performance enhancements based on hard data versus anecdotes.

Your new measures and measurement skills also lay the foundation for those ongoing measurement systems that can do so much to create a more responsive company. Learning from your mistakes and applying good data collection and measurement "habits" will make the long-term goal of measurement systems that much more achievable. We'll pick up the theme of measurement systems in Step 5 (Chapter 17), where we review how to combine all the key elements of the Six Sigma methodology and system to drive sustained success and continuous improvement.

Measurement Dos and Don'ts

Do—Set measurement priorities that match your resources.

If you can afford and have the knowhow to begin measuring all core processes, go for it. Most companies have more limited resources, though, and in those majority of cases you should target measurement where the knowledge gained will be most helpful—and is feasible to obtain.

Do—Consider ways to measure Service as well as Output factors.

For simplicity's sake, we've focused our examples and discussion on the more concrete Output Requirement measures. Measuring performance and defects on key Service dimensions may be just as useful however, in helping you to identify improvement projects.

Do—Practice continuous improvement of your measurement.

Good business measurement is not easy. The people-aspects of mea-

sures can be just as important—and challenging—as the technical side. Expect to make mistakes and to learn, as you and your organization become more "measurement-savvy."

Do—Stop measures that are not needed or useful.

If there isn't a good reason to keep up with a measure, abandon it. If you aren't on your toes, a measurement bureaucracy can arise that protects all *measures—then the objective becomes "measure for measurement's sake."*

Don't—Use all the measurement formats available.

Sigma, Yield, DPMO, First-Pass—they all have their place. But remember to use the measures that are most meaningful for your business and process.

Don't—Ignore other measurement options.

Existing or alternative measures such as Control Charts/SPC (covered in Chapter 18), process capability (Cp, Cpk), Cost of Poor Quality, etc. have their place, too, and also can aid you in selecting improvement projects.

Don't—Expect the data to confirm your assumptions.

Often, people will find that the baseline data they gather is right in line with what they thought. It seems to be just as often, though, that measures bring a big surprise. When that happens: pay attention. Dig deeper if you have to, but don't dismiss the data as "Impossible!"

CHAPTER

15

Six Sigma Process Improvement

(Roadmap Step 4A)

Introduction and Key Deliverables

This is the chapter in which the Six Sigma engine really gets revved up. As we take you through the process improvement steps, both here and in the next chapter, the goal is to help you match or exceed the gains described back in Chapter 1. (see Fig. 15.1).

Our plan, mentioned earlier, is to illustrate the paths that go through Define, Measure, Analyze, and Improve by telling you a story, one that reveals how a typical team tends to work through a typical project. We'll mix the story with fascinating interludes in which we explain actions and tools. Of course, no team or project is really "typical"; each is unique and poses special challenges. Still, an example will give you a better "feel" for the work that needs to be done—and for how to do it well.

By the way, you may have noticed that we've left off the "C" in DMAIC. Control is the end of DMAIC, but really the *beginning* of the sustained improvement and integration of the Six Sigma system. So, we'll tie Control tools and concepts into our discussion of Step 5 in Chapter 17: Expanding and Integrating the Six Sigma System.

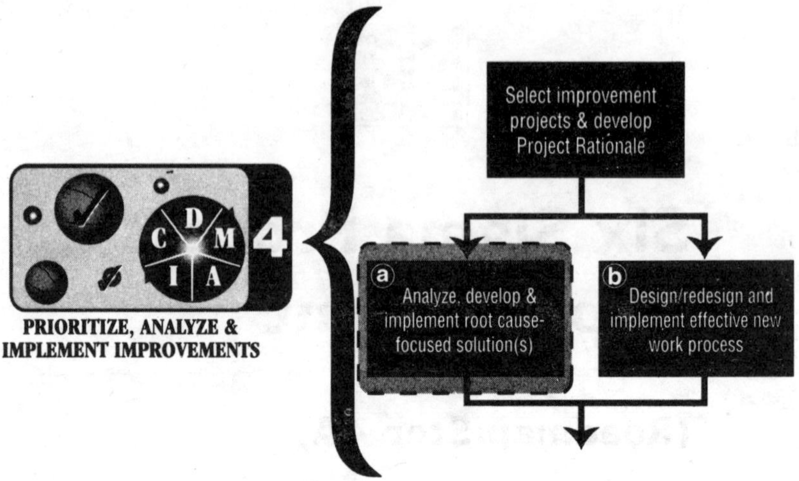

Figure 15.1 Six Sigma Roadmap Step 4A

Focusing Your Attention

Many of the basics of DMAIC (for example, the elements of a Project Charter) we'll deal with in this first chapter, while we'll focus on variations for design/redesign projects in Chapter 16. If you expect to be involved in process design/redesign, you'll want to review both chapters. If your only interest, for now, is in process improvement (i.e., incremental change), you can concentrate on this chapter. Also, since we covered many of the basics of measurement in Chapter 14, our review of the Measure phase will cover how a team might apply the concepts—for example, by selecting measures and developing baseline data. In Analyze, we'll get into how to *use* measures to find out why things are happening in the process.

Tools: Handling with Care

We will be describing and giving examples of a number of common and/or valuable improvement tools and techniques that support the DMAIC process. Our emphasis will be on which tools to use, when, and why—one of the biggest challenges for organizations and teams embarking on a Six Sigma effort. In the References section we've listed other resources where you can get more details on the techniques.

Whenever we teach improvement tools, there's a worry that people will misuse or abuse them. Having a variety of tools to apply to different business problems is important, but people can become "tool-happy."

Here are some things to keep in mind:

Tool Use Guidelines

1. *Have a clear objective, whenever you decide to use a tool.* Never use a tool just because "it's in the book" or "we haven't done that one yet." Only pull out a hammer if a nail needs pounding.
2. *Consider your options, and select the technique that looks most likely to meet your needs.* With the variety of techniques in the Six Sigma toolkit, there's often more than one method that *might* be of help. Be careful of which one you try.
3. *Keep it simple; match the detail and complexity of the tool with the situation.* The most basic tools should be used the most often. If you're using detailed statistics for every problem or project, it's likely you're over-complicating things.
4. *Adapt the method to your needs.* While some organizations or consultants like to play "tool police," it's okay to create your own variations on a method; *if,* that is, a) you don't make a change that no one else can understand, and b) you don't end up drawing faulty conclusions from it.
5. *If a tool isn't working, stop.* Consider every tool you use a "trial"—if you don't get the answer you need or if it isn't working, try something else.

Overview of the Process Improvement Story

Growth with Some Pains

The market for handheld dictation and note recorders has been growing like gangbusters. Businesspeople have gotten so used to talking into their cell phones while in the car, walking down the street, in restaurants, etc., that apparently when there's no one left to call they still like to chat away—to themselves. A new array of devices has been introduced that take advantage of digital memory and minidiscs. As a result, consumers have a variety of types of recorders to choose from—all of them lumped into a product category called "Auto-Talk Devices."

In the past year-and-a-half, one of the Auto-Talk leaders, AutoRec, Incorporated, has made a breakthrough by linking various dictation format devices with voice-recognition technology. Now, people can actually have their utterings converted into *text* automatically. A new market has opened up for AutoRec in the sales force automation arena, meaning for instance that account executives can more easily keep notes on their clients and prospects, as well as dictate letters and proposals without the need for administrative support.

The challenge, however, is to meet the very specific requirements of AutoRec's growing group of corporate accounts. Because the Auto-Talk devices have to interface with a client's existing technology—laptops, networks, word-processing and contact-list applications, etc.—each large order for a sales group needs to be specially designed and produced. Unfortunately, the number of deliveries that turn out *not* to meet client specifications has always been high, and it's growing. AutoRec's leadership group, having heard about the big impact of Six Sigma improvement efforts at other companies, decided to see if the methods would help them to address their problems.

"We only have a few months," said AutoRec's CEO, "before someone matches our technology and clients start looking elsewhere. We've got to get our [*censored*] act together, or we'll be called Auto *Wreck!*" (Which, in fact, they already were.)

The leadership team put together a Project Rationale statement:

Mistakes in deliveries to customers are affecting almost 40 percent of our shipments. Rework costs are up to $300,000 per month, and 2 of the top 25 companies in the country who've been considering major orders now say they need assurances we can deliver. If we don't improve our effectiveness in meeting customer requirements, we risk slipping behind TalkNBox [key competitor] when they introduce their voice integration system in the Fall. This team is charged to find out why we are making so many out-of-spec deliveries—and to get results fast.

A team was chosen consisting of seven people coming from different functions within AutoRec, including two from Assembly (manufacturing), and one each from Order Administration, Procurement, Product Design, Shipping, and Sales. Initially the team was going to number only six, but the VP of Sales insisted on having a representative. (For guidelines on project team selection, see Chapter 9.) The Director of Product Design was selected to be Team Leader. The Leader and team members attended a one-week workshop that gave them an overview and key methods for executing a Six Sigma–focused process improvement project. The CEO visited each team member personally, to pledge support for the project.

In the AutoRec team's training, they were given an overview of the five phases of the DMAIC model. Since the team knew that time was of the essence, they realized they would have to focus on *fixing* the problems in their current processes: there would be no time to attempt to redesign their workflows.

The Back-and-Forth Nature of Process Improvement

Before we take the AutoRec story any further, we should emphasize an important fact: the DMAIC cycle is *not a purely linear activity.* As any team begins probing, gathering data, etc., they almost invariably make discoveries about the problem and process. These revelations mean that the project Goal, for example, can be revised even up to the point of implementing solutions. Or, after testing a solution, a team may need to do more "Analyze" work. In general, improvement teams can plot their progress using the D-M-A-I-C phases, but overall it's an *iterative* activity.

Define: Clarifying the Problem, Goal, and Process

The Define phase sets the stage for a successful Six Sigma project by helping you to answer four critical questions:

1. What's the *problem* or opportunity on which we will focus?
2. What's our *goal?* [That is, what results do you want to accomplish, and by when?]
3. Who's the *customer* served and/or impacted by this process and problem?
4. What's the *process* we're investigating?

In documenting project goals and parameters at the outset—in what's usually called the "Project Charter"—improvement teams can help ensure that their work meets with the expectations of their organization leaders and project "Sponsor."

Getting Started on the Project Charter

At the AutoRec group's first meeting, the agenda contained one item: "Define the Problem." A couple of team members questioned why that would take an entire meeting, since the Project Rationale given to them by the executive team had stated the situation pretty clearly. In the first five minutes of discussion, though, several different "takes" on the issue were identified, including these:

- Customer expectations for the AutoRec units are too high.
- People on the assembly floor are making mistakes that lead to product errors getting to customers.
- Order specifications somehow are not being followed properly, meaning that products aren't configured to customer requirements when shipped.
- Late deliveries are creating angry customers, who take it out on AutoRec when they find the slightest thing wrong with the units.
- Clients' sales staff—i.e., end users of AutoRec's products—don't understand how to use the units.

With such a wide range of notions about the problem, the team decided to write a general Problem Statement, which they would refine as more data were gathered.

The team also prepared an initial Goal Statement, which identified the results they would work to achieve. Some of the members were uncomfortable with the deadline they set—but agreed that they did need to aim for early successes.

"Well," concluded the Sales department member, "these are pretty general statements. We're going to have to get some more specifics pretty quick."

Six Sigma Project Charter

There are many options for developing and formatting a Charter. The AutoRec team has so far done only the two most essential Charter elements. Here's a rundown of many of the most common items included in a Project Charter, as well as some guidelines for producing your own project document.

The Problem Statement

This is a concise and focused description of "what's wrong"—either the pain arising from the problem or the opportunity that needs to be addressed. In some cases the Problem Statement can be a distilled version of the Project Rationale; but usually a team will need to define their issue much more specifically, since even the best Project Rationale statements will be pretty broad.

A Problem Statement, and the process of writing it, serve to:

1. Validate that the Project Rationale has been clearly understood by the improvement team
2. Solidify consensus and "ownership" of team members around the problem to be addressed
3. Ensure that the team is beginning to focus on a problem that is neither too narrow nor too broad
4. Assess the clarity of the data supporting and helping to define the problem
5. Establish a baseline measure against which progress and results can be tracked

This last benefit, the baseline measure, may not exist when the team first meets—so it's an example of one of the elements of the Problem Statement that would need to be clarified over time. Figure 15.2 summarizes the four key questions you should pose as you develop a Problem Statement.

The Goal Statement

Problem Statements and Goal Statements are a matched pair. While the Problem Statement describes the pain or symptoms, a Goal Statement defines "relief" in terms of concrete results. Goal Statement structure can be pretty well standardized into three elements:

1. *A description of what's to be accomplished.* The Goal Statement should start with a verb: "Reduce . . ."; "Increase . . ."; "Eliminate . . ." (But try to avoid "Improve," as it's too vague.)

Problem Statement Structure	
What?	◆ Which process is involved? ◆ What is wrong? ◆ What is the gap or opportunity?
Where?/ When?	◆ Where do we observe the problem/gap? ✓ department ✓ region ✓ etc. ◆ When do we observe the problem/gap? ✓ time of day/month/year ✓ before/after X ✓ etc.
How big?	◆ How big is the problem/gap/ opportunity? ◆ How will we measure it?
Impact?	◆ What's the impact of the problem/opportunity? ◆ What are the benefits of action/ consequences of inaction?

Figure 15.2 Elements of a Problem Statement

2. *A measurable target for desired results.* The target should quantify the desired cost saving, defect elimination, or time reduction, etc., in percentages or actual numbers. If it's too soon to even guess, leave a "placeholder" to indicate where you plan to add the target later. The measurable target is what your team and business leaders will use to gauge the project's success.
3. *A project deadline and/or timeframe for results.* The date set in the early part of the project may need to be revised later, but establishing a deadline helps to rally resources and commitment and shorten project cycle times.

A suggestion: For clarity, you may want to include *two* deadlines in a Goal Statement—one date for implementing solutions, the second for when you expect to show measurable results.

Many teams say that agreeing on the Problem and Goal is one of the most challenging aspects of their Six Sigma project. Individuals from different parts of your company may see the issue very differently, making consensus hard to come by. Moreover, the initial drafts tend to be based more on guesses than on hard data, so there's more room for disagreement. One way to avoid Problem and Goal "wheel-spinning" is to remember that these statements will *evolve* as you gain more knowledge about the process and data. (It's common to describe a Project Charter as a "living document," which somehow suggests to us a B-movie scene: "Look, Professor, it's *breathing!*")

Constraints and Assumptions

This section of a Charter—which might also be called "resources and expectations"—helps you to clarify and document the limitations, and other relevant factors that may affect your team's efforts. One common example is time availability: Are improvement team members expected to spend 100 percent of their time on the project? Will there be sufficient resources to cover their "regular" jobs? Some possible solutions may be "out of bounds"—for example, you may decide that a major Information Technology upgrade just isn't feasible for the time being. Realities such as these are best clarified upfront, so that teams don't go down the wrong path or cherish any false expectations.

Not all the elements noted in this category are necessarily limiting, either. An assumption may be that "The team will make all key decisions about the solutions to be implemented." Or: "The finance department will provide one full-time person to help the team gather Cost of Poor Quality data." Other assumptions may define the anticipated frequency of team meetings, contributions of the Sponsor, and so on. Even if constraints and assumptions aren't made formal elements of the Project Charter, just asking the questions around them is a good idea.

Initial Problem or Opportunity Data

Since you don't want the Problem Statement to run longer than two or three brief sentences, any measures or facts that you feel are relevant to identifying or understanding the problem can be summarized in a separate section of the Charter. You can update this data as you go, or just leave it "as is" as a record of the facts you had available at the outset of the project.

Team Members and Responsibilities

A Project Charter may also list the people who'll be involved in the Six Sigma project, including team members, support people, coach or consulting staff, and project Sponsor or Champion.

Team Guidelines

Expectations as to how the team will collaborate can also be incorporated into the Charter. These may include team Groundrules; roles for managing meetings; decision processes; or other aspects of teamwork.

Preliminary Project Plan

Final deadlines alone won't keep most teams on track throughout the course of a Six Sigma project. Identifying and setting dates for key milestones helps keep energy levels higher and creates a sense of urgency. Having team members commit voluntarily to the milestone dates—rather than imposing them—usually is preferred, but sometimes a little pushing is needed, especially if all team members continue to work at their "regular" jobs.

Note: An additional element of a Project Charter that's included in some organizations is known as the "Scope." We'll wait till we look at Process Design/Redesign to discuss Scope, as it's more relevant to those projects.

Completing the Project Charter

It had taken the AutoRec team an entire two-hour meeting just to prepare their initial Problem and Goal statements. Prior to the second meeting a couple days later, the Team Leader drafted several other pieces of the Charter, including a list of team and project participants and constraints and assumptions.

A heated discussion arose about the expectations swirling around how much time team members were to devote to the project: the draft Charter indicated that each member of the team would carve out 25 to 50 percent of his or her schedule for the project. "I've got work stacked on my desk," said the Procurement group member. "I can't be in meetings for two hours every other day without some relief." Others had similar complaints. The Team Leader agreed to talk to their Sponsor to ensure that people would have time freed up for the project.

So far, the Problem Statement was vague on the size of the problem. Then the Shipping Department team member spoke up: "I finally found some figures on the bad deliveries," she explained. "It turns out about 8 percent of orders are arriving late, and 30 percent are not configured properly, with a few miscellaneous problems here and there."

Based on the new data, the team revised the Problem Statement and completed their initial Charter. (See Figs. 15.3 and 15.4.)

Six Sigma Customer Delivery Team:

Project Charter

Problem Statement

Forty percent of orders delivered to AutoRec corporate clients are not meeting customer requirements, including 30% rejected for out-of-spec units and 8% noted as late deliveries. These defects are hurting our image, creating customer dissatisfaction and costing us roughly $350,000 per month to rework rejected orders. Continued high levels of delivery errors threaten our position as leader in this growing industry.

Goal Statement

Reduce delivery errors by 70% (to less than 12%) and cut rework costs by 50% by the end of Q3 of this year.

Constraints

Team members will be expected to devote 25 to 50% of their time to the project. Back-up support for their existing jobs will be... [*to be reviewed with Sponsor*].

Assumptions

No reasonable solutions will be considered "out of bounds," however, the focus of the team will be on improving existing processes, not on designing or redesigning processes.

Team Guidelines

The team will meet at least once a week, Tuesday mornings from 9am to 10am. Decisions will be made by consensus, guided by criteria analysis where needed. If consensus can't be reached, the Team Leader will make the final call.

CHARTER: Draft One, Page One

AutoRec

Figure 15.3 AutoRec Team Project Charter (page 1)

Project Charter, continued

Team Members

The team is comprised of the following members:

- Ravi Gosai, Order Administration
- Al Johnson, Product Design (Team Leader)
- Daphne Martin, Manufacturing
- Mike Moshivitz, Manufacturing
- May Yamamoto, Sales
- Elena Zarzuela, Procurement
- Arnold Ziffle, Shipping

Other key players include:

- Pat DeLia, VP of Customer Satisfaction - Sponsor
- Martin Wyck, Six Sigma Coach
- Eleanor Carajota, Finance liaison/support
- Bob Megabyte, IT liaison/support

Preliminary Project Plan

To achieve our goal and results by our target date, the team will have to work aggressively and rapidly. The following are milestones for completing each phase of the DMAIC process:

DEFINE - March 15
MEASURE - April 15
ANALYZE - May 15
IMPROVE - June 15
CONTROL - July 15

CHARTER: Draft One, Page Two

Figure 15.4 AutoRec Team Project Charter (page 2)

Identifying and Listening to the Customer

Here are some of the practical benefits of using a "Voice of the Customer" assessment in the Define phase:

1. Ensuring that the problem and goal are defined in terms that truly relate to key customer requirements
2. Avoiding cost- and time-cutting solutions that actually hurt service to or relations with customers
3. Providing information on possible "Output" measures that may need to be tracked as solutions are implemented
4. Giving team members practice in, and reinforcing the importance of, focusing work on the *customer*

If your organization already has an effective VOC strategy and the data are accessible (as described in Chapter 13), it may be easy for a DMAIC team to validate customer needs and specifications. Without good "upfront" sources, however, getting the relevant customer input may take time and money. Under pressure to get results, your process improvement teams will have to balance the *ideal* of having a thorough understanding of customer requirements with the need to keep the DMAIC project moving.

Getting in Touch with Customers

At the end of their meeting to finalize the Project Charter, the AutoRec "We Deliver" team (their new name) agreed that May, from Sales, and Arnold, from Shipping, would make contact with several sources to get a better idea of how the delivery problems were affecting Corporate Account customers.

Because of the need for speed they decided to divide the work, with each focusing on one source of customer data:

1. May would put together a brief phone survey, and phone about 10 sales managers and 10 IT managers to develop a detailed list of customer requirements and priorities.
2. Arnold meanwhile would review letters and complaint forms from corporate customers, to see what patterns emerged or conclusions could be drawn from it.

After a week, May and Arnold got together to compare findings. What they learned was a bit of a surprise: Corporate clients were not nearly as concerned about quick delivery of orders of AutoTalk devices as they had thought.

"All the customers told me they are eager to have the systems to boost their groups' productivity," May noted. "But if they had to wait a few weeks or a month, it wouldn't be a huge issue."

The data Arnold culled from complaint forms and letters was indicative, too. "It took me about three hours just to separate the corporate account items from the rest; they were all mixed together! But I could only find six forms or letters that had anything to do with late deliveries, and they were pretty mild. The clients whose systems couldn't be used right away were almost unanimously livid—there were over 150 of those."

Customer: Corporate Sales Department

Output: "AutoText" Devices & Support Materials

Weight	Customer Requirement	Type
10	Compatible with existing hardware	DI
10	Compatible with existing software	DI
8	Accuracy of voice translation to text (at least 95% accurate)	SA
5	Usable by reading instructions in 5 minutes or less	SA
5	Correct Quantity	DI
3	Delivered on date noted on Purchase Order	SA

SA = Satisfier
DI = Dissatisfier (minimum requirement)
DE = Delighter

AutoRec

Figure 15.5 AutoRec customer requirements weighting and type

May and Arnold prepared a one-page summary of their findings for the team. (see Fig. 15.5).

When the other team members saw the list and the data, their jaws dropped and eyes widened (it's an expressive group). The top priority for everyone at AutoRec had been to ship the systems *as soon as possible.* The rationale was that, as the "only game in town," AutoRec needed to get its products to customers fast.

"The customer's sense of urgency doesn't seem to be nearly as intense as ours is," May explained. "Fast is fine, but not a big deal. *Wrong* is, however, a big deal."

The team left the meeting with some things to think about.

Identifying and Documenting the Process

A final, essential Define activity is to develop a "picture" of the process involved in the project. Some groups are tempted to skip this step, but there are several strong reasons to make it a "must" at the outset of any DMAIC project:

- *Putting the problem in context.* Understanding how the work flows in and around the problem will help clarify the various factors that may influence performance.
- *Refining the Scope of the project, or focusing analysis.* A quick way to help a team concentrate its attention is to create a diagram of their process. It's typical to recognize that the process described is so huge that some immediate narrowing of focus is needed.
- *Revealing possible "obvious" root causes.* We don't advocate conclusion-jumping, but sometimes just documenting how the process is working—or *not* working—will help a team see the cause of the problem.
- *Clarifying Inputs, roles, and supplier/customer relationships.* This can help team members to better understand one another's role in the process and to see how they contribute to the project. It also can help to determine if the team has the right mix of members.
- *Helping to target what and where to measure.* Having a broad view of the process makes tangible where key data may be needed and/or available.

Choice of Process Diagrams: SIPOC or Detailed

An important question to raise, with respect to documenting a process early in a DMAIC project, is this one: How much detail do we need? As usual the answer is, "It depends." But in general we suggest that you begin with a SIPOC diagram, as introduced in Chapter 12. Once that has been completed, you can decide whether a more detailed process map is needed. The AutoRec team elected to do a high level SIPOC map, shown in Fig. 15.6.

With a SIPOC diagram, customer requirements, and Project Charter completed, a team may be ready to move into the Measure phase of DMAIC. An optional "final" task would be to create a detailed process map to use in helping to identify where to implement measures—but only when and where it's really needed. It's best to avoid too much detail too soon.

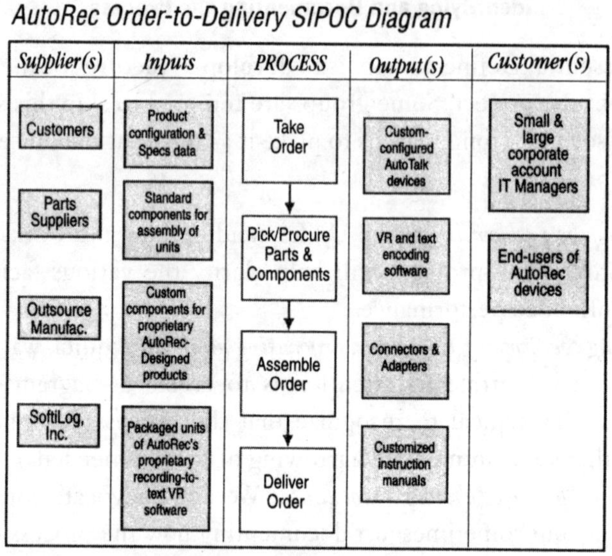

Figure 15.6 AutoRec Order-to-Delivery SIPOC diagram

Define "Dos and Don'ts"

Do—Make Problem Statements as specific and fact-based as they can be.

Focus on what's observable and confirmed, not on suspicion or assumptions.

Do—Use the Charter to set direction and to gain agreement on the problem, goal, and project parameters.

Take the time to address questions or uncertainties with the team and sponsors early. *This will help to smooth the path for the project.*

Do—Keep the Charter "visible," and revise it as needed.

It's a tool to keep things focused, and a "living document."

Do—Listen to the Voice of the Customer.

Six Sigma is all about customer-focused improvement. Even efficiency-enhancing projects need to pay close attention to value and impact on customers.

Don't—Describe suspected causes or assign blame for the Problem.

A key to Six Sigma improvement is the assumption that you do not know the cause of the problem—even if you have some guesses.

Don't—Over-publicize preliminary Goals.

It's okay to set ambitious targets, so long as they don't lead to false expectations.

Don't—Over-"wordsmith" the Charter.

Easier said than done, since people like to get the wording of these statements "just right." Taking a long time, however, can kill enthusiasm and commitment.

Don't—Get mired in process detail.

A basic high-level view of the process is essential, but usually is enough at the beginning of the project. Create detailed process maps only where that extra information will be immediately useful.

A checklist for the Define phase can be found in the Appendix (page 386).

Measure: Baselining and Refining the Problem

Measurement is a key transitional phase, one that serves to validate or refine the Problem and to begin the search for root causes—the objective of Analyze. Measure addresses two key questions:

1. What's the focus and extent of the problem, based on measures of the process and/or outputs? (This is commonly called the "Baseline Measure.")
2. What key data may help to narrow the problem to its major factors or "vital few" root causes?

Note: For some background info on how to execute measurement, see Chapter 14.

Planning for Measurement

Prior to their next meeting, Al, the AutoRec Team Leader, sent an e-mail asking each member to bring along some ideas as to what measures would best build understanding of the delivery problems. The team posted and grouped the measures into two broad categories: Output or Input/Process. After eliminating duplicates, their list looked like this:

OUTPUT MEASURES:

- Number of defects by type of defect
- Proportion defective and yield (overall, and by customer type)
- Output Sigma

INPUT/PROCESS MEASURES:

- Discrepancies between order form and final shipment
- Cycle time per major process phase
- Pulse rate of Shipping staff on last day of the quarter
- Time between ordering and receipt of parts
- Average days that parts inventory are on hand

Unfortunately, the team realized, existing data on defective deliveries and the customer complaint forms did not have enough detail to really help them narrow the problem. They therefore had to develop a new data collection plan.

"If we can see whether the specs on the order forms are the same as what's shipped," noted Daphne from Assembly, "we'll know if it's a mistake in the order-taking or somewhere later in the process."

By the end of the meeting the group had decided to focus on three measures. Over the next few days, subgroups of the team developed a description of the purpose, and operational definitions for each:

- *"Delivery Defects."* This measure actually would identify a variety of factors, including date of delivery, type of delivery defect (four categories or opportunities), product type (e.g., microcassette or digital memory), customer type, and salesperson.

- *"Process Cycle Time."* The team decided to follow a sampling of orders through the entire process, and to gather cycle time data for each phase. To do this they created a simple "traveler" checksheet, to be attached to the documentation that followed each job from order entry to shipment.
- *"Order/Shipment Discrepancy."* For this measure, the team was able to use existing ("historical") data from "bad" deliveries. They were checking to see, as Daphne had suggested, if the *orders* were wrong, or if somehow the problems were arising during the process.

Measurement Choices

Decisions on what to measure are often difficult, both because of the many options available as well as the challenge of collecting data. In process improvement efforts, the need to collect data in several phases is one of the main reasons that projects can often take months to complete. Every team needs to make its measurement choices carefully. Sometimes it's not possible to do the measures you'd *like* to do, so the ability to find alternatives or else make the best use of the data you *can* gather is important. Over time, improvement projects will tend to go faster as measurement choices and resources improve. Part of the art of Six Sigma is to base decisions and solutions on *enough* facts to be effective and to learn how to better use data over time.

Gathering and Interpreting AutoRec Data

It took the full month allotted in their preliminary plan for the team to gather data on their three targeted measures. They were fortunate, because the data collection period covered the end of the first Quarter of the year, so they could see how the process performed during both calm and busy cycles. (They knew it was important for data to be representative of how work levels and other factors vary over time.)

Here are the conclusions they drew from each of the measures:

- *"Delivery Defects."* The data gathered on this key output measure (actually, several measures) was compiled in a spreadsheet. As Elena from Procurement noted, "There are lots of things we could look at in this data!" For the time being, though, they developed two views of the data:

1. The performance of the process was determined to be a DPMO of 122,800 or 2.7 sigma.
2. Defect data was broken down by type and displayed on a *Pareto Chart* (explained below). This revealed that most of the problems related to incompatibility, with hardware problems showing the most incidents.

- *"Process Cycle Time."* Average cycle time, from order entry to delivery, was found to be 17.3 days. A breakdown of the time involved in the major process steps (from the SIPOC diagram) showed that the largest amount of that time was devoted to Order Assembly—11.6 days.
- *Order/Shipment Discrepancy.* For this measure, the team was able to make use of existing data on defective deliveries. They were checking to see whether the orders themselves had been done incorrectly or if the problems were arising somewhere later in the process. The data were conclusive: For about 93 percent of the defective orders they examined from the previous four months, the Order Specification Sheets (OPS forms) were different from what was actually shipped to the customer. They also checked a significant proportion of those to find that the OPS forms were accurate—that is, the information did reflect the proper customer configuration.

Altogether, the data gave the AutoRec team a much clearer picture of the problem, and helped them to narrow their focus as they begin the search for root causes of the defective deliveries. They were able to update their Problem Statement based on the findings in Measure:

Forty percent of orders delivered to AutoRec corporate clients are not meeting customer requirements, including 30 percent for Hardware and Software incompatibility problems. These defects are hurting our image, creating customer dissatisfaction, and costing us roughly $350,000 per month to rework rejected orders. Continued high levels of delivery errors threaten our position as a leader in this growing industry.

The Transition from Measure to Analyze

The main requirement, before declaring yourselves ready to begin Analyze, is to have at least one solid, repeatable measure confirming—and often clarifying—the problem or opportunity. This should be the measure you'll repeat during and after solutions are implemented, to track the effects of your improvement. Another common result of Measure is a new, more sophisticated set of questions about your problem. Those questions are a good sign: They show you're thinking about how you can *investigate* the problem, versus just coming up with off-the-cuff solutions.

Measure "Dos and Don'ts"

Do—Balance Output with Process/Input measures.

Make sure you're tracking impact on the customer and end product/service, even if your focus is on boosting efficiency.

Do—Use measures to narrow the problem.

Try to find the most significant components of or contributors to the problem, so that your analysis and solutions will be well targeted.

Do—Anticipate what you'll want to analyze later.

Try to reduce the cycles of data collection by gathering facts that will help you to find the root cause.

Don't—Try to do too much.

Even though you want to "get a jump" on Analyze, don't get greedy and try to measure too many things at once. Focus on the measures that you're pretty sure you will use and that you can complete in a reasonable time frame (one week to a month is a good rule of thumb).

Don't—Skip the key steps in measurement.

Taking the time to create good operational definitions, collection forms, sampling plans, etc., and testing your measures before launching them, avoids worthless data and frustrating re-measures.

A checklist for the Measure phase is provided in the Appendix (page 387).

Analyze: Becoming a Process Detective

Analyze is the most "unpredictable" of the DMAIC phases. The tools you use and the order in which you apply them will depend a lot on your problem and process and on how you approach the problem. Like a detective story, you can try to anticipate what will happen next, but often as not you'll be surprised. One of the most valuable lessons of the Six Sigma approach, in fact, is that the "usual suspects" (the causes you *think* are at the root of the problem) often turn out not to be "not guilty," or else just accomplices to the *real* culprit. (Hey, we're on a roll with this detective thing!)

When your teams—and business leaders—see their hunches go wrong a time or two, it teaches everyone to be wary of their assumptions and educated guesses. Don't *ignore* past experience or intuition, but to rely on them alone can let the real criminals go free to cause further problems. (*End* of detective analogy.)

The Root Cause Analysis Cycle

We can represent Analyze, as applied in process improvement, as a *cycle* (see Fig. 15.7). The cycle is driven by generating and evaluating "hypotheses" (or "educated guesses") as to the cause of the problem. You can enter the cycle either at point (a)—by looking at the process and the data to identify possible causes—or point (b)—where you *start* with a suspected cause and seek to validate or refute it through analy-

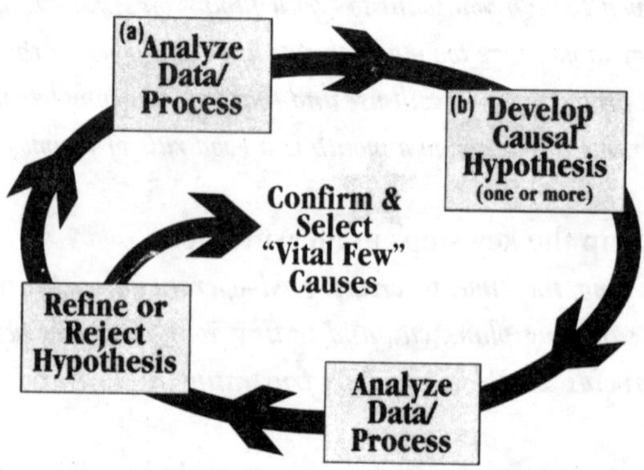

Figure 15.7 The root cause hypothesis/ analysis cycle

sis. When you find an hypothesis is not correct, you may have to go back to the beginning of the cycle to come up with a whole new explanation. But even "incorrect" causes are actually opportunities to refine and narrow your explanation of the problem.

Key Analysis Strategies

As the Analysis Cycle diagram indicates, there are two key sources of input to determine the true cause of your targeted problem:

- *Data Analysis.* Use of measures and data—those already collected, or new data gathered in the Analyze phase—to discern patterns, tendencies, or other factors about the problem that either suggest or prove/disprove possible causes.
- *Process Analysis.* Deeper investigation into and understanding of how work is being done to identify inconsistencies, "disconnects," or problem areas that might cause or contribute to the problem.

  These two strategies, combined, produce the real power of Six Sigma analysis. Independently, either can give you a pretty good idea of a likely root cause, but your knowledge will always be lacking unless you can bring data and process findings together.

The two biggest mistakes in Analyze, for process improvement teams, are these:

1. To shortcut the cycle prematurely, declaring the suspected cause "guilty" and moving to solutions without sufficient evidence—much like convicting the wrong person;
2. To get stuck on the cycle, never being convinced you have sufficient data and never mustering the confidence to apply solutions to the most probable cause.

It's especially important at the early stages of Six Sigma to avoid these two extremes. With practice, a team can develop good habits and a good sense of what is enough, but not *too much,* analyzing of the problem. As we work through Analyze and look at the AutoRec team's story, we'll explain how you and your teams can try to avoid these pitfalls.

Preparing the Initial Line-Up of Causes

"In our Six Sigma workbook," Ravi, from Order Administration, reminded the team at their next meeting, "it says there are two major strategies in analyzing a problem: examining the process, or examining the data. Which should we use?"

"That's not an either/or question" was the response. It came from Martin Wyck, the Coach working with the team who was sitting in on the meeting. "It's usually better to look closely at both the data *and* the process," he added. "You can get clues from both sources, and when the clues match up you really learn about the problem."

"I'll buy that," Ravi agreed, and the rest of the team concurred. They had trouble, however, agreeing which to do first: delve into the data, or look at the process in more detail.

However, at the suggestion of Elena from Procurement, they decided to start not with data *or* process analysis, but with a list of possible root causes to consider. Using a Cause and Effect diagram the team brainstormed all the possible causes that might create the high level of bad deliveries. They then narrowed the list down to several "prime suspects" or, more technically, "causal hypotheses." Perhaps:

- Order Specification forms were being entered incorrectly into the procurement system
- Parts vendors were mislabeling items, so that the wrong connectors and adapters were being packed into the shipments
- Errors were being made when shipments were rushed out to meet delivery deadlines
- Assembly staff, being hired at a rate of several dozen per month, were not adequately trained, and were mixing up digital and tape-recording devices
- Shipments were being mixed up at the dock, mislabeled, and sent to the wrong customer

"But these are just *guesses!*" commented May from Sales.

"That's true," responded Coach Martin. "What you've done is put some of your hunches down on paper. So now, you can look at the data and the process to see if they make sense. But the *real* cause might be something not even on this list."

To take their Analysis further, the team divided up their assignments: three of the members would work on a more detailed process map of the Procurement, Assembly, and Shipping activities, while the other four looked more deeply into the data they'd already collected.

Starting Points for the Root Cause Cycle

The AutoRec team has chosen a common way to begin their analysis: by developing a list of potential causes or "causal hypotheses." The tool they chose—the Cause and Effect or Fishbone diagram—has for years been one of the favorites for quality teams, and still is used by Six Sigma improvement teams.

The Cause and Effect Diagram

Cause and Effect analysis lets a group start with an "effect"—a problem, or in some cases a desired effect or result—and create a structured list of possible causes for it. Benefits of the Cause and Effect diagram include the following:

- It's a great tool for gathering group ideas and input, being basically a "structured brainstorming" method.
- By establishing categories of potential causes, it helps ensure that a group thinks of many possibilities, rather than just focusing on a few typical areas (e.g., people, bad materials).
- It helps get the Analyze phase started. Using a Cause and Effect diagram to identify some "prime suspect" causes, as the AutoRec team has done, provides the focus to help begin process and data analysis.

The Cause and Effect diagram also brings us back to the issue of *variation* that we introduced back in Chapter 2. We noted that a business process has variation of two types. Upstream from the customer (in the Inputs or Process), we call factors of variation "the Xs." The downstream or Output variation that is the result of the changes in the Xs we call "the Ys." We can apply the same principle of X and Y to the Cause and Effect model: the "effect" or problem is the Y, and the possible root causes that appear on the "bones" are the Xs.

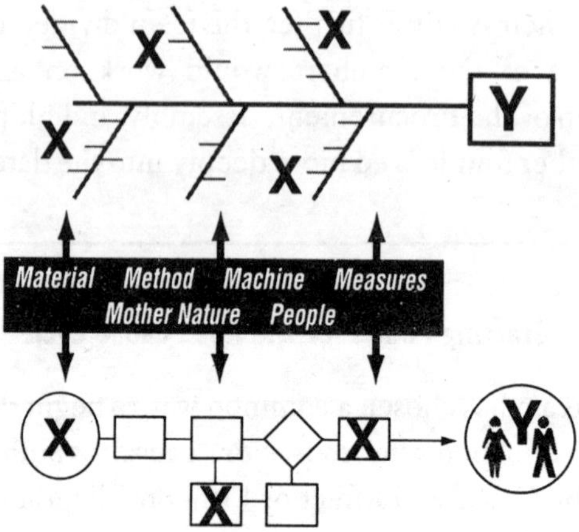

Figure 15.8 Process map and Cause and Effect diagram showing causes of variation in upstream (X) and downstream (Y) factors

As shown in Fig. 15.8, typically there are six major factors described that cause variation in a business process—sometimes called the "5Ms and 1P":

- *Material*—the consumables or raw inputs that are used in the process
- *Method*—procedures, processes, work instructions
- *Machine*—equipment, including computers and non-consumable tools
- *Measures*—techniques used for assessing the quality/quantity of the work, including inspection
- *Mother Nature*—the environment in which the work is done, or which affects any of the other variables; may include "facilities," not just the natural environment
- *People*—bipedal primates native to most continents on earth; reportedly show signs of intelligence

As we move deeper into root cause analysis, we'll likely be examining all of these potential causes of variation so as to target the so-called "vital few" Xs, or causes, that contribute most to the problem.

The AutoRec Process

There were nine people in the conference room on the morning set aside to build a complete process map of the AutoRec process from procurement through shipment. One or two representatives from each area involved in the process had been invited to attend, to ensure broad input into the map.

"We want to look at the process 'as is,'" explained Team Leader Al of Product Design. "We'll be checking this with other people, so it doesn't have to be perfect, but we definitely do not want to describe the process the way it ought to be done, or the way the execs think it's being done."

It actually took two two-hour meetings to create the full map of the process. Between the sessions a preliminary draft was created (using a process-mapping software program) and circulated for feedback, which led to some corrections.

One interesting part of the process involved the links between Procurement and Assembly. Procurement's strategy has been to keep a month or more of stock on hand in the case of small items like connectors and adapters as well as software packets, since they aren't expensive and don't tie up a lot of capital in inventory. That leaves them time to focus on ordering more complex custom parts like recording-device components.

In Assembly, for each order that's received a "kit cart" is prepared with bins for all the items needed, based on a Bill of Materials generated by the computerized configuration software. For each order, a "twosome" that is assigned primary responsibility for ensuring that the materials get delivered on time. After the kit cart is ready, the twosome pulls all available inventory of key components for the recording devices and submits an order to Procurement for any items not available. Because volume has grown so dramatically and continues to increase, almost every order requires a special purchase of items for the recorders.

For the smaller items like connectors and adapters that are kept in quantity, supervisors in the Assembly Store Room check stock levels every week to see what's needed. When pieces are low, they e-mail a list of low inventory items to the Procurement department for reorder.

Looking at the process, the group took note of the difference in how the two types of parts were being ordered, as something to look into further. One of the people in the meeting, from Assembly, commented that some of the adapter and connector parts are *always* "on order," while others run out only rarely.

The other "discovery" from the meeting involved responsibility for and participation in getting shipments made on time. While

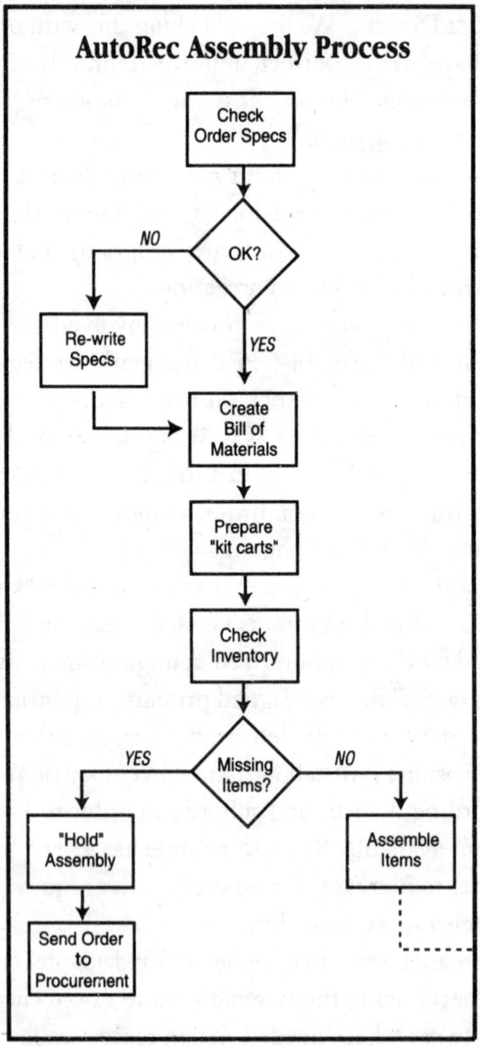

Figure 15.9 AutoRec Assembly process map (partial)

everyone at AutoRec knows the high priority the company has placed on on-time delivery, the folks in Shipping seem to be most attentive to dates, and will check with Assembly on orders when deadlines are getting close. "We go in and help them complete the kit carts pretty often," explained one of the Shipping people. "We get a bonus every month based on the number of on-time deliveries, so we probably take it a little more seriously."

The "We Deliver" team members exchanged looks when they heard that comment, and after the meeting agreed that here might be a clue to the problem: Shipping people were involved in doing Assembly's job.

A segment of the process map is shown in Fig. 15.9.

Process Mapping and Analysis

Process Maps are among the most essential tools of Six Sigma, in which improving, designing, measuring, and managing processes are the primary focus. The basics of a process map are simple: a series of tasks (rectangles) and decisions/reviews (diamonds), connected by arrows to show the flow of work. The AutoRec example is a standard business process map; later we'll see some variations on the Process Map theme.

As you build Process Maps for your Six Sigma projects, you are likely to find that some of the most enlightening information comes right in the actual "map creation" sessions, as people start to hear about how work is done and processes managed in other parts of the business. When a process is documented and validated (i.e., checked with others who do the work to see if the map matches "reality"), you can analyze it for some of the following specific problem areas:

- *Disconnects.* Points where handoffs from one group to another are poorly handled, or where a supplier and customer haven't communicated clearly on one another's requirements.
- *Bottlenecks.* Points in the process where volume overwhelms capacity, slowing the entire flow of work. Bottlenecks are the "weak link" in getting products and services to customers on time and in adequate quantities.

- *Redundancies.* Activities that are repeated at two points in the process; also can be parallel activities that duplicate the same result (e.g., entry of the same data into different departments' systems).
- *Rework loops.* Places where a high volume of work is passed "back" up the process to be fixed, corrected, or repaired.
- *Decisions/Inspections.* Points in the process where choices, evaluation, checks, or appraisal intervene—creating potential delays. These activities tend to multiply over the life of a business and/or process.

Fun with Data Analysis at AutoRec

When the "We Deliver" subteam working on data analysis met to plan their approach, they started by looking at the list of possible causes to see how data might support or refute them. As a reminder, the initial hypotheses were these:

- Incorrectly entered Order Specification forms
- Mislabeled connectors, and adapters being packed into the shipments
- Errors made due to the rush to meet delivery dates
- Untrained Assembly staff, hired at a rate of several dozen per month, were mixing up digital and tape-recording devices
- Shipments being mislabeled at the dock and sent to the wrong customer

Since quantities shipped usually were accurate, the team ruled out "Mislabeled Shipments" as the root cause. "You'd expect to see the quantities to be all wrong," noted Ravi from Order Administration. "I don't think I've ever had two orders that wanted the exact-same number of units."

The group agreed to look more closely at the largest category of defect from the initial breakdown: hardware incompatibilities. The team was able to construct a "second-level" Pareto Chart focusing on the hardware incompatibilities, shown with the "first-level" which showed the major issues involved incompatible connecters and adaptors (see Fig. 15.10).

"But I know we're sending adapters and connectors," said Arnold from shipping. "This still doesn't explain why they're wrong."

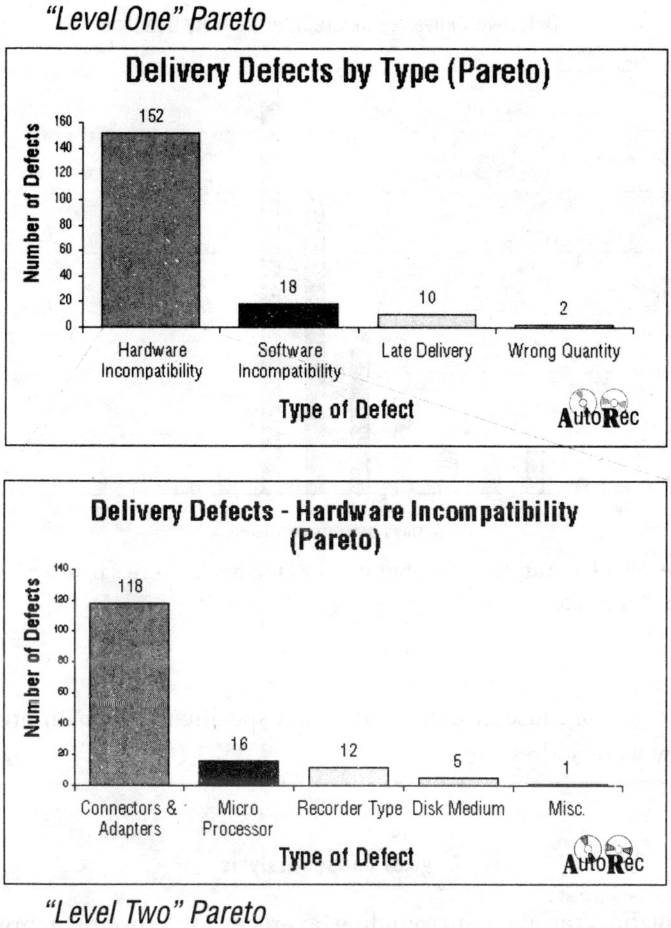

Figure 15.10 AutoRec level 1 and level 2 Pareto charts

One issue they investigated required some statistical analysis. A hypothesis suggested that the rush to get orders out was causing the problem. They first developed a Histogram showing distribution of defective shipments, based on how many days before or after a scheduled delivery date the order was shipped to the customer (see Fig. 15.11). Clearly, rushing seemed to be an issue. However, when they stratified the defective data by *type* of defect they found—using "Analysis of Variance" or "ANOVA" (see Chapter 18, page 360)—that the pattern for rushing was no different for Hardware Incompatibility than for any other type of defect. So, while "rushing" seemed to

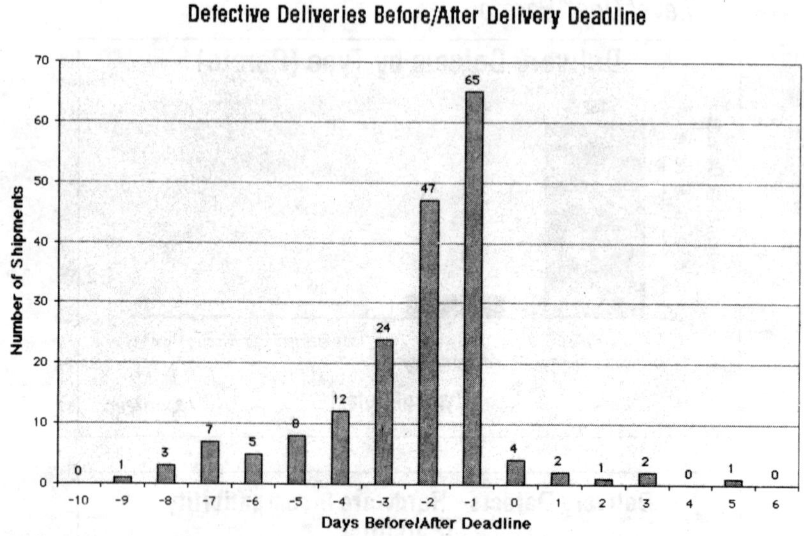

Figure 15.11 AutoRec distribution of defective deliveries by days before or after "due date"

be a *general* cause of defects, it wasn't specific to the main problem they were addressing.

Logical Cause Analysis

Investigating the data surrounding a process improvement problem requires discipline, an open mind, and a mix (strange as it may seem) of logical and creative thinking. Armed with a pool of (accurate) data of the kind the AutoRec team has collected, you want to use the data, and other available facts, to surface new cause hypotheses or to objectively "test" existing hypotheses to see if they fit the data.

The method of logical cause analysis is an approach that all of us use intuitively, at least some of the time. For example if a small child tells you "Doggie ate cookies," yet you see crumbs all over his or her face, you are skeptical of the child's "hypothesis." Or if your car (SUV) won't start—the motor doesn't make a sound—but the lights, radio, wipers, power windows, etc. all work as usual, there's evidence that the battery is *not* the problem. In both these cases what you *observe* (the facts) doesn't fit the hypothesis.

The beauty of the logic-based approach (technically, this is "deductive" logic) is that you don't need to be an "expert" in a subject or technology to contribute to the narrowing down of possible causes. Another benefit of this Logical Cause Analysis is its objectivity and emphasis on facts. The technique (it's also an attitude) is driven by questions, and supported in most cases by "stratified" data about the process, problem, or product. (We've already talked about gathering stratified data in Chapter 14—now we can see how to use it.) Typical logical analysis questions for you to pose when involved in a DMAIC project include:

- What types or categories of problems are more common? What's different about the most common types?
- Are there locations (regions, places on the item itself) where the problem is greater? How are those places where the problem occurs more unusual?
- What are the times, days, weeks or conditions when the problem is most prevalent? What's going on that's unique during those times?
- What factors or variables change as the problem changes (or "correlate" with the problem)?

These and other questions support the analysis cycle by narrowing the problem, eliminating possible causes (an important step in finding the real cause), and/or validating hypotheses. If your team has not included stratification factors in your initial data collection, the ability to do this analysis will be more limited; as we've noted, however, more than one round of data collection is not uncommon.

Visual Tools for Data Analysis

Often, the best way to learn from your data is to literally "see" the answers to the questions you pose. We've already seen a couple of these visual data analysis tools in the AutoRec case; here we'll provide background and examples of four of the most common techniques and how they can be used.

Pareto Chart or Pareto Analysis

The Pareto is used to stratify data into groups from largest to smallest. A specialized form of bar chart, the Pareto helps you identify the most common occurrences or causes of a problem. To use a Pareto Chart, however, you need to make sure you have discrete or category data—it won't work with measures like weight or temperature (i.e., continuous data). Pareto analysis is based on the "80/20 Rule"—the notion that 80 percent of the costs or pain in an organization are created by just 20 percent of the problems. The numbers aren't always exactly 80 and 20, but the effect is often the same. You can use a Pareto Chart to:

- Sort problem data by region, and find which region has the most problems
- Compare defect data by type, and see which defect is most common.
- Compare problems by day of the week (or month, or time of day), to see during which period the problems occur most often.
- Sort customer complaints by type, to see what the most common complaints are.

Histogram or Frequency Plot

Histograms are used to show the range and depth of variation in a group of data (aka "population"). A Histogram technically shows continuous data only, while a Frequency Plot can display discrete "count" data (e.g., numbers of defects). Both show data along a continuum or increasing quantity on the horizontal (x) axis and the number of frequency of occurrences/observations on the vertical (y) axis. In process improvement, groups of data on the continuum are grouped and displayed as a bar chart; the more "classic" view of a Histogram, though is known as the "bell-shaped curve." You can use a Histogram or Frequency Plot to:

- See the range and distribution of continuous factors (e.g., weights for each shipment; dollars spent per purchase; size of each hole; reboot time for each computer).
- See the variation and performance around a customer specification/requirement (e.g. size, cycle time, temperature, cost) (*Note:* continuous factors only.)
- See how many defects occur on each unit in a group of defective items (when there are multiple opportunities for error). (These may include discrete characteristics.)

- See how key "count" characteristics in a group or population are distributed (e.g., customers by number of purchases per year, suppliers by score on our quality audit).

Run Chart or Time Series Plot

A Run Chart shows the variation in a process, product, or other factor *over time*—a very valuable tool for understanding processes, which by nature are ever-changing. The Run Chart (also called a "Trend Chart" or "Line Graph"), and its cousin the Control Chart, show how things change from moment to moment, day to day, etc.—making them the best tools to track ongoing activity or performance. In structuring a Run Chart, the horizontal or x axis is *always* the time or sequence of occurrence moving from left to right. The vertical (y) axis can represent any continuous or count measure, including percentage, number of defects, and temperature. As each observation, or sample of observations, is made, it's noted in the proper time-order at the value observed.

You can use a Run Chart or Time Plot to:

- See the degree and pattern of variation in a process or product over time; for example, how much difference there is in test data from day to day; or how much variation occurs in process cycle time from item to item.
- Identify possible timing patterns in variation; for example: Is there a weekly cycle? Do certain events seem to match changes in the process?
- See how a process or key factor is responding to change; e.g., how process improvements are impacting performance; how the new phone system is affecting caller hold times.

Scatter Plot or Correlation Diagram

The Scatter Plot shows the link or "correlation" between two factors that vary by count or on a continuum. Scatter Plots show potential causal relationships between one factor and another. As a simple example, daily high temperatures and ice cream sales would tend to be correlated: It's reasonable to conclude that hotter weather causes people to buy more ice cream. It can be dangerous, however, to assume that a correlation guarantees that one factor causes the other. Chlorine sales at pool supply stores, for example, may increase as ice cream sales do (i.e., they're "positively correlated"); but we're pretty sure one doesn't cause the other. Another cause—hotter weather, perhaps?—happens to affect both.

Nevertheless, Scatter Plots can be a great tool for you to use to test the links between the suspected causes of a problem. A strong correlation can be a pretty good indicator that your hypothesis is valid, as long as you apply common sense when drawing your conclusions.

There are actually several types of correlation you may find:

- *"Positive Correlation."* Mentioned already, this is the relationship in which an *increase* in one factor tracks with an *increase* in the other.
- *"Negative Correlation."* In this case, an increase or decrease in one factor matches the *opposite* effect in the other.
- *"Curvilinear Correlation."* This is the Scatter Plot version of "what goes up, must come down." For some factors, a positive or negative correlation may exist up to a certain point, at which it actually turns into the opposite.

When there is *no* correlation, the points will literally be scattered all around the chart like a cloud—meaning that a change in one factor had nothing to do with a change in the other. You can measure the strength of the link between two factors statistically—which is pretty easy to do, with the formulas built into most spreadsheet programs.

You can use a Scatter Plot or Correlation Diagram to:

- See the degree to which one factor's increase in value or performance is linked to the increase or decrease in another.
- Test the relationship between a suspected root cause of a problem and the level of the problem (defects, costs, etc.).

Bringing Data and Process Knowledge Together

Back at AutoRec, two subteams had been working on process analysis and data analysis for the delivery defects problem. The full team then convened, to share their findings. While they realized they hadn't yet gotten to the true root cause of the problem, they were ready to formulate some more refined hypotheses. They noted the most revealing facts so far:

1. The most common defects in deliveries were due to incompatible connectors and adapters, accounting for about 60 percent of the bad deliveries.

2. Connectors and adapters were being carried in inventory, not ordered on a "just-in-time" basis. Ordering for those parts was triggered when the Store Room in Assembly noticed that stock was low.
3. Defective orders tend to be those shipped just before the due date; however, all types of defects occur in the same pattern—indicating that rushing alone isn't the reason for the high level of adapter/connector incompatibilities.

A couple of suspected causes—order entry mistakes and mislabeled shipments—had been eliminated. Inadequate training of the Assembly staff did not appear a strong possibility, as it was felt that other problems would be found that were not seen in any of the data.

There was a heated discussion about what to do next. A couple of members (we'll protect their identities) wanted to simply tell customers they'd get their orders a little later, and lengthen the lead time that Sales promised for delivery.

The other view was expressed by Al, the Team Leader. He noted that the company might be hurt even *more* in the long run if it slowed delivery time just to cut defects. "If TalkNBox can fill orders faster than we can when their products come out, it *will* become important to customers, and we'll be left in their dust."

Finally, two "next steps" were agreed to:

1. Al would confer with Pat DeLia, the team's Sponsor, to get an executive perspective on the problem and on the issue of delivery cycle times.
2. The team would think about the problem, and bring other ideas on where to go next with their analysis to a half-hour "update" meeting the following day.

Narrowing Down the Root Causes

The next day, Al brought feedback from the team's Sponsor to the group. "Pat was pretty adamant that we not lengthen delivery commitments," he said. "It'll reduce our capacity in the long run, and we're still looking at significant growth if we can keep our edge on TalkNBox. So we really need to figure out why the connectors and adapters are wrong so often."

The next person to speak up was Elena from Procurement: "I've been thinking a lot about this. One thing we haven't thought about is that we never had this level of rejected deliveries a year and a half ago, when the AutoTalk systems first came out."

"So what's different now from back then?" Al asked. "I mean, other than we have more people and more customers and might be out of business in six months if we don't figure out this problem."

"That's easy," said May from Sales. "The product mix."

"Right!" said several people at once. May pulled out a brochure and opened it to a chart that broke down AutoRec sales between tape and digital memory recording devices. It showed that as sales had grown, tape devices had slipped from being almost 80 percent to now being about 30% of total units shipped (see Fig. 15.12).

"So if this has changed," asked Ravi from Order Administration, "how would it cause our problem?"

Daphne and Mike from Assembly explained that the connectors and adapters for the two types of products are different, though in a plastic bag it can be hard to tell them apart. After some more discussion, they came up with a *new* root cause hypothesis:

Connectors and adapters for tape media recording devices are being mistakenly shipped with digital memory devices, making them incom-

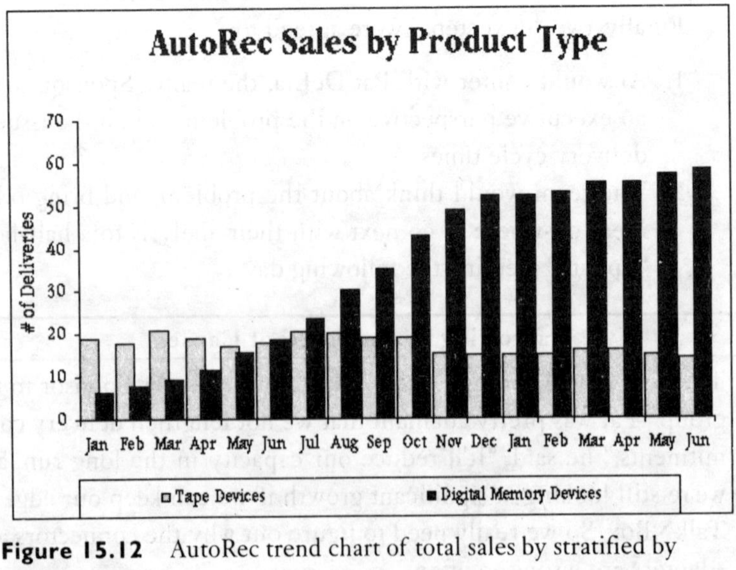

Figure 15.12 AutoRec trend chart of total sales by stratified by product type

patible with the recorders and causing customers to report unusable deliveries.

"But wouldn't we know that?" asked Ravi, a little incredulously.

Daphne and Mike again explained to the team that, when a shipment is reported "defective," they immediately go to work to reassemble and ship it correctly. "To be honest, we haven't had time to do a post-mortem to figure out what the real problem was," Mike explained. "When the returned items come back from the customer, the Returns groups just puts anything that's still usable back in inventory."

"How can we test this cause?" Al asked the group.

"Easy," said Arnold, "if the wrong connectors are going in with digital memory units, those are the ones that should be involved in the bad deliveries." Arnold volunteered to use their spreadsheet to do a comparison by product type. Meanwhile, Elena from Procurement, who'd been quiet for a while, said she was going to check out another hunch.

The End of the Detective Trail

Arnold's chart brought applause from the team (see Fig. 15.13). "I guess that settles it," said Al. "Or does it? I'm still not clear on why the wrong cables are going into the shipments."

"I told you I had a hunch," Elena from Procurement spoke up, "and I was right. We place orders for connectors and adapters with our software system—we call it an 'MRP' system—based on a usage forecast. Turns out the forecast hasn't been updated for 13 months—so we always order a lot more tape device parts than digital."

After more discussion, all of the pieces fell into place; it turned out many digital unit orders were being held up in Assembly because of the shortage of correct connectors and adapters. As the delivery deadline approached, and Shipping became more insistent about getting the orders ready, they would "help" in Assembly and—innocently, but ignorantly—include the wrong parts to complete the shipment. Out the shipments would go—on time, but destined to be rejected because the connectors and adapters would not work.

"This is a great example," someone commented, "of how when a problem is big enough, there's plenty of blame for everyone."

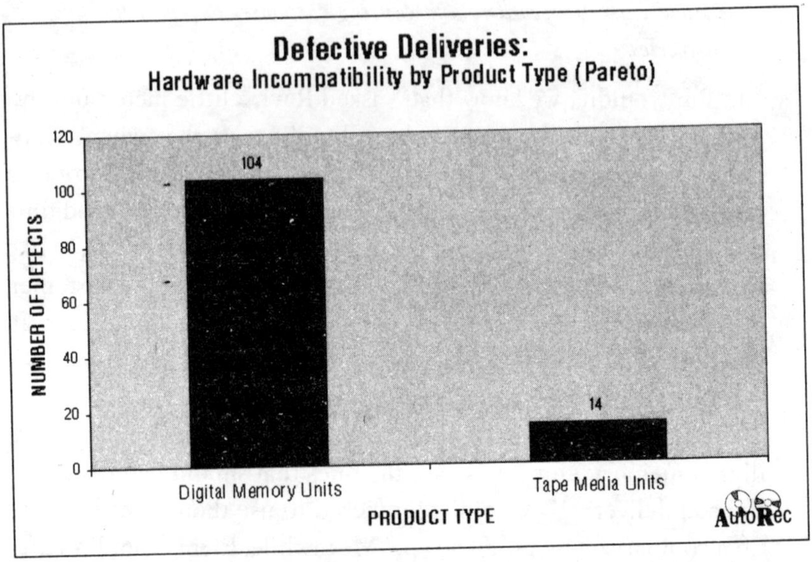

Figure 15.13 AutoRec defective deliveries by product type (Pareto)

Completing the Analyze Phase

There's no such thing as absolute certainty of a root cause. Here are some final steps that will help you to confirm your causal hypothesis and move into the Improve phase:

1. *Verify the cause through logical analysis.* Test the cause against the data you've gathered and ask: "Does this explanation fit the facts, including both what we see *and* what we don't see happening?"
2. *Check the cause through observation.* Visit the process or the place where the cause is suspected to be happening, to see if you can watch it in action.
3. *Confirm your suspicions with people who know.* Talk to people involved in the work—customers, suppliers, or subject matter experts—to get their validation—or refinement or rejection—of your hypothesis.
4. *Apply the "Confidence Test."* As a team, see if you can reach consensus on the following questions:

   - Are we comfortable that we understand enough about the process, problem, and its root cause(s) to develop effective solutions?

- Is the value of further confirmation of our conclusions worth the additional time, resources, and momentum?

If your answers are "Yes" and "No," you're ready to move on to Improve.

Analyze "Dos and Don'ts"

Do—Carefully state your causal hypotheses.

Avoid the tendency to describe suspected causes vaguely or too briefly (e.g., "Bad training," "Defective parts"). General cause statements are not only hard for people to understand, they're difficult to disprove. Rather, create a clear explanation *of the factors you suspect, and how you think they cause the problem.*

Do—Be skeptical about your hypotheses.

The real cause should fit with the data and the process. If it doesn't, don't bend the data to fit—consider what other causes or other facts may be involved.

Do—Apply common sense and creativity.

Statistical techniques have their role, but not as big a role as the ability to ask good questions, recognize patterns and trends, and challenge cause assumptions by setting up logical tests—which can take some creative thinking.

Don't—Over-analyze.

The degree and depth of analysis should be adjusted based on benefits and risks.

Don't—Under-analyze.

Too many shortcuts, or failure to understand the process, can lead to solutions that either miss *the root cause, or solve one problem while creating others. If you really understand the process and problem, you can move to solutions. If not, consider more investigation.*

A checklist for the Analyze phase is provided in the Appendix (page 388).

Improve: Generating, Selecting, and Implementing Solutions

All the work of Defining, Measuring, and Analyzing process problems pays off in the Improve phase—*if* your team and organization handle it well. Lack of creativity, failure to think solutions through carefully, haphazard implementation, organizational resistance—these are all factors that can squelch the benefits of a Six Sigma project. Fortunately, after the "spade work" of investigating a problem is through, most teams find new energy when they begin to ask the questions that drive Improve:

- What possible actions or ideas will help us address the root cause of the problem and achieve our goal?
- Which of these ideas form workable potential solutions?
- Which solution will most likely achieve our goal with the least cost and disruption?
- How do we test our chosen solution to ensure its effectiveness—and then implement it permanently?

We'd suggest it's important during Improve to look for ways to *maximize* the benefits of your efforts. If there are ways your limited solution can help remedy other issues, you should take that advantage—as long as the risks are acceptable. Too often, teams apply *narrow* solutions when they might have achieved more with just somewhat greater creativity and a broader perspective.

The Storm Hits at AutoRec

"In our workbook," Ravi of Order Admin spoke up at the team's next meeting "it says the best way to start the Improve phase is to come up with a lot of ideas of how to solve the problem, and then use those to develop workable solutions." (Ravi had become something of a DMAIC process expert, and several times had helped keep the team on-track by reminding them of key steps.)

After a 20-minute brainstorming session, the team had about 40 ideas, including some pretty good possibilities. But they wanted more input. Daphne from Assembly recommended they try a "billboard" approach to get other people's input. "We've been so close to this problem for a while, I'm not sure my creativity is really good."

Martin the Coach offered to post flip-chart paper in strategic spots around the three AutoRec buildings to get ideas from other AutoReckers (what employees call themselves). At the top of each poster he wrote: "How do we stop shipping the wrong connectors and adapters in customer deliveries? Give us your ideas!" It worked. After three days they had 40 more suggestions.

Idea Generation, Objectives and Methods

A Six Sigma organization—empowered with systems to understand customers and measure processes—can be a great place for creative thinking. Ideally, new ideas stretch the envelope, provide new perspectives on how we work, and pose challenges—and they can be a lot of fun.

Unfortunately, people at work are used to being rather practical—which is okay when you're implementing a solution, but not so cool when you're trying to think "outside the box." Here are some of the basics of effective idea generation and ways to help you broaden your thinking, even in the practical environment of a DMAIC project.

Keys to Brainstorming Success

1. *Clarify the objective of your brainstorming.* Unless everyone has the same purpose in mind, ideas will be a jumble. Another important objective is "quantity," as well as "quality." Setting number targets (for example, "let's generate 30 ideas in the next five minutes") can help boost the numbers of ideas—raising the odds of a breakthrough.
2. *Listen to and build on the ideas of others.* Brainstormers need to pay attention to other people's ideas and not get totally wrapped up in their own thought processes. The "spark" of one person's suggestion may light a larger creative flame in another's brain—but not if no one's listening.
3. *Don't judge, criticize, or comment on ideas.* This may be the most frequently missed "key to success." However, the typical brainstorming session—one idea, followed by five minutes of discussion—tends to keep the really new ideas at bay.
4. *Avoid self-censorship.* The most insidious, evil form of judging ideas happens in *your own head!* Most of us are conscious of how our ideas

make us appear to others. Remember, however, that your "goofy idea" may be the spark for another person's genius. (In brainstorming statistics, we call that "an assist.")

5. *Abandon assumptions and be wild.* Much easier said than done, of course. There's always plenty of time for the practical and analytical considerations in the Improve phase. Doing the same old thing won't get you to Six Sigma.

Other practical considerations for idea generation include the following:

- *Time and Place.* Avoid times of low energy or high distraction, or places where people will tend to think more practically.
- *Participation.* Usually more is better (up to a point, of course), so expanding to include other groups and individuals is quite common. On the other hand, people may be less free with their ideas when "the boss" is in the room.
- *Understanding of the Idea Development Process.* People will be more comfortable if they understand how you plan to narrow and synthesize the ideas into workable solutions.

Once you're loaded with ideas, great and not-so-great, the next challenge is to turn them into real *solutions.*

The Calm after the Storm

A veritable blizzard of sticky notes was plastered across the "We Deliver" team's meeting room—ideas from their brainstorming session and the "billboards" they'd posted around the hallways. The team first eliminates redundant ideas, then used the Affinity method to silently organize the remaining ones.

What emerged were five broad categories of ideas:

1. Changing the MRP system. (This one, everyone agreed, was a no-brainer.)
2. Changing the performance incentives for on-time delivery.
3. Broadening the responsibility for preparing shipments.
4. Reorganizing the Assembly Storeroom.
5. Improving the ease of telling tape media parts from digital memory parts.

Through a round of "multivoting," in which each person voted for several of his or her preferred ideas, the list was narrowed to about 12 ideas.

"I don't think we can do all of these," said May from Sales.

"Absolutely not," agreed Al. "If we go to the leadership team with a laundry list like this, we'll get tossed out." Ravi, ever-watchful of the DMAIC process, suggested they try combining ideas into some more-coherent solutions. The group agreed to think and confer informally for a couple of days, and get back together to try to hash out a final solution on Thursday.

The Plan Comes Together

At their next session, all of the team members had fresh input on the various ideas still under consideration. Eventually those were boiled down to two main options, which they called their "Solution Statements":

1. To eliminate hardware incompatibilities in shipments to Corporate clients, change the MRP formula for reorder quantities of connectors and adapters to match the current product mix. Also, change the labeling on connector and adapter packaging to make them easier to identify.
2. To eliminate hardware incompatibilities in shipments to Corporate clients, include all parts—including connectors and adapters—in the just-in-time ordering system, eliminating all product parts from the Assembly Store Room. Change performance criteria so that Procurement, Assembly, and Shipping personnel are all evaluated on meeting delivery schedule correctly.

The team soon began calling the two solutions the "safe option" and the "risky option," as the second choice clearly involved more substantial changes. They set up the following list of selection criteria, to help them choose the most appropriate solution:

- Cost to implement
- Cost to operate
- Ease of implementation
- Likelihood of achieving Project Goal

- Additional/long-term benefits
- Buy-in from the organization

Setting up a Criteria Matrix, the team compared their two options. The implementation and operating costs between the two were about the same. While Solution 1—the safe option—was clearly easier to implement, the team wasn't convinced it would achieve their goal or offer the benefit of addressing some of the other defective delivery issues, such as software incompatibility. And although changing performance criteria was a potential area to meet some resistance, they felt they could get people in Procurement, Assembly, and Shipping to understand the need for the changes.

"We're going to have to work a lot harder to make Solution 2 work," Elena from Procurement said, "but it is basically a much better solution. Option 1 is more of a band-aid."

Because AutoRec's leadership team was meeting the following day, most of the team members stayed late that night, preparing an initial implementation plan while Al finished work on a presentation of their recommended solution to the senior managers. By 10 A.M. the next day, they had the go-ahead to convert to the Just-in-Time ordering and work out new performance criteria across the three key order fulfillment functions.

Synthesizing and Selecting Solutions

Ideas generated in the Improve phase are like raw material: They need to be refined to have real value to the organization. Usually, Six Sigma solutions will be combinations of ideas that together make up a plan for results, whether it's reduced defects, faster cycle times, enhanced value for customers, etc. It's important to recognize that solution selection may not be an either/or choice. Combining several actions into one plan is okay. On the other hand, a "shotgun" solution that sprays many different mini-fixes at the problem can be a big waste of resources.

Solution Statements

The "Solution Statement" is a clear description of a proposed improvement. The value of the Solution Statement is that it ensures a thorough definition and understanding of the idea under consideration. We recommend that your teams consistently create these statements to ensure that solutions have been well thought through. The Solution Statement becomes the project objective once you've chosen a solution to be implemented. It also becomes the last of the four key statements a DMAIC team should create in the course of a process improvement project (Problem Statement, Goal Statement, Hypothesis Statement, Solution Statement).

A criteria-based choice is a way to show the rationale behind a recommended solution—which is why Al of AutoRec was able to get the senior managers' approval so quickly. A Cost/Benefit analysis can be incorporated into the decision process as well.

Now let's take a moment to summarize the key steps leading up to a final DMAIC solution:

1. *Generate solution ideas.* Use brainstorming, common sense, and other techniques like best practices analysis, expert input, etc. to create a broad array of possibilities to deal with the root cause.
2. *Narrow options, and create "Solution Statements."* Refine the ideas into workable approaches that can be implemented in the process/business. Describe them in a formal "statement."
3. *Select the solution to be recommended/implemented.* Review your "short list" of options and identify the solution to be implemented to achieve your goal. Be aware that other potentially terrific solutions *may* be put on a plan for later implementation.

Implementing Process Improvements

This midpoint in the Improve phase is a major threshold for a team. After what are usually weeks of talking, measuring, and analyzing, they're finally going to *do* something. Depending on the nature of the solution, a team may need other knowledge and resources. The atmosphere changes from one of reflection to one of action.

While the potential benefits increase as actual improvement gets closer, the risks increase as well. To launch solutions successfully you should focus on the "four Ps": Planning, Piloting, and Problem Prevention:

- *Planning.* Changing or fixing a process demands strong project management skills. Having a solid implementation plan that covers actions, resources, and communication is key, and more critical as the complexity of the solution increases.

- *Piloting.* Trying solutions on a limited scale is a must. The chances of unforeseen problems are high, and the "learning curve" can be steep when changing to a new way of doing things.
- *Problem Prevention.* Asking tough questions like "How could this thing crash and burn?" can seem like negative thinking when you're in the midst of an exciting improvement project, but it's key to ensuring that your team has thought through as many possible difficulties as it can—and is prepared to deal with them proactively.

Putting the Solutions in Place

The AutoRec team got busy right away on planning for their solution. Realizing that their proposal had two major elements—switching to just-in-time inventory (JIT) and developing the new performance criteria—they set up two parallel implementation teams. The original Project Charter had included an IT support liaison person, Bob Megabyte, but the performance criteria changes clearly would call for some help from Human Resources. Thus the VP of HR agreed to let Bonnie Fitz, one of the most experienced people in the HR group, become part of the implementation team.

Each implementation team put together a plan to pilot its solution. For the JIT effort, one vendor of adapters was chosen to try out the new ordering and delivery procedure for a two-week trial. There were a few bugs, but it worked out. The main challenge was getting people in Assembly and Procurement, and the vendors, to get used to a new way of handling the adapters. Once AutoRec's people had gone through the change with one vendor, though, they were more comfortable with making the switch for other vendors.

Because their biggest fear was that a vendor wouldn't meet its short-turnaround delivery commitments, Procurement and Assembly agreed to have a backup supply on-hand so the new system wouldn't cause even more late or bad deliveries if it didn't work. (They only had to use the backup connectors for one shipment.)

For the new performance criteria, one of the "problem prevention" techniques chosen was to let AutoReckers have input into the new system. Since many of the people already knew of the havoc created by bad deliveries, they were pretty open to change. In fact, one of the suggestions was to measure not just on "on-time" delivery but actual speed of order fulfillment. The plan was begun first in Assembly, and went well. Within a month the new guidelines and performance criteria were in effect for all three groups.

Measuring Results

The "We Deliver" team continued to measure delivery defects during the planning and piloting effort. It was interesting to see that, once the cause of the problem had been uncovered, some improvement happened right away. As each element of the solution was rolled out, the level of defective deliveries dropped sharply, as the team's Run Chart showed (see Fig. 15.14).

Other reasons for defective deliveries were reduced, too. The level of coordination between Procurement, Assembly, and Shipping increased substantially as they were all given a clear, common performance standard: Get orders out as early as possible, but get them done *right.* Informal "teams"—helped by the data the "We Deliver" team had developed—started to look into other causes of bad shipments. They were able to change some of their procedures to avoid those, and rush shipments eased up somewhat, as well. With the reduction in incompatibility defects and other benefits, the DPMO for the process was cut from 122,000 to 39,000—a Sigma level of about 3.3.

Concluding the Project

With results beyond even their ambitious Goal, the "We Deliver" team was a proud group. They had worked with managers in the key functions affected by the project to transition the improvements to their responsibility. However, since we'll be talking about the Control phase later, we'll leave the AutoRec group to enjoy their post-project party (complete with DJ) and their new commitment to Six Sigma improvement.

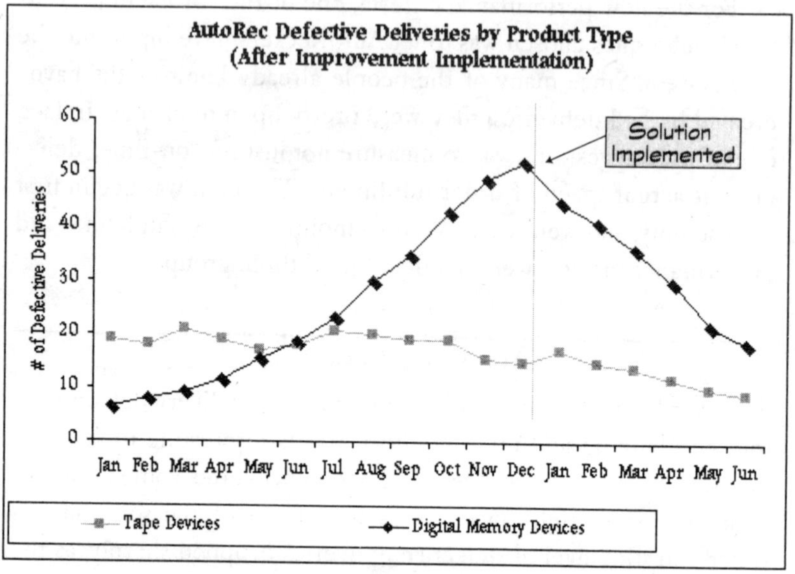

Figure 15.14 AutoRec run chart showing defect levels before/after DMAIC solution

Completing the Improve Phase

It can take a while to test solutions, measure results, and ensure the success of a DMAIC project. A final, critical element of the implementation is to capture data to track the impact of the changes as they take effect—both to tally the results and to look for, and respond to, any possible glitches.

Improve "Dos and Don'ts"

Do—Look for really innovative solutions.

Every Six Sigma project is an opportunity to take your business performance to a new level. While Process Design/Redesign is usually the approach that yields "exponential" improvement, any solution can be a home run.

Do—Target your solutions.

Keep your goal in mind at all times. Don't let the thrill of brain-

storming and developing solutions lead you into other changes that don't directly impact the problem you've been assigned to address.

Do—Plan carefully and proactively.

Rushing to implement a solution can undermine all your efforts. Processes are stubborn, and people are creatures of habit. You have to approach any solution with the realization that it will work only if you do it right the first time.

Don't—Implement full-scale the first time.

Failure to pilot solutions is an almost guaranteed disaster. You can recover from small setbacks and manage limited problems; you may not *recover if your solution backfires on the organization.*

Don't—Forget to measure.

Measures help you see what's working and what isn't, they prove your results, and they convince others that this improvement stuff, well, it's okay! Without measures, your results are only anecdotes and your successes a matter of opinion.

Don't—Forget to celebrate successes.

Six Sigma improvement is a thrill. Share it and enjoy it when it works.

A checklist for the Improve phase can be found in the Appendix (page 389).

If Your Company Isn't AutoRec

And of course, it isn't. This story we've told, and the one on Process Design/Redesign we'll tell in the next chapter, reflect just some of what an improvement project is like. Most projects are likely to encounter a few more bumps along the way than the "We Deliver" team did. On the other hand, many projects are simpler than theirs was, just as plenty are more complicated. But more than on the details of this project, we hope you will focus on the *process* the team followed:

1. They encountered a problem and clarified it. *Define!*
2. They measured the problem and narrowed it. *Measure!*
3. They delved into data and the process, learned about the problem, and figured out what was causing it. *Analyze!*
4. They considered the cause, and targeted solutions to eliminate the cause and achieve the improvement they'd committed to. *Improve!*

Amidst the plethora of tools, questions, and challenges, it really is as simple as that.

CHAPTER

16

Six Sigma Process Design/Redesign

(Roadmap Step 4B)

Introduction and Key Deliverables

The ability to create new or wholly-renewed process was described in Chapter 2 as a critical "core competency" for 21st-Century organizations. To achieve Six Sigma levels of performance and keep pace with market and technology changes, both Six Sigma improvement strategies—improvement and design/redesign—will be needed. This "reinventing" activity—focused on *exponential* versus incremental improvement—is our focus in this chapter (see Fig. 16.1).

Critical Steps toward Process Design/Redesign

The DMAIC process, applied to designing or redesigning a business process, can be revealed to you by asking a few key questions:

- What extent or "scope" of activities will be subject to our process design?
- What are the critical outputs, output requirements, and service requirements that the new process must be able to achieve? What new standards should the process be able to meet in the future?

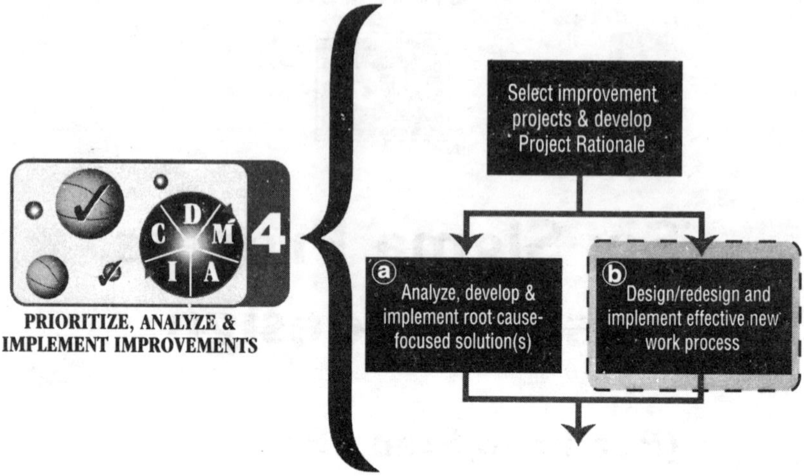

Figure 16.1 Six Sigma Roadmap Step 4B

- What internal performance goals are key to the success of the new process (speed, cost, ease of use, flexibility, etc.)?
- What will the new flow of work and assignment of responsibilities look like? How can we improve on our first-pass redesign?
- How will we test, refine, and transition to the new work process?
- How will we manage the organizational impact of a substantial change in how we accomplish this work?

Before we look at how to answer these questions, though, let's explore some of the key issues relating to *why* and *when* Process Design/Redesign is needed.

Benefits of "Six Sigma Design"

Since many companies tried "reengineering" during the 1990s, it would be legitimate to wonder: "How is this different?" For one thing, "Six Sigma Design" includes tools to design new products and services, not just processes. In fact, several of the advanced Six Sigma techniques covered in Chapter 18 are commonly applied to creating high-performing, low-defect new products. For *Process* Design and Redesign—our focus in this chapter—Six Sigma offers a chance to improve on some of the shortcomings of past reengineering campaigns. The following are some of the key differences.

Emphasis on Value and Customer

Many large-scale reengineering initiatives of the past were thinly disguised campaigns to downsize the organization. These reengineering efforts were too often made without adequate consideration given to the needs of *customers*—not to mention the impact on reengineering "survivors." The starting point for process design/redesign in the "Six Sigma generation" will be on enhancing value to customers and making major strides in productivity, speed, and efficiency.

A Scalable, Focused Method

Redesign efforts under Six Sigma will focus on specific segments of a business or on critical change opportunities. The result will be smaller, more manageable design and redesign projects—again in clear contrast to the sweeping efforts of the 1990s. Rich Lynch, co-author of the book *Corporate Renaissance,* a work on the "how-to" of reengineering, notes that the long execution times of past reengineering projects constituted a key reason why top leaders lost commitment for the effort. More focused design projects will be easier to manage and faster to complete—though they almost always will be longer than process improvement projects.

Broader Application of Design/Redesign Efforts

Making Process Design/Redesign a standard part of the Six Sigma system will allow for broader participation and a better range of ideas and skills. Many early reengineering projects were assigned to an elite group, or a major consulting firm, with the rationale that such critical decisions needed to have top talent behind them. However, ideas that look terrific at the 30,000-foot level may not be practical when implemented. At the same time, people close to the process—accustomed to doing things a certain way—may be unable to "think outside the box" in seeking new ways to design their work.

Process Design/Redesign success depends on a balance between "break-the-mold" creativity and practical implementation. Involving a broader range of people in your design/redesign efforts will help your business to learn that it must not just *fix* problems, but also *design* processes that work.

Applying Technology Wisely

One of the often-cited "drivers" of reengineering is improvement in information technology (IT). But IT change has proven to be a sharp double-edged sword, when it comes to streamlining processes and improving service to customers. The Internet, database technology, customer relationship management (CRM) systems, and the increasing processing power of computers have enabled many companies to better manage inventories, respond faster, tailor their offerings, and so on. In many cases, business processes have been completely redesigned so as to take advantage of technological capabilities.

The other edge of the technology sword, however, has been the tendency to take on huge systems-upgrade projects and to expect them to magically produce dramatically better business processes—a notion now proven to be overly optimistic. Complicated, corporate-wide IT solutions are, if nothing else, very complicated (also expensive, risky, and challenging). The many stories of delays, frustration, patched-together fixes, and unmet needs in major IT projects signal that systems changes may be better off scaled-down—just like reengineering efforts.

The link between Six Sigma process design and IT change is getting stronger, as companies find the two coming together naturally. At General Electric, Six Sigma Design is now part-and-parcel of many IT efforts: It's been a requirement since 1998 that any significant system or software implementation be guided by GE's Process Design/Redesign model. In fact, the corporate leader of GE's Six Sigma initiative in its first two years, Gary Reiner, was also the company's Chief Information Officer.[1]

Getting Started on Process Design/Redesign

The decision as to when to take on a process design or redesign is usually not black-and-white. In the Process Redesign "story" to be introduced in a moment, the team decides early on that they need to redesign an inadequate process. In other instances, however, it will be *during* the DMAIC effort that a team will decide—with their Sponsor's approval—that a design or redesign is needed. Let's get the background on the case example, and then explore when to take up the banner for design/redesign.

Overview of the Process Redesign Story[2]

Slow Bubbling at COLA

As companies have become more dependent on information technology, the risks of major system outages and crashes have become enormous. As Internet service disruptions have shown, the potential liability for loss of service—not to mention potential lost information and revenue—can threaten the very existence of companies in the technology business. Fortunately, a rule of the free market is: "Where there's risk, there's *insurance*."

In fact, fueled by demand that's been addressed by independent start-ups and new divisions of large insurance companies, IT outage and liability coverage has gradually grown into a big chunk of business for the insurance industry. One of the traditional insurance practices carried over into this new arena is the "letter of agreement." When a large IT provider or major corporation is sold a policy for outage and liability insurance, the "LOA" is the document used to initiate coverage. It's not an official policy, but lays out general guidelines for the insurance to be provided. Legally, after the LOA is complete, the insurance company has 12 weeks to complete the policy, which represents the formal, official contract.

The people at COLA—"Computer Outage Liability Assurance"—have been *increasingly* worried about the impact of the so-called "12-Week Limit." (COLA is an independently-operated subsidiary of mammoth insurance leader III—International Insurance and Indemnity—known in the trade as "Number Three.") There are a number of issues that have been recognized pertaining to the standard four-month policy-writing effort:

- The efficiencies of an 8- to 12-week contract-writing process are questionable. COLA CEO R.O. Biere (known as "Rute") has commented on a number of occasions: "My grandmother—may she rest in peace—could get a contract done in *six* weeks!"

- Legal issues that arise between the signing of the LOA and completion of the policy—including claims and disputes over coverage terms—keep the COLA legal department on a permanent hiring binge, and cost the company between $2 to $3 million a month.
- COLA customers are beginning to complain vehemently about the lag time between LOA and formal policy. While some industries haven't put up much fuss about the 12-Week Limit, in the IT business 12 weeks can cover two mergers and three product life cycles. Often, new LOAs are written for a client before the policy for a first one is ready. Even customers who haven't had to file claims say they're feeling vulnerable with only "semi-official" coverage.
- Insurance regulators are rumored to be considering cutting the 12-Week Limit, perhaps in half.

COLA's Process Improvement Projects

Over the past year and a half, COLA has launched several projects in an effort to reduce the time it takes to get a policy completed. In each case, some progress has been made: One project team, discovering that LOAs were being handled on a "Last-In, First-Out" basis, cut last-minute and late policy writing by about 20 percent. Another project changed the way its LOAs are written so that it will be easier to transfer basic terms to the formal policy.

And yet despite those efforts, the average time it takes to complete a policy at COLA is still 10.4 weeks after the signing of the LOA. That's down from 11.2, but remains a long way from what customers are asking for.

Essential Conditions for Process Design/Redesign

The people at COLA face a dilemma that will become increasingly common for Six Sigma organizations: Which approach to improving our business is best in this situation? COLA's leaders *could* take an improvement-based approach; after all, they have been successful with earlier projects. On the other hand there's concern that additional Process Improvement projects—even effective ones—won't be enough.

We've been asked by business leaders if there's a formula for deciding when to launch a redesign effort. Our honest answer is "No," since there are simply so many variables to consider, from the scope of the process you want to change, to your willingness to undergo business upheaval, to the urgency of the need for major performance gains. We can offer an assessment model, however, based on two major conditions—*both* of which must be met if process design/redesign is going to work:

Condition #1: A Major Need, Threat, or Opportunity Exists

The "benefits" side of the design/redesign equation can emerge out of various sources or threats. Although there's some overlap in the following list, it does give you some situations in which a new process may be needed:

- *Shifts in customer needs/requirements.* Newly emerging needs, more stringent demands, changes in the customer's market and industry—all these put pressure on your business to make dramatic changes in services, product features, delivery capability, etc.
- *Demand for greater flexibility.* Increasingly segmented or individualized customer demands mean that your processes need to handle a wider range of needs and requirements. Your current processes may not be ready to meet a "one-size-fits-one" objective.
- *New technologies.* Whether they are perceived as a threat or an opportunity, your organization needs to accommodate those advances that impact your products and services. Note that new technologies may have nothing to do with your products or services themselves: Books are pretty much the same as they ever were, but the Internet is demanding new processes among booksellers.
- *New or changed rules and regulations.* Deregulation has had a huge impact on processes in many industries over the past 20 years or so. New laws—the Americans with Disabilities Act, or the air and water pollution guidelines—have had significant effects, too. Companies that respond to those changes quickly and decisively may gain a big edge.
- *Competitors are changing.* Others serving your market, or new entrants, may be tapping into needs or opportunities you've missed. When the competition is getting an edge, it may be time to look for ways

to leap over them in terms of value, speed, or any other key competitive factor.

- *Old assumptions (or paradigms) are invalid.* This is the internal "wake-up-call" version of some of the elements noted already. Sometimes the shifts in customer demands, markets, technologies are observed by a business, but still not understood or heeded.

  A sad anecdote will illustrate here. We worked with a once-successful high-tech firm that enjoyed a couple of years as the shining star in the technology universe before suffering a near-fatal decline. One of the factors we observed just as the star began to fade: Their customer base had evolved from a self-sufficient, highly technical end-user to a more "average," non-technical user. Despite that shift, the company had no dedicated customer support resources. The company's engineers—supposedly dedicated to all-important new-product design efforts—were constantly being pulled away to deal with existing customer issues. Meanwhile, a major new product was two years overdue. Yet there was no hint of an effort to change the situation.

  Process Redesign is sometimes needed to jolt the people and the assumptions that govern an organization out of their reverie that things are just fine the way they are.

- *The current process is "a mess."* We like that phrase a lot more than a technical definition such as "The current process is not capable"—"capability" being a statistical definition—or "The process has reached its entitlement." (Makes you want to respond: "Whatever!") Statistical or technical assessments of a process alone can't tell a business leader if a process warrants redesign. For example, a woefully "incapable" process can in many cases be improved substantially through some well-executed improvements (i.e., not a redesign). Other processes—like the one at COLA—are so littered with problems or with old, ingrained ways of doing things that trying to just weed out root causes would be fruitless.

Condition #2: You're Ready and Willing to Take On the Risk

The "dangers" of Design/Redesign aren't trivial. But they can be managed, of course, so the real question is: "Are we ready and able to take this project to completion?" The following are some of the requirements for taking on the added risk of a redesign effort.

- *Longer lead-time for change is acceptable.* In many cases, designing or changing a process takes more time than you'd expected.
- *Resources and talent are available.* You can't expect to just swap an old process for a new one. You'll need people on the redesign team who understand the customer, services/products, process, technology, and people. The chances of needing capital investment, new IT systems, and even the right new people increase whenever you take on a complete "rethinking" of your work.
- *Leaders, and the organization as a whole, will support the effort.* Consensus needn't be total, since some resistance is guaranteed, but the ability to make a convincing case in favor of process redesign is a huge advantage. Leaders need to be ready to make painful choices, too, since new processes realistically may mean fewer people.
- *The "Risk Profile" is acceptable.* Significant change brings more chances for mistakes, opposition, technical problems, and so on. You should consider whether a more limited approach (e.g., a Process Improvement project), represents the safer bet.

Moving to Redesign

COLA CEO Rute Biere and his top lieutenants have been talking about the need to make more progress in shortening the policy completion process. "I think we have an opportunity," said Marketing VP Sal Sparilla. "Our latest Voice of the Customer data show a huge dissatisfaction among IT executives with our performance and with the way the whole outage liability sector is dealing with policy cycle time."

"I know there are a lot of problems in the policy-processing area," confessed VP of Policy Administration Di Edsota. "I can give you seven or eight projects we could launch today—but I still can't guarantee we'd achieve what we want. This 12-Week Limit is just ingrained in how this industry has been working for a long time."

The executive group was concerned, though, about the organizational trauma that might come from trying to remake the policy-writing process. The challenge of managing large-scale change was daunting, to say the least. Finally, though, the group agreed—or was compelled to agree by Rute Biere's strong insistence—to set up a team to explore a ground-up redesign. "It may be the only way," said Biere.

Since launching its process improvement effort a little over a year earlier, COLA had not done any Process *Redesign* projects. One *new* process had been created, to cross-market backup power systems as a joint venture with an equipment manufacturer. "That was easier, though," noted the director of the COLA Management Process (the name for their Six Sigma initiative), Juan Callorrí. "We weren't trying to replace an existing process with a new one."

At a meeting the following week, Callorrí brought a draft Project Rationale to the executive group.

Project Rationale

The Information Technology industry, our market, is driven by a need for speed. Unfortunately, the administrative activities at COLA and other insurers in the outage liability business have not yet responded to that critical need. Where our customers are asking for policies in days, we're taking over ten weeks. Though that's better than the industry average, we're vulnerable to either faster competitors or possible self-insurance by our customers.

We need to completely rethink and redesign our approach to getting policies completed and into the hands of our customers. In doing so, we can offer major benefits to our insureds and to prospective customers, improve our profitability, reduce frustration for our associates, and position COLA for faster growth.

In reviewing those words, several of the executives commented that the thought of cutting policy lead time dramatically was exciting.

"Yeah," said Chief Counsel Tom Collins, "but kind of scary, too."

Define: Defining the Redesign Goal, Scope, and Requirements

COLA Forms a Redesign Team

When word got around that the policy development process was going to be redesigned, there was a mixed reaction around COLA. Some people were pleased and felt it was an overdue decision; others either didn't understand the reasoning or were just afraid of the change. Nevertheless a number of people came forward right away, to volunteer for the redesign team. The first choice was Team Leader: Toni Kwahter. Toni had been at COLA for two and a half years, and was well respected throughout the company. As a former underwriter, she had the core credentials for an insurance company, plus she'd worked for several years at a network systems company and knew the mentality of COLA's customers. Her current position was as head of Customer Relations.

Working with Di Edsota, the VP of Policy Administration, and with the consultant who would be advising the team, Art Glass, Toni selected a team that included a cross-section of the processes and functions in the company:

Bev Ehridge	Human Resources
Ike Scube	Underwriting
Bob Tull	Legal
Colleen Waters	IS (Information Systems)
Tye Neebublscz	Policy Administration

When the team met for the first time, Toni presented the Project Rationale and told the group they were in for a challenging effort. "There are a lot of people who'll say that what we want to accomplish—to get a contract completed fast—is either impossible or unnecessary. We're going to have to be change agents for the company, and as we put together our Charter we want to be focusing on the opportunity we have to make a big impact on our company and especially on our customers."

The Design/Redesign Charter

The basic purpose of the Project Charter in a process redesign effort are the same as in an improvement project: to set direction and to define project parameters. The spirit of the Design Charter, however, should be somewhat different. While the work of a Process Improvement team is to analyze and fix problems, in redesign the intent is more far-reaching: to design and bring to fruition a new way of doing key work in the organization. It may not be awe-inspiring to outsiders, but to people in the business the sense of purpose should be strong. Without a—here's that word—"vision," the level of creativity and energy the team exhibits may be weak and the new process only incrementally better than the old one.

Also, it's okay here for the Problem and Goal statements to be a little more vague, since the focus is often on more global rather than specific issues. Measures are still important, but a Goal Statement that's too concrete can actually *lower* the bar for the team. To people with backgrounds in the technical side of quality, for example, these ideas may seem to lack rigor. The rationale, though, is that the level of benefit being sought through Six Sigma Design requires a sense of passion and purpose beyond what's typical for a Process Improvement project (though passion is a good thing for those teams, too).

The COLA Team's Problem, Goal, and Scope

The team at COLA decided they should give their project a name, to bring some focus to their activities. They agreed to "The Limit Busters" since they were trying to break away from the 12-Week Limit concept that had so upset their customers. It took longer to come up with a Problem and Goal Statement, but the final drafts were finished at the end of a tiring, day-long meeting.

Problem Statement

Completion of insurance policies for COLA clients takes an average of 10.4 weeks. While previous efforts to improve our turnaround have reduced the number of policies not meeting the industry-standard 12-Week Limit, we are still far short of the speed being demanded by our customers in the computer and networking industry. If we don't substantially reduce our policy completion time, we risk losing existing and potential customers to self-insurance or to faster competitors. Seeing a dramatic improvement in our processes is key to COLA's survival and growth.

Goal Statement

Our Goal is to redesign COLA's Policy Completion Process—from signing of the Letter of Agreement to execution of policy documents—to an average of 1.5 weeks by the end of the current fiscal year. In doing so, we will enhance COLA's competitive strength and profitability, and set a new performance standard for our industry.

One of the initial decisions The Limit Busters team made in developing its Charter was in relation to the project "Scope." This was incorporated into the Goal Statement in the form of the phrase "from signing of the Letter of Agreement to execution of policy documents," and quickly became one of the most controversial parts of the meeting.

"Can we really redesign that *entire* process?" asked Bev Ehridge from HR. "That's a huge amount of activity."

"No kidding," agreed attorney Bob Tull. "It seems like too much to get our arms around."

After several rounds of debate, Toni (Team Leader) asked the group's Consultant, Art Glass, for his thoughts. "Well," he said pausing reflectively and stroking his beard, "I'd say two things." He paused again. "Maybe three." (The team had been warned that Art was brilliant, but it took some time to get the brilliance out of him.)

"Number One, you may *have* to take on the entire process to meet your goal. After all, to cut four-fifths, or four-and-a-half-fifths, or even five-sixths of the time out of your process, you may need to look everywhere to cut time from the work. Number Two [he was picking up momentum now], you're right that it will be harder to manage a bigger scope—so you may want to narrow it some if you can. Number Three, which I guess I *do* have, you can *adjust* your scope later to meet the needs of your projects and according to the information gained through your further efforts.

"I'd recommend," he concluded, "that you leave it as is, and review or revise it as you get more data."

At that point the team felt much better about their draft, and agreed to leave the scope as written for the time being. They also were glad to have had Art's input, though as one anonymous team member commented to another later: "We're lucky this is a non-smoking building. Give that guy a pipe, and we'd be listening to him for hours."

The Project/Process Scope

The term "scope" generically describes the size of a problem or the breadth of a team's focus. In Six Sigma projects the term has a more specific definition; by "Scope," we mean the *boundaries* of the process that the project team will seek to design or redesign. Thus the Scope describes the "playing field" or the limits within which all process activities will be considered to be fair game for redesign. Defining Scope can be useful in Process Improvement projects, too, as this can give a team guidelines on where their solutions can be implemented.

Selecting Project Scope

Selecting the *right* scope for a project can be the big challenge. As shown in the COLA team's Goal Statement, a Scope is identified simply by naming the process(es) involved and specifying the *starting* and *ending* points of the steps to be redesigned:

- "We'll redesign the Invoice Payment process, from receipt of invoice through clearing of checks from our account."
- "Our scope for the new Packing Process will start with the labeling of filled product containers, and end with palletizing for shipment."

Having a SIPOC diagram or a more detailed process map helps you to define the scope, because it allows a team to literally *draw* the process boundaries on the diagram.

The choice of scope is often a subjective judgment. Each of the above examples, for instance, could have been broader or narrower and still have been "correct." The debate that transpired among The Limit Buster team at COLA, then, is pretty common; the Scope can be and often is adjusted over the course of the design project.

The following steps to take, and questions to ask, will help you to clarify the scope of your project:

1. *Name the process.* It's better to *avoid* department names (e.g., "The Sales Process") so that you will clearly distinguish redesign (changing how work gets done) from reorganization (changing the reporting structure in a group or function). For instance, make it

    - The "Invoice Payment Process," not "Accounts Payable."
    - The "Service Call Dispatch Process," not the "Tech Support Process."

2. *Identify the end point.* The most important element of a process is its final product, service, or output. The best guideline is to define the end point where the "thing" being processed is passed on, completed, to the customer or next process. Ask:

   What is the key Output of the process? Who is the customer? What's the best "final step" for us to consider within our scope? Can we realistically hope to "redesign" work activities up to that point?

3. *Define the starting point.* The next step is to clarify the "upstream" boundary of the process to be designed. If there's a clear trigger or initiating point for the process—e.g., a customer call, a work order, receipt of raw materials or parts—the starting point can be easy to describe. In other cases, especially with internal process activities, it may be more subjective. Ask:

   At what point or with what action does the process begin? What key Input or handoff would make a reasonable starting point?

4. *Test the scope.* As the boundaries of the process take shape, the team needs to be wary of describing an overly vast or too-narrow chunk of activities. The balance here goes back to our two generic criteria, Meaningful and Manageable. Ask:

   Do the boundaries as defined include the activities necessary to achieve our Goal? Can we effectively design and manage all the activities within our current scope? If we change and improve these steps, will we truly be able to "raise the bar" of performance, efficiency, competitiveness, value, etc.?

Ensuring a Manageable Scope

One approach that fits well with today's need for speed and its constantly changing business environments is the "staged" redesign of a process. After establishing a vision and goals for the "new generation" performance of an entire process, executives, process owners, and/or project teams can segment the design effort into stages, in which a complete overhaul of the work process is undertaken in two or more successive (or, less often, concurrent) projects. If, for example, your company needed to redesign its Service Delivery process so as to enhance global capability, the entire effort might be "scoped" into three stages: 1) Service Ordering; 2) Order Preparation; and 3) Order Delivery and Completion.

Whenever you are tempted to take on a larger Scope, remember the following rule: As the "width" of the process boundaries widens, complexity tends to grow geometrically. One of the challenges of Six Sigma Design is that you are not changing *just* the process within the Scope, but also potentially all the current inputs and interfaces in the project. A redesign project of fairly limited Scope may have from two to eight key interfaces and various other minor ones. As you expand the boundaries, that number could grow dramatically. If Input requirements change, you may need to "renegotiate" with many more Suppliers—making the whole effort a lot more challenging.

Putting the Scope on Paper

The team at COLA reviewed their initial Problem and Goal Statements with the company leadership group. They also included a SIPOC diagram of the Policy Completion Process (Fig. 16.2) which they were able to "borrow" from one of the teams that had completed one of the earlier process improvement projects.

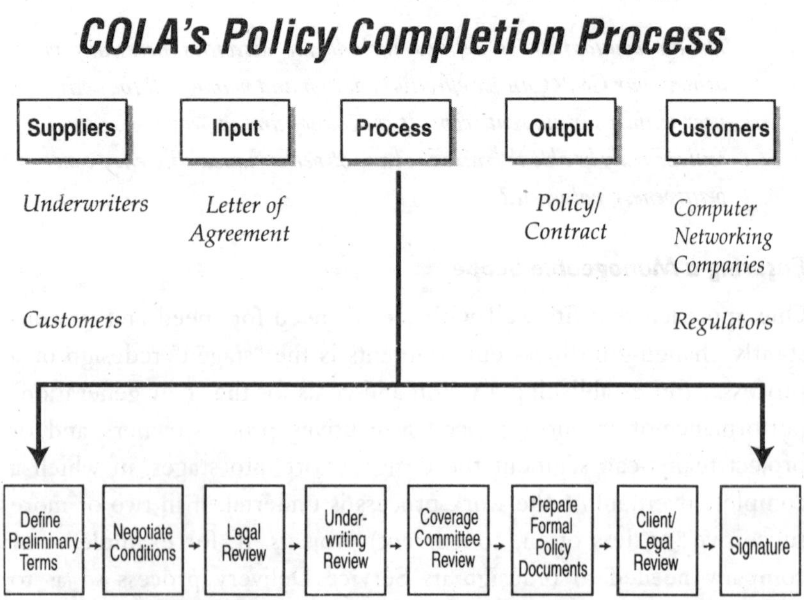

Figure 16.2 COLA's Policy Completion SIPOC diagram

Defining and Revising Process Outputs and Requirements

The most thrilling and inspiring Process Design/Redesign stories come from the groups who took advantage of their projects to redefine their understanding of customer requirements—in some cases, even to change *customers'* understanding of their requirements. In this step, as in many of the activities of Process Design/Redesign, a fundamental objective is to *question existing assumptions* about what's important, why it's needed, and how it can be accomplished. The trouble is, assumptions are hard to abandon.

We know of a training company, for example, that spent significant resources—including buying a printing operation—based on the assumption that customers "needed" high-quality, multi-color-printed training workbooks. In spite of an increased insistence on the part of clients for "custom" and "tailored" training, the firm kept printing materials in large quantities on traditional printing presses. A lot of the stuff ended up getting scrapped, since custom materials were usually used only in small volumes.

Finally, the company awoke to reality: Customers cared much less about color or fancy printing and much more about having training fit their specific needs. That delayed revelation enabled the training company to switch its production to "demand publishing" (printing small runs on black-and-white high-speed laser printers), close its warehouse, and sell the printing operation. All because what they'd "grown up" believing to be important to training buyers was no longer valid.

Steps to Clarify the Output and Requirements

The Output and Requirements form the "reason for being" (or in the French, *raison d'être*) of the process. Over the course of the design effort, however, you'll want to take the following actions and pose the following questions:

1. *Define and reexamine the process output.* Ask:

   - What is the current Output or end product of the process?
   - Is this Output still the best "thing" to fulfill the needs and objectives of the customer?
   - What other alternatives—products or services—might we offer instead, or how might the nature of the Output be changed?

2. *Clarify and scrutinize the key requirements of the Output.* Ask:
   - What features or characteristics of the Output make it useable by/effective for the customer?
   - What other features or characteristics are not being met?
   - What are the needs or changing requirements of our *customers'* customers that we can help them meet more effectively?
   - What other opportunities are there for the product/service to be more valuable, useable, and convenient for the customer?
   - What lessons or other needs can we identify by understanding how the customer uses the Output?
3. *Review and re-test Output and Requirements assumptions with customers.* Ask:
   - How can we check the validity of our, or the customers', assumptions about what's required?
   - What recent data confirm these requirements? Which pieces of data could be questioned?
   - Are there different groups within the process "customer base" that should be addressed separately?

All of those questions reflect our point that if ever you're going to break the "paradigms" on which your process is based, *now is the time to do it.* One of our colleagues has the groups involved in redesign efforts actually write out all their assumptions about a process on sheets of paper and then *tear them up,* to symbolize making a deliberate break with the past.

The COLA Team Visits Customers

The Limit Busters team decided they'd put some heavy emphasis, early in their project, on gaining a renewed understanding of their customers' computer system outage insurance and other areas where COLA could add value. They began by doing a thorough review of existing Voice of the Customer data, noting each key Output and the Requirements.

Next, the team scheduled a series of telephone and in-person meetings with the Risk Management staffs, senior managers, and legal departments of a cross-section of customers. Those discussions proved very enlightening. They began to realize that they might "delight" their customers not only by completing policies faster, but also by making the policy documents themselves easier to understand. They completed their Define phase by creating a preliminary set of Output design specifications for the Policy Completion Process.

Process Design/Redesign Define Dos and Don'ts

Do—Think *big* in terms of results, benefits, and scale of improvement.

Inspired and enthusiastic people tend to be more creative and to persist in spite of resistance. The design team members need to view themselves as "change agents."

Do—Define a Scope that balances opportunity with risk.

You may gain more with a larger scope, but the complexity grows rapidly. Adjust the scope as needed during the project.

Don't—Assume that the Output and Requirements are "static."

Use the Design/Redesign as an opportunity to establish new standards or even to change the "solution" delivered to customers.

Don't—Wait to prepare the organization for change.

A change management plan should be part of the initial work of a Design/Redesign team, in collaboration with the project sponsor and team leaders.

Measure: Establishing Performance Baselines

The COLA Team Checks Its Levels

The process redesign team at COLA already had pretty good data on the *overall* Output cycle time for the Policy Completion process. They realized, however, that if they were to gain a better understanding of the current process performance, it would help to have information on how that time was being used *within* the process. They also decided to add a new, previously missing measure, based on the new feedback from customers: length of policy documents.

The team formulated a data collection and sampling plan, using a "traveler" checksheet to get a view of how long each step in the process was taking. They hoped to be able to see if document size had any impact on processing speed. With the data in hand, they were ready to push ahead into the Analyze phase.

Overview of Measure and Design/Redesign

There are few, if any, key differences between the work of a team in the Measure phase of Process Design/Redesign and the Process Improvement projects. If anything, measurement can be simpler, since the objective of a process design is not to ferret out root causes but just to understand enough about the current process to ensure that the new one can achieve dramatically improved performance. As always, be sure any measure you decide to implement has clear objectives and value to the overall project goal.

Benchmarking and External Measures

External measures are one dimension of the Measure phase that can bring special benefits to a Process Design/Redesign effort. (Process benchmarking is an option for improvement projects, too, but tends to have more applicability when the process itself is being revamped.) Benchmark measures help to establish a point of comparison between your performance and that of other, comparable processes.

Often, the best candidates for benchmark measures are *not* your direct competitors. For obvious reasons, it can be hard to get them to share information. Moreover, industry "inbreeding" can see to it that the worst (not best) practices are replicated throughout a business sector. As you consider other places to gather data or conduct measures outside your organization, ask: "Who does this *really* well, and how can we set a higher standard and learn *better* practices?" From an access and cooperation perspective, looking at other divisions, business units, or acquisitions *within* your overall organization may be a good source for benchmarking data, as well.

Defining Future Measures

One of the tasks of the Six Sigma Design process that is often begun in the Measure phase is to establish measures to be used later in testing design options. Using requirements identified in Define, you can develop specific measurable factors to be evaluated, using process simulation tools and/or methods like Design of Experiments.

Setting up these measures early should not "lock them in," but helps to ensure that key requirements are adhered to throughout the design effort.

Process Design/Redesign Measure Dos and Don'ts

Do—Ensure that you have solid baseline performance measures for the process in all key requirements.

As you confirm results and track performance of the new process, you will need to compare to the baseline data.

Do—Look for information that will help you to identify redesign opportunities, both inside the process and outside the organization.

The intent here is to find ways to build in those better performance practices that measures can help you to identify.

Don't—Go on a hunt for root cause data when you plan to redesign the process.

Unnecessary measures not only can waste your time, but also can hamper creativity by burdening people with too much *data about the current process.*

Analyze: Building a Foundation for Redesign

Dissecting the Baseline Data

The measures the COLA team collected have proven to be quite enlightening. As they had suspected, the cycle time for most of the nine major steps in the Policy Completion Process was in a pretty tight range. They displayed the times per step on a bar chart

(Fig. 16.3). However, when they prepared a Scatter Plot diagram looking at the relationship between document length and *total* cycle time, the data were more revealing (see Fig. 16.4).

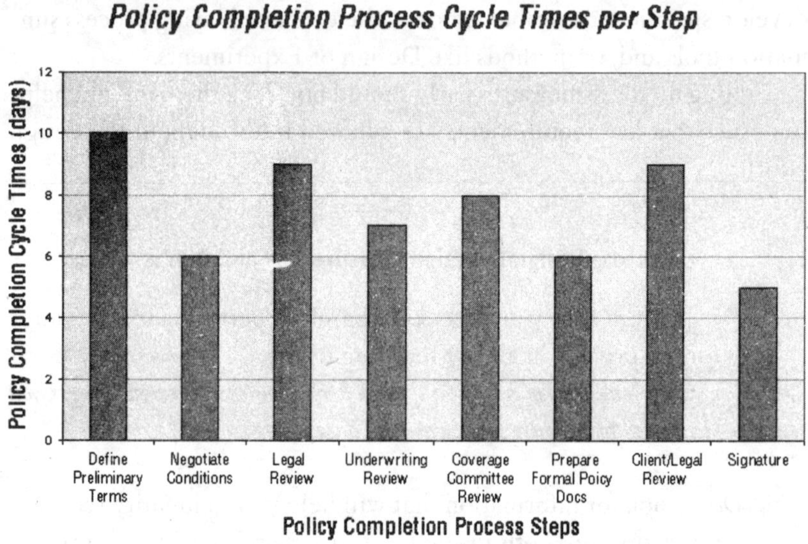

Figure 16.3 COLA Policy Completion Process cycle times per step

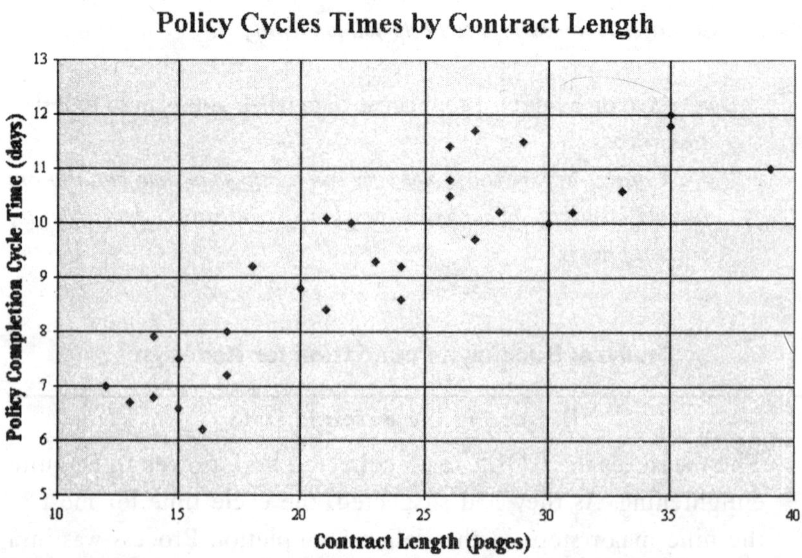

Figure 16.4 COLA scatter plot of policy cycles times (Y) by contract length (X)

A Closer Look at the Process

Despite the findings so far, there was still a lot of skepticism among the team members that redesigning the process really could get them close to their goal of a one-and-a-half-week policy completion. After a longwinded preamble, consultant Art Glass suggested that the team do a "value and time analysis."

"What's that?" asked Bob from Legal, immediately regretting having tossed a question to Art.

Fortunately, for Bob, Art's answer was surprisingly brief: "That's how you figure out how much of the work in the process is really important, and how much time you're spending on it."

Process Design and Analyze

In Process *Improvement,* the Analyze or root-cause-finding stage is pivotal. By contrast, once your organization or team has decided to undertake the *Redesign* of a process, root-cause analysis is no longer critical. The objective instead is to create a new process that applies new workflows, procedures, technologies, etc. to meet a significantly higher level of performance. Over-analysis can actually hamper redesign by locking the current way of doing things into people's heads. At the same time, as the COLA team has discovered, some helpful lessons as to *how* a redesign might lead to a dramatic performance improvement can arise during Analyze.

Process Value Analysis

As processes get more complex, they tend to insulate people from the real reason that customers patronize a business. "Value Analysis" is a way of reemphasizing the key raison d'être of a business or process by looking at work from the external customer's point of view. In the analysis, we assign each process step to one of three categories:

1. *Value Adding.* These are tasks or activities that are valuable *from the external customer's point of view.* That last bit is critical, because almost any step can be justified in *someone's* eyes. "We do this because the boss wants it" does not mean that a task is adding value to the customer.

Here are the three criteria you should consider in relation to taking customer-value-adding steps:

a. The customer cares about and/or would pay us for this activity if s/he knew we were doing it.

b. Some change is being made to the service or product. Hence, just moving things around is usually *not* value-adding.

c. This is the first and only time we're doing it. (Fixes, rework, replacements, etc. only correct mistakes made before; they don't *add* value.)

2. *Value Enabling.* There is a class of activities that allow you to do work for the customer more quickly or effectively, meaning you can deliver products or services sooner, at less cost, with greater accuracy, and so on. You need to be careful, though, not to let all the steps that don't fit the "value-adding" category become "value-enabling." There are usually very few in this group.
3. *Non-Value-Adding.* These are the "rude awakening" aspects of a process, because in most organizations there are *lots* of non-value-adding steps. The kinds of activities that fit in this category include rework, as well as:

- Delays
- Inspections
- Reviews
- Transport (from one location or step in the process to another)
- Internal report and justifications
- Setup and preparation

The Non-Value-Adding category can seem rather brutal. For when you get right down to it, most of what happens in a typical organization does not, in the eyes of the customer, add value. You the reader (our customer) probably don't care that we have purchased special book-writing software that sets off an alarm every-so-many-words to remind us it's time to say something witty. As far as you're concerned, you're paying for the value we offer, not for the costs we incur to make it better, right? It hurts to admit we may have wasted money on this software, but that's the harsh reality of non-value-added activities. It's a sure bet ther are a *lot* of things done in your company "in the interest of the customer" that the customer really doesn't give a hoot about.

Balancing Value-Adding and Non-Value-Adding Tasks

Realistically, it would be a *bad* idea to eliminate every non-value-adding task. Filing tax returns, for example; or providing benefits to your employees; or backing up your computer files—these usually are non-value-adding from the customer's point of view but nonetheless in the best interest of your company if you want to stay in business.

As another example, take customer credit checks. These are a smart business practice to protect you from deadbeats and slow payers. Even though they don't add value from the customer's point of view, you probably won't want to abandon them. On the other hand, realizing that they really are *not* value-adding helps you to put those activities in perspective. You *could* speed up or even eliminate credit checks without much risk of customers complaining. And in fact, instant credit checks have become increasingly important in financial services, as companies look for ways to reduce a non-value-adding activity's impact on customers—while still, of course, limiting the business's risk.[3]

Value Analysis Steps

To do an effective Value Analysis, you need a pretty detailed view of the process. Otherwise, the technique is pretty easy:

1. Identify and map the process to be analyzed.
2. Categorize each step, according to the criteria noted above, as value-adding, non-value-adding, or value-enabling.
3. Compute the proportion of activities that falls in each of those categories, and review the "balance" between value- and non-value-adding work.

The COLA Team Conducts a Value Analysis

It took the COLA team several days to prepare more detailed maps of the processes in the Policy Completion process. Next, they organized the process map into a "deployment" or "cross-functional" format, showing departments and the customer along the top, with process steps falling in the appropriate columns. At the right, they categorized each step as value-adding (VA), value-enabling (VE), or non-value-adding (NVA).

Their overall findings revealed that of 45 basic steps in the process, 4 were value-adding (8.9 percent), 2 were value-enabling

(4.4 percent) and the remainder—39 steps, or 86.7 percent of the tasks—were non-value-adding. "I guess that makes sense," commented Team Leader Toni, "insurance or risk protection is what we sell, not documents."

Colleen Waters from IS voiced the view that, since several of the non-value-added steps were things they could not just eliminate without risk of prosecution under the law, they still hadn't proved the process could be cut to 1.5 weeks.

"Well," agreed Toni, "we still need to factor in the time dimension."

Process Time Analysis

To the three categories of Value Analysis, we can add two aspects of Time Analysis to our understanding of the process:

1. *Work Time.* The time actually spent *doing* something to the product or service as it flows on its way to the customer.
2. *Wait Time.* The time the product or service spends waiting for something to be done. Imagine a bunch of parts, a stack of applications, or truckloads of product all sitting around twiddling their thumbs (if they had them) waiting for someone to come and work on or move them. This is also called "queue time," "staging time," or just "delay."

Time analysis can be another shocker, if no one has paid attention to it before. It may not be news to you, but there's often a *lot* of idle time in business processes. Where cycle-time improvement has been a priority, time analysis has been a tremendous benefit to cutting process turnaround to minutes instead of hours, days instead of months. The need for speed—from "Just-in-Time" delivery to rapid product cycles to time-based competition—has driven some of the most impressive improvements in corporations around the world over the past 15 years.

Time Is on Their Side (Yes, It Is)

As the COLA process redesign group looked at time data from the perspective of the entire process, it became an even bigger revelation than the Value Analysis.

"Okay, I'm convinced," said Colleen of IS when she saw the figures. The team had done a ballpark estimate of the amount of "work time" needed for each step in the process, and then reviewed and revised their estimates by talking with people doing the work. When the team totaled all the possible time, they found that of the roughly 10.4 weeks (52 days) the average policy took to be finished, only about 8 days of that time was actual work time—15.4 percent of the total.

Factoring in the value analysis data was even more revealing: A big chunk of the work time was devoted to non-value-added steps. Overall, they estimated that just 3 percent of the total time of the Policy Completion process was spent working on value-adding activities, or less than two days.

"Twelve-Week Limit," you are *history!*" exclaimed Ike from Underwriting.

"Not so fast," cautioned consultant Art, in no danger of breaking any speed records himself. "You won't be able to just eliminate all the steps and idle time in the existing process and expect the current levels of performance to be maintained at an adequate level while keeping clear controls on the . . ." Anyway, the gist was that the real solution would come from rethinking how COLA could prepare policy documents, and find a way to do it under the new parameter of 1.5 weeks. The team agreed they were ready to start their design work.

Wrapping Up Analyze

Value and Cycle Time analyses are very helpful tools you can use in Process Design projects to confirm—or raise questions about—the feasibility of achieving dramatic improvements in process efficiency and effectiveness. Some of the most powerful "ah-has" we've heard come when people see how much of their work and time actually is essential. These techniques can also be useful in Process Improvement activities, or if a team is uncertain whether they should try to fix a process or redesign it.

As revealing as this kind of data can be, though, it needs to be used carefully. For one thing, you may not be ready to redesign the process; that means you can't, as Art Glass said, just boot out all the non-value-adding work and declare wait time to be forbidden. Moreover, these non-value-added tasks—some of which can be critical to the *company*—represent people's jobs. Telling a large percentage of the people working their tails off every day that their work is "non-value-adding" could create repercussions you'd rather avoid.

Process Design/Redesign Analyze Dos and Don'ts

Do—Use process analysis to clarify the potential for redesign gains.

Look for data to support your conclusion that redesign is necessary—and for ways it can be done that will help you to achieve your goal.

Do—Be ready to revise your plans based on what you learn.

For example, if you find that a single solution will achieve big gains without the need for a complete redesign, change your focus. Don't redesign if you don't need to.

Don't—Start analyzing every problem in detail.

Keep a broad perspective on the process. The more you delve into specifics, the harder it may be to design without ingrained assumptions.

A Minor Revolt

"I'll just have to explain to people what's going on." COLA CEO Rute Biere was talking at an emergency meeting of the company's leadership group in the wake of sudden rumors of massive layoffs. "We won't gain anything by keeping quiet," he said.

Toni Kwahter, who was included at the meeting, spoke up: "It's possible we may have opportunities to reduce some head count, Rute. Isn't that still an option?"

"It may have to be, Toni," Biere agreed. "But I'm also expecting that the growth we can achieve, if you can come up with a faster process, will give everyone plenty of chances to stay on board. But we can't sugar-coat it, either: There may be some cuts—we can't have people sitting around doing nothing."

Policy Administration VP Di Edsota (the redesign team sponsor), offered an apology: "Well, Rute, I have to confess that Toni and her team had asked me a couple of times to have you make a more direct announcement about the project and our possible plans. But I've not been as pushy as I should have been."

"You know," noted COLA Management Systems director Juan Callorrí, "I think lots of companies are going to have to deal with these kinds of issues more and more. When you become more proactive about improving your business—or staying abreast with customers and competitors—it means more change, more often. But we have to learn how to manage the implications better."

The following day, all associates at COLA received an e-mail from Rute Biere that read in part:

> *To continue to grow our business and meet the increasing demands of our customers for fast response to their risk-management needs, COLA must solidify its policy agreements much more quickly, but with the same accuracy and professionalism on which our reputation has been based. The team now seeking to redesign our Policy Completion process has taken on the goal of cutting policy turnaround from over 10 weeks to less than 2 weeks. Our intent is not to cut staff, but there is the possibility some positions will be eliminated in changing how we approach this important work. It's also possible we may add staff. I promise to do a better job than I have in keeping you all posted on this effort, and I ask for everyone's support on this initiative. If we succeed, it will mean significant new opportunities for COLA and all our associates.*

Over the next few days, COLA senior leaders held a series of luncheon discussions with staff. While there was still some concern among the employees, the general mood became much more positive when the story behind the rumors was clearly explained.

Improve: Designing and Implementing the New Process

Envisioning, designing, and then operationalizing a new work process can be an almost schizophrenic effort. The team needs to display different "personalities" as it tries to break down accepted norms and fears, identify new workflows and procedures, and then construct a new way of doing work that is practical, cost-effective, free of problems and rework, and shows quantum gains in performance. An extra challenge comes from the fact that your existing processes are "comfortable" to the people who work in them every day.

Steps in the Improve Phase

The best path for process design to follow, in light of these common fears and the "multiple personalities" required, is to alternate between the creative and the analytical, adding detail and refining the design as you go. The initial "design" phase is followed by the "refinement" phase during which more work is done to test, refine, and foolproof the process, and finally by the "implementation" phase where the

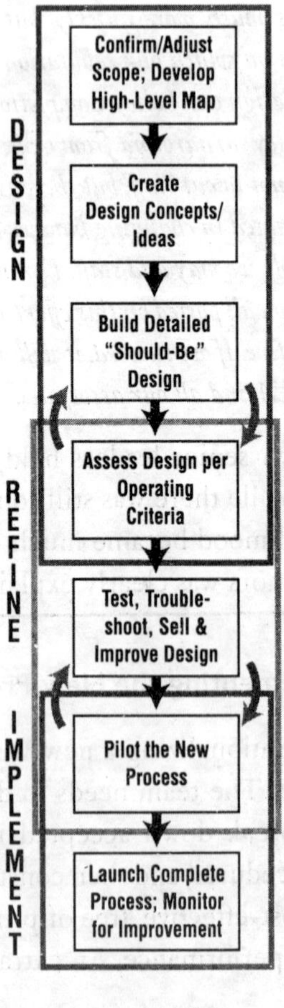

Figure 16.5 Process Design/Redesign Improve phase high-level steps

process is put into full operation. Fig. 16.5 presents a guide to the high-level set of steps for the Improve phase, from design through implementation.

Working at the High Level

A little shaken by the worries their project had aroused, the Limit Busters team spent the first part of their next meeting reviewing their Project Charter and reaffirming the essential need to redesign the Policy Completion Process from the ground up.

To begin rethinking the process, they decided to find an offsite location to help them get away from their thinking about how the process was done *now*. With the coaching of Art and Juan, they mapped out a process for their design work that included several rounds of creative design, followed by scrutiny and analysis, then implementation.

Early in the design discussions, the team agreed on one important feature of the streamlined process: the contract document itself would have to be dramatically simplified. "It wasn't part of our plan, but the effect of these 30-page contracts is pretty obvious. We can move things through faster and customers will be a lot happier with something they can maybe understand," said Tye from Policy Administration.

A shorter contract, of course, would have to be legally sound and acceptable under insurance regulations. The COLA legal department would have to be supportive, too, or the whole idea could be derailed. Bob Tull from Legal volunteered to put together a separate contract redesign team; it was agreed he and Tony would meet with Di Edsota from Policy Administration and Bob's boss, Chief Counsel Tom Collins, to get their support for the contract revision subproject.

Other design principles or ideas the team discussed included:

- Limiting and/or eliminating reviews
- Creating more standard contract features as "building blocks" for policies
- Front-loading some decisions into the Letter of Agreement
- Taking wait time out of the process

- Electronic transmission of documents
- Assigning an "owner" or "coordinator" to each contract, that person being responsible for its timely completion

The final action in the offsite was development of the high-level process diagram (see Fig. 16.6). "We had eight steps and now we have four, so that's a start," noted Bev.

Essential Ingredients for Process Design

As a team begins to "build" the new process, it's important to check that all the right ingredients are in place. Some of these are pretty commonsensical, while others may not be so obvious:

✦ *Clear goal, objectives, and/or vision.* These help the team see where you want the new process to be. They serve as a beacon, like the green-and-white signal light of a distant airport.

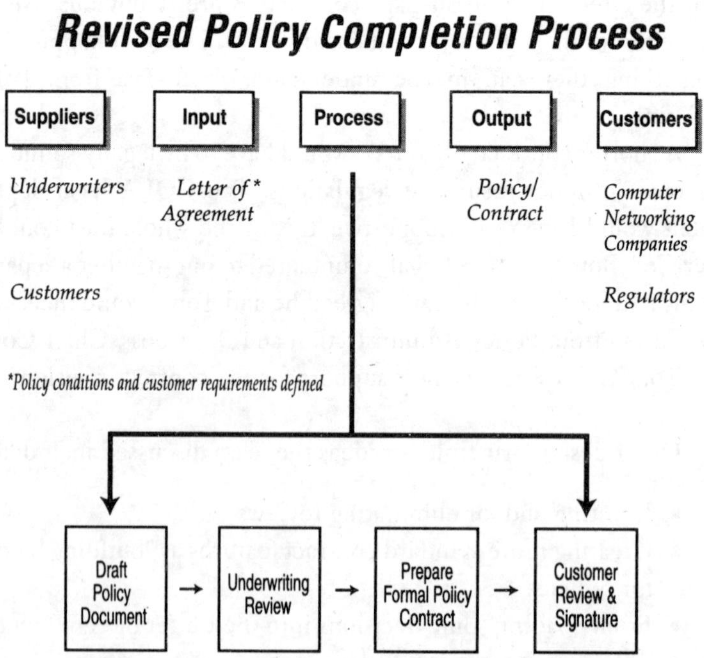

Figure 16.6 COLA Policy Completion SIPOC diagram after redesign

- *A well-defined process Scope.* Any significant refinement in process/project Scope should be checked with the Sponsor and/or business leadership.
- *Willingness to change the rules.* Unfortunately, the obstacles to new process ideas often are *unconscious* assumptions or beliefs about how things are or should be done. It can take a concerted effort by a team—and by their colleagues who will live in the new process—to overcome their old assumptions.
- *Creative thinking.* The ability to imagine and find ways to achieve a new level of performance can play a big role. So can "creative borrowing" of best practices from organizations.
- *Technical/implementation knowledge.* As ideas come into focus, the ability to assess their practicality and to make them a reality requires greater performance.
- *Assessment/operational criteria.* If the redesign Goal is like an airport beacon, then evaluation and operating criteria for the new process are the airport's runway lights: They guide you to the right path for a "smooth landing." Defining these criteria in advance can actually help people be more creative, by them giving guidelines and also the security of a "good" way to evaluate ideas.
- *Time.* To quote Thomas Paine: "Time makes more converts than reason." Having the time to think and to get comfortable with new approaches is essential to creativity and "buy-in."
- *Trust.* "Trust" is a key principle and ingredient for Process Design success. For example, many non-value-added process activities are based on the *possibility* that someone will make a mistake simply because we can't trust them not to. But a basic premise of smooth process flow is that if people understand what's required of them, and have the proper support and skills, they *will* get the job done.

Adding Meat to the Bones: The New Process Emerges

The COLA group elected to work in two subteams to start building the new process flows. While one of the subteams went right to work mapping a "Should-Be" process on the wall, the other brainstormed ways to shorten the process time and still get contracts written with adequate input from customers to meet their coverage needs. ("Fast, but wrong, is not an option," commented Bob Tull.) As they developed their new process maps, both teams discussed whether each step was value-adding or value-enabling. Any non-value-added steps were starred for later review.

Overall, several innovations were envisioned in the new process flow:

- Letters of Agreement would include a coverage code corresponding to policy "templates." The policy contract would be put together more quickly based on the codes and templates.
- Policy conditions (i.e., requirements of the client that ensure they will not be an undue risk) would also be defined in "packages." These would be described in the LOA so that Policy Completion would be able to simply include the correct conditions (if any) in the contract.
- A Policy Completion "Coordinator" would be responsible for each new policy assigned to him or her. Each Coordinator would work with no more than two Sales/Underwriter teams, to ensure consistent knowledge of the customer up and down the process.
- Each Letter of Agreement/New Policy would be given a number at the *beginning* of the process, instead of in the middle as had been the practice. Policies could be tracked in the Policy database, with cycle-time guidelines for each step in the process. Alerts would be issued if a policy missed a deadline.
- Legal staff review of policies would be eliminated, except for coverage over a certain amount (this representing a very small percentage of policies).
- Meanwhile, a dedicated Underwriter group—initially, two people—would be set up in the Policy Completion group, to review questions that didn't need to be presented to the customer.
- As already decided, policy contracts would be simplified, with a goal of an average length of eight pages. Review copies would be e-mailed to customers for review, with explicit guidelines and highlighted text to help them review the key points requiring their scrutiny. When the two sub-teams shared their ideas and merged their "Should-Be" process maps, they had reduced the number of steps in the process to 16 from 45.

Process Flow and Management Options

There are many options which, depending on the product/service and work being done, can improve the performance of a process. Some principles that apply in many process design situations include the following:

- *Simplification.* The fewer the steps and the more consistent the path, the better your ability to eliminate defects and control variation. You can have fewer "handoffs," fewer people ("too many cooks..." and all), fewer non-value-adding activities. Simplification can be a reason to *avoid* automation when it's less complex to do work manually.
- *Straight-Line Processing.* If tasks can be arranged in sequence, this will help you to avoid communication and coordination issues. The straight-line path is the easiest to track and manage.

  A big disadvantage of the straight-line path, however, is that it can add time to the overall process by delaying the start of each task until the previous one is done.
- *Parallel Processing.* Doing tasks "in parallel," or concurrently, reduces overall process cycle time. For example, in a new product development effort, several components can be designed independently, then integrated into the completed product. The challenge of parallel flows you might call the "right-hand/left-hand" syndrome: Changes or decisions are made in one path of the process that the other paths don't know about. The result is a problem "downstream" in the process when the paths converge.
- *Alternate Paths.* Preplanned flexibility in how work is done, based on customer needs, product type, technology, etc., is increasingly important in an environment where every product or order is unique. Alternate paths allow you to handle work according to any number of factors. For example when you go to the hospital, there are different "paths" to being admitted depending on the urgency of your condition. The risk of having alternate paths, however, is that it means you have to keep track of and manage various ways to handle an item in the process.
- *Bottleneck Management.* In almost any process, there are points where capacity or cycle time causes a slowdown or backup. In bottleneck

management, the process flow is "widened" so as to streamline the entire process. But *beware!* Adding people or equipment may *not* be the best way to widen the bottleneck. Consider also how the product, service, or task/procedure could be changed to eliminate the slowdown. Also, be advised that eliminating one bottleneck may just create another one farther downstream in the process; that means that bottleneck management should be undertaken with a "whole process" perspective.

- *Front-Loaded Decision Making.* Because decisions can be challenging, there's a natural tendency to defer them until later in the process. But that delay may force a lot of work to be based on assumptions that later are proven to be wrong. Pushing decisions upstream in the process can reduce the probability of rushed efforts or rework later. In our COLA project example, one of their design decisions is to require earlier clarification of policy terms and conditions—a front-loaded decision—so that the actual policy completion process can move forward unheeded.
- *"Standardized" Options.* This is a way to simplify decisions yet still offer flexibility by defining a fixed number of options and preparing the process to handle them. The output of this design would be a "semi-custom" product or service. Depending on the number of elements to be selected, there still can be a large number of possible end products. One of the most familiar examples of this approach is found in the car business. Manufacturers offer a set of color "packages" and other options that you can choose from, but you can't just get the beige carpet with the blue exterior unless it is one of the packages. In a service example, the COLA team took this approach when they elected to establish set policy components to speed up completion of contracts.
- *Single Point of Contact or Multiple Contacts.* These are the two ends of the customer-interface spectrum. In the "single contact" option, a customer and/or order is assigned to a person or group which maintains responsibility for the item as it's processed. Another term for this is the "case worker." If you call a customer service number and are told to "always ask for Amy," you're dealing with a single-point-of-contact process. (Unless they have a lot of Amys...) "Multiple contact" processes are usually backed up by strong customer and/or

order tracking systems. They allow any person on the system to follow and respond to customer requests and questions. We use a travel service in which we enter an ID code at the beginning of the call; then the agent who takes our call will have our latest travel data right up on their computer screen when they say "Hello." They can then make itinerary changes, answer questions, and so on.

These are some of the more common options you should consider when exploring process designs for your organization. Variations on all of these themes have been around for a long time. One of the most important advances in management thinking in recent years nas been to define these options more clearly, and to allow for more conscious decisions about which approach works best for a particular organization or process. The most important question, of course, is: "Which design will work—and work best—for the customer?

Reviewing and Refining the Design

There is a variety of useful techniques to help you evaluate and improve the initial process design. During this effort, more details and subcomponents of the new process can be developed as well. Some of the more helpful methods for the refinement phase include the following:

- *Process Walk-Throughs and Simulations.* Even process "talk-throughs" are a good way to validate how things will work; surface possible problems; determine where greater detail is needed; and so on. Some process-flow software will let you run sample scenarios of different options to see the impact on costs, cycle time, etc. More elaborate simulations can be done on computers, as well, though the costs there can be high.
- *Moments of Truth Assessment.* Identifying and assessing the key points of customer interface in the process should be a priority. You may have a terrific new approach that will provide faster, better products to customers; but if customers are treated badly or ignored during the process, they may end up less happy than they were before.
- *Focus Groups and Feedback Sessions.* Broader feedback, especially from customers and/or people familiar with the process, can surface con-

cerns and issues you never even dreamed of. Much as you may not *like* people to shoot holes in your brilliantly designed new process, better to have it happen early, and in a meeting room, than on the day the new process is launched. Seeking input from people also helps gain their support, or at least lets them know their opinions are valued. Be careful, though, not to just listen politely and then totally ignore feedback offered.

- *Potential Problem Analysis.* Every process has plenty of potential problems. A process design team can't deal with every possible problem, but it can try to identify the big ones and prepare proactive steps to eliminate or mitigate them. In potential problem analysis, the basic strategy is to focus on critical steps or milestones in the process and ask: "What could go wrong?" Then, concentrating on the higher-probability, higher-impact problems, you can develop *preventive* actions—ones that reduce or block the effect of causes of the problem—or *contingent* actions—measures designed to contain or overcome the consequences of the problem. (In Chapter 18 we'll review a more detailed variation of potential problem analysis: "Failure Modes and Effects Analysis," or FMEA.)
- *Unintended Consequences Analysis.* This approach takes the "big picture" view in considering the impacts of a new process and of the various procedures, forms, systems, etc. it will entail. Implementing a new process is like tossing a rock in a pond: The effects spread out to the surrounding water (i.e., people and processes) in all directions. Those waves of change may create other problems you never anticipated; potentially big ones. Understanding the interconnectedness of processes is key to doing a good analysis of potential consequences. You can trace the effects of, say, new requirements, upstream, to see who they will affect and how. Conversely, new procedures or service changes need to be followed downstream, to note where they may cause unforeseen difficulties.

Most critical in all of these testing and refinement activities—and you should choose the ones that will be of most help to your project—is to learn from them and to adapt/improve the process so that it incorporates those lessons.

Winning Support for the Plan

An important part of the refinement process, with an eye on effective implementation, is to gain acceptance of a Process Design—or a Process Improvement. A couple of approaches can help any leader or group to deal with the challenge of gaining support:

- *Strategic Selling.* By "strategic selling," we mean focusing your efforts on key influencers and decision makers who can help build support for the plan—and offer useful suggestions on how to improve it. It's best to start with people who are likely to look with favor on your ideas. Usually that will mean focusing on the management and executive levels, but you shouldn't necessarily stop there. Important influencers can exist in many parts of an organization.
- *Force-Field Analysis.* This is a tool used to identify and analyze the factors, pro and con, to any change or idea. Force Field begins with structured brainstorming and then leads to a discussion and to planning on how to deal with those elements or issues that oppose your new idea. A key premise is to concentrate on changing or weakening the opposing or restraining forces. When you push harder on the "Driving Force" side, the other side usually just pushes back harder.

Fine-Tuning the Policy Completion Process

Though the COLA team was pretty pleased with the new process design they'd come up with, they realized it wasn't a cinch to get everyone's approval. They also knew that a lot of details would need to be worked out before they could launch anything.

Their first step was to present the plan to the executive group. Actually, they'd met prior to the presentation with their sponsor, Di Edsota, as well as with the head of Sales, Phil Cooler, to review the plan. They felt Phil's support would be especially important since they were asking salespeople to put more detail into LOAs—which might add some time to the selling process. They also knew, though, that Phil was a strong proponent of Six Sigma and would see the strength of their reasoning.

The top managers had some concerns, especially about the notion of eliminating the legal review. It would also mean the likely layoff of about 20 attorneys—which wasn't the initial objective of the project. In the end the leaders agreed to let the team move forward with the work to refine the process plan and make sure it would operate as envisioned.

Before "unveiling" the process to any other groups in the organization, the team decided to do some of its own tough evaluation of the process, and gave Bob Tull the go-ahead to start working on the policy contract templates. The first analysis they did was a "walk-through" of each step in the new process design. By taking an entire day, they were able to flesh out some of the more important procedures for the process and identify where others would need to be developed.

The walk-through also caused one aspect of the new design to be placed on the "questionable" list: the database tracking of policies. "As busy as things are in the IS [Information Systems] group," said Toni, the team leader, "this may hold up the entire project—and I'm not sure if manual tracking won't work just as well for now."

Their next step was to divide the work into two main areas:

1. Analyze the process for potential problems.
2. Prepare an initial piloting plan.

Their potential problem analysis turned up a number of possible trouble spots that they were able to address. One, for example, was described as follows:

Process Step: Customer Contract Review
Potential Problem: E-mailed review file is edited by the customer on-line, making it difficult to track revisions and ensure legal validity of the document.
Preventive Action: Send customers a "mark-up" file, on which they can add comments and changes but not actually edit the document itself.
Contingent Action: None

Focusing on the Process

The next refinement action was to review the still-evolving process design in a series of "focus group"—type meetings with COLA associates. There was a back-and-forth debate on whether to have cross-functional meetings or to focus on one department at a time.

In the end they split the difference: Three sessions would be held, each with one or two representatives from Policy Administration, Underwriting, Sales, Accounting, and Claims. They decided to do a special session with a couple of folks from Legal; in light of the potential layoffs, it was thought not to be a good idea to involve them in the cross-functional sessions.

A lot of preparation went into the sessions. First of all, the team wanted to present the process in a positive light, and accurately. Second, they wanted to ensure that people didn't "clam up" and not offer helpful criticism. Most of the reaction was positive, though, and it was clear that the communicating Rute Biere had done since the "mass layoff" rumors hit had helped to prepare people well for the coming changes. At the same time, there were some stern critiques along with the helpful suggestions. A lot of unforeseen issues were raised, which gave the team more food for thought and led to more ideas on how to make things run smoother.

At the end of a series of revisions to the process, Toni, Bev Ehridge, and an Accounting manager prepared a budget for the implementation. It included severance packages and outplacement services for attorneys, and costs for moving some staff locations, as well as salaries for an additional two Underwriters. Toni met alone with Rute Biere and Di Edsota and presented the updated plan and budget. She sent an e-mail to the team as soon as the meeting was over: "It's a go!"

Implementing the New Process

To repeat the point about implementing Six Sigma solutions from the last chapter: You should *always* start with a "pilot" rather than with a full-scale launch. Piloting gives you an opportunity to test the assumptions, procedures, and people-challenges of the new process, try out your measurement systems, and limit any damage that might occur if things don't go perfectly—which they *won't.*

Piloting Approaches

There are various options open to you when preparing a pilot. The most sophisticated pilots can be used as "experiments" to compare different approaches and identify the best combination of factors for effective, efficient performance. Some broad choices for pilot strategies—which also influence how you eventually implement the process permanently—include the following:

- *Off-line pilot.* Like a laboratory test, in this approach the pilot is really a "dummy" operation that resembles/replicates the real world. The Output of this approach may end up not being sold or delivered to customers, but its "quality" can still be evaluated to check the effectiveness of the process. In some companies a "pilot plant" is used to test new processes and equipment, and/or to develop products for test (i.e., pilot) marketing.
- *Selected times.* A defined-length pilot offers a couple of advantages:

  1. Participants know the test has a defined end point, so they may approach it with more of an open mind.
  2. The post-pilot period offers "downtime" for corrections or refinements that may be harder to accomplish if the pilot continues to operate.
  3. Comparative measures can be even more revealing. For example, if improvements are seen during the pilot period, but then disappear afterwards, it adds validity to the conclusion that the solution (not some other unknown factor) created the gain.

- *Selected items or customers.* In essence, this approach creates an "alternate path" in which a certain type or number of real items is sent through the new process. This piloting strategy can lend itself well to a "parallel" implementation in which more and more work is moved over to the new process.
- *Selected locations.* If you have different regions or locations, you can "switch" one site to the process as the pilot, gather data and refine the operation, and convert other sites as appropriate.
- *Selected solution components.* Rather than testing the entire new process, different parts of the change can be tried independently. For more on this approach, which works best as an experimental method, see the information in "Design of Experiments" in Chapter 18.

These pilot strategies can all be "mixed and matched." For example, you might conduct an "off-line" pilot of one component of the new process; or, you could do a time-limited test at one location. Depending on the Scope, complexity, and potential risk of your new process or solution, piloting in several dimensions and/or phases can be key to ensuring that the full implementation goes as smoothly as possible.

Preparing for Takeoff

The Limit Busters' piloting plan called for a selected group to try the new process in parallel with the existing one for a four-week period, taking all the new Letters of Agreement from two Sales Associates. The Sales and Underwriting members of the team had actually already begun preparing their prospective customers for the more detailed decisions that would need to be made before signing the LOAs. So far, clients were showing no resistance to defining their coverage requirements more explicitly in advance of the LOAs, and the extra detail wasn't adding much time to the sales cycle. "If you can get my policy ready faster," said one Internet Services Provider CEO, "a little upfront work is not a problem."

The team had agreed that each Policy Coordinator would keep track and measure the progress of his or her contracts "manually" (i.e., not on a central database). "This has been a lot of work," Tye Neebublscz of Policy Administration told the pilot group, "but it's really been fun, too. I'm getting more and more excited as we go."

After the first four-week pilot, there would be a two-week evaluation period. At that point it would be decided if a second pilot was needed. Assuming that it wasn't, the plan was to have the pilot group convert to the new process full-time, then shift the rest of the group and make the shift-over in two phases.

At the end of the meeting, consultant Art Glass made a brief (for Art…) speech about the excellent work the group had done. The design team later explained to the pilot participants that Art actually had been a huge help in their effort. "You just have to get used to him."

Look at this COLA *Fizz!*

Like almost any pilot, the four-week test of the new Policy Completion process experienced a few road-bumps. The "predefined coverage" categories and the new policy templates weren't well matched, so it took the Policy Coordinators some extra work to clarify just what clauses and endorsements would be needed. Having a "team" approach made that go smoother, though, since the Coordinators were in close touch with their Sales/Underwriting partners most of the time. They also found that it hadn't been routine in the past to get customers' e-mail addresses, so when the time came to send out policy documents for review, they had to call the customer's office first to get the address.

With the COLA people really "on their toes" and concentrating on getting the Policy papers finished in less than eight days, the cycle times were close to the target, especially as the pilot progressed. It was a little hard to manage the client review time; sometimes it would take four or five days to get the papers back. But when the customers *did* turn their review around in a day, the total cycle times were less than one week.

At the end of the pilot, the full group held an assessment "debriefing" session. These are among the refinements they identified:

1. Include customer e-mail addresses on LOA data sheets.
2. Clarify a primary and an alternate person to review the documents on behalf of the client (so that there would be a "backup" if the primary person happened to be out of the office).
3. Adjust the coverage codes and policy templates, so that the right items could be included in the policy documents.
4. Inform clients one day in advance of e-mailing policy documents for review, and send a client-reminder e-mail two days after transmission of the review documents.

The team realized that their measures weren't as clear as they should be, and that the role of the customer needed to be taken into account. Therefore they resolved to change the cycle time goal to make it more specific namely:

> *Maintain a 7-working-day* average *cycle time per month, with a maximum cycle time (in the event of client delays) of 2 weeks.*

The operational definition for a cycle-time measure was updated to clarify that the "clock" would start on the day LOAs were signed by the customer, except for those signed after 3 P.M.

which would be measured starting the following working day. Any policy contract would be considered a cycle-time "defect":

1. Completed in more than 8 days if signed off on by the customer in three days or less; *or*
2. Completed in more than 10 days if signed-off on by the customer in more than three days.

The other primary Output measure of the Policy Completion process, "Contract Accuracy," would continue on unchanged.

Over the four-week period the average cycle time was 8.5-days, with only 5 of the 150 policies processed taking more than 10 days. The team—both the design group and those in the pilot process—were confident that these refinements, with some "learning curve" time would allow them to meet their goal.

The Final Process Rollout

It's a big mistake to get over-confident after a successful pilot. The pilot is usually a much more controlled situation than real life, with fewer variables to manage and fewer people involved. Other problems are almost sure to arise in the conversion from test to final rollout of a new process. Some of the critical ingredients—all pretty commonsensical, but worth noting nonetheless—of a successful launch of a redesigned process include the following:

- *Training.* New approaches need to be learned, old habits broken.
- *Documentation.* References on how to do things; answers to frequently asked question; process maps; etc.—all of these are important.
- *Troubleshooting.* Responsibility needs to be clear with regard to who will deal with the issues that arise.
- *Performance management.* Keep your eyes open for needs/opportunities to revise job descriptions, incentives, performance review criteria.
- *Measurement.* Results need to be documented.

The COLA Team Declares Victory

Six months after the first pilot of the new Policy Completion Process, the people at COLA were beginning to wonder how they ever could have lived with the old "twelve-Week Limit." There had been some glitches in the rollout of the new process throughout the rest of the company. Not all Salespeople were ready to do the extra work on the LOAs the new process required. A couple of them actually had to be let go.

Nor were customers always as quick to turn papers around as had been hoped. Over time, the organization learned ways to better prepare its customers to be ready for the reviews. And even though the shorter policy documents were a huge hit, eventually COLA added to the process a "documents review appointment," during which Policy Coordinators would walk through policy with customers (usually by phone). That new "Moment of Truth" actually turned out to be a big customer satisfaction-booster.

The "before and after" report tells the story (see Fig. 16.7). Even with a much tighter customer requirement, process performance

Policy Completion Process: Comparative Performance Data

Measure:	Before Redesign:	After Redesign:
Total Cycle Time	**10.4 Weeks**	**8.2 Days**
Average Pages/ Contract	**26.3 pages**	**9.2 pages**
In-Process Revisions/ Contract	**7.1 revisions**	**.4 revisions**
DPMO (rounded)	**321,000**	**75,000***

***Based on new 8-10 day completion requirement**

Figure 16.7 COLA "before and after" results report

and capability have improved. Staff in Policy Administration, Underwriting, Sales and Claims have discovered that their work is much more rewarding without the constant confusion over coverage terms that would come up during the 10 weeks it *used* to take.

In the annual report of International Insurance and Indemnity (COLA's parent), the subsidiary was singled out for its Six Sigma Design effort:

> *In one of the fastest-growing markets in the insurance industry, Computer Outage Liability Assurance (COLA) has established itself as the leader in responsiveness, customer focus, and understanding of the needs of its high-tech customers. "Without COLA's work," said the top executive of NetSetGo, the fifth largest ISP in the finance sector, "many companies might have had to close because of undue liability risk. Their work is literally keeping us in business." COLA CEO R.O. "Rute" Biere is projecting 35 percent annual growth over the next five years. This year, Biere was named to the III Board of Directors.*

Process Design/Redesign Improve Dos and Don'ts

Do—Concentrate on seeing the process in a new way.

Try to identify what rules or assumptions govern today's process and ask: "Are these valid? Why? How can we make them invalid?"

Do—Set performance criteria to analyze the design.

Give the team a framework to assess their creative ideas against the practical reality of the process.

Do—Refine and enhance the process iteratively.

Get feedback, use simulations, walk through the process and add detail as you go.

Do—Pilot the process, in multiple phases when warranted.

It may take longer, but the chief benefit will be a smoother final implementation.

Don't—Run a "downtime" pilot.

Test the process in a variety of conditions, including when things are "really busy."

Don't—Assume everyone will love the new process.

Even if it's only unconscious, resistance will come up. Respond to it, and learn from it. But also be ready to enforce new procedures when people are downright belligerent.

Don't—Take your eye off the process.

Expect problems, and you'll be ready for them. Stay alert throughout the duration of at least one process cycle. Prepare to transition to "Control."

CHAPTER

17

Expanding and Integrating the Six Sigma System

(Roadmap Step 5)

Introduction and Key Deliverables

Imagine you have decided to lose some weight by using the new Six Sigma Diet Plan. With the help of a well-defined problem ("I'm 25 pounds over my optimal weight"), some carefully recorded, valid measurements, a review of your eating and exercise processes, and the advice of a doctor and some fitness instructors, you implement a solution of changed diet and increased exercise. You are so successful that you go beyond the goal you set for yourself and lose 27 pounds. And just in time for Thanksgiving!

How might this success story end? As with Six Sigma, so with diets: It depends.

Old habits are hard to break. Maybe you pile on an extra helping of stuffing, skip jogging on rainy days, order *whole*-milk lattes instead of non-fat. And before you know it the scale is back up where it started. The alternative takes more discipline: You decide to control your weight by keeping an eye on your eating and exercising processes and by keeping some charts on your weight and eating patterns. You even manage to get your cholesterol down, and people say you're looking great.

Six Sigma companies face much the same challenge as the dieter. When Process Improvement or Design projects achieve their goal of reducing defects, discipline is essential to sustain the results. It's more complicated than losing weight, of course, because a process involves many people, not just the dieter. Do Six Sigma gains ever fade when solutions are turned over to full-time operations? Do dieters ever gain back lost pounds?

Even when improvement "sticks," a Six Sigma company faces another challenge similar to the dieter's: Those first few pounds tend to come off easily, but they get harder to shed as you go. Without a sustained, focused effort, the beginning drive for improvement will lose energy and your company will become a *former* Six Sigma organization.

Step 5 Overview

In this chapter, we explore both the short- and long-term challenges of sustaining Six Sigma improvement and building all the concepts and methods of Steps 1–4 into an ongoing, cross-functional management approach. The key actions to be taken in Managing Processes for Six Sigma Performance (see Fig. 17.1) are these three:

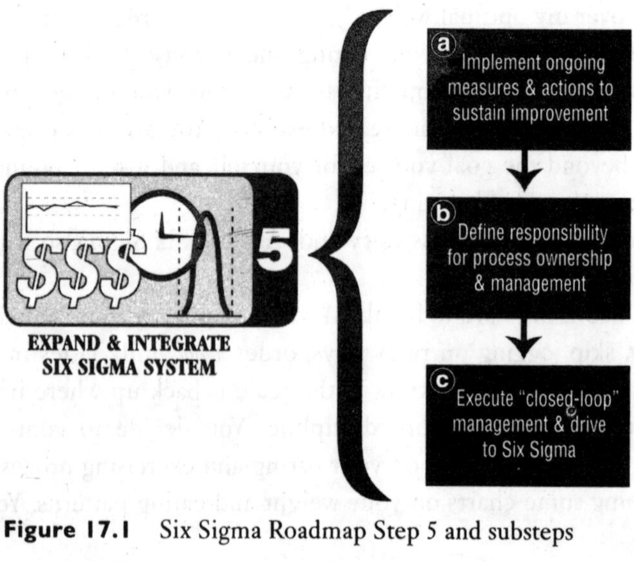

Figure 17.1 Six Sigma Roadmap Step 5 and substeps

1. Implement ongoing measures and actions to sustain improvement (the "Control" phase of DMAIC).
2. Define responsibility for process ownership and management.
3. Execute "closed-loop" monitoring and drive on toward Six Sigma performance.

Step 5A: Implement Ongoing Measures and Actions to Sustain Improvement (Control)

Our first consideration is how to solidify the immediate gains made through Six Sigma efforts. It is at the end of a Process Improvement or Design/Redesign effort that the results achieved are most vulnerable. A team alone can't keep its efforts from fading away. The ensuing subsections give you the essentials of sustained improvement.

Build Solid Support for the Solution

Being smart about getting others to understand and buy in to your solutions is a recurring theme in Six Sigma, and the need to "sell" the solution doesn't stop. Some of the most important considerations here include the following:

- *Work with those who manage the process.* It helps if those who must manage new and improved processes also participated in their creation. When this is not the case, teams and project sponsors have to carefully explain the benefits of the improvement. If there's a process "owner" to take over responsibility for your solution, that can make the task simpler.
- *Use a "Storyboard" with facts and data.* The project Storyboard tells the background, plot, and outcome of your Improvement Project in words and pictures. Being able to show why and how the change you've developed makes sense for your business's customers will go a long way to convince people that the new approach is the right one.
- *Treat the people managing and using the new process as your customers.* Tailor your pitch and product to the internal groups you're selling to. Results need to be expressed in terms each group understands. For example, people in Customer Support will be happy to hear "reduced customer complaints," but may not care much about

"additional referral business." When people are being asked to do new or extra work as part of the solutions, explain clearly how other aspects of their job will get easier.

- *Create a sense of purpose and enthusiasm.* Sharing "credit" for the solution and building a sense of participation isn't just a good selling tool, it's also realistic. As we've noted, no Black Belt or team can even hope to make a meaningful improvement happen on their own.

Document the Changes and New Methods

In the minds of many people, the thought of documenting a procedure or process—even one they've created themselves—falls somewhere between the thrill of dental work and the ecstasy of filing income taxes. But documentation is a necessary evil, and can even be a creative undertaking in itself. A successful Six Sigma organization will have to look for new and better ways to make documentation usable and accessible, to get away from the horrors of all those huge procedures manuals and process descriptions guaranteed to cure insomnia.

What follows are some general guidelines that will help people to actually follow your directions and/or documentation:

1. *Keep the documentation simple.* Write in direct, jargon-free sentences. If you have to use specific terms that someone new may not understand, include a definition or glossary. Explaining the meaning of TLAs and FLAs (three-letter and four-letter acronyms) is important, too. If a lot of detail is needed, consider including it in the support or reference materials, so that people can get the *basics* easily, and more background as needed.
2. *Keep the documentation clear and inviting.* Using pictures and flowcharts whenever possible can make your message clearer and more accessible. Use of white space, bullets, various fonts, and highlights will make the documents both easier to navigate and more appealing to the eye—a pretty important criterion in today's visually-oriented world.
3. *Include options and instructions for "emergencies."* One of the ways to ensure that your new processes and procedures aren't abandoned is to plan and document ways to adjust them under various conditions. Include information on how to identify problems or issues, too.

4. *Keep the documentation brief.* Yep! (Actually, there's more....) If you want a good guide to brief instructions, read cake recipes. Usually they're models of clarity and brevity. By contrast, check the operating instructions for a VCR. The longer instructions are, the less likely it is that people will have time to read or understand them.
5. *Keep the documentation handy.* One sign that an organization really isn't taking Control seriously are documents that are hard to find, either physically or on the computer. This sends the implicit message that—despite all of someone's hard work and analysis—you can feel free to do any old thing you care to while working on this process. But guess what? That old devil, Variation, will be sneaking in whenever this happens, and it won't be for your company's good.
6. *Have a process for updates and revisions.* It's not enough to say "we've gotta keep this up-to-date." Documentation, like measurement, is a process that needs to be *designed* and managed, with document tracking and revision a key part of it. The need for revision should be one of the most important considerations in designing the documents to start with: The more complicated they are, the harder it will be to update. But the less often they are revised, the more likely it is that people will ignore the documentation.

There is, of course, a risk of creating a documentation bureaucracy. Having a "Document Control" department has worked fine for some companies. Our recommendation, though, is to try to keep ownership of documents close to the work, in the hands of those people who are best able to judge *what* needs to be documented, to what level, and when it should be revised. Guidelines to maintain consistency across the organization are important as well.

Service Comes to Live at Up-Home

Up-Home is a small but successful chain of retail stores that sells "contemporary country" home furnishings in 17 locations in the Mid-Atlantic states. Up-Home carved its "niche" by being the first store of its kind to sell products that had a country look but had been updated to contemporary tastes. People wanting their décor to be "cozy" but not old-fashioned have been terrific customers for Up-Home.

As the market for home furnishings has diversified, however, Up-Home had begun to see some decline in its sales. Looking at their prospects, company leaders and store managers concluded that their *products* could still outshine their competition, but that the real edge would come from the *service* provided to their customers. Up-Home subsequently launched a transformation effort based on the Six Sigma system with the theme "Making People Feel Up-Home."

One of the first projects completed was the development of a new furnishings loan-out process. Up-Home salespeople (called "neighbors") and folks in advertising began to actively promote the option of trying out items in people's homes to make sure they actually worked well. The "Take it Home" process was piloted at two stores before being implemented chainwide; the tests showed it to be a huge success.

Take it Home was not a simple process, however, because it involved issues such as inventory, delivery, potential damage, and the risk of theft. The team that developed the process worked out as many issues as possible in the design phase, and then fine-tuned the various procedures during the pilot with the active participation of the management and staff of the two pilot locations.

The result was a kickoff campaign for the full rollout of *Take it Home* that created a lot of excitement throughout Up-Home. Salespeople from the pilot stores gave testimonials about the stronger relationships they were able to develop with customers. Sales figures showed an almost immediate 25 percent jump after the launch of the program.

In addition to a series of training programs held at each location to explain the new process and tasks, each store associate was given a personalized "How to help *'Take it Home'*" guidebook. The most useful was an extensive intranet site that provided complete instructions on how to handle questions and issues as they arise—linked to a "bulletin board" where issues and questions were posted. A section with maps of the key process elements was one of the most popular sites. A committee made up of representatives from each store was responsible for reviewing and updating the site as adjustments were made to the process.

To make sure no store associate created a problem for customers due to uncertainty about the "*Take it Home*" policy and procedures, each staff member was given three "your call" opportunities per month, in which whatever they decided to do was okay. The only requirement was that they be posted on the bulletin board.

Establish Meaningful Measures and Charts

Imagine you're the coach in a football game in which you aren't quite sure of the score or how much time is left in the game. How do you know what plays to call, how to handle that fourth-and-one situation, whether to let the clock run or call time-out? Well, your experience may lead you to some pretty good guesses, which is what many managers rely on much of the time.

Now that you're successfully invested in Six Sigma projects, however, you put your victory in jeopardy if you revert to the management guessing game. You avoid guessing, on the other hand, by employing well-chosen and well-implemented measures to track your process and solution. By now, we expect that you understand some of the basics and tools of measurement covered in previous chapters. Thus the two questions in Step 5 become: "What measures do we continue to use?" and "How do we make them useful?"

Selecting Ongoing Measures

We've already looked at several ways in which you can categorize measures: Input, Process, and Output; Efficiency and Effectiveness; Predictors (Xs) and Results (Ys). One of the first rules with ongoing measures is to include a balance among these categories so as to give a full picture of the organizational system. For example, measures of defect levels will tell you how well you're meeting customer requirements, but in-process measures are better at giving you early warning of *pending* problems. Financial measures are useful, but other data can be more indicative of what's happening to drive the dollars.

Another consideration is rate of change. Things that change more frequently—especially factors that can impact customers, product, or service quality, and costs/profits—should go higher on the measurement priority list. You can't ignore the more slowly changing factors, but it may be possible to keep an eye on them through different mechanisms than an ongoing measure.

What you measure should also be influenced by what's important at a particular point in time. Some will be long-term "maintenance" measures—of things like defects, cycle time, cost per unit, etc. Other measures will be "situational." For example, in the first few months after a new process has been introduced you may measure several aspects to make sure it's working well, then phase them out once the success of the improvement seems certain. Still other measures may be "improvement-focused." Obvious examples would be those initiated during a DMAIC project to gather data on a problem or causes, or those tied to a business imperative such as a new-product launch.

Finally, you can test each possible measure with our favorite two criteria: *meaningful* and *manageable.* Will the data from the measure really help track the business and lead you to make better decisions, and will the resources and logistical issues behind getting the data be affordable?

Using Your Ongoing Measures

As with any product, the more you can tailor how measures are designed and reported—the better. Some people love the detail, and aren't happy without a full spreadsheet of numbers. Others want the barest synopsis.

As a general rule, however, simpler, graphical measurement reports work best. They're quicker to read, make for easier comparisons, and can be colorful. The kinds of charts we've already mentioned, such as Run or Trend charts, Pareto charts, and Histograms, along with many other familiar "data pictures," can be the workhorses of measurement reporting. Another technique, profiled in the following chapter, is the Control Chart. This helps you to see at a glance how much variation is occurring in a process and whether the process is "in control."

As data are collected at various points throughout the organization, the need to summarize *many* measures—so that top leaders can effectively get an idea of what's happening in the trenches—becomes critical. One of the most popular and useful tools you can use to reach that high-level view is the "Balanced Scorecard," popularized by Robert Kaplan and David Norton.[1] A Balanced Scorecard (or BSC) is a flexible tool for selecting and displaying "key indicator" measures about the business in an easy-to-read format. Many organizations *not* involved in Six Sigma, including many government agencies, are using the BSC to establish common performance measures and keep a closer eye on the business.

One of the strengths of the Balanced Scorecard concept is the emphasis it places on four categories of measures: Innovation, Process, Customer, and Financial. So it can offer some help in choosing what to measure. But whether you use a "by-the-book" Balanced Scorecard or develop your own approach, just taking the action of creating an easily digestible array of measurement data can help to ensure that *using* measures becomes a part of the new habits of your Six Sigma organization.

Building Process Response Plans

Given the power of Finnegan's law ("Murphy was an optimist"), we can rest assured that sooner or later something will go wrong in any process—even one that has been improved by a crack Six Sigma team. Having advance guidelines on when to take action and what to do is part of the "Proactive Management" practice of any Six Sigma company.

A process Response Plan includes three major elements:

1. *Action Alarms.* With clear standards in place at key points in the Input, Process, and Output phases of a process, and measures tracking performance, "trigger points" can be set at which some action needs to be taken to correct a problem or concern. For example, if test data show circuit boards approaching the edge of their rated energy consumption, an engineer may want to begin investigating to see what's wrong. Or if no-shows at a hotel get 5 percent above the seasonal normal, some special contingency plans could be implemented.
2. *Short-Term or Emergency Fixes.* By no means can every problem wait for a chartered team or Black Belt assignment. Having some guidelines on quick fixes mean they can be more effective and less likely to cause the "collateral damage" that often results from haphazard short-term solutions.
3. *Continuous Improvement Plans.* A process for identifying and prioritizing ongoing or serious problems so they can be acted on, feeds into the DMAIC process and other higher-level activities such as strategic planning and budgeting. Guidelines can also be established on how significant a problem or opportunity must be before it qualifies for a continuous improvement action. Continuous improvement plans are a key link in the closed-loop business management system of Six Sigma.

Anticipating possible problems is clearly an important part of an effective Response Plan. Techniques like Potential Problem Analysis and FMEA (covered in the next chapter) can support that effort.

Up-Home Keeps Its Eyes Open

Despite the early success of furniture and decorating retailer Up-Home's new *Take it Home* service and process, the company wasn't ready to declare victory. Each store was asked to keep track of such key variables in the new process as

- Percent of *Take it Home* customers who make purchases
- Dollar volume of *Take it Home* related sales, overall and by Neighbor (sales associate)
- Defect data (e.g., missed or wrong deliveries; erroneous billing; etc.), including a Sigma score
- Damaged/lost merchandise
- Customer satisfaction index data

The data were reported by each location and then summarized for the Up-Home chain as a whole.

A checklist for the Control phase of DMAIC can be found in the Appendix (page 390).

Ongoing Measures and Controls "Dos & Don'ts"

Do—Develop good documentation to support the new process.

Keep it simple, clear, and easy to use, and have a plan for updating the document.

Do—Select a balanced mix of measures to monitor process performance.

Look at results, process variables, customer requirements, and costs. Avoid strictly financial measures.

Do—Create measurement reports that convey information quickly and simply.

Charts and graphs usually are preferable to texts and tables of figures.

Do—Develop a plan to take action in case problems arise in the process.

"Responding" in a preplanned, effective manner is much better than "reacting" in an ignorant panic.

Don't—Leave documents to gather dust.

Designing and finding ways to use documentation helps ensure they'll be kept up-to-date, and will help keep the process from reverting to "bad habits."

Don't—Forget the process maps.

They're the best tools for quick reference and review of workflows, customer/supplier relationships, and key points for measurement. Process maps make changing the process much easier, too.

Step 5B: Define Responsibility for Process Ownership and Management

Six Sigma and the Process Management Vision

As your company adopts and implements the steps on the Six Sigma roadmap, you'll be positioning your organization to adopt the most promising solution to cross-functional barriers and organizational "silos": a *process* management approach. What might this mean, in terms of how your company operates? Well, here are some elements of the process management "vision":

- Business leaders will concentrate on getting work to move effectively and efficiently *across* functions to the benefit of customers—and ultimately, of shareholders.
- Employees will identify as much with the process as with their individual functions/departments.
- People at all levels will understand how their work fits into the process and adds value to the customer.
- Customer requirements will be known throughout the process.
- Processes will undergo continuous measurement, improvement, and redesign.
- More energy and resources will be focused on delivering value to customers and shareholders, rather than be wasted on bureaucracy or in-fighting.

You may notice that this "vision" list closely matches the goals of the Six Sigma system we've been presenting. In fact, such Six Sigma leaders as GE, AlliedSignal/Honeywell and others have already begun the task of making process management a key element in their overall approach. Today only a few steps have been taken in the new direction, but they certainly have helped to blaze a trail ahead.

The Process Owner

Perhaps the most essential step in the transformation to process management is designation of "Process Owners."

The Process Owner's Responsibilities

There's no official job description for a Process Owner, but the following responsibilities are essential to the role in a Six Sigma organization:

- *Maintaining Process Documentation.* The Process Owner is the person who creates and becomes keeper of process design data (i.e. maps, flows, and procedures), background data on customer requirements, and other defining documents of the process—and is responsible for keeping them up-to-date.
- *Measuring/Monitoring Process Performance.* You may already have wondered: "Who's going to *do* all this measurement and tracking of the process?" Process Owners see that the right measures are executed in the right way.
- *Identifying problems and opportunities.* As the primary observer of performance data, a Process Owner is the person who should first see problems as they arise—or to whom other people report the problems or issues they observe. Process Ownership ideally involves the authority to take action to address quick fixes and longer-term solutions.
- *Launching and Sponsoring Improvement Efforts.* When projects to improve, design, or redesign a process are identified, the Process Owner will take up the key role of supporting—if not *leading*—the effort. Just as importantly, the Process Owner "takes the handoff" from an improvement team, assuming the responsibility for maintaining the gain.
- *Coordinating and communicating with other Processes and with Functional Managers.* One of the most important principles behind the Process Owner role is that the work coming *into* and especially *out of* the

process is just as important as the work *within* the process. Some of the biggest obstacles to serving *external* customers come from poor coordination between *internal* suppliers and customers. It's only through upstream and downstream coordination that the Process Owner can remove the barriers or "us-against-them" attitudes that arise in the functional world. A Process Owner has to work *with* Suppliers and Customers to meet the goal of top-level performance. S/he also has to align the various groups in the process to make sure the work flows smoothly and is done well.

✦ *Maximizing Process Performance.* All the responsibilities noted thus far lead to this most-important objective. The Process Owner becomes the key driver to achieve Six Sigma levels of quality, efficiency, and flexibility.

Process Owners in the Organization

Decades of functional management won't give way to a process management orientation overnight—nor is it clear that it *should.* To maintain the "command and control" advantages of the functional system, a hybrid of process and hierarchical structures may be more effective.

In some businesses, for example, there are "levels" of process ownership, with a Core Process owner having two or more Subprocess owners engaged in a process management team. Each of these individuals wears a functional hat as well, but in their role as Process Owners they concentrate on the overall cross-functional operation and on improvement of the process. If these process management layers were to turn into a new reporting structure, it isn't clear how much better it might be than existing organizational hierarchies. This is one of those evolutionary questions about process management that will have to be answered over time and by each organization based on its own needs and experiences.

What *is* clear about Process Ownership is that the emphasis on measuring, improving, and coordinating flows of work calls for a somewhat different, if not broader, set of skills than does functional management. A profile seeking to identify potential Process Owners might include these traits:

- Results-oriented, with an emphasis on "win-win" gains and a focus on the customer

- Respected by senior leaders, middle management, and staff
- Strong business knowledge, with ability to think and work as a "generalist"
- Excellent people skills, especially in the areas of team development, consensus-building, and negotiation
- Skilled in Six Sigma concepts, measurement, and Process Improvement and Design methods
- Ability to share credit for success and to take the responsibility for setbacks

Strong technical knowledge or statistical expertise also can be helpful—but not if they take away from that more important generalist perspective.

Exactly where Process Owner candidates will be found in an organization is anyone's guess. It will likely take some creative talent-scouting to find the right mix of skills and potential to fill the Ownership role in your organization. It's safe to say, though, that old-style authoritative managers won't be right for the role unless they can change their approach. In fact, one of the reasons that Process Management will require a long-term evolution—is the fact that many of today's managers will have trouble adapting to the new "horizontal" approach. It may take a whole new generation to really develop the talent needed for the new role.

Where to Put Process Owners?

We laid the groundwork for an answer to this question back in Chapter 12, where we explored Core and Support Processes. As your organization prepares its inventory of critical or strategic processes, you are also setting the stage for designating *owners* of those processes. In larger organizations—as in the organization noted above—having "layers" of ownership is the best option. No one person can oversee a single large, diverse process. Where responsibility for a larger process is divided, those Owners would form what some companies call a Process Management Team, or PMT.

It's also important that Process Owners be deployed at an *operating* level of a business. We've seen situations where a company with several divisions created a "macro" process management system at the corporate level. Unfortunately, while there were definitely common processes in the different divisions, each was unique and required focused ownership at the division level. The firm struggled for a while, before realizing and correcting its mistake.

Can Process Ownership reach all the way down to the departmental or functional level? The answer is a qualified "Yes." There clearly are processes *within* a function, and these can be managed with many of the same methods and measures as cross-functional processes. Nonetheless, we say the shift to process management at the department level is best driven by a change in focus, rather than by creating a new "Process Owner" assignment within functions. Individuals are already in place to manage functions: VPs, directors, managers, etc.

Owning Up-Home

Top management at Up-Home was very pleased with the results of the design and management of the *Take it Home* process. They were early in their Six Sigma effort, though, and still unsure whether or how the concept of "process management" would fit in with a dispersed retail operation.

The launch of the new process seemed however to provide a good opportunity to test how the Process Owner role would work, and to see if it would add value to the organization and its customers. After a discussion of the idea of creating a *Take it Home* process owner, top management agreed that it did meet several important criteria:

- It was a cross-functional process, involving many of Up-Home's departments
- It was a continuing effort, not just a marketing campaign, and hence an appropriate choice for establishment as a key business process
- The ability to measure, assess, and improve the *Take it Home* process would be key to its continued success. As customer needs, product mixes, competition, and so on changed, it was likely the process would need to adapt.

One question provoked some debate: Could a Process Owner really oversee an activity being carried out at 17 different locations? The decision was to designate a companywide *owner* of the process, and to assign a process *coordinator* at the store level. (Some of the coordinators would cover two or three locations.)

Selecting the Process Owner was, fortunately, pretty easy. One of the members of the team that had designed the new process, Margy McMahon, had already exhibited the kind of leadership and process perspective that seemed ideal for such an important cross-functional activity.

Margy's first task was to pull together many of the documents and notes prepared by the design team—which no one had touched since the pilot—and create an overall process guidebook. When that was ready, she set out on a tour of Up-Home stores to begin selecting Process Coordinators.

Step 5C: Execute "Closed-Loop" Management and Drive to Six Sigma

Establishing process management is both the end of our Six Sigma Roadmap and the *beginning* of becoming a real Six Sigma organization. Any business or process that has followed the Roadmap through at least steps 1, 2, and 3, will be forming the key elements of the Process Management approach. Let's briefly review these steps and their contributions:

1. *Identify core processes and key customers.* Defining the process, its key steps, customers, and outputs creates the blueprint for Process Management.
2. *Define customer requirements.* Process goals and performance standards, determined by market and customer needs, are the "*raison d'être*" of any process. Understanding those requirements in concrete terms helps you to answer that basic question: "Manage the process to do *what?*"
3. *Measure current performance.* Measurement in the process management system will provide ongoing, essential feedback on results (Ys) and key process factors (Xs).

As your efforts at Six Sigma mature, Process Improvement and Design/Redesign (DMAIC) become the strategies that drive work processes to ever-higher Sigma levels and respond to customer demands for new products, services, or capabilities.

Tools for Process Management

Every tool we've described or mentioned—as well as those we'll review in the next chapter—plays a role in helping to manage processes. A couple of other methods, however, can be of particular value to the Process Owner as he or she strives to keep a process running smoothly and improving continuously.

Process Scorecards or Dashboards

The Process Scorecard, like the Balanced Scorecard mentioned earlier, provides a summary update on key indicators of process performance While the Balanced Scorecard typically provides organizationwide data, the Process Scorecard would be designed for a specific process. It can include "alarms" to show if and when a key indicator is nearing a problem level. For example, by noting the specified delivery time on a cycle-time chart, a Process Owner could see whether times are close to exceeding the requirements. Some companies, including a number of GE businesses, actually provide tailored Process Scorecard data to *customers,* telling them "here's how our process is performing for *you.*"

Customer Report Cards

Timely customer feedback is a key ingredient in optimized process performance. One of the focused tools that can support that need—an element of the overall Voice of the Customer system—is a Customer Report Card. Ideally, it provides representative data (i.e., an accurate, unbiased sample) of how well the process is meeting customer needs. The best Customer Report Cards are more than "surveys" or "complaint data"; they provide input that is meaningful both to the customer and to the company on performance, concerns, etc.

In business-to-business relationships these Report Cards can be tailored specifically to the client, so that the "grades" or other feedback provided has been selected on the basis of each customer's unique needs and priorities.

Process Management Finds Up-Home

Six months after Margy McMahon was named the first Process Owner at Up-Home—overseeing the new *Take it Home* product trial process—company leaders were becoming convinced that the

Process Management approach could be a big benefit to the organization as a whole.

For one thing, Margy and the network of Process Coordinators in the stores had made some significant contributions to the *Take it Home* process's continued success. For example:

- Three months after the process was launched, lost items began to climb. Margy and the Process Coordinators were able to determine that some of the Up-Home sales associates were failing to record complete address data and were unable to recontact customers to get the items back. A simple fix solved the problem.
- By tracking the types of products where *Take it Home* led to the highest sales increases, they were able to anticipate additional inventory needs and gear up for higher demand. This not only allowed for additional sales, but also gave Up-Home an opportunity to get discounts from vendors.
- In a number of instances where squabbles arose between the Sales and Product Delivery departments, Margy and/or the Process Coordinators were able to keep things from getting

Take-it-Home PROCESS SCORECARD (Quarterly Summary)

Measure	Target	Performance JLY	AUG	SEP	Notes
New Products Added	6 per Month	●	●	○	Quarterly Target Exceeded
Defects per TIH Item Loaned (DPU)	.01 (99 % Yield)	○	○	◒	Total DPU of .031
TIH Volume Growth	6% Month-to-Month	◒	○	◒	Quarterly Target Met
% TIHs Purchased	75%	◒	○	○	Average 68% for Qtr.
% Customers Rating TIH "Excellent"	95%	◒	●	●	Strong positive comments
Sales Increase due to TIH (estimate)	20%	●	●	●	25% Increase, approx. $8 mill.

● - Above Target ◒ - At Target ○ - Below Target

UpHOME

Figure 17.2 UpHome Take it Home Process Scorecard

out of hand. Maintaining the focus on the customer, the issues were resolved to everyone's satisfaction.

The Process Scorecard Margy created for Take it Home helped everyone keep up-to-date on the performance of the process [see a sample of it in Fig. 17.2].

As a first step in expanding the Process Management approach, Up-Home's leaders scheduled a half-day meeting, to begin mapping out all their core business processes....

Moving toward Six Sigma

We began this chapter with an analogy of regaining lost weight after a bout of successful dieting. We suggested that some companies, like complacent and undisciplined dieters, are doomed to backslide when they shift their attention to seemingly more "urgent" issues. We also noted that the gains of Six Sigma will come somewhat easily at first, like those first few pounds in a diet, but that the last few "Sigma points" will be hard to rack up in the drive for *Six* Sigma.

The Process Management discipline is where the momentum to "keep losing weight"—or defects—will come from. It's the mechanism which ensures that your firm will make measures and improvement a daily responsibility, not just an occasional task. Moreover, as your business progresses down the Six Sigma Way, you'll find more opportunities to use sophisticated tools to move past Four and Five Sigma. We'll look at the advanced Six Sigma tools in the next chapter.

Managing for Six Sigma Performance "Dos and Don'ts"

Do—Document the steps and lessons in Process Improvement and Design/Redesign projects.

A project storyboard will be helpful to "sell" the solutions, and as an aid to future improvement teams.

Do—Develop a complete plan to Control the process and maintain the gains.

Selling, documenting, measuring, and responding are essential to solidify success—and become key inputs to the Process Management system.

Do—Carefully define the role and responsibilities of a Process Owner for your organization.

As a new player on the business landscape, a Process Owner and those who work with him/her need a clear idea of the Owner's function and objectives.

Don't—Take on process management without careful upfront consideration.

As useful as this discipline and resource can be, an all-out process management implementation may not make sense. If necessary, try it out and learn (i.e., pilot the concept) before you create unnecessary business upheaval.

Don't—Create process reports and documentation that end up being just as under-used as your current ones.

Focus first on information you know you or others will need, and add to it as need be.

CHAPTER

18

Advanced Six Sigma Tools: An Overview

IN OUR JOURNEY along the Six Sigma Way so far, we've concentrated on those tools that drive much of the improvement in most organizations and processes. What Motorola discovered when it initiated Six Sigma, other businesses have learned since: Many problems and opportunities can be addressed with techniques that anyone can use. On the other hand, one of the keys to the success of the Six Sigma system has been the application—by teams and by specially trained Black Belts—of more sophisticated tools that bring more power to the Learning and Improvement efforts.

Our objective in this chapter is not to make you an expert in any of these advanced methods. We will try, though, to make you familiar with *what* some of the most common Six Sigma techniques are, *why* they can be helpful, and *how* they can be applied to Process Design, Management and Improvement. Each of the "power tools" we'll cover has one or more specific applications, and like any tool these can be misused or unproductive if not chosen and applied with care.

We've sequenced the methods in this chapter based on their most common use in the Six Sigma improvement effort, as noted in italics:

- Statistical Process Control and Control Charts—*problem identification*

- Tests of Statistical Significance (Chi-Square, *t*-tests and ANOVA)—*problem definition and root cause analysis*
- Correlation and Regression—*root cause analysis and prediction of results*
- Design of Experiments—*optimal solution analysis and results validation*
- Failure Modes and Effects Analysis—*problem prioritization and prevention*
- Mistake-Proofing—*defect prevention and process improvement*
- Quality Function Deployment—*product, service, and process design*

Statistical Process Control, and Control Charts

Statistical Process Control, or SPC, involves the measurement and evaluation of variation in a process, and the efforts made to limit or "control" such variation. In its most common application, SPC helps an organization or Process Owner to identify possible problems or unusual incidents so that action can be taken promptly to resolve them—in other words, to *control* the performance of a process.

When and Why to Use SPC/Control Charts

Use of SPC and Control Charts constitutes the ideal way of monitoring current process performance, predicting future performance, and suggesting the need for corrective action. Control Charts, which are pretty easily understood after just a bit of instruction, can be a very effective communication tool. Quite a few companies we've worked with post Control Charts for key processes in readily accessible areas—giving visibility to daily activities, trends, and patterns, and warnings of possible problems. This practice can get everyone involved in the company's management and problem solving.

Control Charts have three significant uses in the Six Sigma system:

1. In the early "Measure" activities of a DMAIC project, they help teams identify the type and frequency of problems or "out-of-control" conditions. They can even suggest what type of investigation or corrective action might prove most effective.

2. In piloting or implementing a Process Solution or Change (in the Improve or Control phases), they help track results, showing how variation and performance have been affected and perhaps even suggesting further areas of work or investigation.
3. Third, Control Charts act as an ongoing alarm system, alerting the observer to unusual activities in the process and triggering the process "Response Plan" discussed in Chapter 17.

You can think of SPC/Control Charts in that third application as being a smoke detector in your house: When it has batteries, is properly placed, and someone is around to hear it, it can sound the alarm in ample time to keep the place from going up in flames.

What Does the "Control" in SPC/Control Charts Mean?

"Control" means keeping a process operating within a predictable range of variation. The objective is to maintain the stable, consistently good performance of a process. In SPC, we're adding the notion of *statistical* control to the discussion. Thus to figure out whether a process is statistically "in control" or "out of control," you have to begin by actually measuring a process over time and then examine the variation in the data you've gathered. With enough data you can calculate what are called "Control Limits," thereby taking a first step in checking to see how well the process is working.

Let's take an example. Imagine you're managing your company's e-mail system, and you want to know how much variation exists in the number of e-mail messages sent per hour. To get an answer, of course, you have to gather some data. So, after compiling hourly volume-levels over a month (using excellent data-collection methods, no doubt), you plot e-mail traffic volumes on a Run or Trend chart (i.e., in time order). Next, you use that data to calculate the Control Limits—UCL, for "Upper Control Limit," and LCL, for "Lower Control Limit"—and you add those to your chart along with a line indicating the average or mean. You now—voilà!—have a Control Chart (see Fig. 18.1).

If you continue to gather data on e-mail traffic, the Control Chart will give you the ability not only to track changes in e-mail volume, but also to be able to see if and when the process is "out of control," or operating in a way that is no longer predictable.

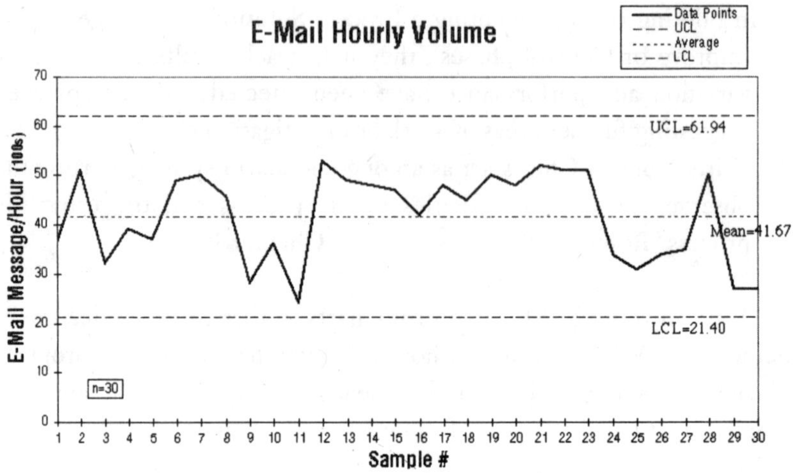

Figure 18.1 Example: Control chart of e-mail volume

Control Chart Alarms

Because we expect that variation in a process under normal conditions will be "random," there are several indicators of an out-of-control situation:

- *Outliers*—any point outside the control limits
- *Trends*—a series of points continually rising or falling
- *Shifts,* or *Runs*—a continuous sequence of points above or below the average
- *Cycles,* or *Periodicity*—a series of points alternating up and down or trending up and down in "waves"
- *Tendencies*—situations in which the points continually fall close to the center line or to either of the Control Limits

Control Charts and Customer Requirements

One of the misunderstandings about Control Charts is that being "in control" means the same thing as being "good." If a computer repair shop decides to measure its turnaround time on routine repairs, it might create a chart showing a process under perfect control. The problem however is that while their average turnaround is five days, customers want these jobs done in *two!*

Remember that these two types of "limits" we've introduced in this book (Control and Specification, not Outer and City) are developed very differently: Control Limits are calculated from actual process data; they can change as the process performance changes over time. Specification Limits come from the *customer;* they change only as the customer's requirements change.

Using Control Charts

The basic steps for implementing SPC should be familiar by now: Decide on the critical measures, implement a Data Collection Plan, plot the data, view the results, and take appropriate action. It's very much in line with the "closed-loop" system that is the foundation of the Six Sigma organization. Plotting and testing the data can be easily accomplished using statistics software. Simply enter the data or copy it from a spreadsheet, select the chart type and the tests from menus, and there you have it—a Control Chart.

Choosing the right type of Control Chart to use is important. There are several factors involved in determining which chart format fits your situation. For example if you have a continuous data measure (weight, time, temperature, etc.) you'll use one of two types. SPC books usually feature handy guides to selecting the appropriate chart.

No business should be creating new Control Charts all the time, since they are of real value only in monitoring changes in process performance. Therefore you should only occasionally have to confront the question: "What type of Control Chart should we use?"

SPC and Control Chart "Dos and Don'ts"

Do—Gather, plot, and review data promptly.

A key to the value of SPC is to get early warnings of problems or opportunities. If your data-collection systems and reporting take days or weeks to create reports, or if no one looks at them, why waste the resources?

Do—Choose and prioritize measures carefully.

One or two really meaningful Control Charts can be a big help. Having 10 or 15 mildly interesting ones only mean you'll quit looking at them soon.

Do—Set and fine-tune your alarms.

Use what you learn about the process to improve your response plans. The more promptly and effectively you can take action on key events, the more likely you are to keep customers and shareholders smiling!

Don't—Recalculate control limits too often.

Since the control limits are a function of the data, they could *be adjusted almost continuously—but that would make it much harder to detect "alarm" conditions. It's best to recalculate the limits only following a known process change. (When using software to present and test the Control Charts, set your preferences so as to prevent the recalculation of the control limits!)*

Don't—Assume perfect data.

Regular checks on the quality of your data collection—using methods like Gage R&R—are important to ensure that alarms aren't based on problems with the data itself.

Finally, remember that SPC and Control Charts are methods for *monitoring* and *understanding* your process. They do nothing to *solve* problems or improve your performance, unless you take corrective actions or apply Six Sigma improvement methods.

Tests of Statistical Significance (Chi-Square, t-test, ANOVA)

When you measure and analyze a process or product, it's often possible to draw valid conclusions simply by *looking* at the data.

There are times, however, when the lessons of the data are not obvious—or certain. You may look at your data and say, "I don't see anything to help me here!" Or you may have a pretty good hunch about what's going on, but want to be *extra* sure your conclusions are supported by the data. In these instances we can apply more rigorous *statistical* analysis methods to find or confirm trends or patterns in your data.

Uses of Tests of Statistical Significance

Tests of Statistical Significance are some of the most important techniques used by statisticians to look for patterns or to test their suspicions about data. In Six Sigma these tools have various possible applications, including:

- Confirming a problem or meaningful change in performance
- Checking the validity of data
- Determining the type of pattern or "distribution" in a group of continuous data
- Developing a root-cause hypothesis based on patterns and differences
- Validating or disproving root-cause hypotheses

Basics of Statistical Analysis: The Null Hypothesis

A 10-day heat wave hits your town and people say: "It's global warming!" You hit two holes-in-one in golf in two weeks, and exult "My game's really coming around!" The phone in the office seems to be ringing constantly and everyone says "It's going to be a busy quarter." You see a group of school kids making a lot of noise in the grocery store and say to yourself: "Kids these days just aren't brought up right!"

How valid are these conclusions? It's easy for us to extrapolate broad explanations from simple observations, and in some cases that's not a problem. The fact is, however, that in many instances, the so-called "patterns" we think we see are simply random variations. Wait long enough, and we'll see just as much evidence for a completely *opposite* conclusion. When the cold spell hits its fourth week, someone's sure to speculate on the coming Ice Age. As you hit your fourth bad round of golf in a month, you'll figure you're "past your peak." And so on.

In statistics, we guard against the possibility of "false patterns" tricking us into faulty conclusions by adopting what's called "the Null Hypothesis." The Null Hypothesis states that any variation, change, or difference observed in a population or a process is due purely to *chance*. It's much like the attitude of that ultimate skeptic who won't believe anything unless you "prove it." And often the way we convince a skeptic is not to prove *your* theory but rather to *disprove* any other explanation. That's the approach we take in tests of statistical significance.

Testing for Statistical Significance: Methods and Examples

As with Control Charts, you have several methods to choose from as you proceed to statistically test a hypothesis:

- *Chi-Square* (χ^2) test. This is the technique used with discrete data, and in some cases with continuous data ("Chi" is pronounced *kye*). As examples, you could apply a Chi-Square test so as to
    - Compare defect rates in two locations to see if they are significantly different
    - Check to see if week-to-week changes in customer product choices indicate a meaningful level of variation
    - Test the impact of various staffing levels on customer satisfaction
- *t*-test. You use this method to test for significance when you have two groups or samples of *continuous* data. (As we've noted in Chapter 14, continuous data measures have more power than discrete ones, but you need to be careful because these tests work only if certain conditions are met in the data.) Assuming that your data qualify, you might apply a *t*-test to:
    - Compare the cycle time for a key step in your process at two weeks during the quarter, to see if there's been any meaningful change
    - Examine customer income levels in two regions, to see if one serves significantly higher- or lower- income customers
    - Test to see if the seek-time speed in two lots of disk drives is different
- *Analysis of Variance* (*ANOVA*)—ANOVA is another test of significance for continuous data; unlike the *t*-test, however, it can be used to compare *more* than two groups or samples. (If you find there's a significant difference among three or more groups of data, you have to do more analysis to find out *which* groups are different.) The following examples are the same as those for the *t*-test given above, but with the number-differences shown in italic type:
    - Compare the cycle time for a key step in your process for *each week* during the quarter to see if there's been any meaningful change.

- Examine customer income levels in *four* regions to see if one *or more* serves significantly higher- or lower-income customers
- Test to see if the seek-time speed in *five* lots of disk drives is different

- *Multivariate Analysis.* In the first three methods we've described, the comparisons are based on a single factor or variable: time, income, speed, etc. Of course there may be *other* factors changing between one group or sample. Multivariate Analysis (sometimes called MANOVA) is used to determine the significance of several factors. (It's usually best to do an ANOVA test before doing a Multivariate.)

Basic Steps Taken in Statistical Tests

The good news about applying statistics to business problems these days is that a lot of the grunt-work has been eliminated, thanks to statistical software. The major steps in applying them remain relevant, however, regardless of how quickly the calculations are done:

1. *Identify the issue being analyzed.* What is the key question or concern to which you want to apply a statistical test? Check to make sure statistical validation is really needed; is the answer already pretty obvious?
2. *Formulate your hypothesis and the Null Hypothesis.* Describe in your hypothesis (known technically as the "Alternative Hypothesis") what you think is happening, and then negate it by concluding: "It's actually just random probability that this is what we see" (the Null Hypothesis).
3. *Select the proper statistical test.* Before you make a final choice of a continuous-data technique, you will need to review the data to see if it will work.
4. *Conduct the calculation and review the results.* Basically, there are three possible answers here: a) the Null Hypothesis is proven, meaning this data provides no evidence supportive of your hypothesis; b) the Null Hypothesis is *not* true, based on this data, indicating that some significant factor is impacting the data and hence your hypothesis may be correct; or c) there is an *error,* indicating that something in your data or in the tool you selected isn't right.

Tests of Statistical Significance "Dos and Don'ts"

Do—Make sure the data being used is valid.

A test done using faulty data is meaningless or even dangerous. If for example your sample size is too small, that may cause you to find "significant" differences when they don't really exist.

Do—Select the right kind of test.

For example, if it's discrete data, Chi-Square is the test to use.

Don't—Use your own expertise as a "gut check" of the statistical analysis.

Statistics and experience are meant to work together.

Don't—Consider yourself an "expert" too soon.

There are plenty of complexities and nuances to these tools. "Unusual" situations actually are pretty typical in the real world, and thus it can take more than a bit of experience to learn the ins-and-outs of statistical analyses.

Correlation and Regression Analysis

Correlation and Regression Analysis encompass a family of tools that analyze the relationships among two or more factors. The basics of correlation were introduced with Scatter Plots in Chapter 15 (see the Overview on p. 269 and the example on p. 308). When two factors are "correlated" it means that a change in one will be accompanied by a change in the other. By applying statistical calculations to that data, we can measure the *strength* of a possible relationship among the factors and draw a number of other helpful conclusions besides.

Uses of Correlation and Regression Analysis

Across the various types of Correlation and Regression you will find tools that can help you to:

- Test root-cause hypotheses by seeing if there's a link between the suspected cause (the X) and the response or output (the Y)

Table 18.1 Correlation Test Example.

Unit or Item:	Factor 1 (X, or independent variable):	Factor 2 (Y, or dependent variable):
Copier	Time elapsing between maintenance	Copy defects

- Measure and compare the influence of *various* factors (Xs) on the results (Y)
- Predict the performance of a process, product, or service under certain conditions.

Correlation and Regression can be used *only* when you have data for two or more factors that are matched on individual items. (This contrasts with the statistical tests we've just seen, which compare *groups* of data.) Table 18.1 shows a situation in which you might test a correlation.

To do a correlation analysis there, you would need to have data *both* for Time between Maintenance *and* for Copy Defects from Copier A, B, C, etc.

Particularly in analyzing causes, and depending on the nature of your data, Correlation and Regression tools can bring some important advantages over such tools as Chi-Square and ANOVA. They allow you to see finer patterns in smaller samples of data, and to see how the changes in different variables directly affect a "unit."

Types of Correlation and Regression Analysis

Again, computers, spreadsheets, and statistical software have made these tools accessible to many people. Here are some of the common uses, and a few key concepts:

- *Correlation Coefficient.* The same data used to draw a Scatter Plot can be "crunched" into a number—noted *r*—that tells you whether and how strongly the factors are correlated. The *r* correlation coefficient ranges from −1 to 1; generally an *r* score of below −.7 or above .7 would be worthy of serious further investigation. (Negative *r* results indicate a negative correlation.)

- *Correlation Percentage.* Another number, r^2, is preferred by many because it reflects the amount or percent of variation in the Y or dependent factor that seems to be caused by the X factor. (You get r^2 just by "squaring" *r*.) For example, let's say you found an apparent positive correlation for the time between copier maintenance and copy defects, with an *r* value of .72. You'd get an r^2 of .52—meaning that roughly 50 percent of the increase in defects correlates with the time between maintenance. Note that how you will interpret and respond to either *r* or r^2 will depend on the purpose of your analysis and on your type of data.
- *Regression.* The various forms of regression analysis concentrate on using existing data to predict future results. The most common is "Linear Regression" (or "simple" regression), which is used for two variables. We can illustrate by using our copier example.

Percy's Copy Repair

Percy's wants to show clients the value of its maintenance service contract. Having gathered data on the relationship between Time Maintenance and Copy Defects, they found that defect rates tend to increase by 15 percent for every two-week period without maintenance. Using the tool of Linear Regression, they were able to predict to a prospective customer that by the third month after their last "emergency" service call, they'd be getting about 25 percent "defective" copies. The prediction turned out to be pretty accurate, and now the customer has a bi-weekly service agreement with Percy's.

- *Multiple Regression.* Multiple regression, like Multivariate analysis, examines the relationship among *several* factors and the results. In a process environment, examples could include all those shown in Table 18.2.

  Using Multiple Regression, you would be able to quantify the impact of each of these Xs on the Ys—and to see how they interact. In more advanced applications, Multiple Regression is applied to create *models* to predict the results when combinations of factors interact under various conditions.

Table 18.2 Multiple Regression Analysis Examples.

Process	Unit or Item	X_1 (Input variable)	X_2 (Process variable)	X_3 (Process variable)	Y (Output or result variable)
Software Installation	Software Package	Size of Software (MB)	Number of Users on Network	Server Processor Speed (MHz)	System Downtime during Install (Minutes)
Hotel Reservation and Check-In	Reservation	Hold time to talk to Reservation Agent (seconds)	Number of days reserved	Number of Agents on duty in Call Center	Time to check in a guest (minutes)

Correlation and Regression "Dos and Don'ts"

Do—Make sure you have paired data.

The ability to do correlation and regression is predicated on how you collect and compile data. If the values of the factors being analyzed don't match for a single item, you can't do correlation analysis.

Do—Use the correlation coefficient and percentage (r and r^2) to better understand Scatter Plot data.

This is one of the easiest statistical indicators, and it can be a huge help to you as you try to interpret the mass of dots on a Scatter Diagram.

Do—Apply more advanced methods—when you're ready—to learn more about your processes and products.

Used properly, correlation and regression can add significantly to your understanding of how and why variation occurs in your business—and how to control it.

Don't—Take predictions drawn from data as "fact."

The predictions made from regression analysis are in most cases based on tendencies. *That means there can still be a lot of variation you don't understand—which can lead to results you didn't expect.*

Don't—Look at the data in only one way.

If a strongly suspected correlation doesn't show up, it may be "hidden." You might want to consider stratifying your data, or gathering them over a longer period, before you conclude absolutely that there's no relationship.

Don't—Assume that correlation means causation.

As we discussed in Chapter 15, two items that correlate may not cause one another at all—something else may be affecting them both.

Design of Experiments (DOE)

DOE is a method used for testing and optimizing the performance of a process, product, service, or solution. It draws heavily on the techniques just reviewed—tests of statistical significance, correlation, and regression—to help you learn about the behavior of a product or process under varying conditions. What's unique about DOE is the opportunity it gives you to plan and control the variables using an *experiment,* as opposed to just gathering and observing real-world events in the manner known as "empirical observation."

Uses of Design of Experiments

DOE has plenty of potential application in a Six Sigma organization. It can allow you to:

- Assess Voice of the Customer systems, to find the best combination of methods producing valid feedback without annoying customers
- Assess factors to isolate the "vital" root cause of a problem or defect
- Pilot or test combinations of possible solutions to find the optimal improvement strategy
- Evaluate product or service designs to identify potential problems and reduce defects right from "day one."

While DOE tends to be easier to apply to *things* than to people, nonetheless it is possible to conduct experiments in service environments. These tend though to be "real-world" tests in which the variables are controlled in the actual process and the results then compared. For example, a large sales organization tested 14 variables over a four-month period, in an effort to find the best sales-boosting combination. Based on solutions identified in the "field experiment," sales volume jumped by over 50 percent even in the firm's top-producing region.[1]

Basic Steps in Design of Experiments

Basic steps for you to take in a designed experiment include the following:

1. *Identify the factors to be evaluated.* What do you want to learn from the experiment? What are the likely influences on the process or product? As you select factors, keep in mind the importance of balancing the benefit of getting additional data by testing more factors with the increased cost and complexity.
2. *Define the "levels" of the factors to be tested.* In the case of such variable factors as speed, time, weight, etc., you could test them at an infinite number of levels. Thus in this step you choose not only which values, but also how many different levels, you want to test. In the case of discrete data, levels may be "either/or"; for example, in testing a form we could a) include our e-mail address or b) not include our e-mail address.[2]
3. *Create an array of experimental combinations.* In DOE, you usually want to avoid the "one-factor-at-a-time" approach (known as OFAT), where each variable is tested in isolation. Rather, arrays of conditions are examined so as to get representative data for all the factors. Possible combinations or arrays can be generated by statistics software tools or found in tables, and their use helps you to avoid having to test every possible permutation.
4. *Conduct the experiment under the prescribed conditions.* A key here is to avoid letting other, untested factors influence your results.
5. *Evaluate the results and conclusions.* If you're going to see patterns and draw conclusions from DOE data, tools like ANOVA and Multiple Regression are a must. From the experimental data you may get very clear answers, or additional questions may arise that you will then test in additional experiments.

Design of Experiments "Dos and Don'ts"

Do—Be prepared to apply DOE concepts to "real-world" processes.

Outside of Product Design, Engineering, and Manufacturing, most other business activities won't fit in a "laboratory." You may need to conduct your experiments on real people—for example, in piloting a new solution.

Do—Take advantage of experimental "arrays."

One way that the discipline of DOE can bring you big time and resource savings is by producing more data from fewer tests. Done right, you can *take the time to conduct experiments you might otherwise not have considered.*

Do—Include "problem prevention" in your DOE plans.

If something goes wrong in your experiment, would there be serious consequences? If so, you need to plan preventions and contingencies to make sure an experiment doesn't "backfire." For example, piloting a solution with customers is fine, as long as you don't put your business with them at undue risk.

Don't—Fail to consider a variety of factors or influences.

It's the unanticipated variables that "mess up" lots of experiments.

Don't—Get stuck on the experimental treadmill.

As in the "Analyze" phase of DMAIC, you can always do more tests and gather more data. Use DOE as a tool, *not as an* end.

Failure Modes and Effects Analysis (FMEA)

Failure Modes and Effects Analysis is a set of guidelines, a process, and a form to identify and prioritize potential problems (failures). By basing their activities on FMEA, a manager, improvement team, or Process Owner can focus the energy and resources of prevention, monitoring, and response plans where they are most likely to pay off. Borrowed from high-stakes industries like aerospace and defense, FMEA is a more rigorous application of the "potential problem analysis" concept discussed in Chapter 16.

Uses of FMEA

The FMEA method has many applications in a Six Sigma environment, in terms of looking for problems not only in work processes and improvements but also in data-collection activities, Voice of the Customer efforts, procedures—and even the rollout of a Six Sigma initiative. The only prerequisite is to have a complex or high-stakes situation in which you want to place a special emphasis on keeping problems at bay.

How FMEA Works

The steps and key concepts are as follows:

1. *Identify the process or product/service.*
2. *List potential problems that could arise (Failure Modes[3]).* The basic question is: "What could go wrong?" Ideas as to potential problems may come from various sources including brainstorming, process analysis, benchmarking, etc. They can be grouped by process step or product/service component. Avoid trivial problems.
3. *Rate the problem for Severity, Probability of Occurrence, and Detectability.* Using a 1–10 scale, give a score on each factor to each potential problem. More serious problems get a higher rating; harder-to-detect problems also get a higher score. Again, these may be judgments or be based on historical or test data.
4. *Calculate the "Risk Priority Number," or RPN, and prioritize actions.* Multiplying the three scores together gives this overall risk rating. By adding the RPNs from all problems, you get a total risk figure for the process or product/service. (Maximum RPN is 1,000.)
5. *Develop actions to reduce the risk.* Focusing first on potential problems having the highest priority, you then can devise actions to reduce one or all factors: Seriousness, Occurrence, and Detectability. A key benefit of the tool is to make your problem management resources—which always are finite—go to best benefit.

An FMEA Example

Managers and engineers at e-commerce company Nitwit.com wanted to make sure nothing went wrong with its process for updating the on-line catalog. Here are two of the problems they identified and the analysis they did:

1. *The wrong artwork is used with a new item.*
   Severity = 5
   Occurrence = 5
   Detection = 3
   RPN = 5 × 5 × 3 = 75
2. *Buyers can't place an order for an item.*
   Severity = 8
   Occurrence = 5
   Detection = 6
   RPN = 8 × 5 × 6 = 240

Based on this assessment, they focused on the concern about not being able to place orders and developed preventive measures to ensure that all new product numbers are posted to the ordering system.

Mistake-Proofing (or *Poka-Yoke*)

Mistake-proofing can be thought of as an extension of FMEA—or as an extra-disciplined way of shedding those final pounds (i.e., defects) in our Six Sigma diet. Whereas FMEA helps in the prediction and prevention of problems, Mistake-Proofing emphasizes the detection and correction of mistakes before they become defects delivered to customers. It puts special attention on the one constant threat to any process: *human* error.

The basic ideas behind Mistake-Proofing—also known by the Japanese name *Poka Yoke* (*POH-kuh YOH-kay*)—were developed by a management consultant in Japan, Shigeo Shingo. Shingo's ideas were controversial, partly because he proposed a method whereby "inspection" (the word he chose) becomes an integral part of every step in a process, as opposed to being solely a separate responsibility. When one looks more closely, however, one sees that the heart of Mistake-Proofing is simply to pay careful attention to every activity in the process and to place checks and problem prevention at each step. It's a matter of constant, instantaneous feedback, rather like the balance and direction data transmitted from a cyclist's ears to brain, keeping his or her bike upright and on the path.

Uses of Mistake-Proofing

Mistake-proofing can be used to:

- *Fine-tune improvements and process designs from DMAIC projects.* How can those rare, most challenging errors be avoided or managed?
- *Gather data from processes approaching Six Sigma performance.* (The more "perfect" a process is, the harder it can be to measure.)
- *Eliminate the kinds of process issues and defects needed to take a process from 4.5 to 6 Sigma.*

Basic Steps in Mistake-Proofing

Mistake-proofing is best applied after completion of a thorough FMEA prediction and prevention review. Then you can

1. *Identify possible errors that might occur despite preventive actions.* Review each step in the existing process while asking the question "What possible human error or equipment malfunction could take place in this step?"
2. *Determine a way to detect that an error or malfunction is taking place or about to occur.* An electric circuit in your car, for example, can tell if you've fastened your seat-belt. E-commerce software is programmed to tell if any piece of data is missing from a field. In an assembly plant, trays holding parts help the worker to see if an item is missing.
3. *Identify and select the type of action to be taken when an error is detected.* The basic types of "Mistake-Proofing Device" are these:

   - *Control.* An action that self-corrects the process, like an automatic spell-checker/corrector.
   - *Shutdown.* A procedure or device that blocks or shuts down the process when an error occurs. The automatic shutoff feature of a home iron is one example. Another is sophisticated investment software that bars the entry of certain investments in accounts decreed to be off-limits to those investments.
   - *Warning.* As the name implies, this alerts the person involved in the work that something is going wrong. A seat-belt buzzer is an example. So is a control chart that shows that a process may be "out of control." Warnings too often are ignored, so controls and shutdowns usually are preferable.

Coming up with methods to detect, self-correct, block/shut down, or warn of a problem can require real imagination and creativity. Some common types of Mistake-Proofing measures include:

- Color- and shape-coding of materials and documents
- Distinctive shapes of such key items as legal documents
- Symbols and icons to identify easily confused items
- Computerized checklists, clear forms, best-in-class, up-to-date procedures and simple workflows will help to prevent errors from becoming defects in the hands of customers.

Dave Boenitz of semiconductor equipment manufacturer Applied Materials—whom we heard from in Chapter 4—says that Mistake-Proofing has been the focus of their improvement and lean manufacturing efforts. "We've looked for ways to make the assembly so foolproof that it's impossible to assemble it the wrong way. So we've done things like more visual displays; we've got colored schematics of how the part is supposed to go together." Also, a variety of jigs and fixtures are used to make it difficult to assemble items in the wrong way—much like a key that can fit only a certain lock.

Extra care is taken to check the work at each step, as well: "Those people that do the work inspect their product before it moves on; then those people that *receive* it inspect the product. Through this orchestrated movement, they are able to eliminate most of the manufacturing assembly errors that can occur."

Mistake-Proofing "Dos and Don'ts"

Do—Try to imagine all conceivable errors that can be made.

This is where the truly negative and paranoid people in your organization can at last be of real help!

Do—Use all of your creative powers to brainstorm clever ways to detect and correct errors as part of the work process itself.

To leave the detection of defects to downstream inspectors, or to the customers, is to court disaster.

Don't—Fall into the "to err is human" mindset.

"To get things right most of the time" is also a human trait. Find out how your people are self-correcting problems that can't be prevented upstream, and share best practices.

Don't—Rely on people to catch their own errors all the time.

If your process is chugging along at just 2 Sigma, there's no way you can eliminate the "safety net" of downstream inspection.

Quality Function Deployment (QFD)

Quality Function Deployment is a method for prioritizing and translating customer inputs into designs and specifications for a product, service, and/or process. While the detail of the *work* involved in QFD can be both complex and exhaustive (not to mention exhaust*ing*), the essentials of the QFD method are based on common-sense ideas and tools we've already seen.

Uses of Quality Function Deployment

QFD is a robust method having many variations, so its uses can be quite broad. It can be applied to:

- Prioritize and select improvement projects based on customer needs and current performance
- Assess a process's or product's performance versus competitors
- Translate customer requirements into performance measures
- Design, test, and refine new processes, products, and services

QFD is by no means a stand-alone tool. It relies on a variety of other methods—from Voice of the Customer input to Design of Experiments—to work well.

Basics of Quality Function Deployment

A special multidimensional matrix, dubbed the "House of Quality," is the best-known element of the QFD method. A full QFD product design project will involve a series of these matrices, translating from customer and competitive needs all the way down to detailed process specifications. Amidst all the detail included in the QFD documentation, however, lie two core concepts:

1. *The QFD Cycle.* An iterative effort to develop operational designs and plans in four broad phases:
   a. Translate customer input and competitor analysis into Product or Service features (basic design elements).
   b. Translate Product/Service features into Product/Service specifications and measures.
   c. Translate Product/Service specifications and measures into *Process* design features. (How will the process deliver the features per specification?)
   d. Translate Process design features into Process performance specifications and measures.
2. *Prioritization and Correlation.* Detailed analysis of the relationships among specific needs, features, requirements, and measures. Matrices like the House of Quality or the simple L-Matrix (see *Fig. 18.2*) keep this analysis organized and document the rationale behind the design effort.

In essence, the QFD Cycle develops the links from downstream Ys (Customer Requirements and Product Specifications) back to upstream

PRODUCT/SERVICE FEATURES

CUSTOMER REQUIREMENTS	choice of point sizes	variety of ink colors	choice of finishes (gold, marble, etc.)	3 price levels ($12, $40, $75)	available neck chain	non-toxic ink	retailed at jewelers & specialty shops	sold direct through WEB
stylish			●	△	△		●	△
multiple choices	●	●	●	●	○		○	○
safe to use			△		△	●		
value for money	△		△	●			△	●
hard to lose			△		●			

CONTRIBUTION: ● STRONG ○ MODERATE △ WEAK

Figure 18.2 Example: simplified L-Matrix for designing a pen

Xs (Process Specifications) *right in the design process.* With an existing process or product, it can be used to clarify and document those relationships if they've never been investigated before. Another benefit of the House of Quality is a "diagonal" relationship test afforded by the matrix, testing combinations that may not have been considered by our standard human "linear" thought processes.

Quality Function Deployment "Dos & Don'ts"

Do—Adapt the complexity of the method to your situation.

Designing a complex product can involve many layers and much detail. Simply creating measures for an existing process should be much simpler. (Software packages are available for simpler or detailed House of Quality matrices.)

Do—Concentrate on getting good input and data, not just on "filling boxes."

A QFD matrix can have a lot of white space. Often, you'll fill it in best just using your own best judgment; if however you are putting something in a box merely to fill the space, don't.

Do—Use the "competitor analysis" feature of QFD to factor other external data into your designs and specifications.

Design for the customer, with an eye on the competitor.

Don't—Forget to apply other tools to the method.

Design of Experiments, for example, can be critical to maximizing performance on various design features. You also can use tools like Project Charters to help lay the foundation for a design effort.

CONCLUSION

Twelve Keys to Success

AS WE APPROACH THE END of our journey along the Six Sigma Way, we hope it's a *beginning* for you. In some ways, this book has just scratched the surface in outlining the ideas, tools, and disciplines that make up this *system* for management. (Some points we've likely repeated often enough so that the diligent reader by now is saying "*Enough!* I get it!") To wrap up, we'll summarize some of the key points of this book and the experiences of various organizations trying to become "Six Sigma Organizations" with a list of *Keys to Success.* Hopefully, this list will make up for the areas we've not covered in more depth, and help you glean the key points from topics we've covered in detail.

Keys to Success

1. Tie Six Sigma Efforts to Business Strategy and Priorities

Even if your first efforts focus on fairly narrow problems, their impact on key business needs should be clear. Show how projects and other activities link to customers, core processes, and competitiveness whenever possible.

2. Position Six Sigma as an Improved Way to Manage for Today

The methods and tools of Six Sigma make sense for successful organizations in the 21st century. They're a product of lessons learned by enlightened companies and managers, which address the challenges of rapid change, intense competition, and increasingly demanding customers.

3. Keep the Message Simple and Clear

Beware of alienating people with strange terms and jargon that create "classes" in a Six Sigma environment. While new vocabulary and skills are obviously part of the Six Sigma discipline, the core of the system and your company's vision for Six Sigma should be accessible and meaningful to everyone.

4. Develop Your Own Path to Six Sigma

Your themes, priorities, projects, training, structure—all should be decided based on what works best for you. Think about it: Why should there be a rigid formula for an approach to create a more flexible, responsive organization?

5. Focus on Short-Term Results

The proof is in the power of what Six Sigma can do to make your organization more competitive and profitable and your customers more loyal and delighted. Develop and push forward a plan that will make initial achievements concrete in the first four to six months.

6. Focus on Long-Term Growth and Development

Balance the push for early results with the recognition that those gains must lay the foundation for the real power of Six Sigma: creation of a more responsive, customer-focused, resilient, and successful company for the *long term.*

7. Publicize Results, Admit Setbacks, and Learn from Both

Don't expect—or claim—that Six Sigma works perfectly in your company. Recognize and celebrate successes, but pay equal attention to challenges and disappointments. Be ready to continuously improve—and even redesign—your Six Sigma processes as you progress.

8. Make an Investment to Make It Happen

Without time, support, and—yes—money, the habits and existing processes in your business won't change much. The results are likely to bring a quick return on investment, but first you have to *make* the investment.

9. Use Six Sigma Tools Wisely

No single tool or discipline in the Six Sigma system can create happier customers or improve profits. Statistics can answer questions, but can't deliver outstanding service. Creative ideas may hold potential, but without processes to develop and deliver them, they're just dreams. Your success in Six Sigma will depend on applying all the methods, in the right balance, to maximize your results. And using the *simplest* tool that works—not the most complex—should be highly valued.

10. Link Customers, Process, Data, and Innovation to Build the Six Sigma System

These are the core elements of the Six Sigma approach. When you understand your markets, your operations, and can use measures and creativity to maximize value and performance, that's the *potent combination that can make life miserable for your competitors.*

11. Make Top Leaders Responsible and Accountable

Until senior managers—of the corporation, business unit, or even department—accept Six Sigma as part of their jobs (or have it *made* part of their jobs), the true importance of the initiative will be in doubt—and the energy behind it will be weakened.

12. Make Learning an Ongoing Activity

A few months of training, however intensive, won't cement all the new knowledge and skills needed to sustain Six Sigma. Over time, you should look outside the Six Sigma discipline for other methods and ideas that complement the tools we've reviewed in this book.

BONUS—Make Six Sigma FUN!

Yes, this stuff about business survival, competition, and measurement is serious, sometimes confusing, even a bit scary. But the Six Sigma Way opens the door to new ideas, new ways of thinking, and a new breath of success. Putting humor into it and having a good time with Six Sigma will only *raise* your chances for success: Any time people enjoy something, they almost automatically put more energy and enthusiasm into it.

A Final Word

In business-speak we are compelled to use short phrases to describe complicated ideas. "Six Sigma" is no more a *thing* than is "economic policy" or "organizational excellence" or any dozens of other shorthand terms we use everyday. As we've noted from the start of this book, Six Sigma is a *system* that encompasses many concepts, tools, and principles—it's not a *thing*.

We believe—and hope you agree—that there are enough essential, powerful, and valuable elements to make the Six Sigma system, in some way, part of *every successful business*. At the same time, we strongly encourage you to adapt the discipline and methods of Six Sigma to best impact your unique culture, industry, market position, people, and strategy. Our biggest fear is that people will "accept" or "reject" Six Sigma as if it were a *thing* (falling victim to the Tyranny of the Or) and not use it as a flexible system.

Finally, having worked with this big topic and the companies applying it for quite a few years now, we're continually startled at how much we still have to learn and how many new perspectives there can be. We'd be thrilled to hear your comments and new ideas—and your thoughts on whether and how *The Six Sigma Way* has helped you. You can reach us via e-mail at *ssw@pivotalresources.com*.

We hope to hear about your successful journeys on the way to Six Sigma.

APPENDIX

Six Sigma Job Aids and Worksheets

Six Sigma Start-Up Checklist

Part One: Is SIx Sigma Right for us now? ...

Assess the current strategic and performance status of your organization (company, business unit, department) and answer the following:

1. Is change a critical business need or opportunity now, based on financial, competitive or cultural needs? **[YES]** [NO]
2. Can we make a strong strategic rationale for applying Six Sigma (in some form) to our business? **[YES]** [NO]
3. Will our existing management systems and improvement processes be capable of achieving the degree of improvement essential to our continued success? [YES] **[NO]**

If your answers are Yes, Yes and No, you appear ready to explore further how to adopt Six Sigma in your organization.

Part Two: How & where should we start our efforts? ...

Consider the current mix of activities and priorities in the organization and check *one* of the following statements that best describes your situation:

1. The company is ready for and able to focus on an all-out push to create a "Six Sigma organization." ☐
2. There are major, high-priority strategic issues or processes in the business that demand focused improvement resources. ☐
3. Our sense of urgency is such that we need to tackle short-term problems and projects before expanding the Six Sigma process. ☐

If you chose:

1-You may be ready for a full Business Transformation. 2-Your best focus will be on some form of Strategic Improvement. 3-immediate process improvement projects are probably your best starting point.

Figure A.1 Six Sigma Start-Up Checklist

Requirements Definition Worksheet

1. Identify the Output or Service encounter (Moment of Truth)

   ____

2. Define the Customer or Customer segment for whom the Requirement will apply

   ____

3. Note sources of data for "Voice of the Customer" input. (Attach relevant data as needed.)

   ____

   ____

4. Draft Requirement Statement (should include observable, objective factors for verification that requirement has been met).

   ____

   ____

   ____

   Check draft Requirement Statement for clarify, specifics, etc.

5. Note methods for Requirement Statement validation. (Attach validation findings as needed).

   ____

   ____

6. Final Requirements Statement:

   ____

   ____

   ____

Figure A.2 Requirements Definition Worksheet

Define Checklist

1. Define

Instructions:

If you can respond "yes" to each statement below, you're off to a good start with your project, and are ready to move into the "Measure" phase of DMAIC.

For our project we have ...

1. Confirmed that our project is a worthwhile improvement priority for our organization and is supported by business leaders. YES NO
2. Been given (or written) a brief Project Rationale explaining the potential impact of our project on customers, profits, and its relationship on the company's business strategies. YES NO
3. Composed and agreed to a two to three sentence description of the problem as we see it—the Problem Statement—focusing on symptoms only (not causes or solutions). YES NO
4. Prepared a Goal Statement defining the results we're seeking from our project, with a measurable target (or placeholder to add one). No solutions are proposed in the Goal Statement YES NO
5. Prepared other key elements of a DMAIC team charter, including a list of constraints and assumptions, a review of players and roles, a preliminary plan and schedule, and a process scope. YES NO
6. Reviewed your Charter with your sponsor for this project and confirmed his/her support. YES NO
7. Identified the primary customer and key requirements of the process being improved and created a SIPOC diagram of the areas of concern. YES NO
8. Prepared a detailed process map of areas of the process where we expect to focus our initial measurement. YES NO

Figure A.3 Define Checklist

Measure Checklist

2. Measure

Instructions:

If you can respond "yes" to each statement below, you're doing well with measurement, and are ready to move into the "Analyze" phase of DMAIC.

For our project we have ...

1.	Determined what we want to learn about our problem and process and where in the process we can go to get the answer.	YES	NO
2.	Identified the types of measures we want to collect and have a balance between effectiveness/efficiency and input/process/output.	YES	NO
3.	Developed clear, unambiguous operational definitions of the things or attributes we want to measure.	YES	NO
4.	Tested our operational definitions with others to ensure their clarity and consistent interpretation.	YES	NO
5.	Made a clear, reasonable choice between gathering new data or taking advantage of existing data collected in the organization.	YES	NO
6.	Clarified the stratification factors we need to identify to facilitate analysis of our data.	YES	NO
7.	Developed and tested data collection forms or checksheets which are easy to use and provide consistent, complete data.	YES	NO
8.	Identified an appropriate sample size, subgroup quantity and sampling frequency to ensure valid representation of the process we're measuring.	YES	NO
9.	Prepared and tested our measurement system, including training of collectors and assessment of data collection stability.	YES	NO
10.	Used data to prepare baseline process performance measures, including proportion defective and yield.	YES	NO

Figure A.4 Measure Checklist

Analyze Checklist

Instructions:

If you can respond "yes" to statements 5 or 7 below, and have done many of the tasks described in the other statements, chances are good you are ready to begin developing solutions in the "Improve" phase of DMAIC.

For our project we have ...

1. Examined our process and identified potential bottlenecks, disconnects and redundancies that could contribute to the problem on which we are focusing. YES NO
2. Conducted a value and cycle time analysis, locating areas where time and resources are devoted to tasks not critical to the customer. YES NO
3. Analyzed data about the process and its performance to help stratify the problem, understand reasons for variation in the process, and identify potential root causes. YES NO
4. Evaluated whether our project should focus on process design or redesign, as opposed to process improvement, and confirmed our decision with the project sponsor. YES NO

For Process Design/Redesign:

5. Ensured that we understand the key workings of the process so we can begin creating a new process to meet the needs of the customer efficiently and effectively. YES NO

For Process Improvement:

6. Developed root cause hypotheses to explain the problem we're solving. YES NO
7. Investigated and verified our root cause hypotheses, so that we are confident we have uncovered one or more "vital few" root causes that create our problem. YES NO

Figure A.5 Analyze Checklist

Improve Checklist

4. Improve

Instructions:

If you can respond "yes" to each statement below, you've achieved success with your improvement, and are ready to plan to "Control" your process/solution.

For our project we have ...

1. Created a list of innovative ideas for potential solutions. YES NO
2. Used the narrowing and screening techniques to further develop and qualify potential solutions. YES NO
3. Created a "Solution Statement" for at least two possible proposed improvements. YES NO
4. Made a final choice of our solution based on success criteria. YES NO
5. Verified our solution with our sponsor and received buy-in and the go-ahead. YES NO
6. Developed a plan for piloting and testing the solution, including a pilot strategy, action plan, results assessment, schedule, etc. YES NO
7. Evaluated pilot results and confirmed that we can achieve the results defined in our Goal Statement. YES NO
8. Identified and implemented refinements to the solution based on lessons from the pilot. YES NO
9. Created and put in place a plan to expand the solution—with refinements—to a complete implementation. YES NO
10. Considered potential problems and unintended consequences of the solution and developed preventive and contingent actions to address them. YES NO

Figure A.6 Improve Checklist

Control Checklist

5. Control

Instructions:

If you can respond "yes" to each statement below, you've completed all key steps in your DMAIC project and are ready to *celebrate* and maintain your improvement.

For our project we have ...

1.	Compiled results data confirming that our improvement has achieved the Goal defined in our DMAIC team Charter.	YES	NO
2.	Selected ongoing measures to monitor performance of the process and continued effectiveness of our solution.	YES	NO
3.	Determined key charts/graphs for a "Process Scorecard" on this process.	YES	NO
4.	Prepared all essential documention of the revised process, including key procedures and process maps.	YES	NO
5.	Identified an "owner" of the process who will take over responsibility for our solution and for managing continuing operations.	YES	NO
6.	Developed (with the Process Owner) Process Management Charts detailing requirements, measures and responses to problems in the process.	YES	NO
7.	Prepared a Storyboard documenting the team's work and data collected during our project.	YES	NO
8.	Forwarded other issues/opportunities which we were *not* able to address to senior management.	YES	NO
9.	Celebrated the hard work and successful efforts of our team.	YES	NO

Figure A.7 Control Checklist

Six Sigma Conversion Table

YIELD (%)	DPMO	SIGMA
6.68	933200	0
8.455	915450	0.125
10.56	894400	0.25
13.03	869700	0.375
15.87	841300	0.5
19.08	809200	0.625
22.66	773400	0.75
26.595	734050	0.875
30.85	**691500**	**1**
35.435	645650	1.125
40.13	598700	1.25
45.025	549750	1.375
50	500000	1.5
54.975	450250	1.625
59.87	401300	1.75
64.565	354350	1.875
69.15	**308500**	**2**
73.405	265950	2.125
77.34	226600	2.25
80.92	190800	2.375
84.13	158700	2.5
86.97	130300	2.625
89.44	105600	2.75
91.545	84550	2.875
93.32	**66800**	**3**
94.79	52100	3.125
95.99	40100	3.25
96.96	30400	3.375
97.73	22700	3.5
98.32	16800	3.625
98.78	12200	3.75
99.12	8800	3.875
99.38	**6200**	**4**
99.565	4350	4.125
99.7	3000	4.25
99.795	2050	4.375
99.87	1300	4.5
99.91	900	4.625
99.94	600	4.75
99.96	400	4.875
99.977	**230**	**5**
99.982	180	5.125
99.987	130	5.25
99.992	80	5.375
99.997	30	5.5
99.99767	23.35	5.625
99.99833	16.7	5.75
99.999	10.05	5.875
99.99966	**3.4**	**6**

Figure A.8 Six Sigma Conversion Table

Sigma Calculation Worksheet

Sigma levels of a process can be determined several ways. The steps below use the simplest method, based on number of defects at the *end* of a process (usually called, appropriately, "process sigma").

STEP 1: Selecting the Process, Unit & Requirements

- Identify the process you want to evaluate: ____________ **(process)**
- What is the primary "thing" produced by the process? ____________ **(unit)**
- What are key customer requirements for the unit? ____________

  ____

  ____**(requirements)**

STEP 2: Defining the "Defect" and "Number of Opportunities"

- Based on the requirements noted above, list all the possible *defects* in a single unit (e.g. late, missing data, wrong size, delivered to wrong address, etc.). Be sure the defects described can be identified *objectively*.________________________

  ____

  ____ **(defects)**

- How many defects could be found on a *single* unit? ________ **(opportunities)**

STEP 3: Gather Data & Calculate DPMO

- Collect end-of-process data: ______ **(units counted)** ______**(*total* defects counted)**
- Determine Total Opportunities in data gathered:

  # Units Counted x Opportunities = ________ **(total opportunities)**

- Calculate Defects per Million Opportunities:

  (# Defects Counted ÷ Total Opportunities) x 10^6 = ________ **(DPMO)**

STEP 4: Convert DPMO to Sigma

- Use Sigma Converstion table on reverse and note estimated sigma here: ___________

NOTES: 1) The table will give you a very rough range of your sigma level 2) Your sigma figure can vary significantly based on the accuracy of your data and the number of opportunities you identify on a unit.

Figure A.9 Sigma Calculation Worksheet

Glossary

Affinity chart (diagram)

Brainstorming tool used to gather large quantities of information from many people; ideas usually are put on sticky notes, then categorized into similar columns; columns are named giving an overall grouping of ideas.

Analyze

DMAIC phase where process detail is scrutinized for improvement opportunities. Note that:

1. Data is investigated and verified to prove suspected root causes and substantiate the problem statement (see also Cause and Effect).
2. Process analysis includes reviewing process maps for value-added/non-value-added activities. *See also* Process Map; Value-Adding Activities; Non-Value-Adding Activities.

Balanced scorecard

Categorizes ongoing measures into four significant areas: finance, process, people, and innovation. Used as a presentation tool to update sponsors, senior management, and others on the progress of a business or process; also useful for process owners

Baseline measures

Data signifying the level of process performance as it is/was operating at the initiation of an improvement project (prior to solutions).

Black Belt

A team leader, trained in the DMAIC process and facilitation skills, responsible for guiding an improvement project to completion.

Cause and Effect diagram

Also known as a "Fishbone" or "Ishikawa Diagram"; categorical brainstorming tool used for determining root-cause hypothesis and potential causes (the bones of the fish) for a specific effect (the head of the fish)

Charter

Team document defining the context, specifics, and plans of an improvement project; includes business case; problem and goal statements; constraints and assumptions; roles; preliminary plan; and scope. Periodic reviews with the sponsor ensure alignment with business strategies; review, revise, refine periodically throughout the DMAIC process based on data

Checksheet

Forms, tables, or worksheets facilitating data collection and compilation; allows for collection of stratified data. *See also* Stratification.

Common cause

Normal, everyday influences on a process; usually harder to eliminate and require changes to the process. Problems from common causes are referred to as "chronic pain." *See also* Control Charts; Run Chart or Time Plot; Special Cause; Variation.

Continuous data

Any variable measured on a continuum or scale that can be infinitely divided; primary types include time, dollars, size, weight, temperature, and speed; also referred to as "variable data." *See also* Attribute Data.

Control

- DMAIC phase C; once solutions have been implemented, ongoing measures track and verify the stability of the improvement and the predictability of the process. Often includes process-management techniques and systems including process ownership, cockpit charts and/or process management charts, etc. *See also* Cockpit Charts; Process Management
- A statistical concept indicating that a process operating within an expected range of variation is being influenced mainly by "common cause" factors; processes operating in this state are referred to as "in control." *See also* Control Charts; Process Capability; Variation.

Control charts

Specialized time plot or run chart showing process performance, mean (average), and control limits; helps determine process influences of common (normal) or special (unusual, unique) causes.

Cost of Poor Quality, or COPQ

Dollar measures depicting the impact of problems (internal and external failures) in the process as it exists; include labor and material costs for handoffs, rework, inspection, and other non-value-adding activities

Criteria matrix

Decision-making tool used when potential choices must be weighed against several key factors (e.g., cost, ease to implement, impact on customer.). Encourages use of facts, data, and clear business objectives in decision making.

Customer

Any internal or external person/organization who receives the output (product or service) of the process; understanding the impact of the process on both internal and external customers is key to process management and improvement.

Customer requirements

Defines the needs and expectations of the customer; translated into measurable terms and used in the process to ensure compliance with the customers' needs

Cycle time

All time used in a process; includes actual work time and wait time.

Defect

Any instance or occurrence where the product or service fails to meet customer requirements.

Defect opportunity

A type of potential defect on a unit of throughput (output) which is important to the customer; example: specific fields on a form which creates an opportunity for error that would be important to the customer.

Defective

Any unit with one or more defects. *See also* Defects.

Define

First DMAIC phase defines the problem/opportunity, process, and customer requirements; because the DMAIC cycle is iterative, the process problem, flow, and requirements should be verified and updated for clarity, throughout the other phases. *See also* Charter, Customer Requirements, Process Map, VOC.

Discrete data

Any data *not* quantified on an infinitely divisible scale. Includes a count, proportion, or percentage of a characteristic or category (e.g., gender, loan type, department, location, etc); also referred to as "attribute data."

Downstream

Processes (activities) occurring after the task or activity in question

DFSS

Acronym for "Design for Six Sigma." Describes the application of Six Sigma tools to product development and Process Design efforts with the goal of "designing in" Six Sigma performance capability.

DMAIC

Acronym for a Process Improvement/Management System which stands for Define, Measure, Analyze, Improve, and Control; lends structure to Process Improvement, Design or Redesign applications

DPMO, or Defects per Million Opportunities

Calculation used in Six Sigma Process Improvement initiatives indicating the amount of defects in a process per one million opportunities; number of defects divided by (the number of units times the number of opportunities) = DPO, times 1 million = DPMO. *See also* DPO; Six Sigma; Defect Opportunity).

DPO, or Defects per Opportunity

Calculation used in Process Improvements to determine the amount of defects per opportunity; number of defects divided by (the number of units times the number of opportunities) = DPO. *See also* Defect; Defect Opportunity.

Effectiveness

Measures related to how well the process output(s) meets the needs of the customer (e.g., on-time delivery, adherence to specifications, service experience, accuracy, value-added features, customer satisfaction level); links primarily to customer satisfaction.

Efficiency

Measures related to the quantity of resources used in producing the output of a process (e.g., costs of the process, total cycle time, resources consumed, cost of defects, scrap, and/or waste); links primarily to company profitability

External failure

When defective units pass all the way through a process and are received by the customer.

Force field analysis

Identifies forces/factors supporting or working against an idea; "restraining" factors listed on one side of the page, "driving forces" listed on the other; used to reinforce the strengths (positive ideas) and overcome the weaknesses or obstacles

Goal statement

Description of the intended target or desired results of Process Improvement or Design/Redesign activities; usually included in a team charter and supported with actual numbers and details once data has been obtained.

Handoff

Any time in a process when one person (or job title) passes on the item moving through the process to another person; potential to add defects, time, and cost to a process.

Histogram or Frequency Plot

Chart used to graphically represents the frequency, distribution and "centeredness" of a population.

Hypothesis statement

A complete description of the suspected cause(s) of a process problem

Improve

- DMAIC phase where solutions and ideas are creatively generated and decided upon
- Once a problem has been fully identified, measured, and analyzed, potential solutions can be determined to solve the problem in the problem statement and support the goal statement. *See also* Charter.

Input

Any product, service, or piece of information that comes into the process from a supplier.

Input measures

Measures related to and describing the input into a process; predictors of output measures.

Institutionalization

Fundamental changes in daily behaviors, attitudes, and practices that make changes "permanent", cultural adaptation of changes implemented by Process Improvement, Design or Redesign—including complex business systems such as HR, MIS, Training, etc.

ISO-9000

Standard and guideline used to certify organizations as competent in defining and adhering to documented processes; mostly associated with quality assurance systems, not quality improvement.

Judgment sampling

Approach that involves making educated guesses about which items or people are representative of a whole, generally to be avoided.

Management-by-fact

Decision making using criteria and facts; supporting "intuition" with data; tools used include process measurement, process management techniques, and rational decision-making tools (e.g., criteria matrix).

Measure

1. DMAIC phase M, where key measures are identified, and data are collected, compiled, and displayed
2. A quantified evaluation of specific characteristics and/or level of performance based on observable data

Moment of truth

Any event or point in a process when the external customer has an opportunity to form an opinion (positive, neutral, or negative) about the process or organization.

Multivoting

Narrowing and prioritization tool. Faced with a list of ideas, problems, causes, etc., each member of a group is given a set number of "votes." Those receiving the most votes get further attention/consideration

Non-value-adding activities

Steps/tasks in a process that do not add value to the external customer and do not meet all three criteria for value-adding; includes rework, handoffs, inspection/control, wait/delays, etc. *See also* Value-Adding Activities.

Operational definition

A clear, precise description of the factor being measured or the term being used; ensures a clear understanding of terminology and the ability to operate a process or collect data consistently.

Output

Any product, service, or piece of information coming out of, or resulting from, the activities in a process.

Output measures

Measures related to and describing the output of the process; total figures/overall measures.

Pareto Chart

Quality tool based on Pareto Principle; uses attribute data with columns arranged in descending order, with highest occurrences (highest bar) shown first; uses a cumulative line to track percentages of each category/bar, which distinguishes the 20 percent of items causing 80 percent of the problem.

Pareto Principle

The 80/20 rule; based on Vilfredo Pareto's research stating that the vital few (20 percent of causes have a greater impact than the trivial many (80 percent) causes with a lesser impact.

Plan-Do-Check-Act, or PDCA

Basic model or set of steps in continuous improvement; also referred to as "Shewhart Cycle" or "Deming Cycle."

Pilot

Trial implementation of a solution, on a limited scale, to ensure its effectiveness and test its impact; an experiment verifying a root-cause hypothesis.

Precision

The accuracy of the measure you plan to do. This links to the type of scale or detail of your operational definition, but it can have an impact on your sample size, too.

Preliminary plan

Used when developing milestones for team activities related to process improvement; includes key tasks, target completion dates, responsibilities, potential problems, obstacles and contingencies, and communication strategies.

Problem/Opportunity statement

Description of the symptoms or the "pain" in the process; usually written in noun-verb structure: usually included in a team charter and supported with numbers and more detail once data have been obtained. *See also* Charter.

Process capability

Determination of whether a process, with normal variation, is capable of meeting customer requirements; measure of the degree a process is/*is* not meeting customer requirements, compared to the distribution of the process. *See also* Control; Control Charts.

Process design

Creation of an innovative process needed for newly introduced activities, systems, products, or services

Process improvement

Improvement approach focused on incremental changes/solutions to eliminate or reduce defects, costs or cycle time; leaves basic design and assumptions of a process intact. *See also* Process redesign.

Process management

Defined and documented processes, monitored on an ongoing basis, which ensure that measures are providing feedback on the flow/function of a process; key measures include financial, process, people, innovation. *See also* Control.

Process map, or flowchart

Graphic display of the process flow that shows all activities, decision points, rework loops, and handoffs.

Process measures

Measures related to individual steps as well as to the total process; predictors of output measures.

Process redesign

Method of restructuring process flow elements eliminating handoffs, rework loops, inspection points, and other non-value-adding activities; typically means "clean slate" design of a business segment and accommodates major changes or yields exponential improvements (similar to reengineering). *See also* Process Improvement; Reengineering.

Project rationale (aka "Business Case")

Broad statement defining area of concern or opportunity, including impact/benefit of potential improvements, or risk of not improving a process; links to business strategies, the customer, and/or company values. Provided by business leaders to an improvement team and used to develop problem statement and Project Charter.

Proportion defective

Fraction of units with defects; number of defective units divided by the total number of units; translate the decimal figure to a percentage. *See also* Defects; Defective

Quality assurance, or QA

Discipline (or department) of maintaining product or service conformance to customer specifications; primary tools are inspection and SPC.

Quality

A broad concept and/or discipline involving degree of excellence; a distinguished attribute or nature; conformance to specifications; measurable standards of comparison so that applications can be consistently directed toward business goals.

Quality council

Leadership group guiding the implementation of quality or Six Sigma within an organization; establishes, reviews, and supports the progress of quality improvement teams.

Random sampling

Method that allows each item or person chosen to be measured is selected completely by chance.

Reengineering

Design or redesign of business; similar to Process Redesign, though in practice usually at a much larger scale or scope.

Repeatability

Measurement stability concept in which a single person gets the same results each time he/she measures and collects data; necessary to ensure data consistency and stability. *See also* Reproducibility.

Reproducibility

Measurement stability concept in which different people get the same results when they measure and collect data using the same methods; necessary to ensure data consistency and stability. *See also* Repeatability.

Revision plans

A mechanism (process) for updating processes, procedures, and documentation.

Rework loop

Any instance in a process when the thing moving through the process has to be corrected by returning it to a previous step or person/organization in the process; adds time, costs, and potential for confusion and more defects. *See also* Non-Value-Adding Activities.

Rolled throughput yield

The cumulative calculation of defects through multiple steps in a process; total input units, less the number of errors in the first process step number of items "rolled through" that step; to get a percentage, take the number of items coming through the process correctly divided by the number of total units going into the process; repeat this for each step of the process to get an overall rolled-throughput percentage. *See also* Yield.

Run chart, or time plot

Measurement display tool showing variation in a factor over time; indicates trends, patterns, and instances of special causes of variation. *See* Memory Jogger for construction/use tips; *see also* Control Chart; Special Cause; Variation.

Sampling

Using a smaller group to represent the whole; foundation of statistics which can save time, money, and effort; allows for more meaningful data; can improve accuracy of measurement system.

Sampling bias

When data can be prejudiced in one way or another and do not represent the whole.

Scatter plot or diagram

Graph used to show relationship—or correlation—between two factors or variables. *See also* Correlation Coefficient.

Scope

Defines the boundaries of the process or the Process Improvement project; clarifies specifically where opportunities for improvement reside (start- and end-points); defines where and what to measure and analyze; needs to be within the sphere of influence and control of the team working on the project—the broader the scope, the more complex and time-consuming the Process Improvement efforts will be.

Should-be process mapping

Process-mapping approach showing the design of a process the way it *should* be (e.g., without non-value-adding activities; with streamlined workflow and new solutions incorporated). Contrasts with the

"As-Is" form of process mapping. *See also* Process Redesign, Value-Adding Activities; Non-Value-Adding Activities.

SIPOC

Acronym for Suppliers, Inputs, Process, Outputs, and Customer; enables an "at-a-glance," high-level view of a process.

Six Sigma

1. Level of process performance equivalent to producing only 3.4 defects for every one million opportunities or operations.
2. Term used to describe Process Improvement initiatives using sigma-based process measures and/or striving for Six Sigma–level performance

Solution statement

A clear description of the proposed solution(s); used to evaluate and select the best solution to implement.

SPC

Statistical Process Control; use of data gathering and analysis to monitor processes, identify performance issues, and determine variability/capability. *See also* Run Charts; Control Charts.

Special cause

Instance or event that impacts processes only under "special" circumstances—i.e., not part of the normal, daily operation of the process. See Common Cause; Variation.

Sponsor (or Champion)

Person who represents team issues to senior management; gives final approval on team recommendations and supports those efforts with the Quality Council; facilitates obtaining of team resources as needed; helps Black Belt and team overcome obstacles; acts as a mentor for the Black Belt

Storyboard

A pictorial display of all the components in the DMAIC process, used by the team to arrive at a solution; used in presentations to Sponsor, senior management, and others.

Stratification

Looking at data in multiple layers of information such as what (types, complaints, etc.), when (month, day, year, etc.), where (region, city, state, etc.), and who (department, individual).

Stratified sampling
Dividing the larger population into subgroups, then taking your sample from each subgroup.

Supplier
Any person or organization that feeds inputs (products, services, or information) into the process; in a service organization, many times the customer is also the supplier.

Systematic sampling
Sampling method in which elements are selected from the population at a uniform interval (e.g., every half-hour, every twentieth item); this is recommended for many Six Sigma measurement activities.

Upstream
Processes (tasks, activities) occurring prior to the task or activity in question.

Value-adding activities
Steps/tasks in a process that meet all three criteria defining value as perceived by the external customer: 1) the customer cares; 2) the thing moving through the process changes; and 3) the step is done right the first time.

Value-enabling activities
Steps/tasks in a process enabling work to move forward and add value to the customer but not meeting all three of the value-adding criteria; should still be scrutinized for time and best practices—can it be done better?

Variation
Change or fluctuation of a specific characteristic which determines how stable or predictable the process may be; affected by environment, people, machinery/equipment, methods/procedures, measurements, and materials; any Process Improvement should reduce or eliminate variation. *See also* Common Cause; Special Cause.

Voice of the Customer, or VOC
Data (complaints, surveys, comments, market research, etc.) representing the views/needs of a company's customers; should be translated into measurable requirements for the process.

X
Variable used to signify factors or measures in the Input or Process segments of a business process or system.

Y

Variable used to signify factors or measures at the Output of a business process or system. Equivalent to "results." A key principle of Six Sigma is that Y is a function of upstream factors; or $Y = f(x)$.

Yield

Total number of units handled correctly through the process step(s).

References

Process Improvement and Design/Redesign

Ashkenas, Ron, Dave Ulrich, Todd Jick, and Steve Kerr. *The Boundaryless Organization: Breaking the Chains of Organizational Structure.* San Francisco: Jossey-Bass, 1995

Cross, Kelvin E., John J. Feather, and Richard L. Lynch. *Corporate Renaissance: The Art of Reengineering.* Cambridge, Mass.: Blackwell Publishers, 1994.

Davenport, Thomas H. *Process Innovation: Reengineering Work through Information Technology.* Boston, Mass.: Harvard Business School Press, 1993.

Hammer, Michael. *Beyond Reengineering: How the Process-Centered Organization is Changing Our Work and Our Lives.* New York: HarperBusiness, 1996.

Hammer, Michael and James Champy. *Reengineering the Corporation: A Manifesto for Business Revolution.* New York: HarperBusiness, 1993.

Harrington, H. James. *Business Process Improvement: The Breakthrough Strategy for Total Quality, Productivity, and Competitiveness.* New York: McGraw-Hill, 1991.

Holpp, Lawrence. *Managing Teams.* New York: McGraw-Hill, 1999.

Ramaswamy, Rohit. *Design and Management of Service Processes: Keeping Customers for Life.* Reading, MA: Addison-Wesley. 1996.

Stalk, George Jr. and Thomas M. Hout. *Competing Against Time: How Time-Based Competition is Reshaping Global Markets.* New York: The Free Press, 1990.

Voice of the Customer

Carlzon, Jan. *Moments of Truth.* New York: HarperCollins, 1989.

Gale, Bradley T. *Managing Customer Value: Creating Quality and Service That Customers Can See.* New York: The Free Press, 1994.

Heil, Gary, Tom Parker, and Deborah C. Stephens. *One Size Fits One: Building Relationships One Customer and One Employee at a Time.* New York: John Wiley & Sons, 1999.

Kaplan, Robert S., and David P. Norton. *The Balanced Scorecard.* Boston, Mass.: Harvard Business School Press, 1996.

Treacy, Michael and Fred Wiersema. *The Discipline of Market Leaders: Choose Your Customers, Narrow Your Focus, Dominate Your Market.* Reading, Mass.: Addison-Wesley, 1995.

Learning and Innovation

Imparato, Nicholas, and Oren Harari. *Jumping the Curve: Innovation And Strategic Choice in an Age of Transition.* San Francisco: Jossey-Bass, 1994.

Janov, Jill. *The Inventive Organization: Hope and Daring at Work.* San Francisco: Jossey-Bass, 1994.

Senge, Peter M. *The Fifth Discipline: The Art and Practice of The Learning Organization.* New York: Doubleday, 1990.

Organizations and Six Sigma

Breyfogle, Forrest W. *Implementing Six Sigma: Smarter Solutions Using Statistical Methods.* New York: Wiley-Interscience, 1999.

Porter, Michael E. *Competitive Advantage: Creating and Sustaining Superior Performance.* New York: The Free Press, 1985.

Rummler, Geary A., and Alan P. Brache. *Improving Performance: How to Manage the White Space on the Organization Chart.* San Francisco: Jossey-Bass, 1990.

Slater, Robert. *Jack Welch and the GE Way: Management Insights and Leadership Secrets of the Legendary CEO.* New York: McGraw-Hill, 1999.

Tichy, Noel M., and Stratford Sherman. *Control Your Destiny or Someone Else Will: Lessons in Mastering Change—from the Principles Jack Welch Is Using to Revolutionize GE.* New York: HarperBusiness, 1993.

Voice of the Process

Brassard, Michael and Diane Ritter. *The Memory Jogger II.* Methuen, Mass.: GOAL/QPC, 1994.

Fraenkel, Jack, Norman Wallen, and Enoch I. Sawin. *Visual Statistics: A Conceptual Primer.* Needham Heights, Mass.: Allyn & Bacon, 1999.

Kume, Hitoshi. *Statistical Methods for Quality Improvement.* Tokyo, Japan: The Association for Overseas Technical Scholarship, 1985.

Endnotes

Chapter 1

1. Address to General Electric Company Annual Meeting, Cleveland, Ohio, April 21, 1999.
2. Annual Meeting address, April 21, 1999.
3. Address to General Electric Company Annual Meeting, Charlotte, NC, April 23, 1997.
4. Background information on some of Motorola's Six Sigma projects are available on the company's web site. See, for example: www.mot.com/MIMS/MSPG/Special/CLM/sld001.htm.
5. "Six Sigma" was adopted as the theme linking all of AlliedSignal's diverse quality initiatives in about 1995. In a sense Allied's decision, and its influence on GE, are what brought Six Sigma back to its original role at Motorola where, as we've noted, it was a full culture-change process.
6. AlliedSignal, *1998 Annual Report,* p. 8.
7. Quoted in the *San Francisco Chronicle,* August 9, 1999, p. B7.
8. GE Annual Meeting, April 24, 1996, quoted in: Slater, p. 209.
9. *AlliedSignal Annual Report,* 1998, page 2.
10. Quoted in *Fortune,* September 27, 1999, p. 132.
11. See, for example, Ron Askenas, Dave Ulrich, Todd Jick, and Steve Kerr, *The Boundaryless Organization* (San Francisco, Jossey-Bass, 1995).

Chapter 2

1. We owe credit for this phrase to our friend and colleague Chuck Cox, whom we'll be quoting later in the book.
2. The curve metaphor is reflected in a core concept presented by Intel chairman Andy Grove in his book *Only the Paranoid Survive:* the "strategic inflection point." Grove points out that a company's failure to adjust its strategy at the right moment can mean disaster. We'd suggest that there are many smaller "inflection points" that can have a huge impact on a corporation or its business units, and that Six Sigma is a way to better negotiate both the strategic and the daily curves. See Andrew Grove, *Only the Paranoid Survive,* (New York, Currency Books, 1996), p. 32.
3. A couple of points to make our comments more precise: First of all, σ is used to represent the standard deviation of a population or an entire group.

Usually, standard deviations are calculated based on a sample from the population, for which the notation is "s" (for "sample standard deviation"). Thus you'll usually see "s" in statistics formulas, and not σ.

Second, the letter z gets used in this context, too. The distance from the mean in numbers of standard deviations is measured in what statisticians call "z units," but the scale is the same (e.g., 1.65 z units from the mean equals 1.65 standard deviations). Also, the percentage of the sample or population represented by a slice of the "bell-shaped curve" is often called the "z score." So when we noted that 34.1 percent of your trips were between 18 and 20.7 minutes, 34.1 percent is the "z score."

4. We'll see later that the Six Sigma measures have been adjusted to accommodate how processes vary over the long term. Because of this there's a difference between statistical "sigma" and the numbers used in the Six Sigma measurement system. But the basic concept of narrowing variation is the same, no matter what the scale.
5. Michael Hammer, *Beyond Reengineering* (New York: Harper Business, 1996), p. 82.
6. Deming called this the "Shewhart Cycle," after his friend and mentor, Walter Shewhart. It's sometimes called "P-D-*S*-A" for "Plan-Do-*Study*-Act"
7. This particular model got its start at GE Capital and was later adopted by all of GE. The original model—still used in some companies—included only four steps: Measure-Analyze-Improve-Control.

Chapter 3

1. Process Management is covered in some detail in Chapter 17.
2. GE 1998 *Annual Report,* p. 4.
3. AlliedSignal 1998 *Annual Report,* p. 3.

Chapter 4

1. See "Qualcomm: From Wireless to Phoneless." In *Business Week,* December 6, 1999, pp. 96–98.
2. Two-time Malcolm Baldrige Award winner Solectron, mentioned in Chapter 3, is an example of a company that has capitalized on this trend. Solectron is a contract manufacturer of electronics components for a wide array of applications. In the semiconductor industry, there is now actually an association of "Fabless" chip companies—those who do little or no actual product manufacturing.
3. The discipline of Activity-Based Accounting is giving finance people new perspectives and tools to help them link costs and process tasks more closely.
4. See "Cowboy Quality," in *Quality Progress,* October 1999, p. 30.
5. ISO9000 is an internationally recognized set of standards used to validate the consistency of processes, usually in product manufacturing and design but in other areas as well. A company is certified by a recognized independent auditor, primarily indicating that: a) the company has properly docu-

mented processes, and b) the processes are being followed as documented. There are a number of other industry- and customer-specific certifications that manufacturing organizations will seek—usually as a basic requirement for consideration as a potential vendor.

Chapter 5

1. We know of a car dealer who visited Detroit in the 1970s to plead for more fuel-efficient, well-made economy vehicles. After listening (or seeming to), the Big Three executives patted the dealer on the shoulder and sagely counseled: "Just sell what we build."
2. See "Can the New Repairman Fix GE's Appliances Unit?" in *The Wall Street Journal,* November 15, 1999, p. B-1.

Chapter 6

1. Andrew S. Grove, *Only the Paranoid Survive* (New York, Currency Books, 1996).
2. These figures are drawn from the presentation "Training Six Sigma Quality in a Service Organization," given at a meeting of the American Society for Training and Development National Conference in Atlanta, GA, on May 26, 1999.

Chapter 8

1. We've seen some *good* change marketing efforts, too. For example, when a major bank was moving a regional headquarters to a new building and shifting people from offices to cubicles (a very jarring change), the switch was accompanied several months in advance by a slogan ("It's Your Move"), sweatshirts, parties, brochures, etc.—all just to help people feel better about the new environment.

Chapter 9

1. The roles and structure noted here are common to Six Sigma and quality efforts in a number of organizations, including GE.
2. Note that we're focusing here only on Black Belts as the "workhorse" role in most Six Sigma initiatives. Some of the same considerations apply to preparing and deploying Master Black Belts.

Chapter 11

1. This great analogy is borrowed from a book by consultant Jill Janov, who actually came across the "dried peas" effect while learning to write billboard ad copy. See Jill Janov, *The Inventive Organization* (San Francisco: Jossey-Bass, 1994), pp. 11–12.

Chapter 12

1. See a classic study: Alfred Chandler, *The Visible Hand: The Managerial Revolution in American Business* (Cambridge, MA, Harvard University Press, 1977), p. 462.
2. Michael Porter, *Competitive Advantage* (New York: The Free Press, 1985), p. 36.
3. Porter, op. cit., p. 38.

Chapter 13

1. We use the single term "Voice of the Customer" throughout the book, to signify *both* efforts to understand current and future needs of existing and prospective customers, *and* activities to gather information on competitors, new technologies, etc.—also called "Voice of the Market" systems.
2. Cited in *BusinessWeek* e.biz, July 26, 1999, p. 23. Survey conducted by Forrester Research. Used by permission.
3. Note: While most of this chapter is presented with a focus on external customers and markets, we *would* encourage those in *internal* organizations or support processes to adopt a similar perspective, as one that will help them to better understand your customers and "markets."
4. Jan Carlzon, *Moments of Truth* (Cambridge, MA: Ballinger, 1987).
5. We learned of this performance standard from Barbara Friesner, director of training for Loews Hotels, which uses "10, 5, first and last" extensively in their evaluations of service performance. In the next chapter, we'll discuss how Loews measures against this standard.

Chapter 14

1. Bob Lawson and Ron Stewart, *Measuring Six Sigma and Beyond: Continuous vs. Attribute Data* (Schaumberg, IL: Motorola University Press, 1997), p. 16.
2. A warning for the technical types: PPM and DPMO aren't really synonymous, so be careful. Many people assume or intend PPM to signify defectives units—so 6σ would mean 3.4 "bad" units for every million produced. In our electronic components example, however, we noted that each item has roughly 4000 opportunities. Using the DPMO calculation, you would therefore reach 6σ performance with 3.4 defects for every 250 units (250 units × 4,000 = 1,000,000 opportunities). If defects were one to a unit, your Yield would be 98.64 percent and your total *defectives* for every million electronic components would be 13,600. Pretty good for a complex product, but a lot more than 3.4!
3. For our discussion and examples here, we'll assume only *one* defect opportunity in our Sigma calculations. Determining opportunities gets trickier for internal process measures.
4. Another method to calculate the internal yield is called "Rolled Throughput Yield." YRTP is generated by multiplying the yields from each of the substeps. In our example this would be: .98 × .99 × .97 = .94

5. Cost of Poor Quality (which we introduced in Chapter 6) also is known as "Price of Non-Conformance" or "PONC." The related measure, "Cost of Quality," includes the costs of *both* rework and defects (i.e., poor quality), as well as the costs of solutions, prevention, and appraisal/prevention (i.e., achieving good quality).

Chapter 16

1. See "GE's Quality Gamble" in *ComputerWorld,* June 8, 1998.
2. Like the one in Chapter 15, this scenario is based on several real organizations. It has been fictionalized for the reader's enjoyment, and to avoid inflicting any embarrassment on real people.
3. There are other "value" dimensions that influence organizational decisions as well; including, for example, integrity, respect for diversity, environmental consciousness, support for employees' personal lives, and so on. These other factors may serve to justify activities not technically "value-adding" to the customer.

Chapter 17

1. Robert S. Kaplan and David P. Norton, *The Balanced Scorecard* (Boston: Harvard Business School Press, 1996).

Chapter 18

1. See "Numbers Tell the Story" in *Selling Power* magazine, July–August, 1999, pp. 58–64
2. If we wanted to test *where* on the form to put the e-mail address, there could be several more possible "levels." Few factors are *really* binary, but it's often simpler to handle them that way.
3. Some practitioners differentiate between "Failure Modes"—referring to system and equipment problems—and "*Error* Modes" (or "EMEA")—referring to human error. We prefer to combine the two into a single analysis.

Index

About the Authors

PETER S. PANDE

Pete Pande is Founder and President of Pivotal Resources, Inc., an international consulting firm providing Six Sigma implementation, training, and management development services to industries from financial services to high technology. Pete has worked in the organization improvement field for over 15 years, supporting change initiatives in a variety of companies including GE, Citicorp, Chevron, and Read-Rite. He and his wife and two children live in the San Francisco Bay Area.

ROBERT P. NEUMAN, PH.D.

Bob Neuman is a senior consultant and noted speaker in the area of business improvement methods and Six Sigma. His background in Six Sigma and quality systems includes two years with a major California health care system, and consulting work with such Pivotal Resources clients as NBC, GE Capital, Cendant, and Auspex Systems. Bob and his wife live in Davis, California.

ROLAND R. CAVANAGH, P.E.

Roland Cavanagh is a professional engineer who has an extensive background in improving manufacturing and service business processes. His areas of expertise include Process Measurement and Applied Statistics, business reorganization and Six Sigma methods. He has worked with such organizations as America West Airlines, Commonwealth Edison, GE, and Tencor Instruments. Roland and his family make their home outside of Chico, California.

